Dollar Distribution

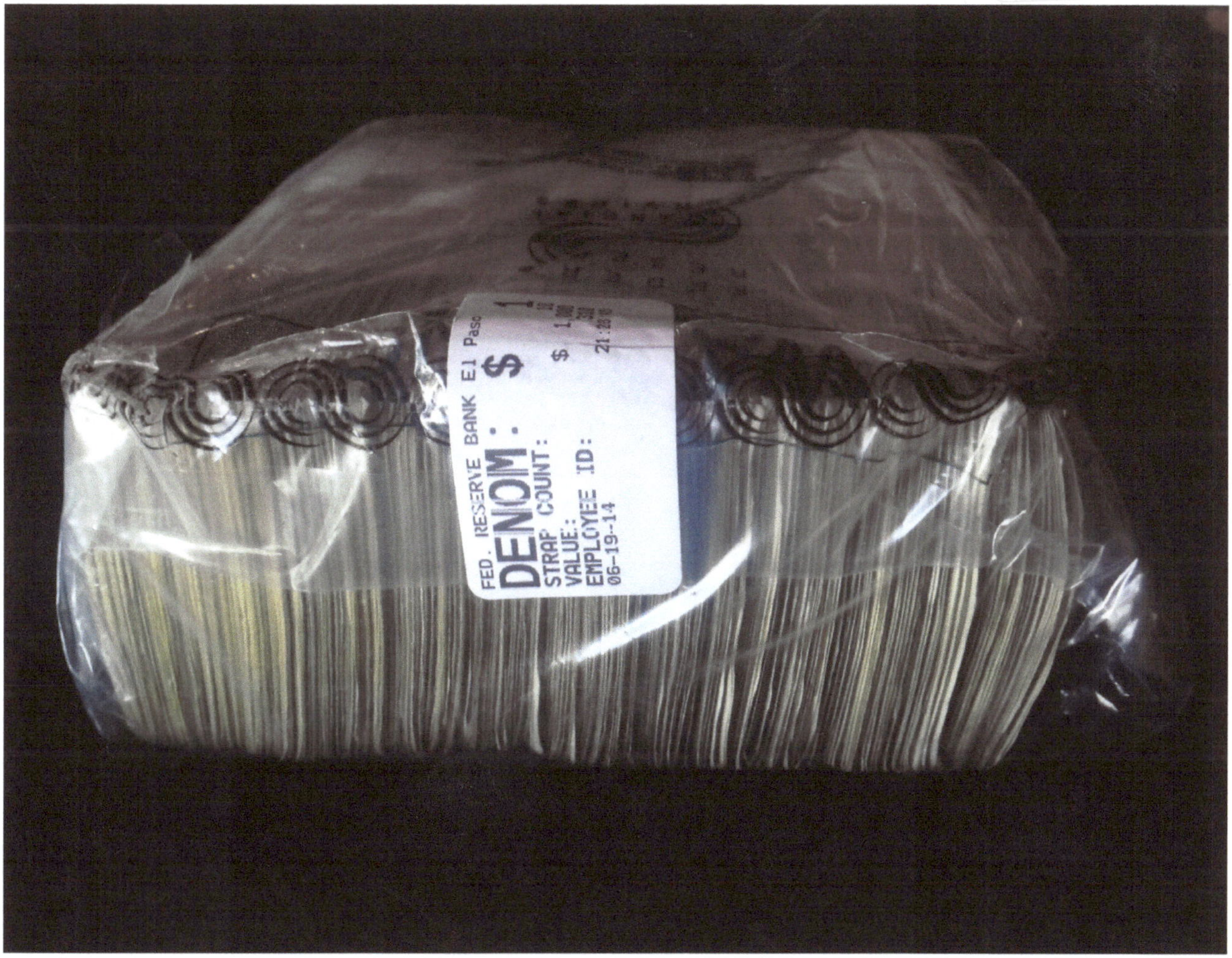

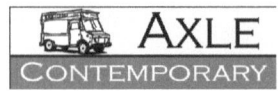

Published by
Axle Contemporary Press
P.O. Box 22095
Santa Fe NM 87502
www.axlepress.com

ISBN 978-0-9858116-8-6

Designed by Matthew Chase-Daniel.

Introduction Photos © 2014 Dianne Stromberg
Other Photos © 2014 Matthew Chase-Daniel

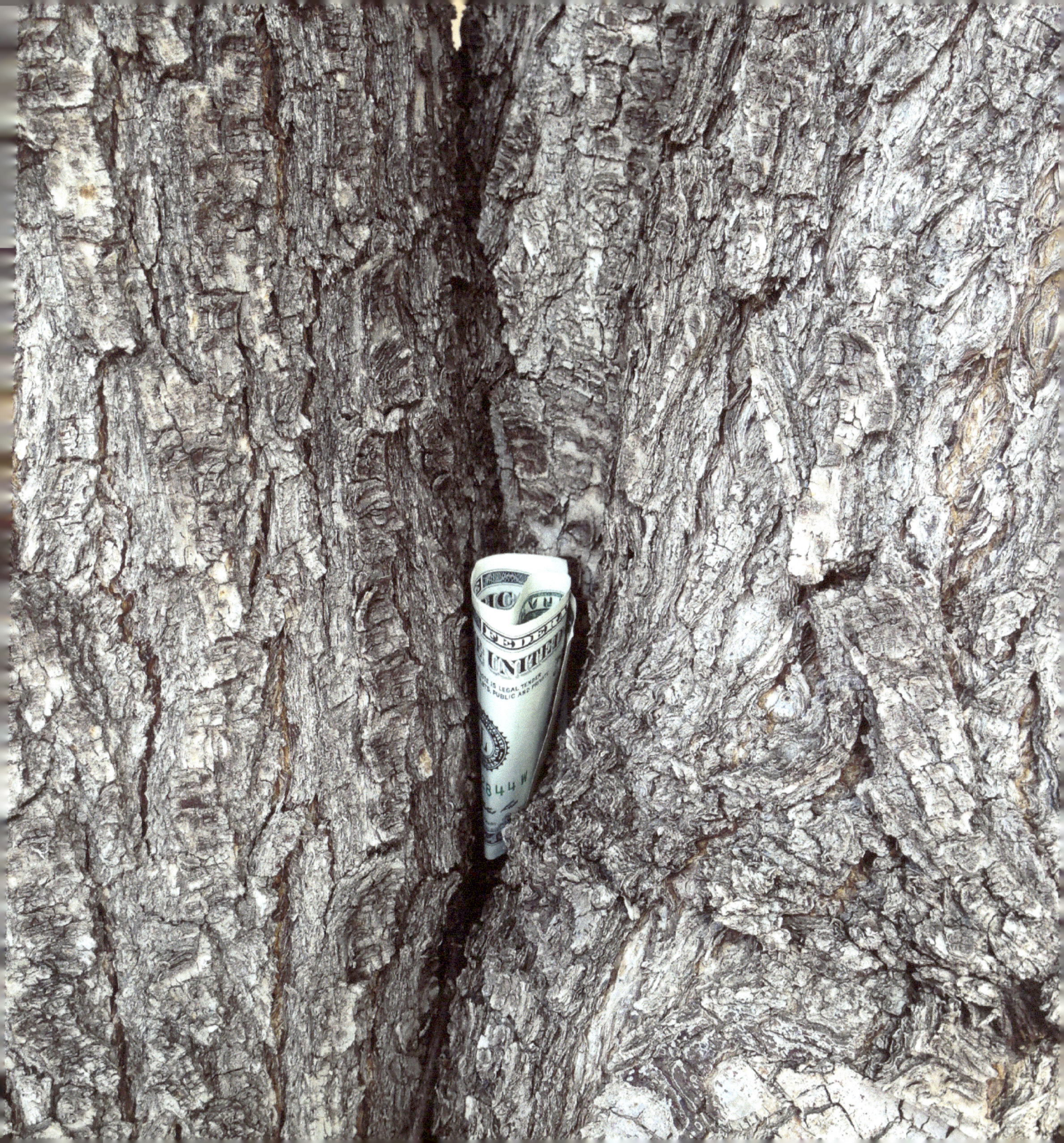

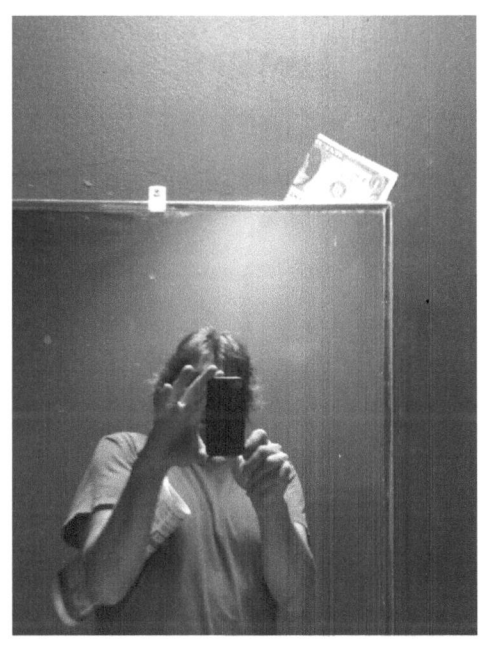

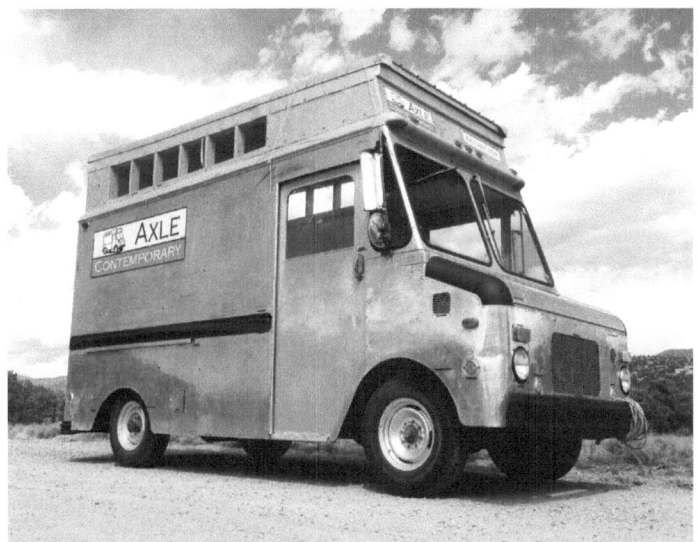

Matthew Chase-Daniel is an artist living in Santa Fe, New Mexico.
See more of his work at www.chasedaniel.com.

Axle Contemporary Press is run by Axle Contemporary, a mobile gallery of contemporary art based
in Santa Fe, New Mexico, founded and run by Jerry Wellman and Matthew Chase-Daniel since 2010.
Info at www.axleart.com.

Axle Projects, Inc. is a non-profit organization supporting the work of Axle Contemporary.
Visit www.axleprojects.org to see how you can support our work.

www.ingramcontent.com/pod-product-compliance
Lightning Source LLC
Chambersburg PA
CBHW050847180526
45159CB00007B/2604

Dollar Distribution

an economic intervention

Matthew Chase-Daniel

Axle Contemporary Press
Santa Fe, New Mexico

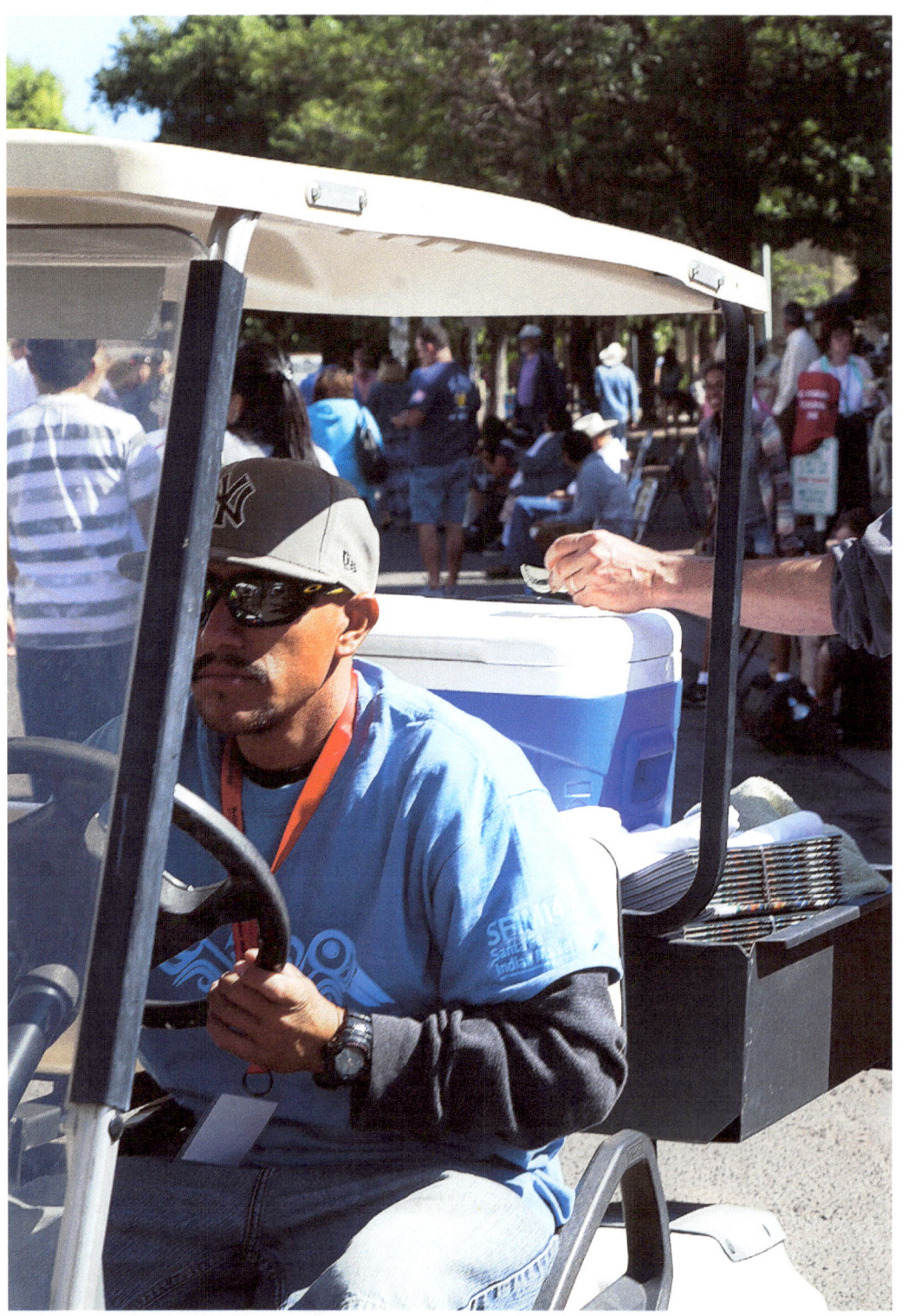

Introduction

Text by Matthew Chase-Daniel
Photos by Dianne Stromberg

Last year, while driving into town, a dollar bill blew past my windshield. Then I noticed a little clump of bills blowing across the road, then cars around me braking and swerving. It wasn't much money at all, but it inspired a strong visceral reaction in all of us there. I got to thinking as I drove away, about money, about cash. It doesn't matter if you are rich or poor, the sight of cash blowing down the road gets attention and provokes reactions and thoughts and reflection of all sorts, positive, negative, joyous, angry, liberated, stressed-out. Cash has so many associations is so prevalent and widespread, can be used for so many different things (but not, I've heard, buying love).

So this blow-by cash experience sparked ideas in my mind as I drove on into town. I decided I wanted to replicate my experience for others, to spark associations and reactions in others by simply leaving some cash around Santa Fe for others to

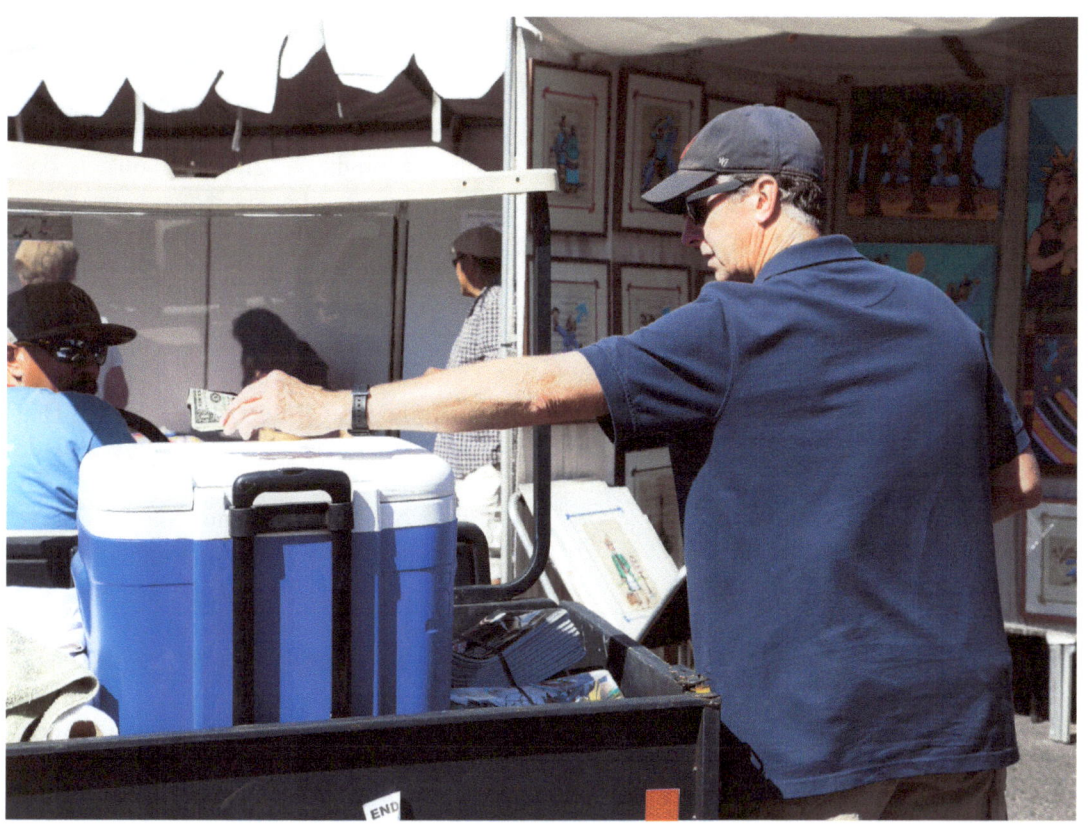

happen upon by chance. Most people (but not all) would be pleased to find a dollar on the street. I decided to use Kickstarter to crowd-source funding for this project. I didn't make any money from the project, nor donate any to it. It's a crowd-sourced pass-through project. And the money wasn't to "fund" the "expenses" of a project. I didn't need to buy a new video projector or rent a performance hall. None of that. All the money given to the project *is* the project. Since my idea was to distribute the money randomly to a large "crowd", crowdsourced funding

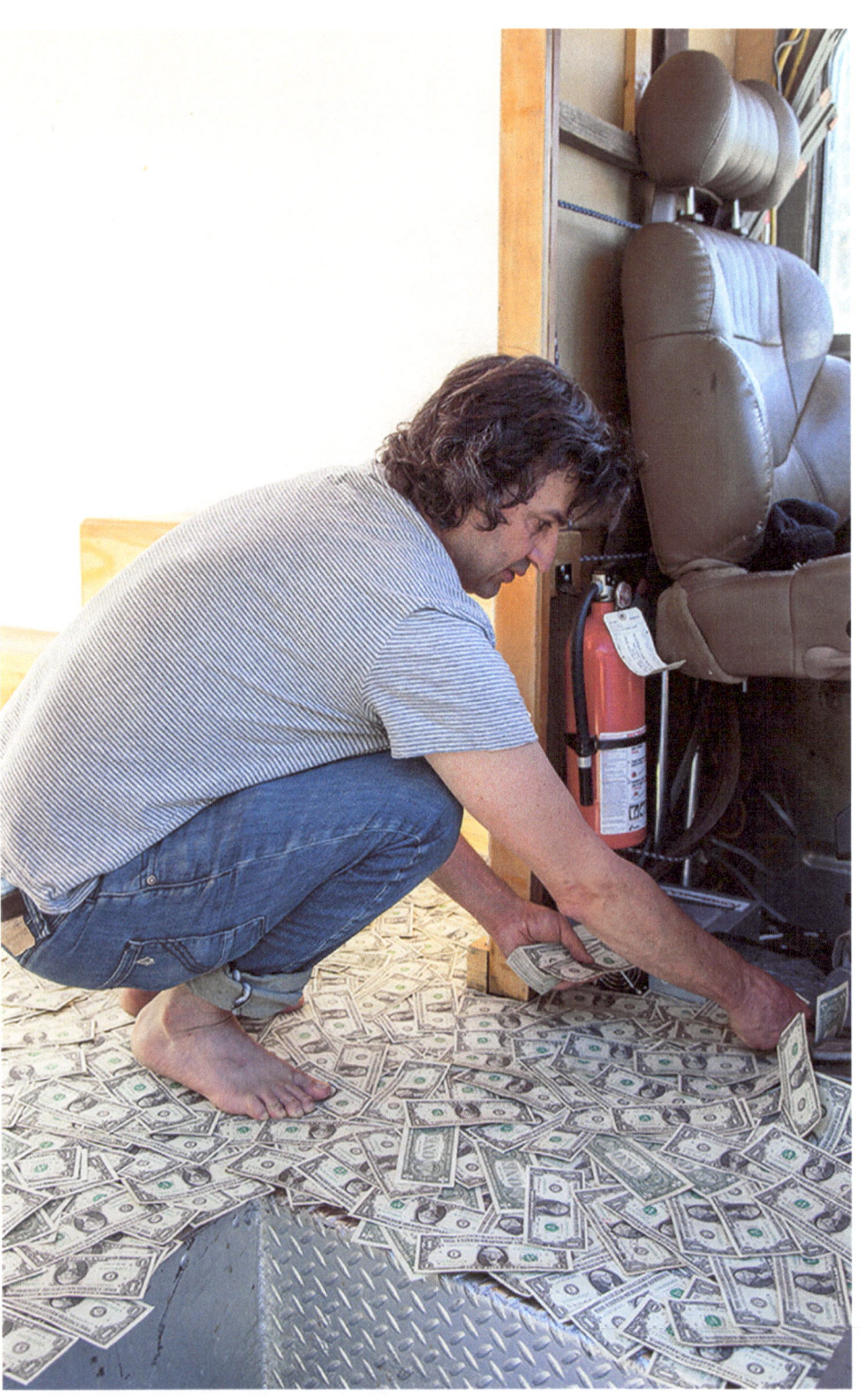

seemed like the logical way to raise the money. Money comes in from a large (and somewhat random) group of people and then quickly flows out to a different (also somewhat random) group of people.

People loved the idea, hated the idea, though it was brilliant, thought is was frivolous, wasteful. Some gave nothing, some one dollar, some 150 dollars, some a jar of pennies. Many just handed me a little cash when I ran into them at the post office or the market. Just the idea of the project provoked a huge range of reactions.

After a month-long Kickstarter campaign, I had raised about $1,500. I went to the bank and withdrew the money, all as one-dollar bills. I wasn't clear how much space that would take. I brought a zippered duffel bag into the bank. It turns out 1,500 bills can be quite compact. 1,000 of them were handed to me fresh from the vault, in a nice brick: 10 banded bundled of 100 ones, sealed in a plastic bag, straight from the Federal Reserve in El Paso. That brick has power. Holding it made me a little giddy and giggly. I brought it home, showed it to my wife, my son, friends. And I worried about it. I was reluctant to leave it locked in my car in a busy parking lot in the middle of the day, tucked away. I worried much more than I would have about leaving a $2,000 computer or a camera. Cash is powerful.

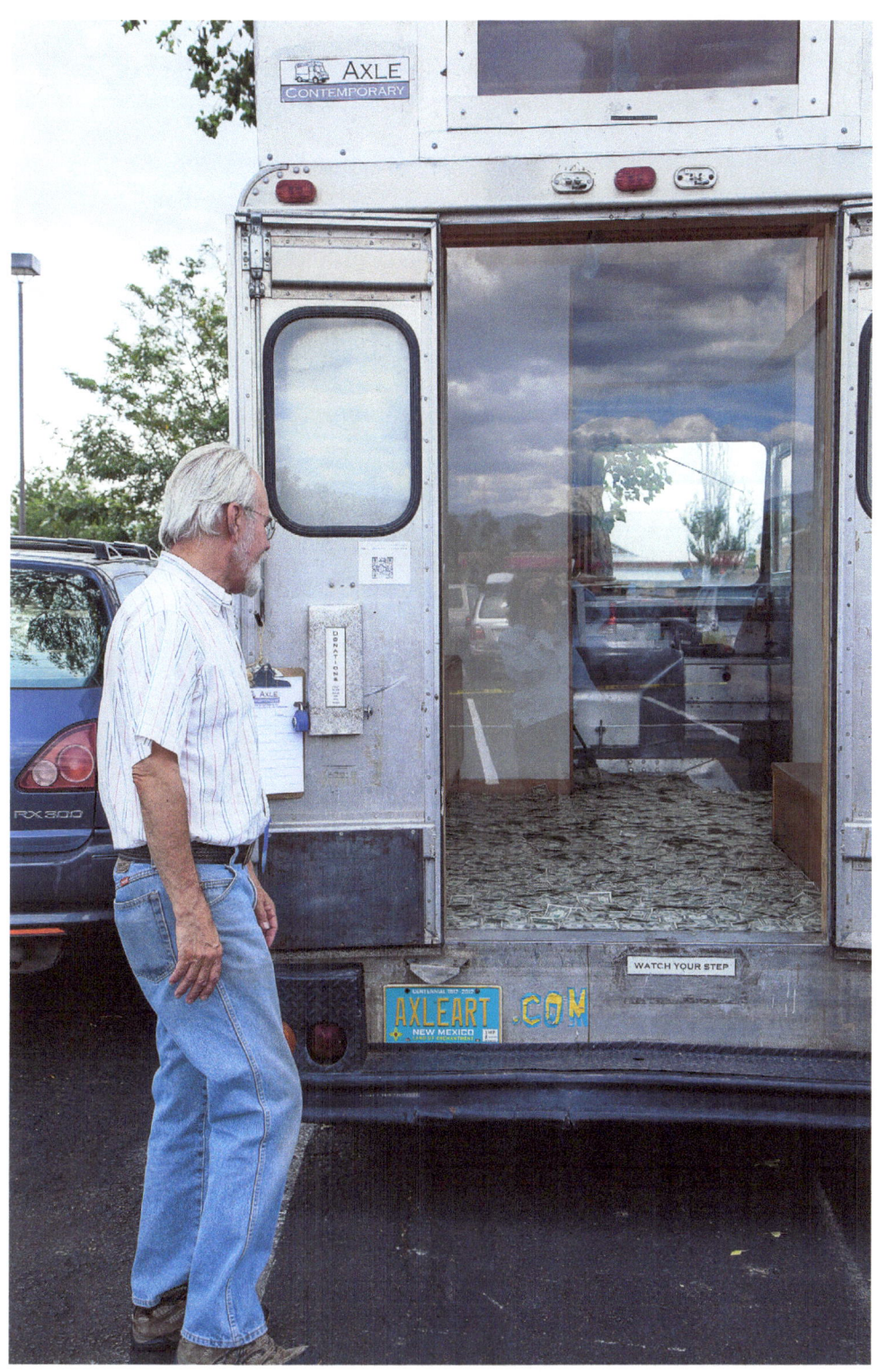

Based on this experience, I decided to create a short exhibition in the Axle mobile gallery. For one day we put the glass on the back door, spread the money across the floor, and I then headed around town to park here and there for an hour or so and show the money. I wanted to provoke and observe the varied reactions that people have to seeing a large amount of cash in a big pile, and also to create awareness of the project in the local arts community.

Then, over the course of the next month, I distributed the bills around town: On city sidewalks, tucked in bushes and sidewalk cracks, pinned to telephone poles, in pockets of thrift-store clothing, in books in libraries, dropped in the midst of busy crowds. 1,500 people had 1,500 unique experiences of finding an unexpected dollar.

Dollar Distribution gives money out to anyone, without discrimination. The cash is found by rich and poor, with no warning or even knowledge of the project by the vast majority of "participants". It is simply invoking that intense feeling (usually but not always a feeling of joy or luckiness or good fortune) that we experience upon finding any dollar bill in the street.

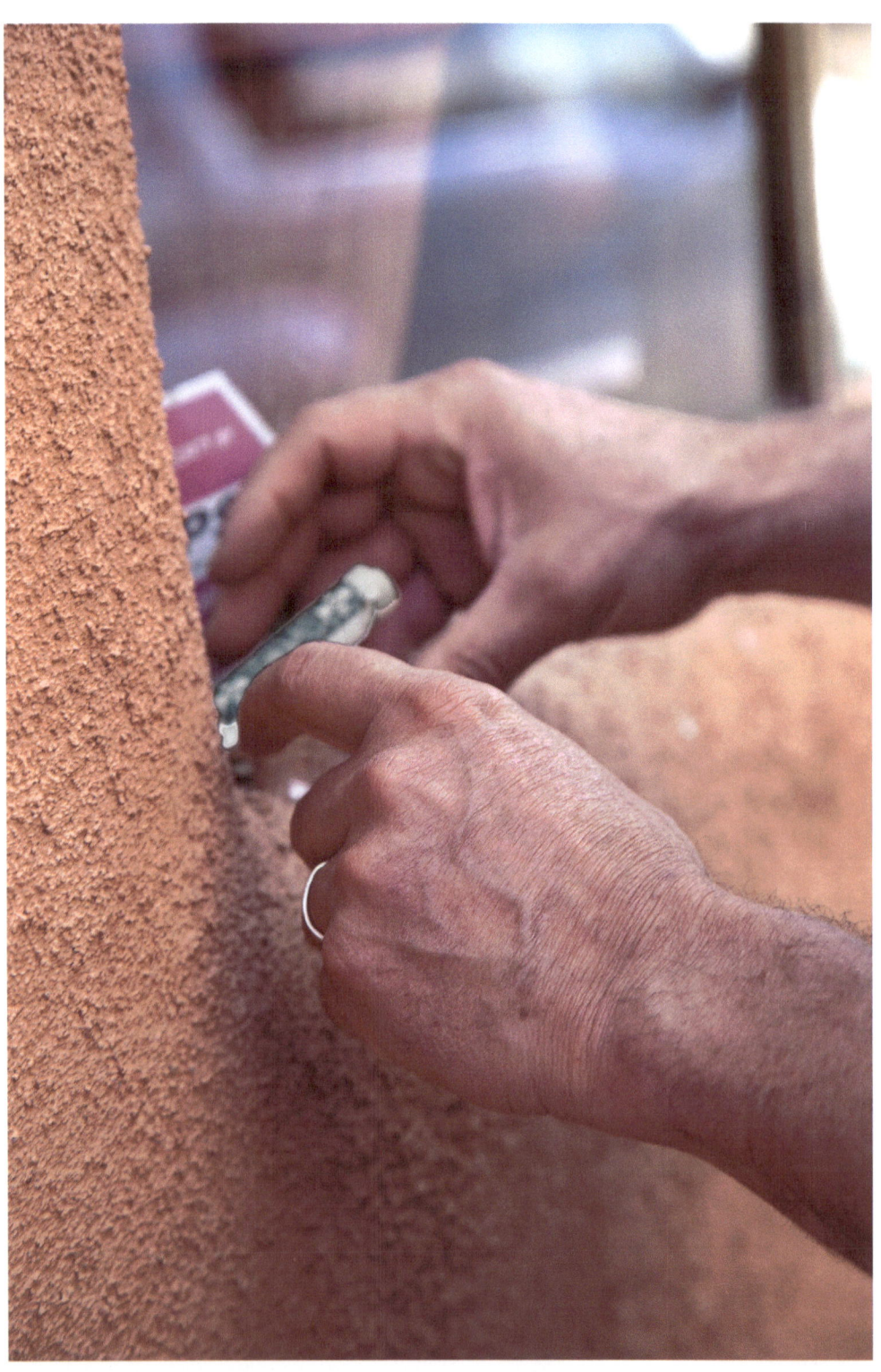

I was able to observe several people finding the cash, but that was limited to perhaps 6 people out of the 1,500 distributed to. It was important to me to remain unobserved while dropping the cash. As this was more important than witnessing or documenting people's reactions, I have very little documentation. Dianne Stromberg followed me around for an afternoon with her camera and was able to photograph me dropping some bills and some people finding them. From the little I saw, people generally just look around to see if the person who "lost" the bill might be around. Once they see that there is no one to return the money to, they pocket the bill and move on.

Distributing the cash turned out to be a lot of work: Heading to parts of town that I didn't usually visit, walking around, and dropping bills in about 50 different spots, every day, 7 days a week, for a month. I had a new and unexpected reaction to holding a big wad of cash by the end. Each day, I'd leave my house with about 50 bills in my pocket. As the day progressed, the wad of cash diminished. During that month, the wad of cash represented work, labor, a task that still needed to be done by the end of the day. Until (and since) that time, a pocketful of cash represented wealth, a resource available in my pocket.

During that time, the meaning was reversed. The cash was work, not like money at all.

The photography that follows began as simple documentation of some of the cash drops. Over time, I began working more on the compositions. The contexts being different, but the dollar bill being a constant. It ended up as a sort of strange portrait of the city.

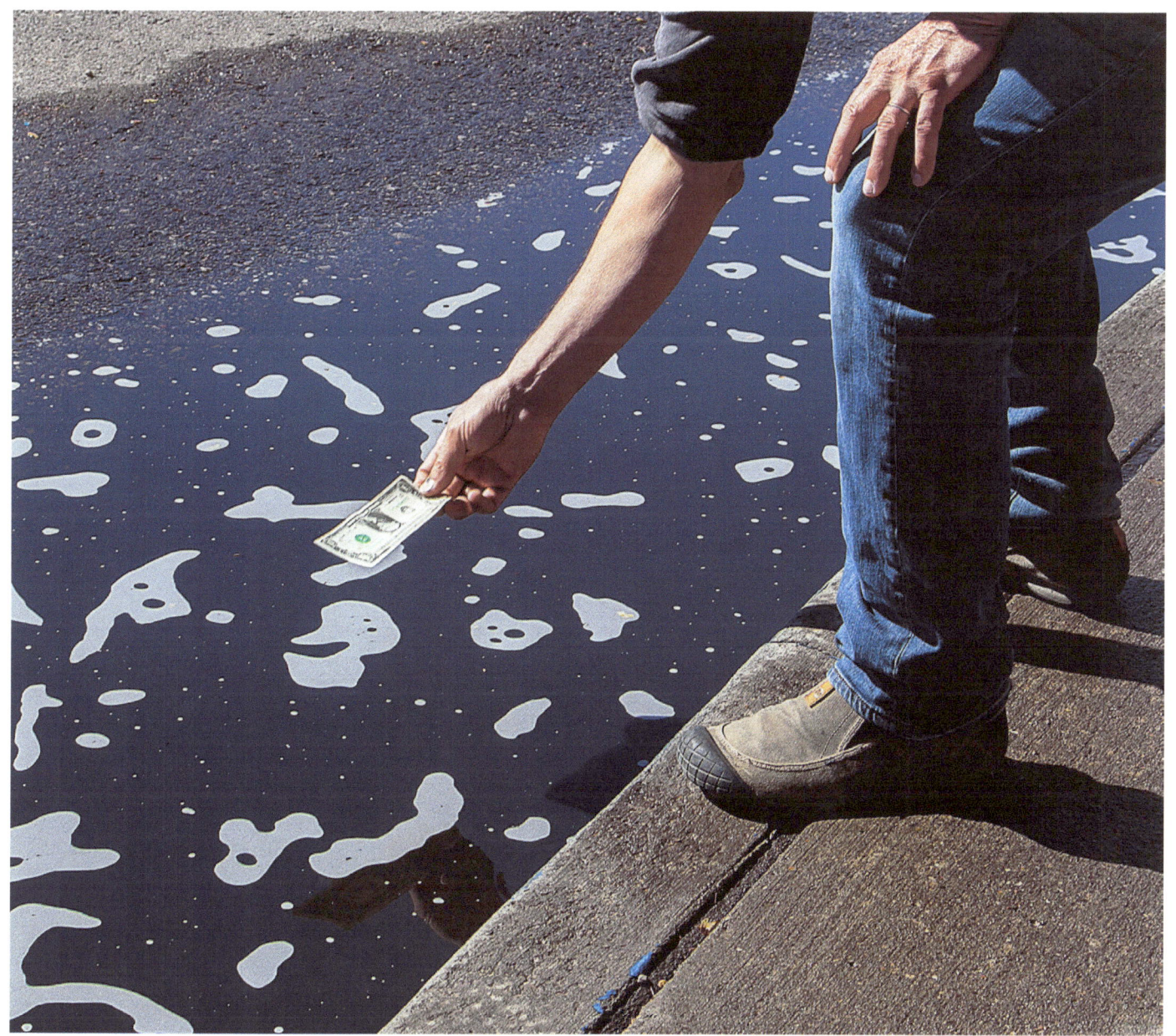

dollar bills

Santa Fe New Mexico

August 19- September 14, 2014

Photographs by Matthew Chase-Daniel

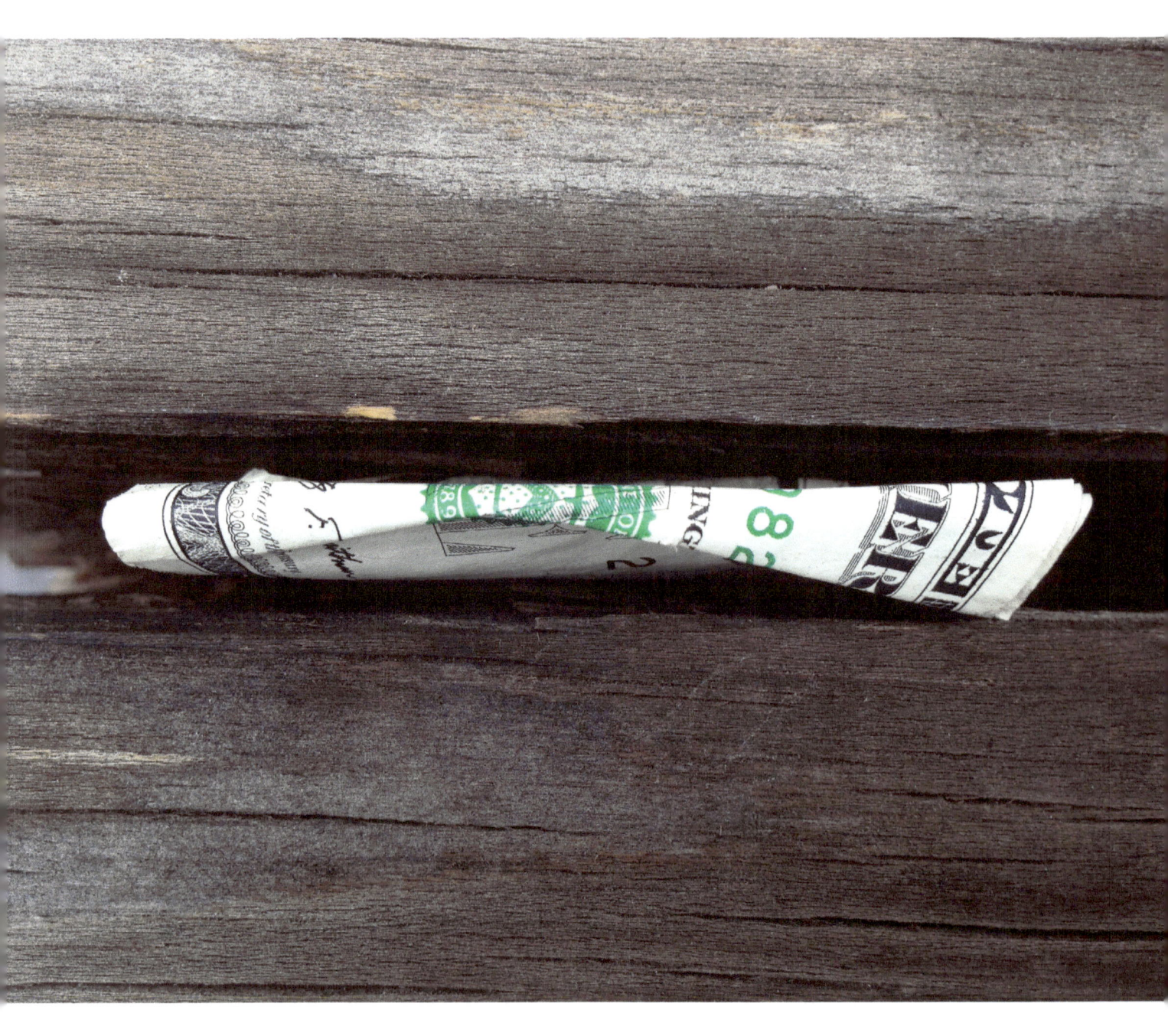

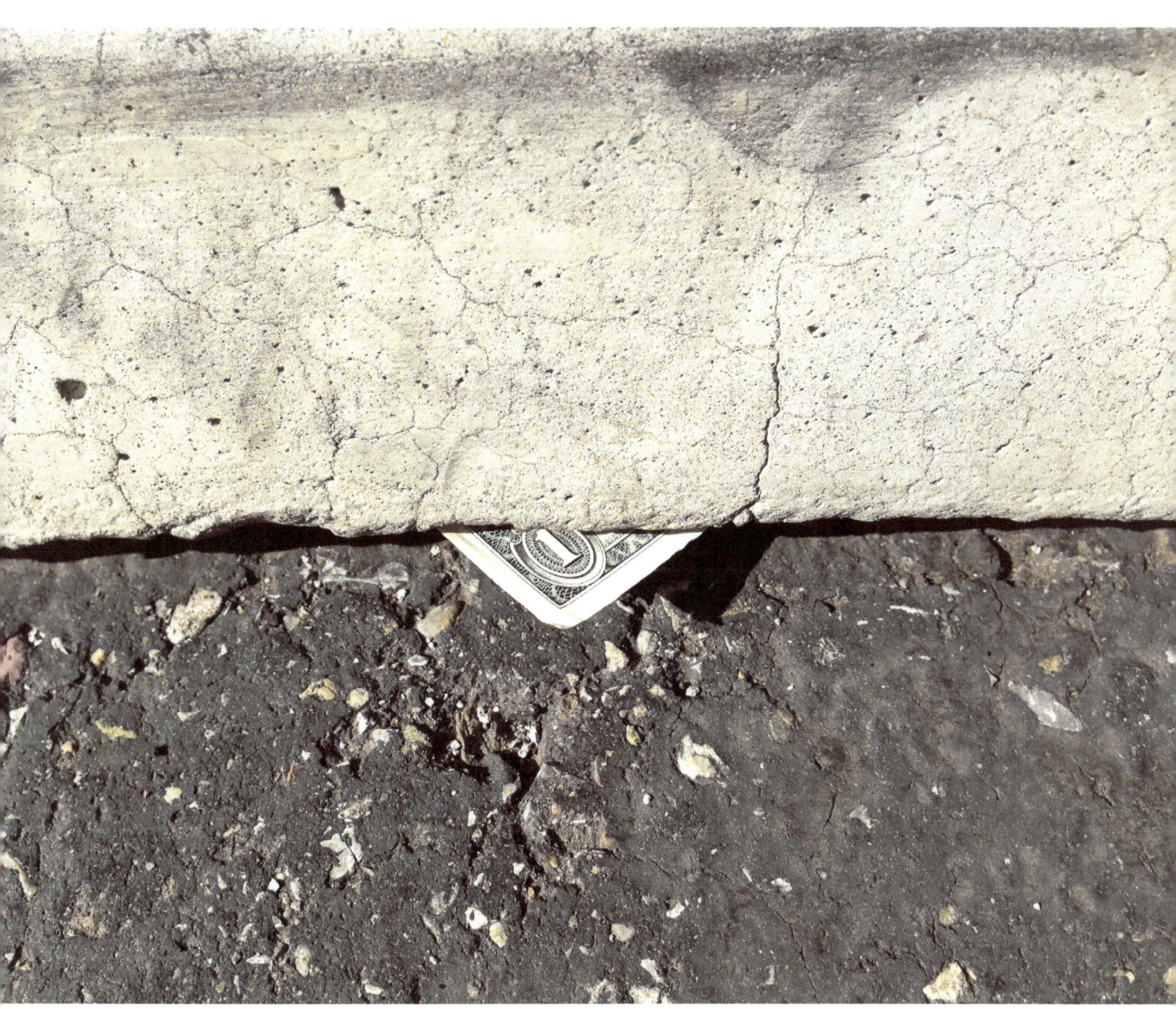

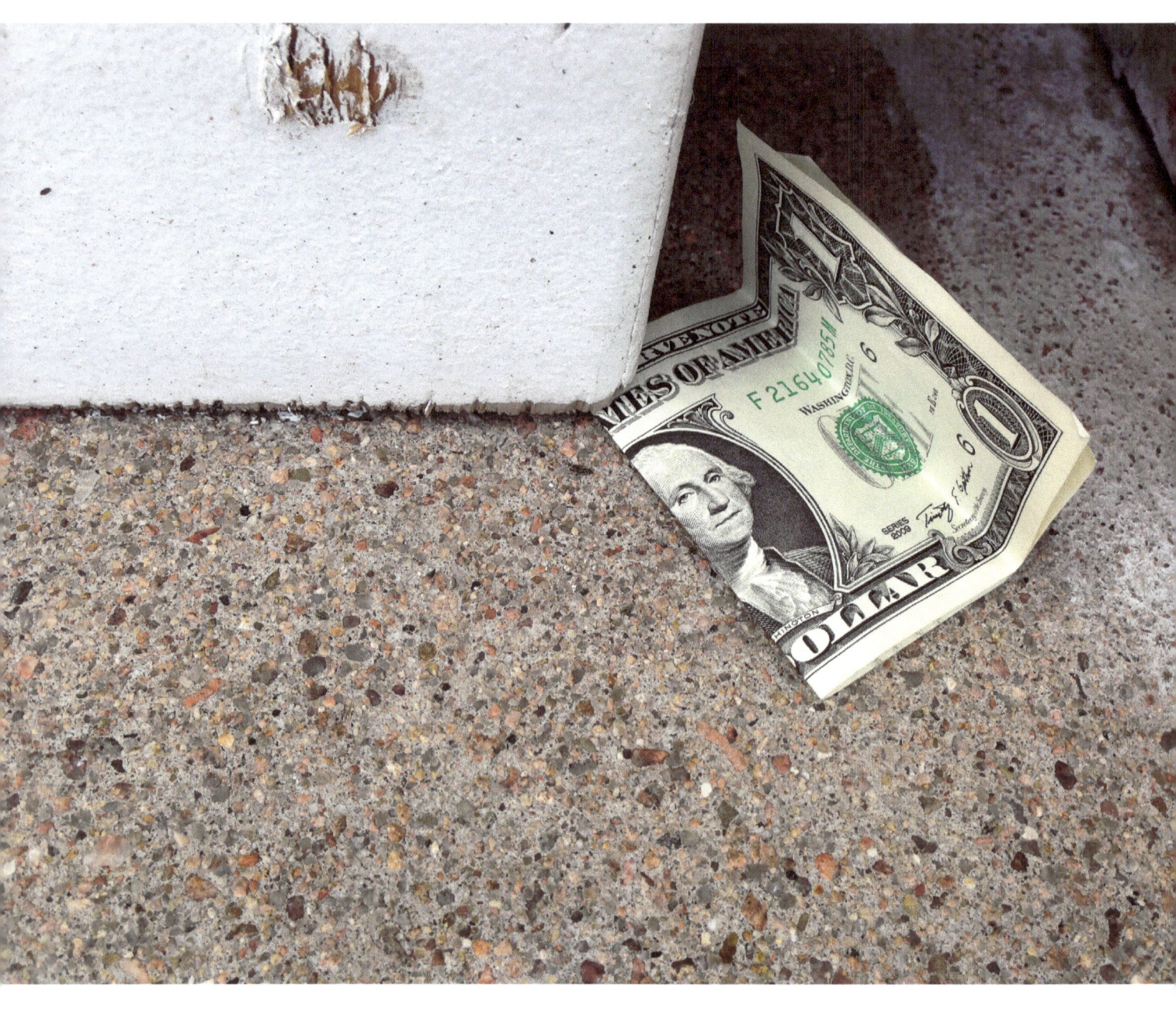

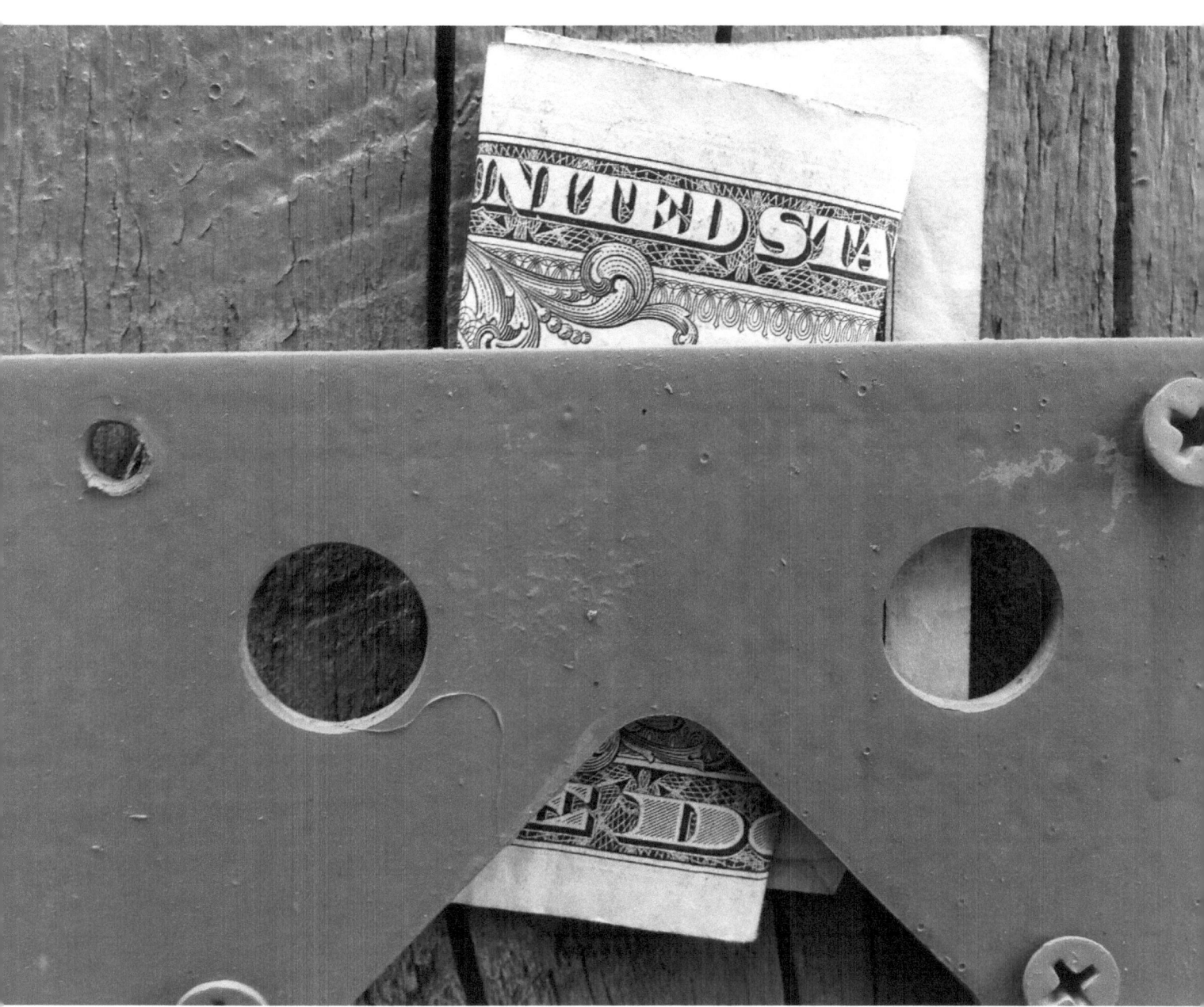

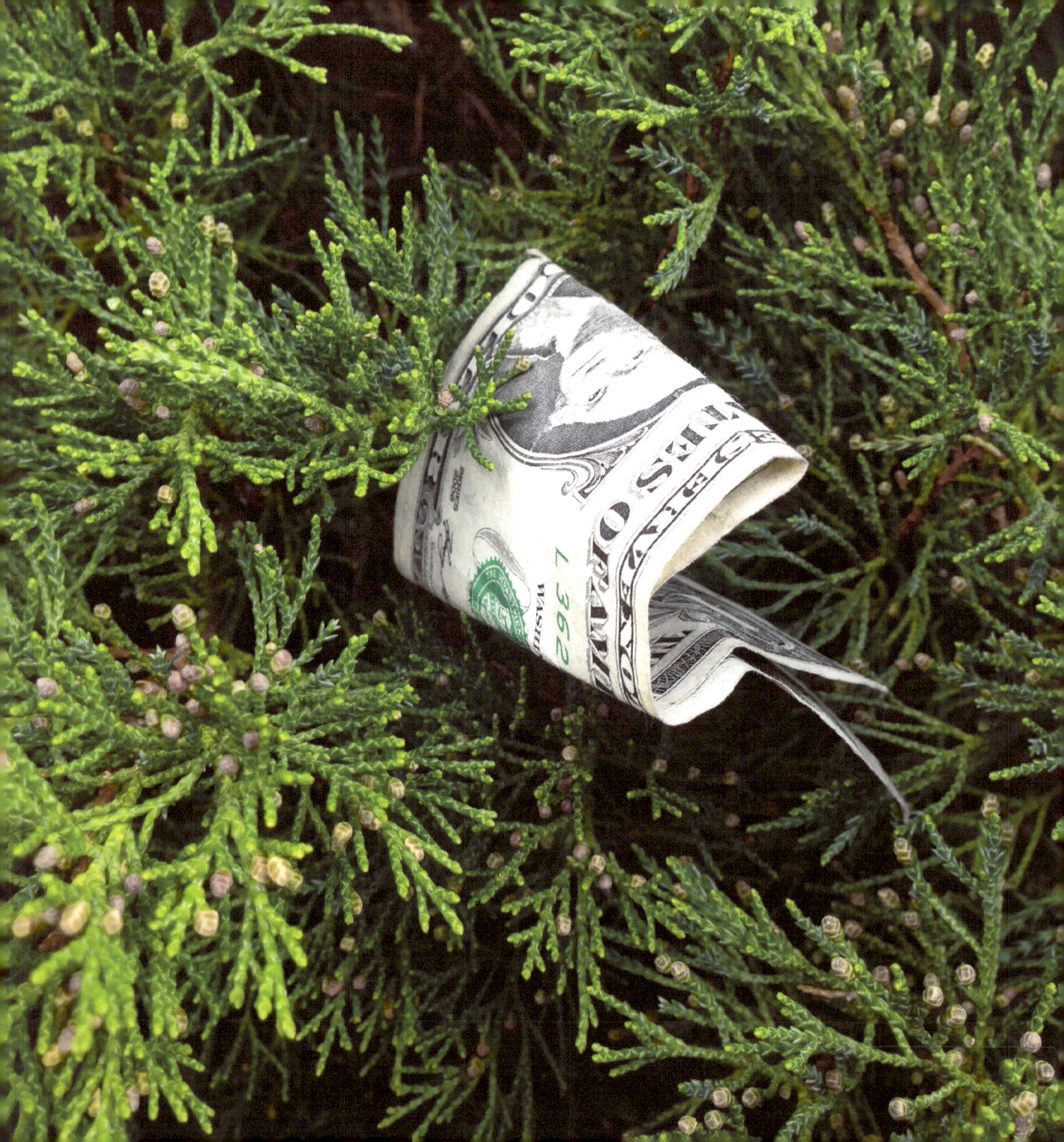

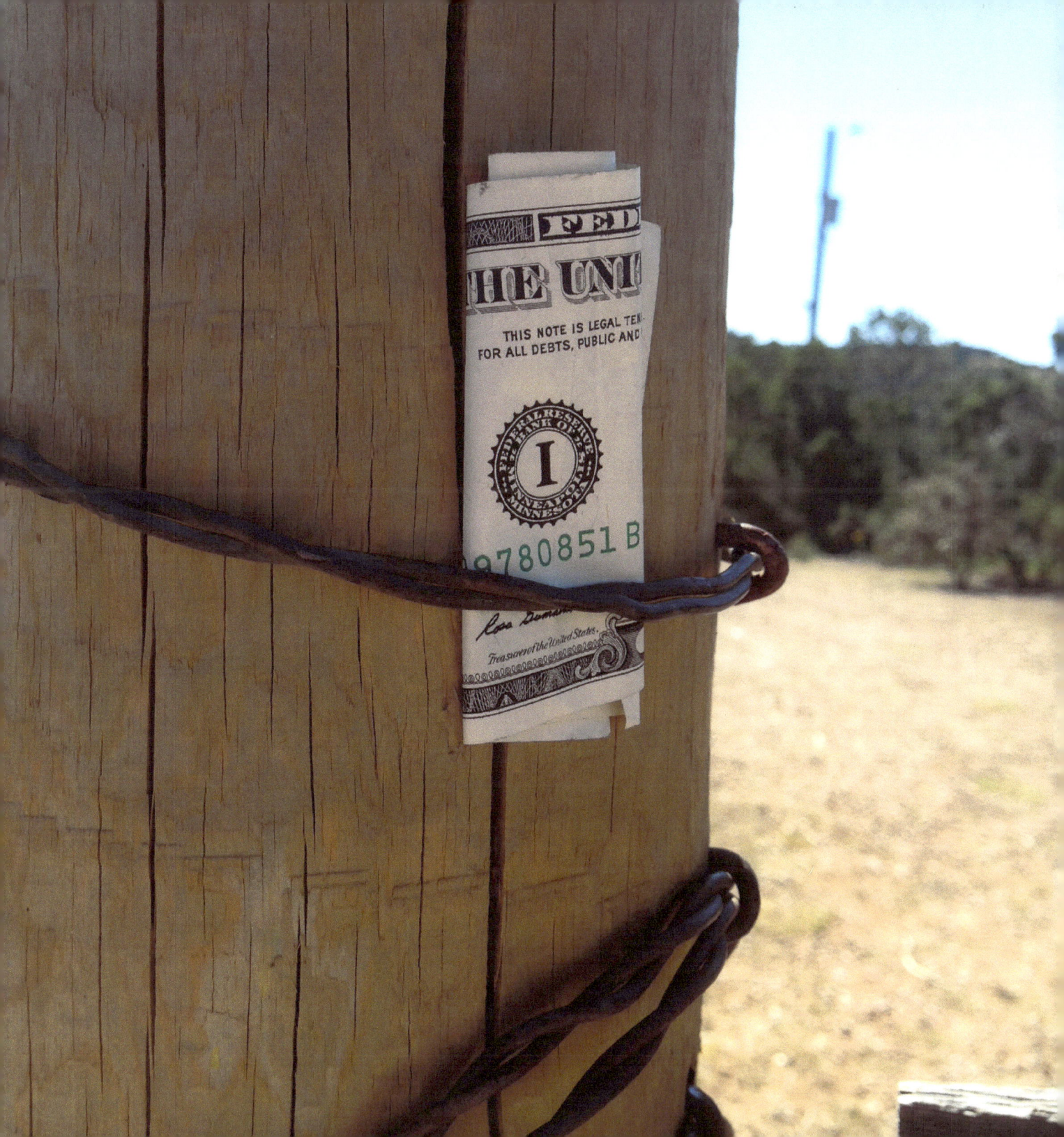

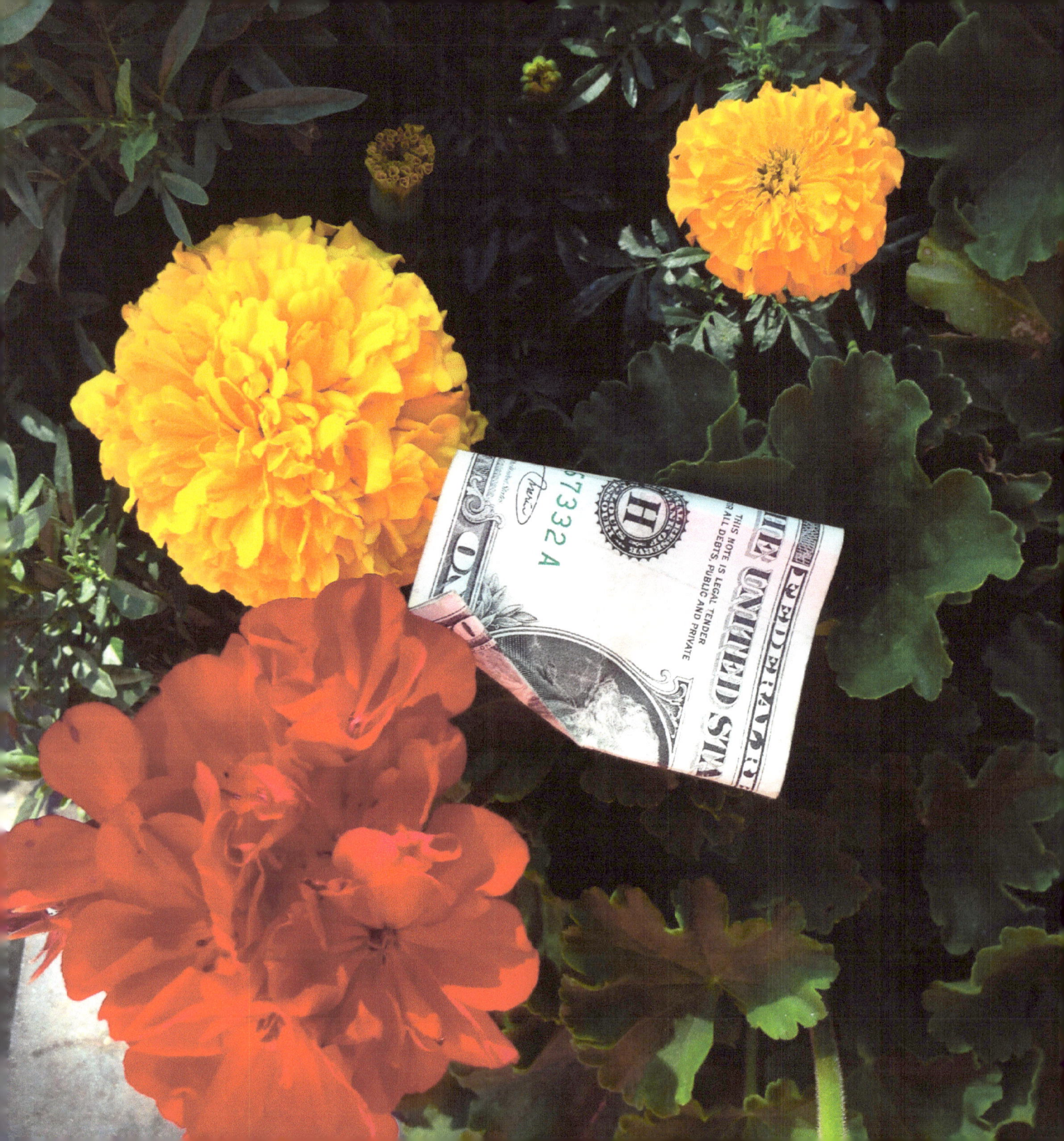

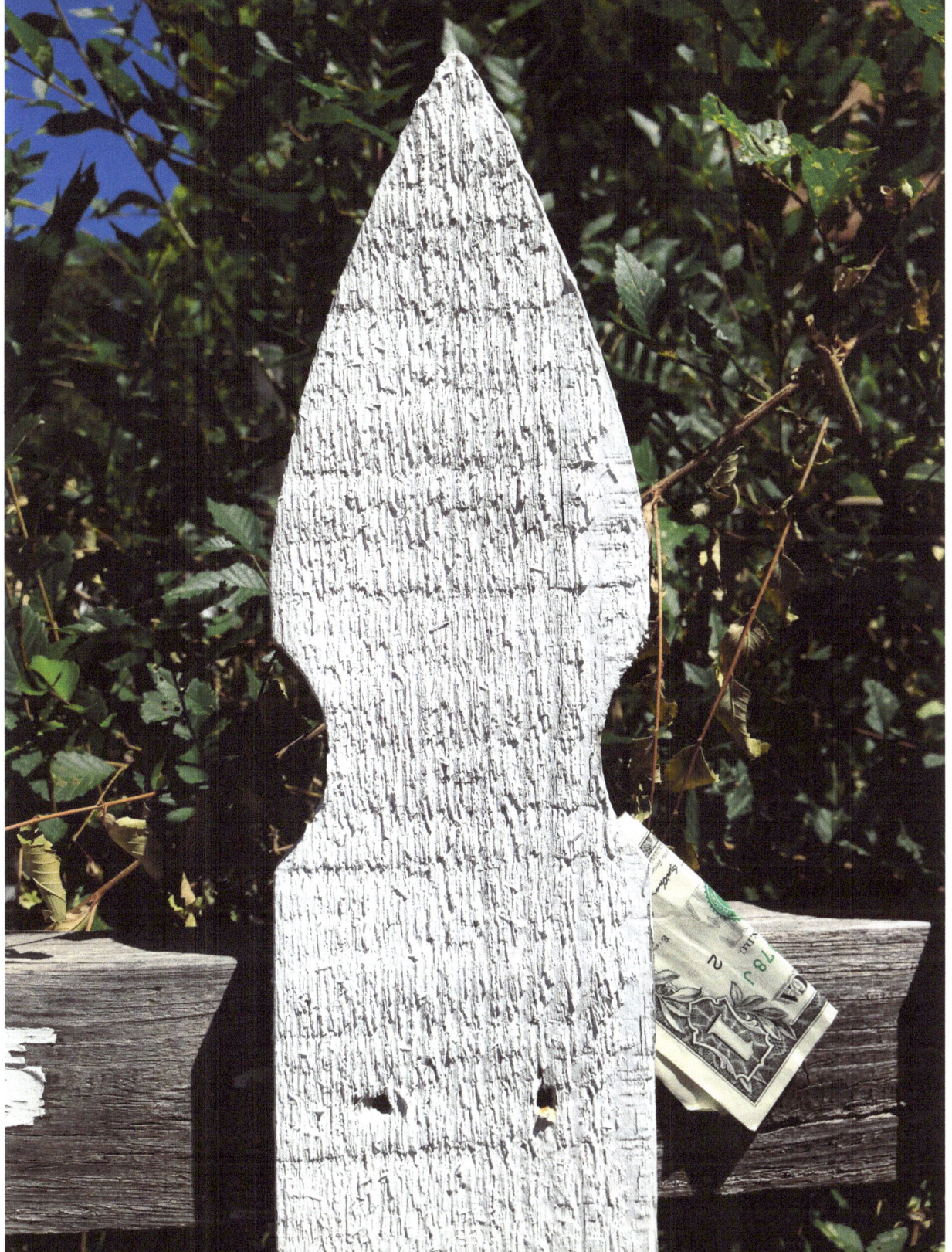

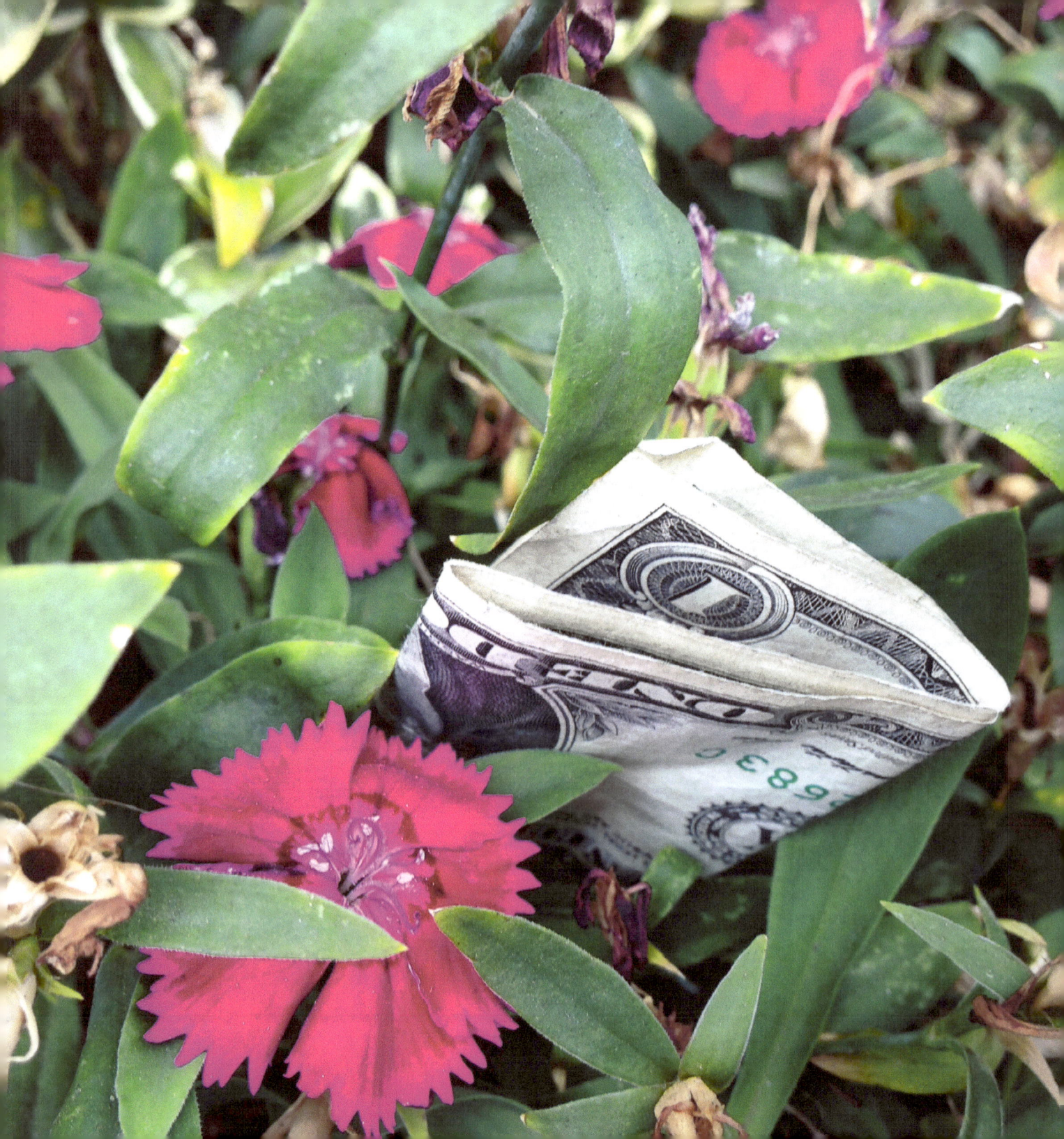

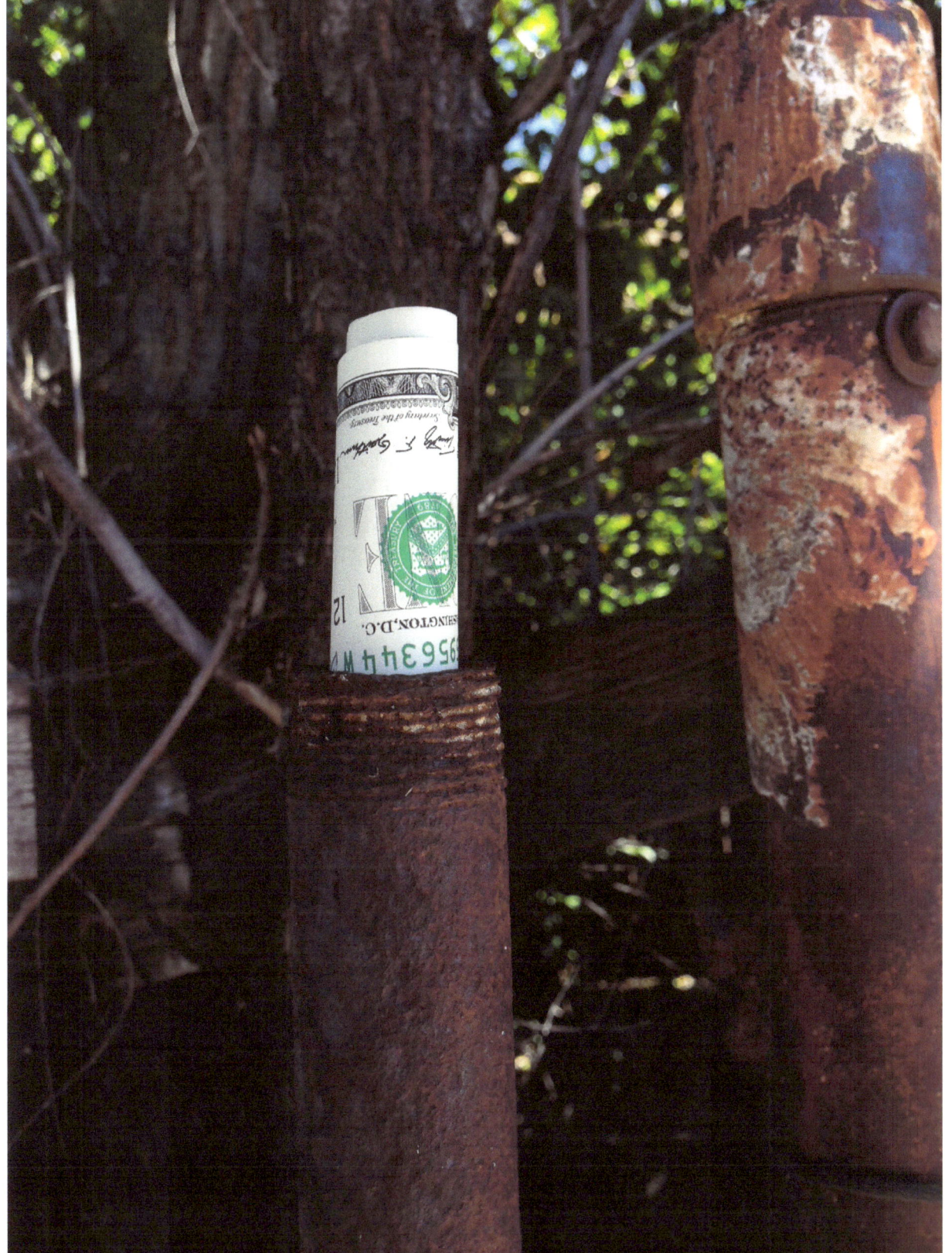

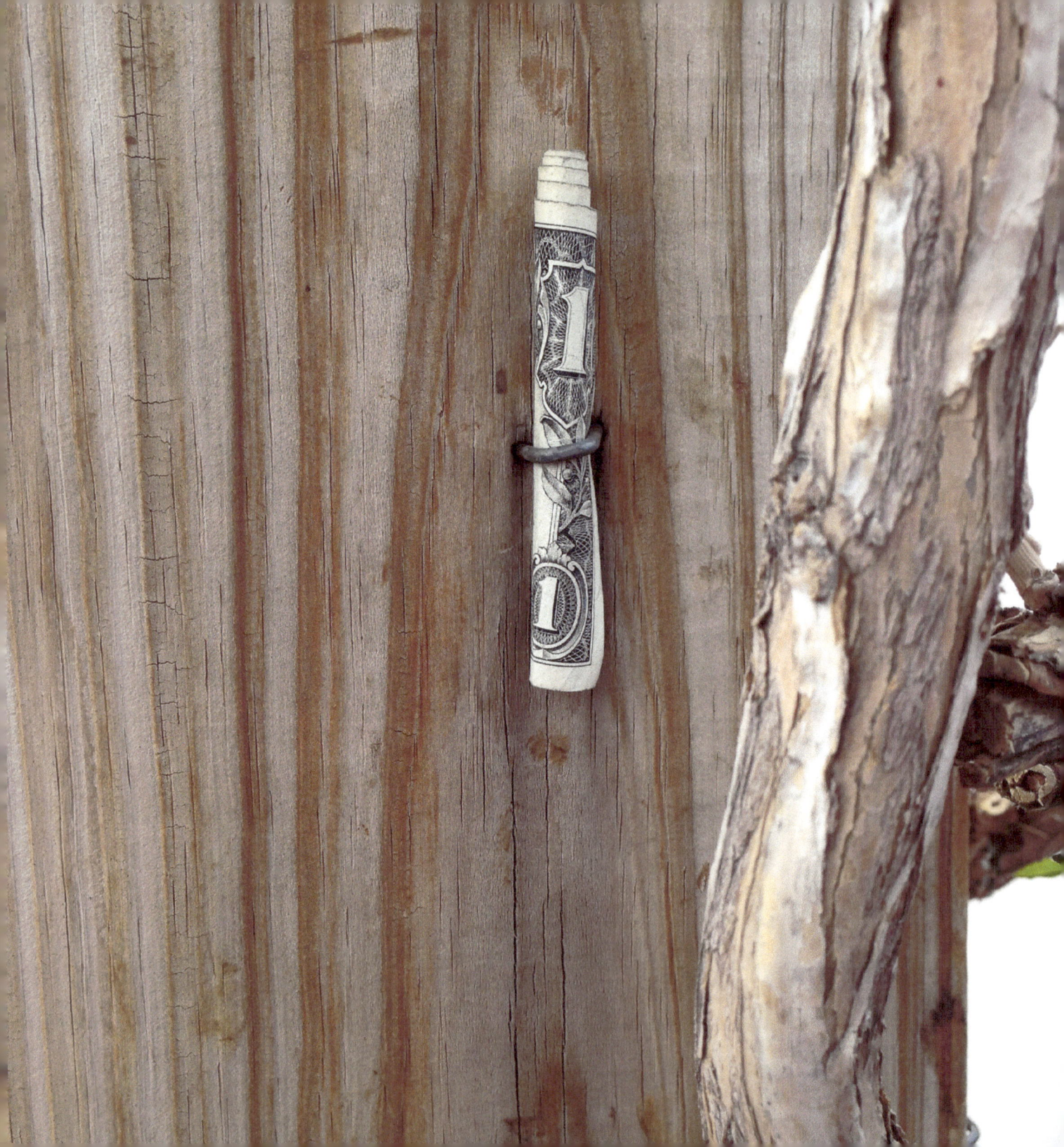

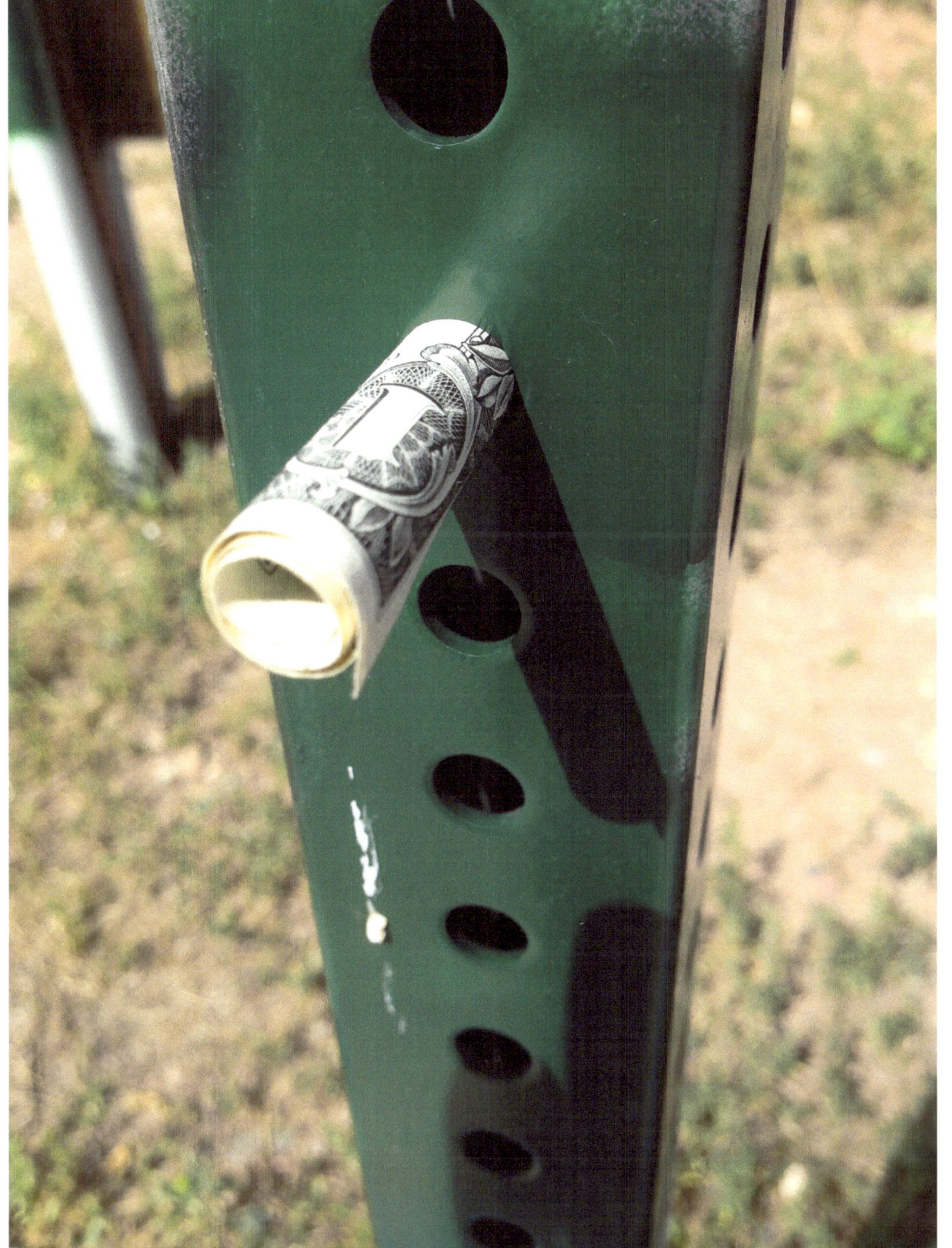

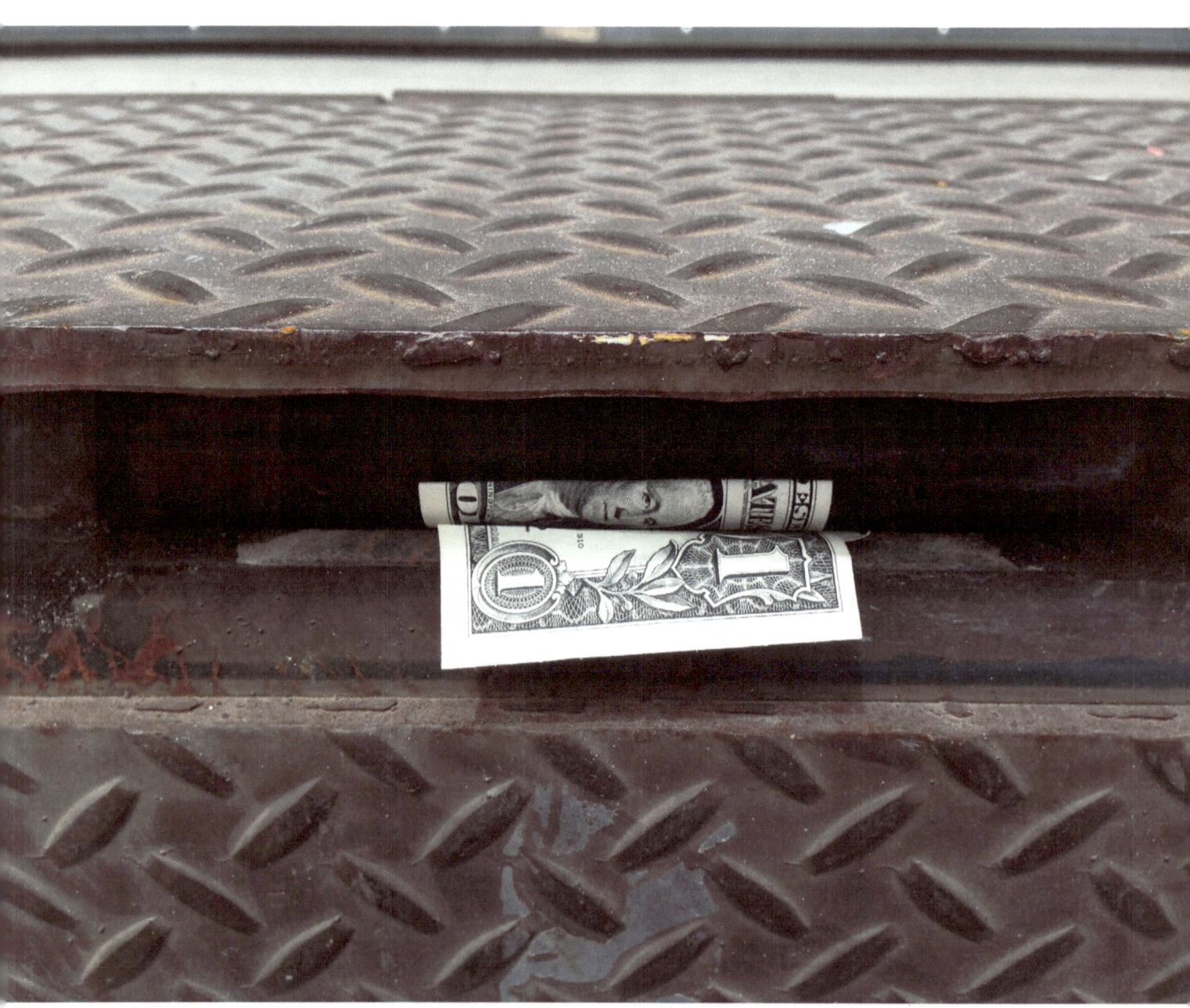

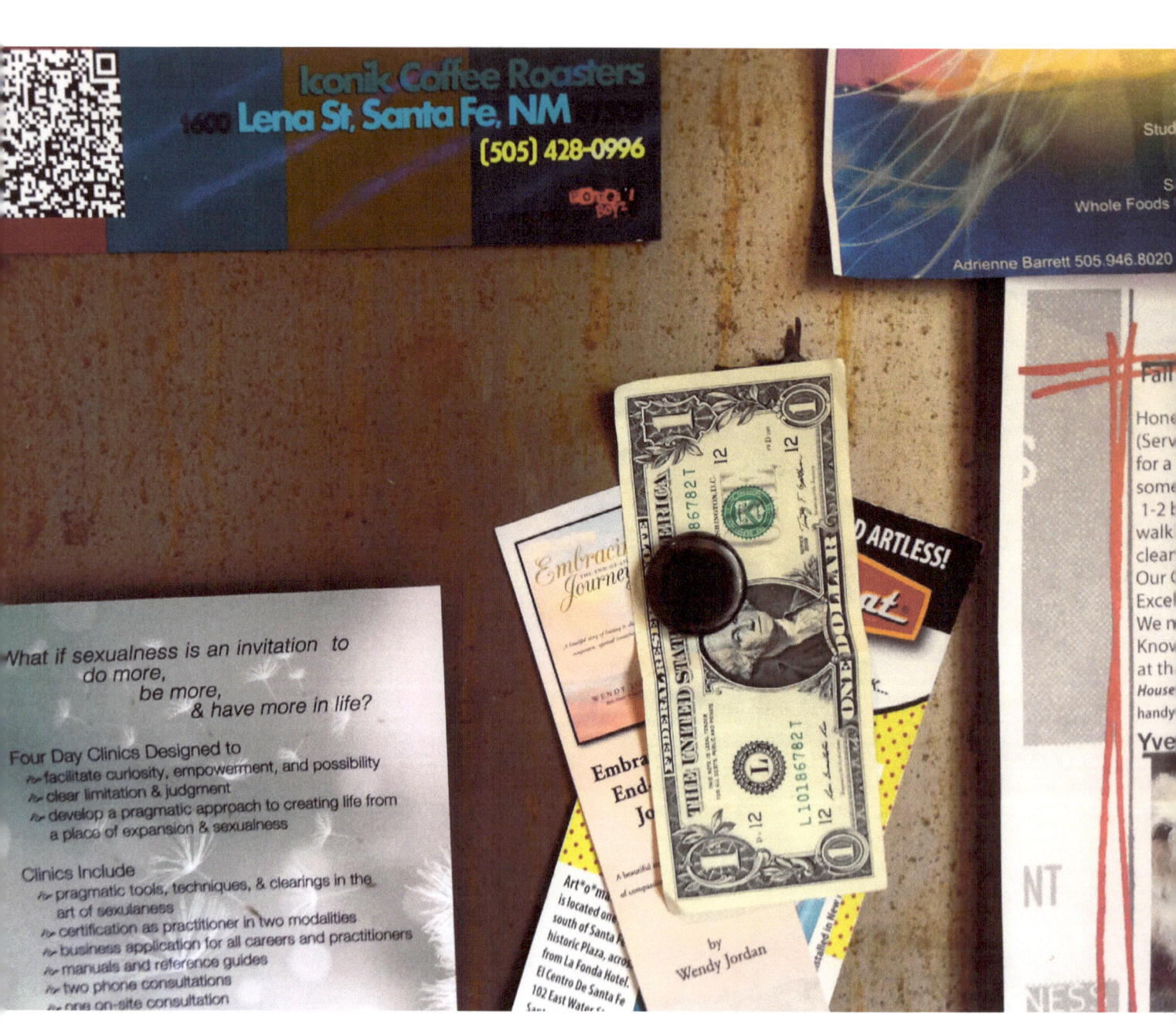

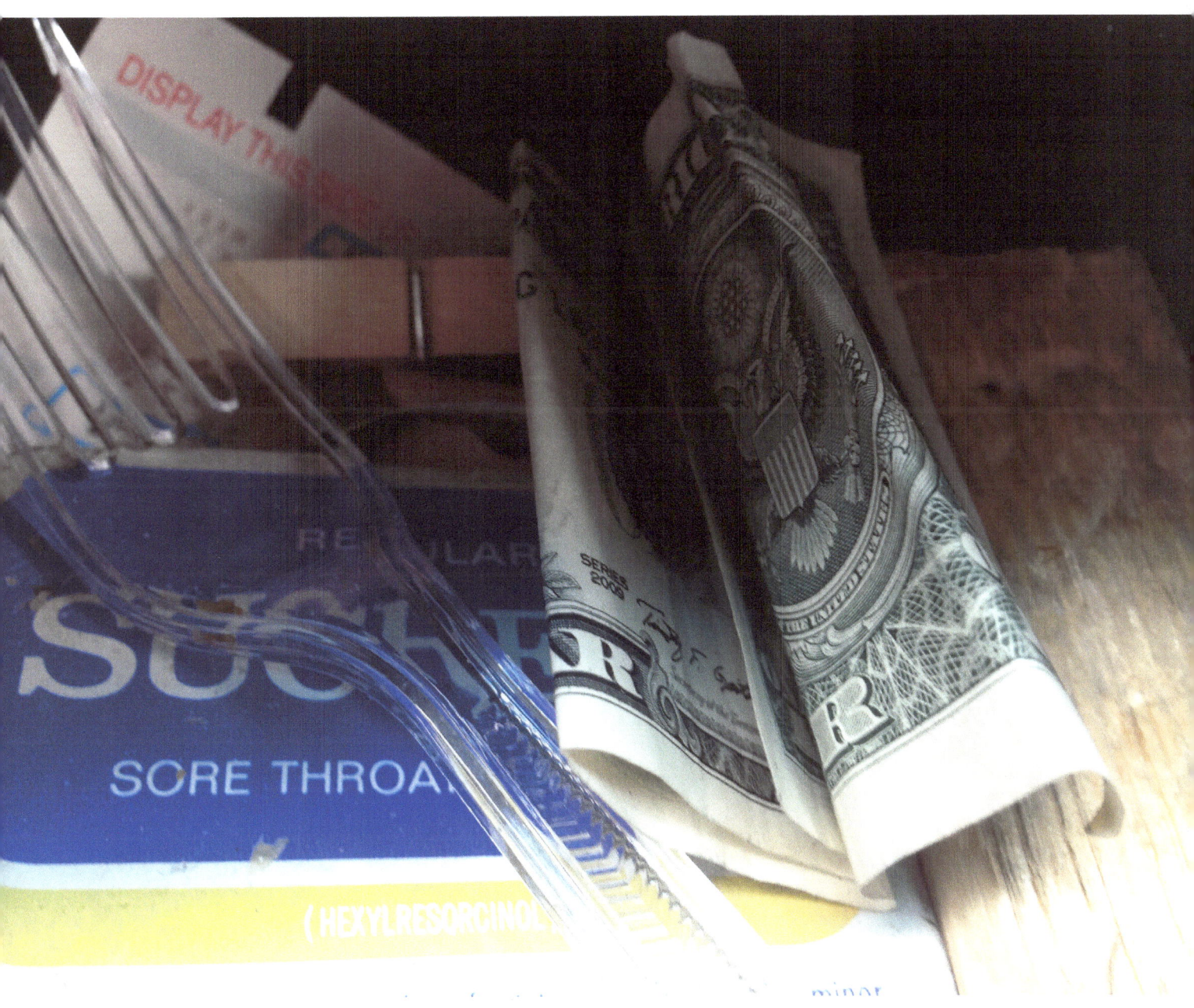

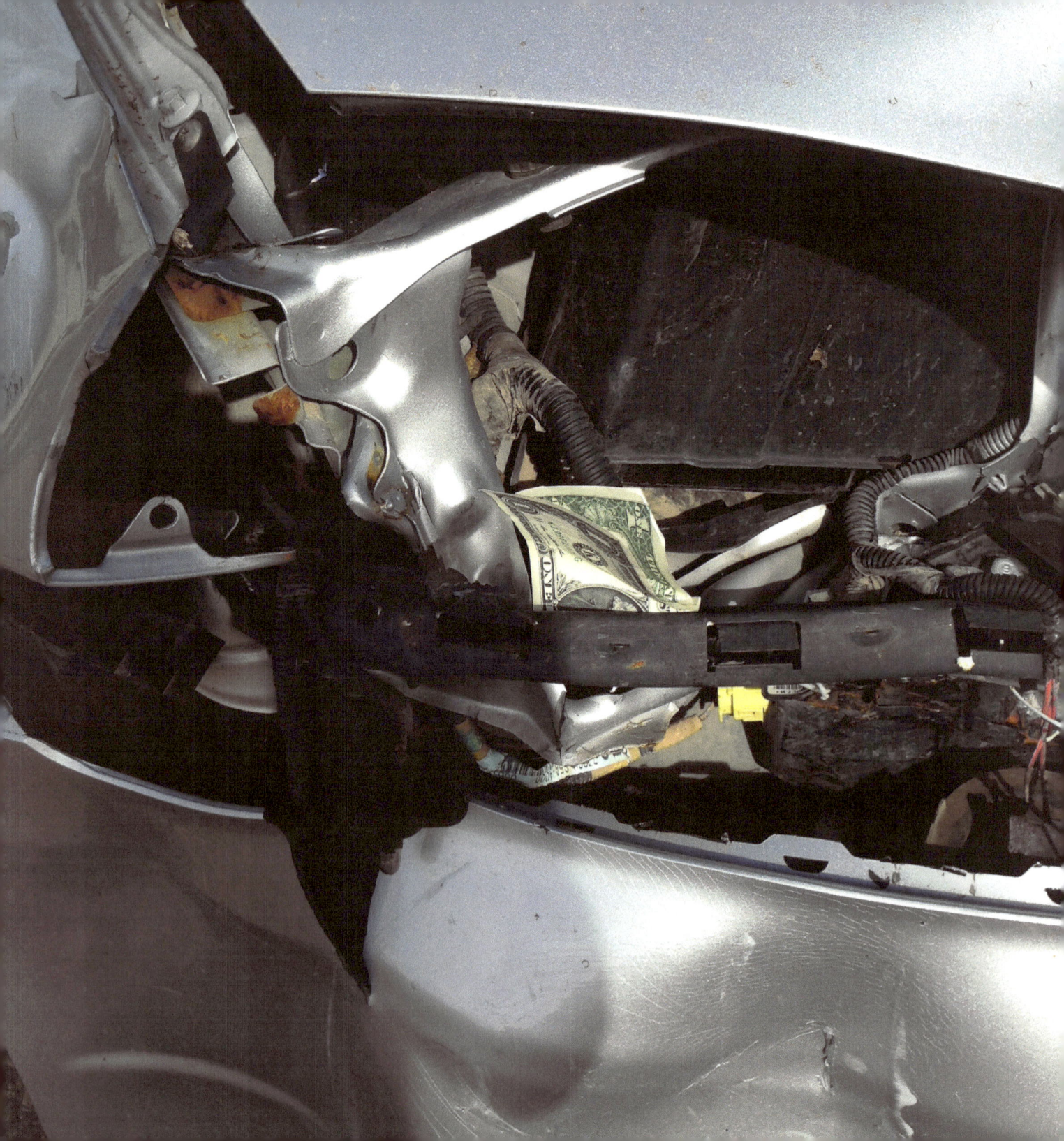

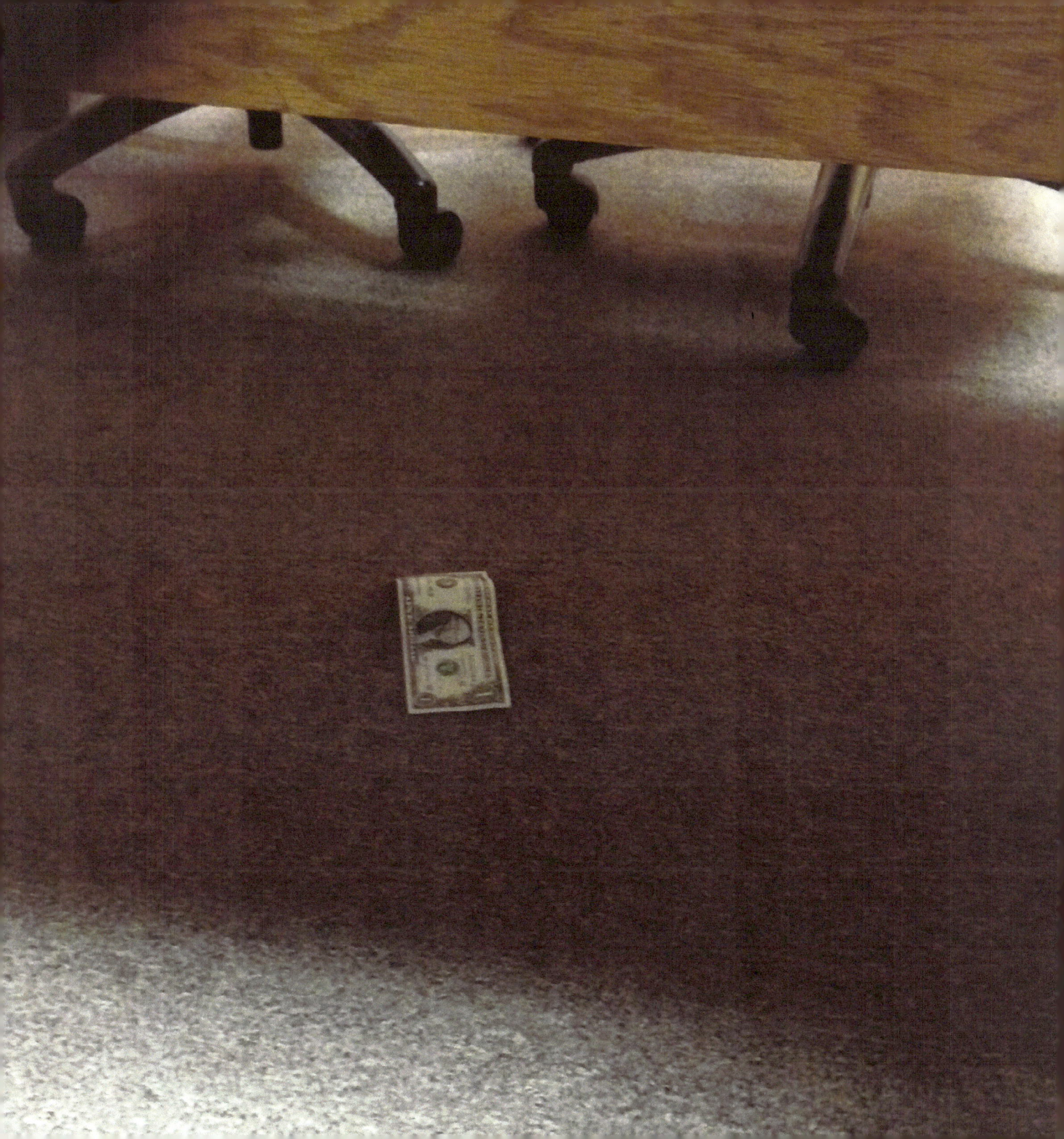

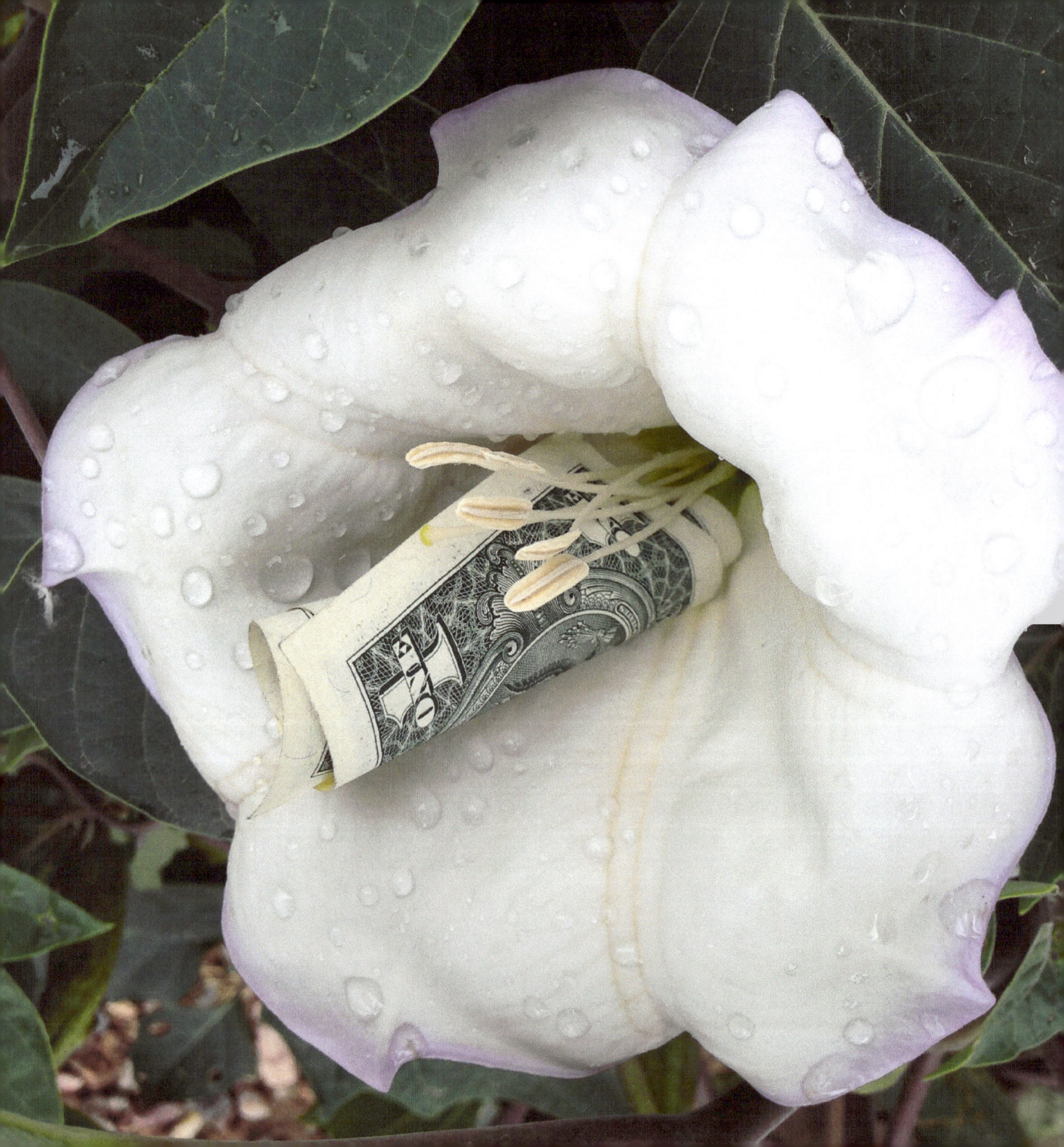

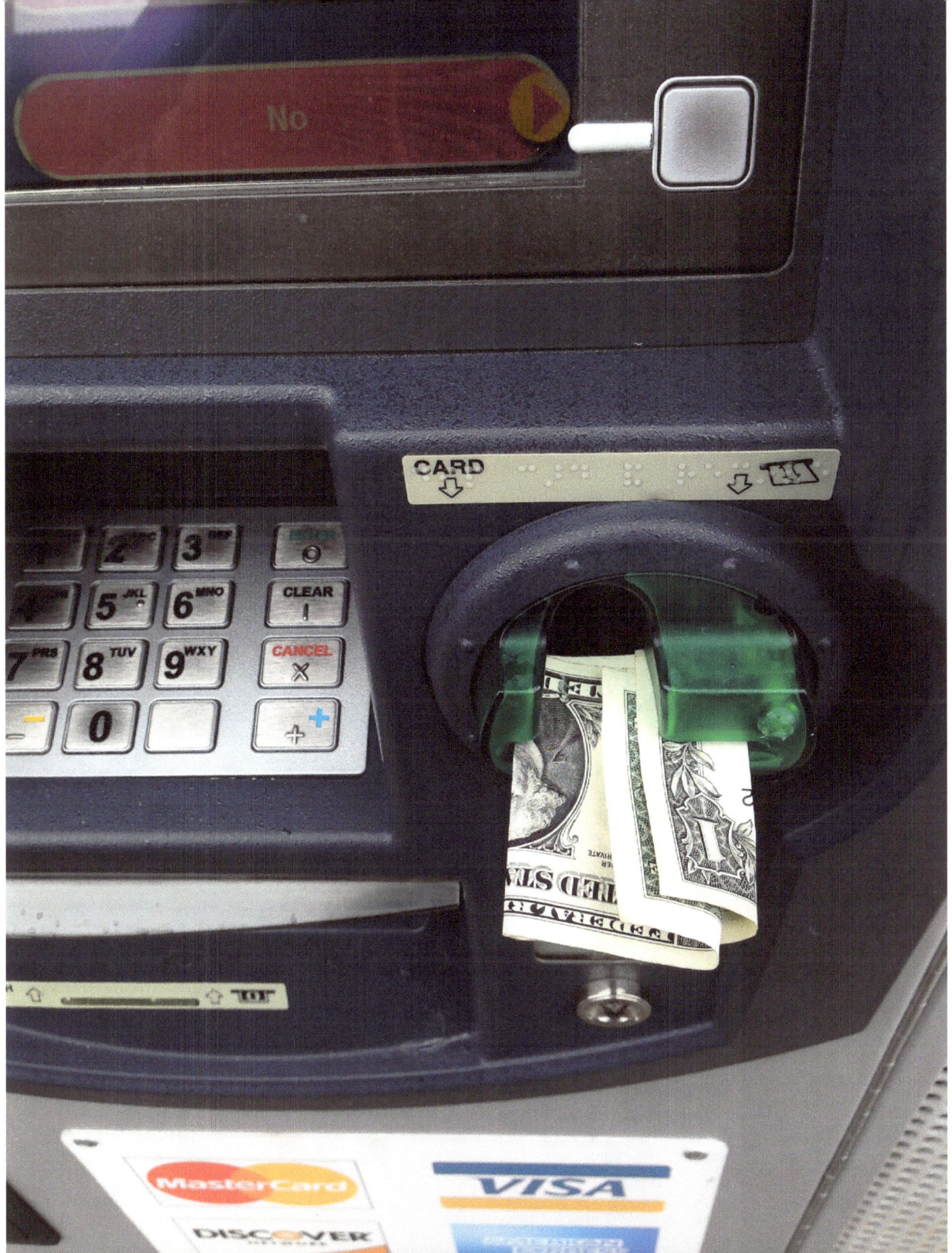

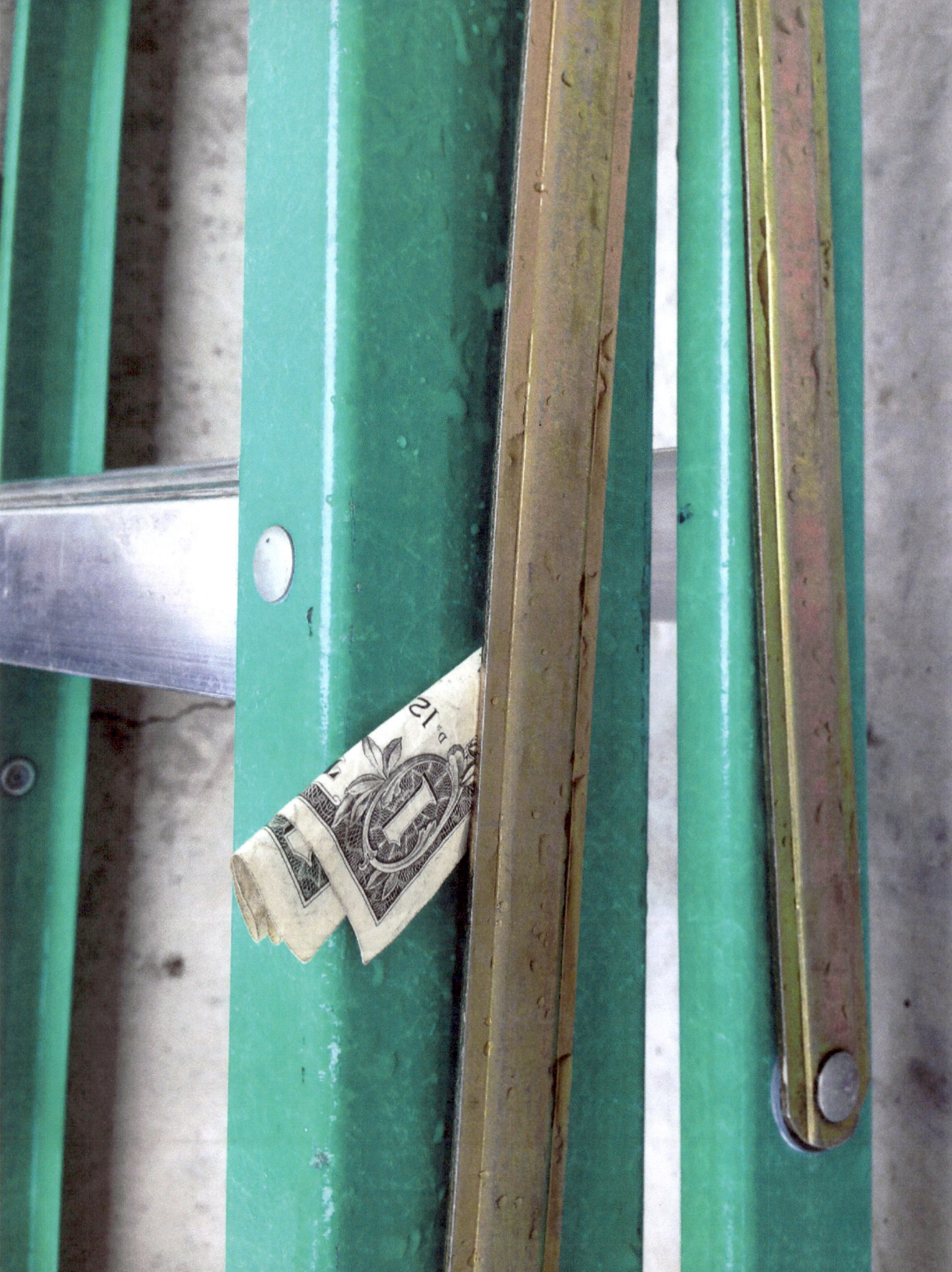

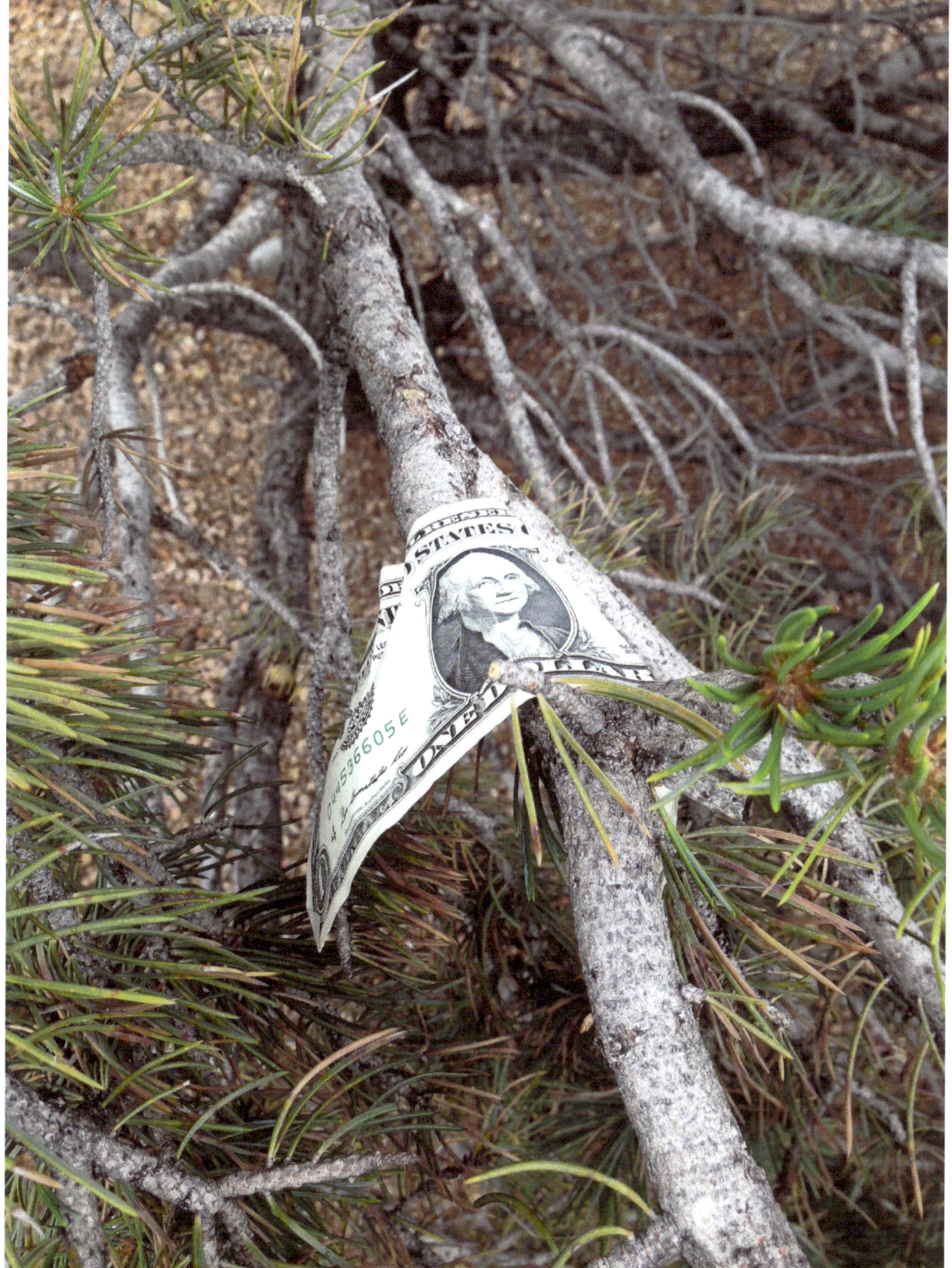

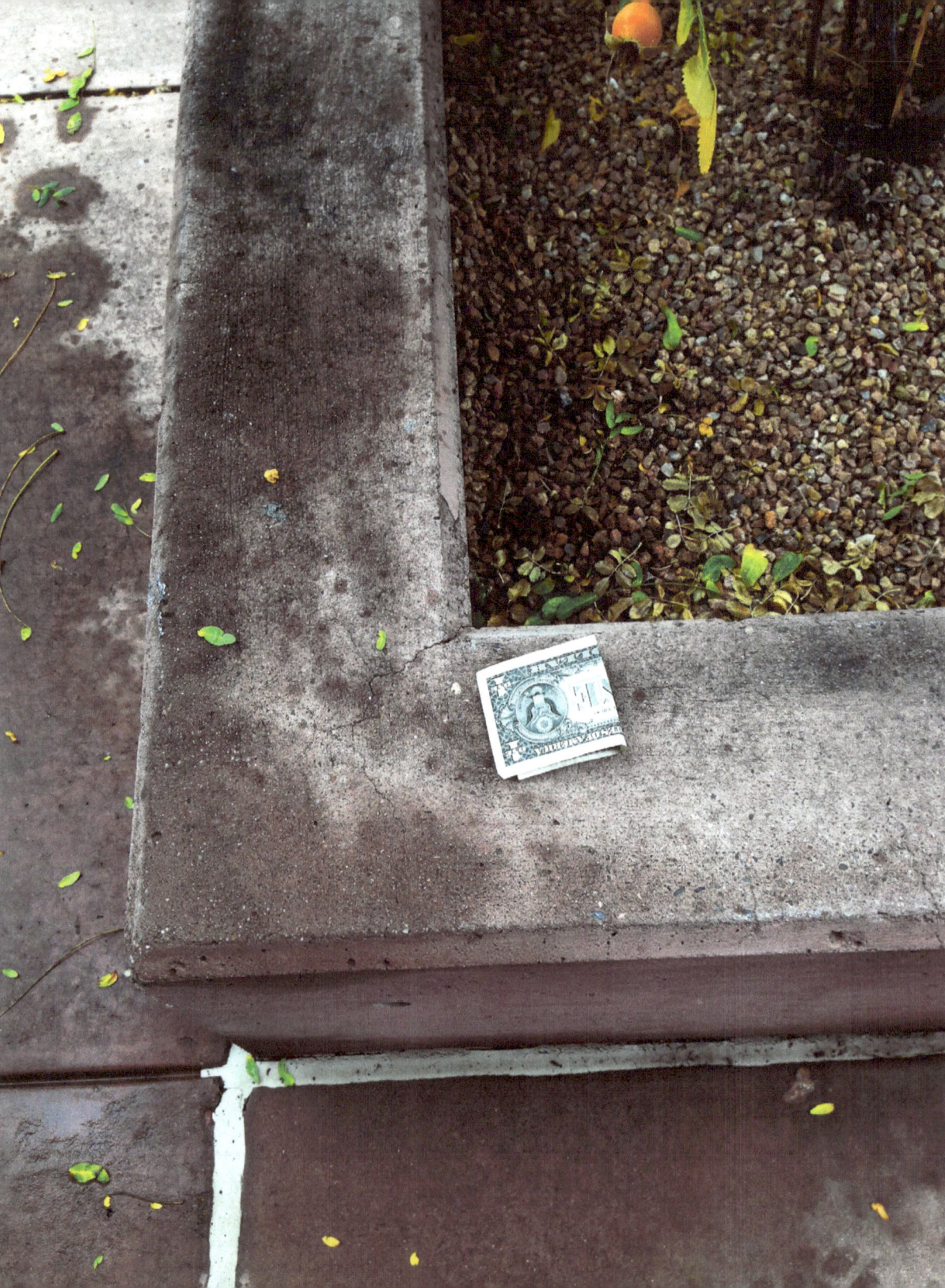

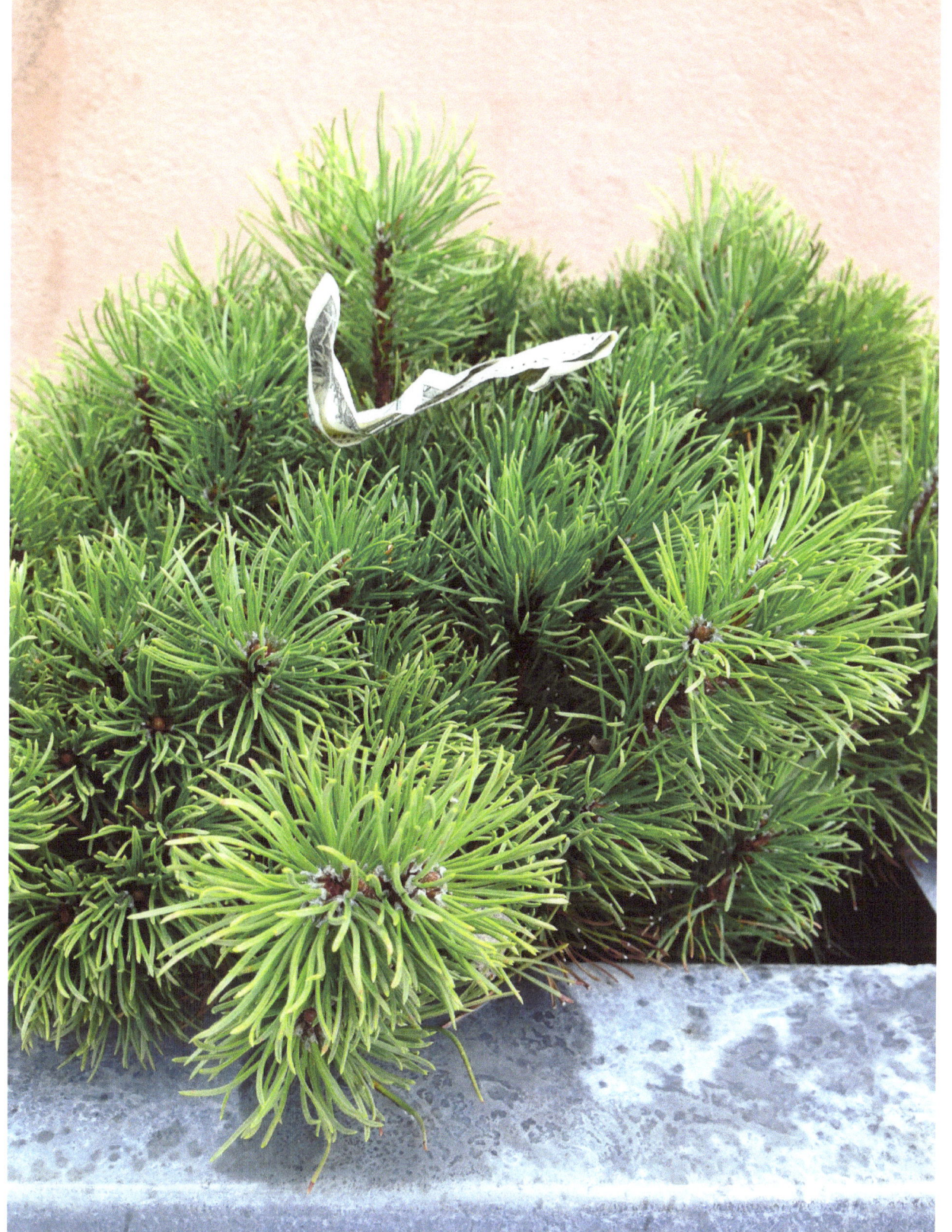

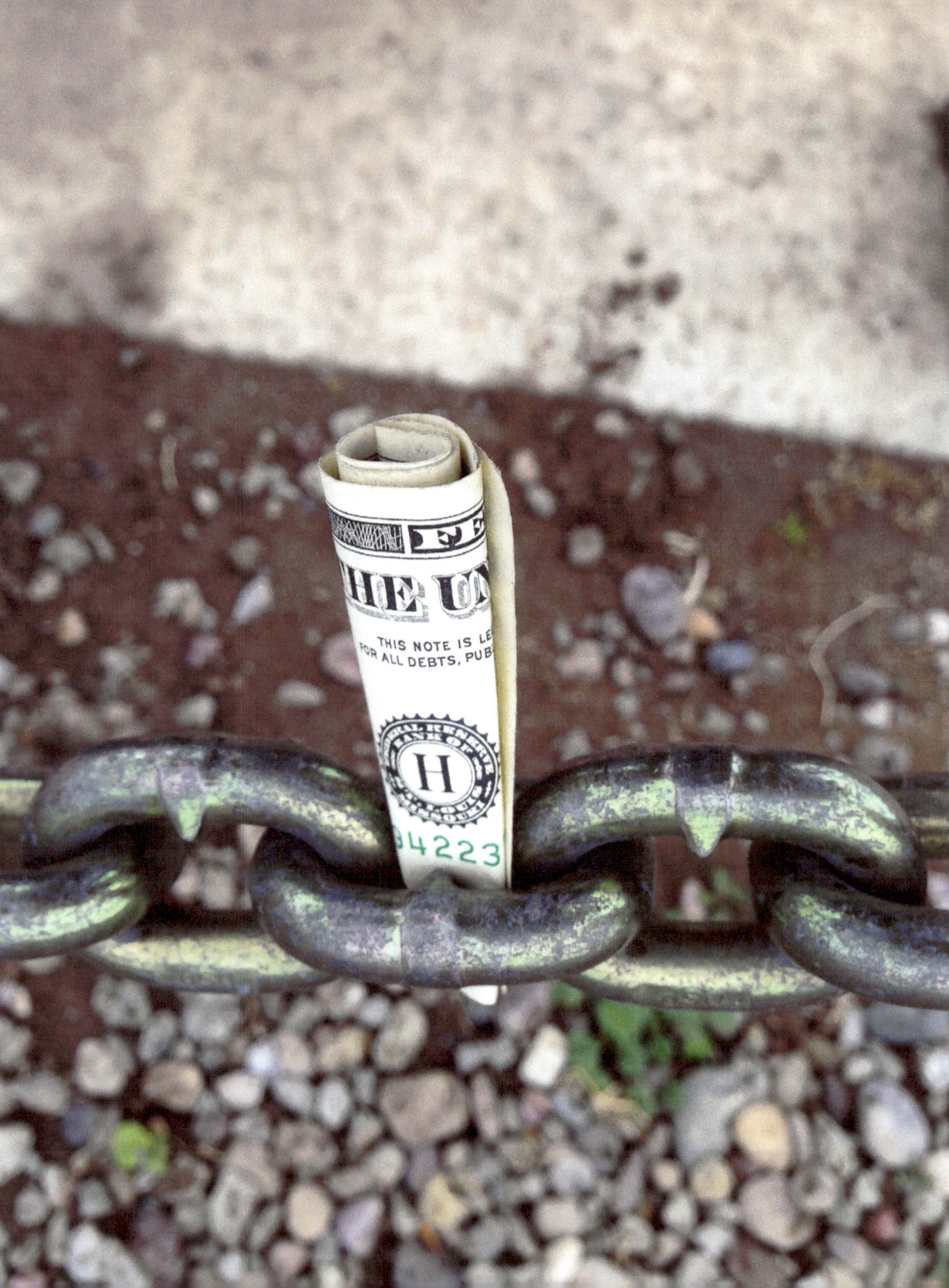

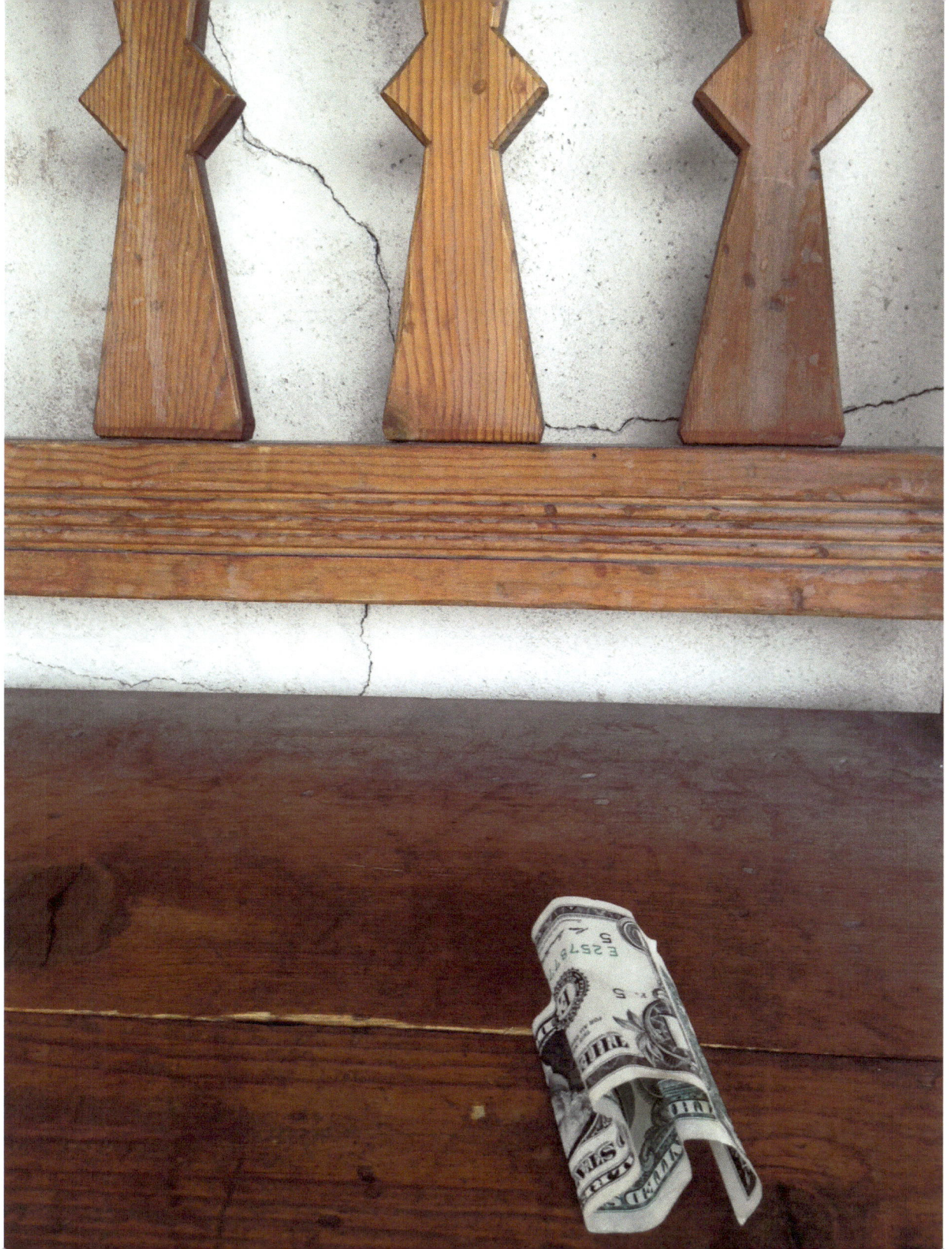

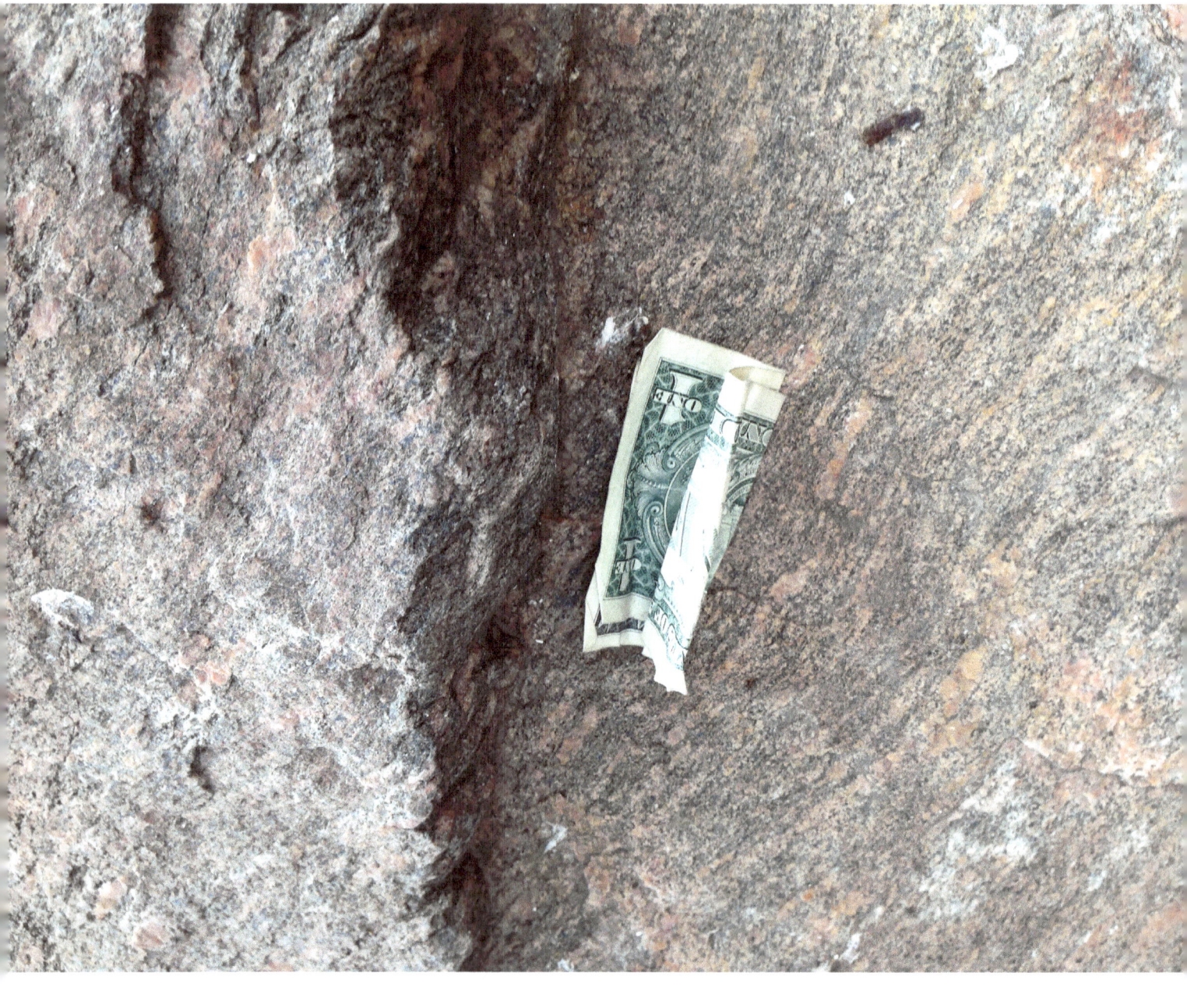

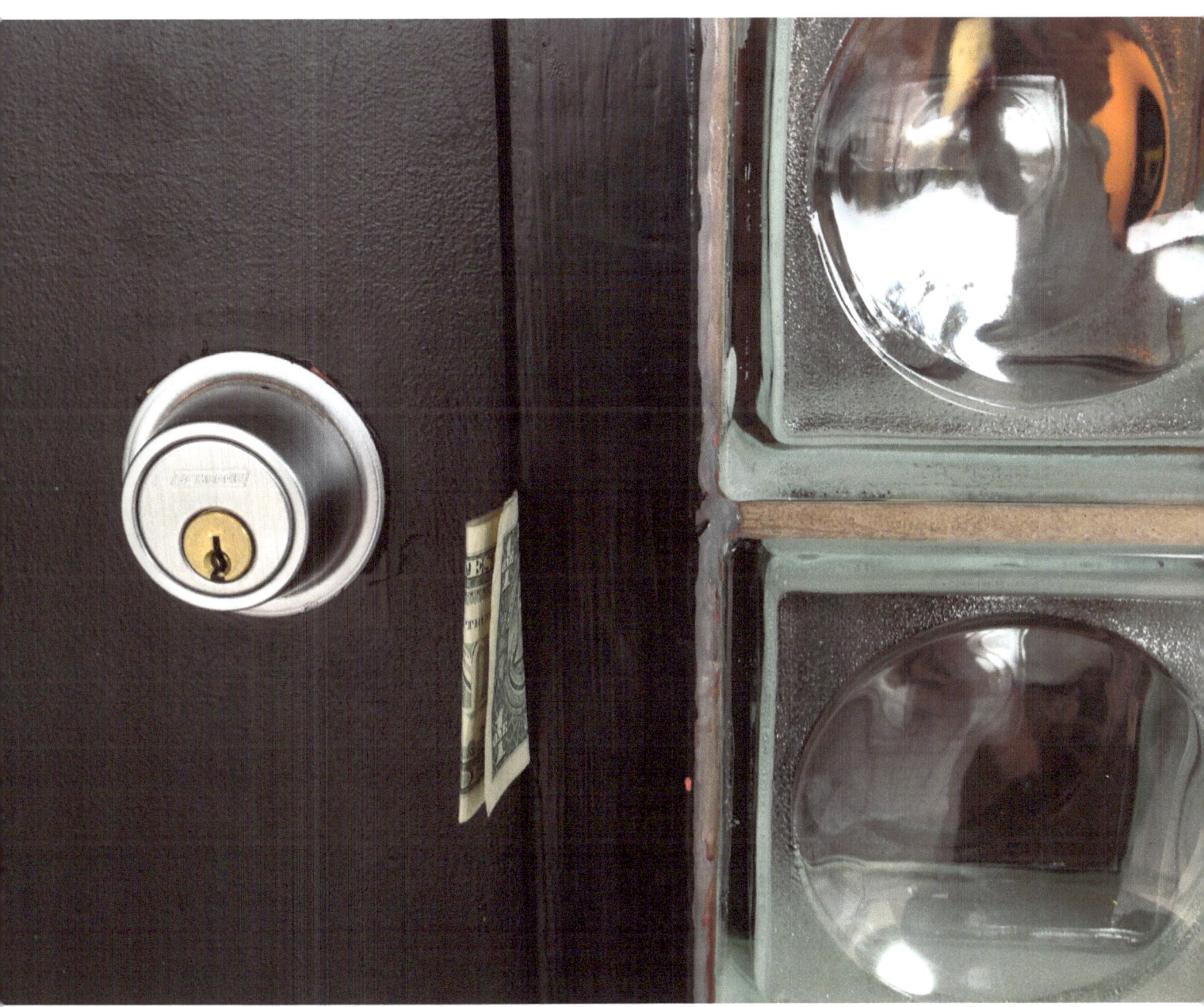

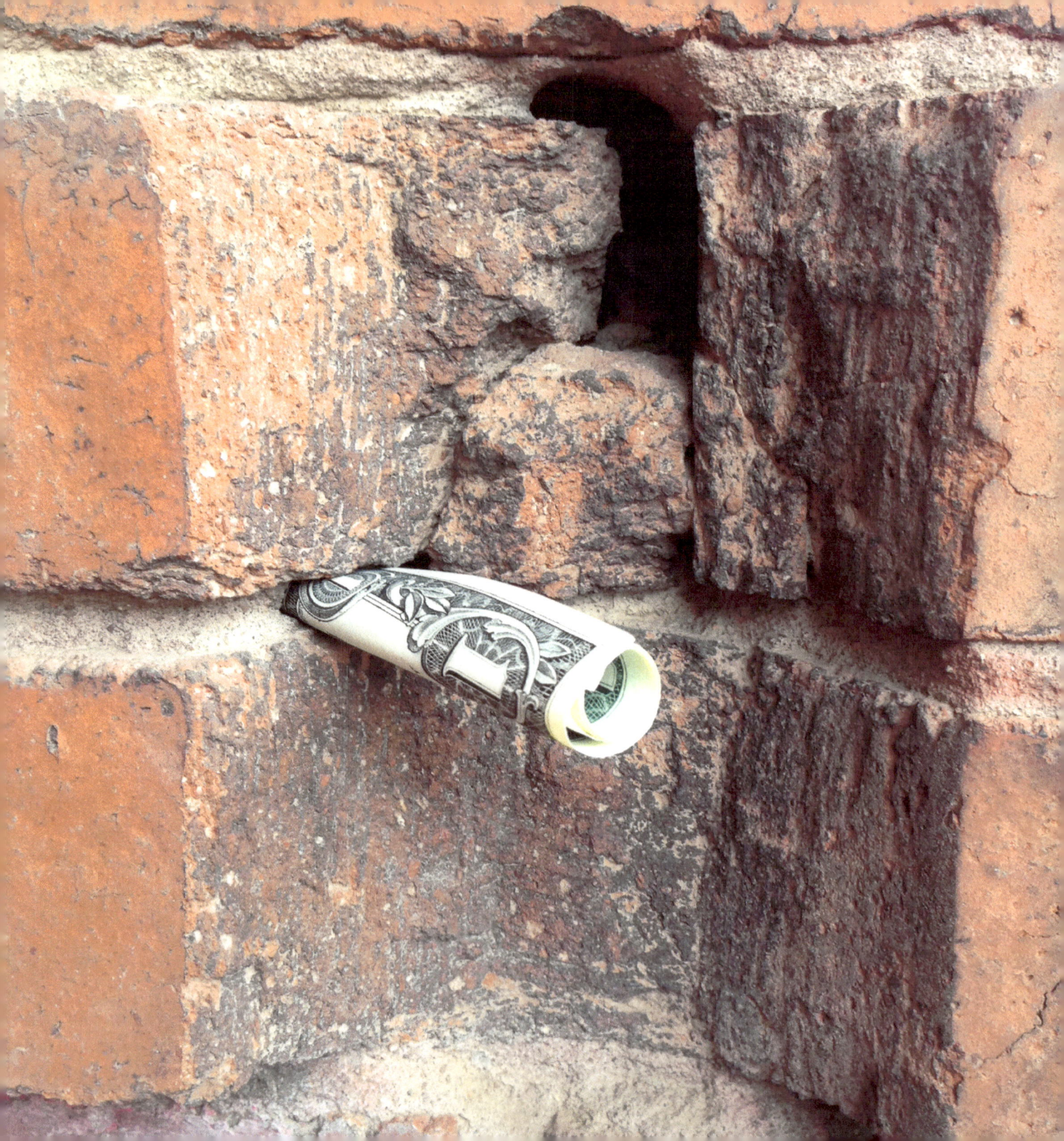

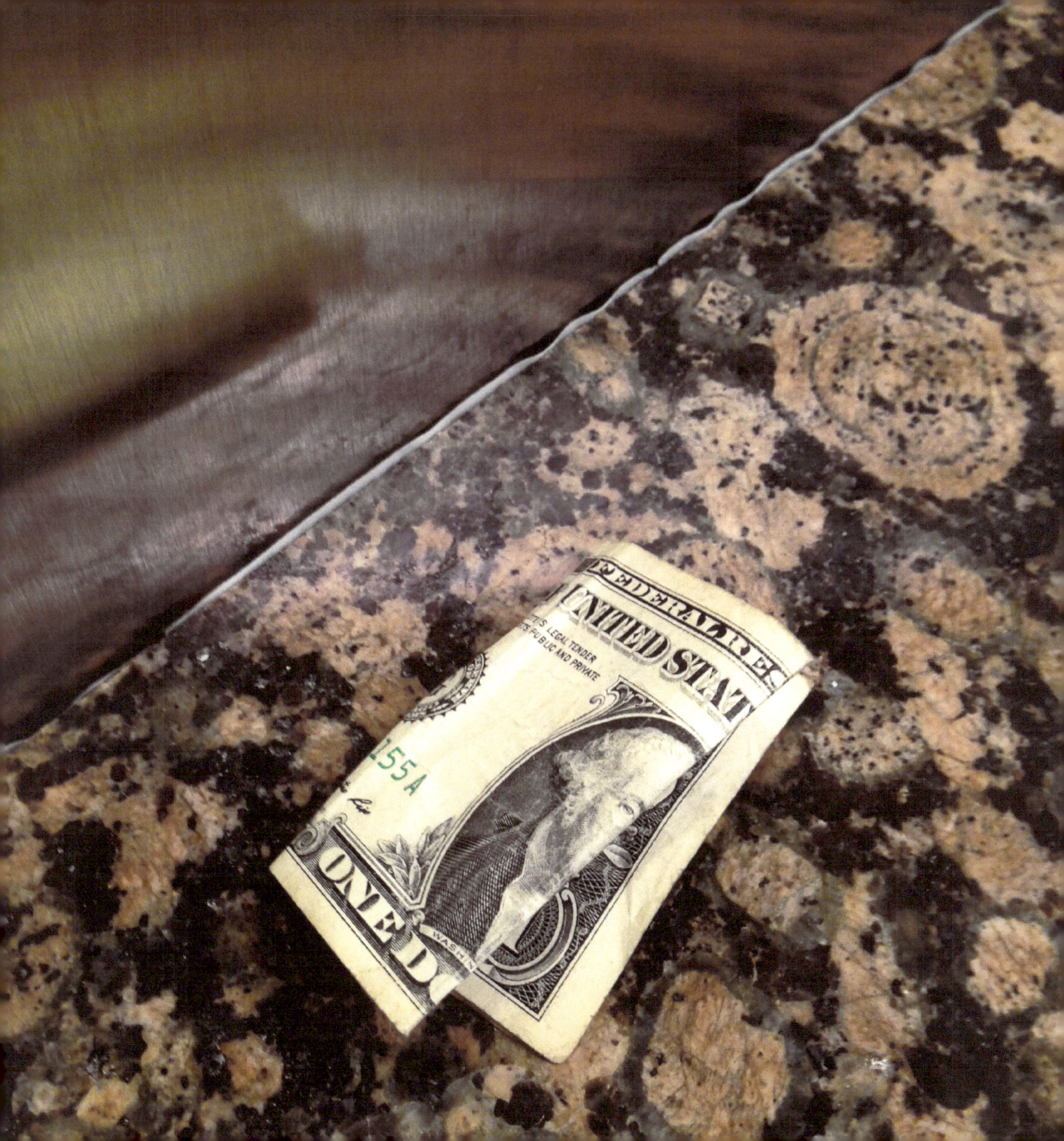

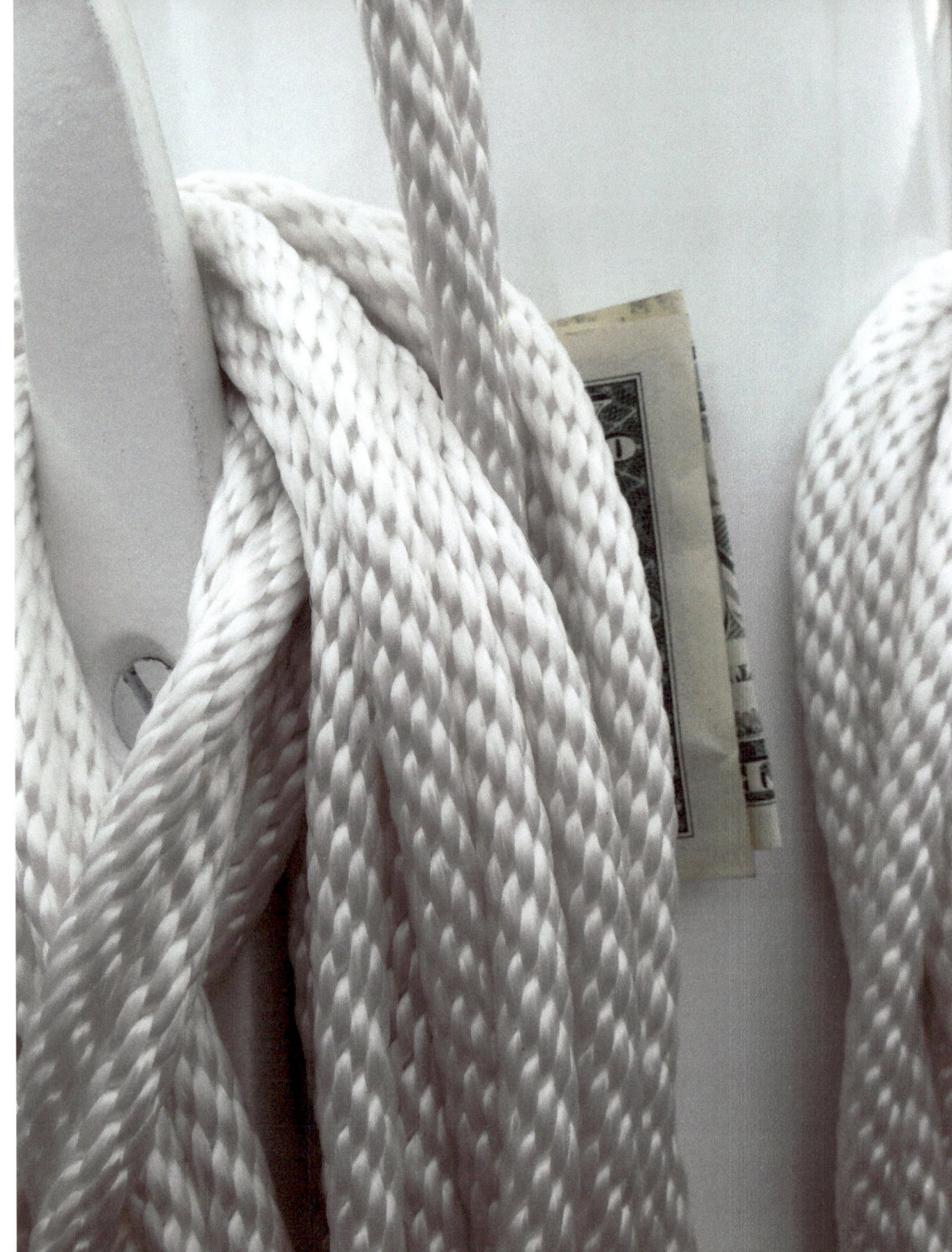

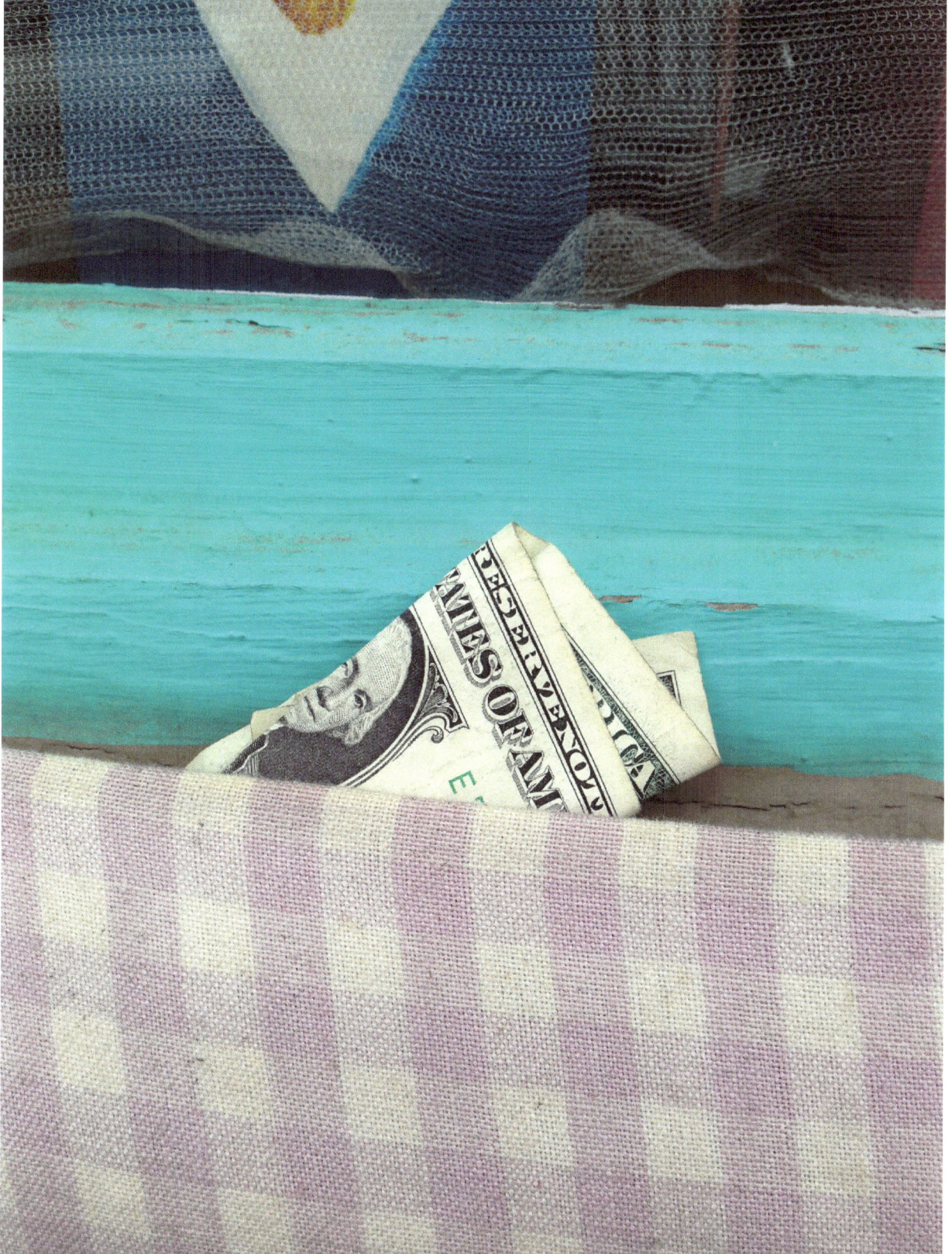

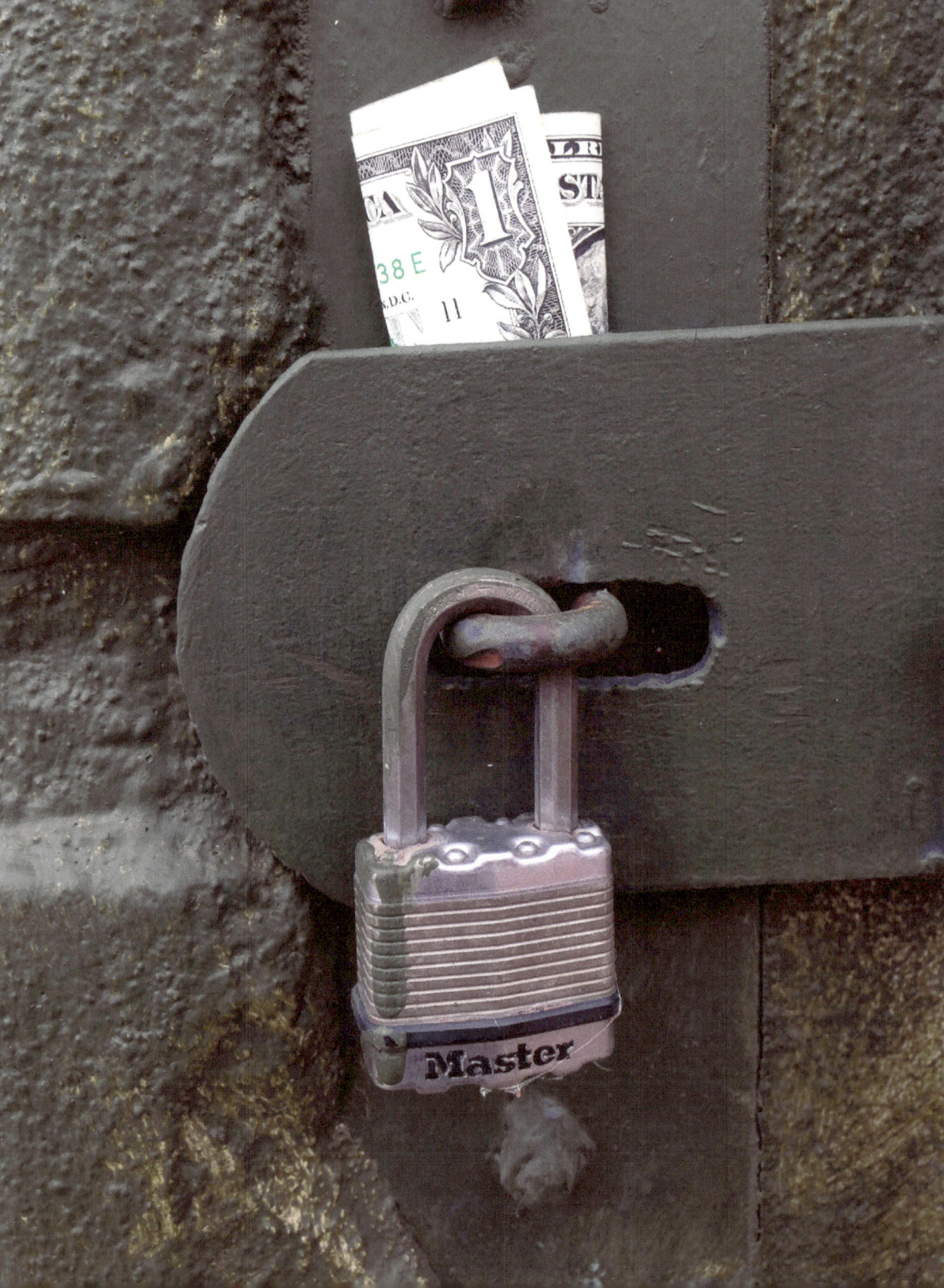

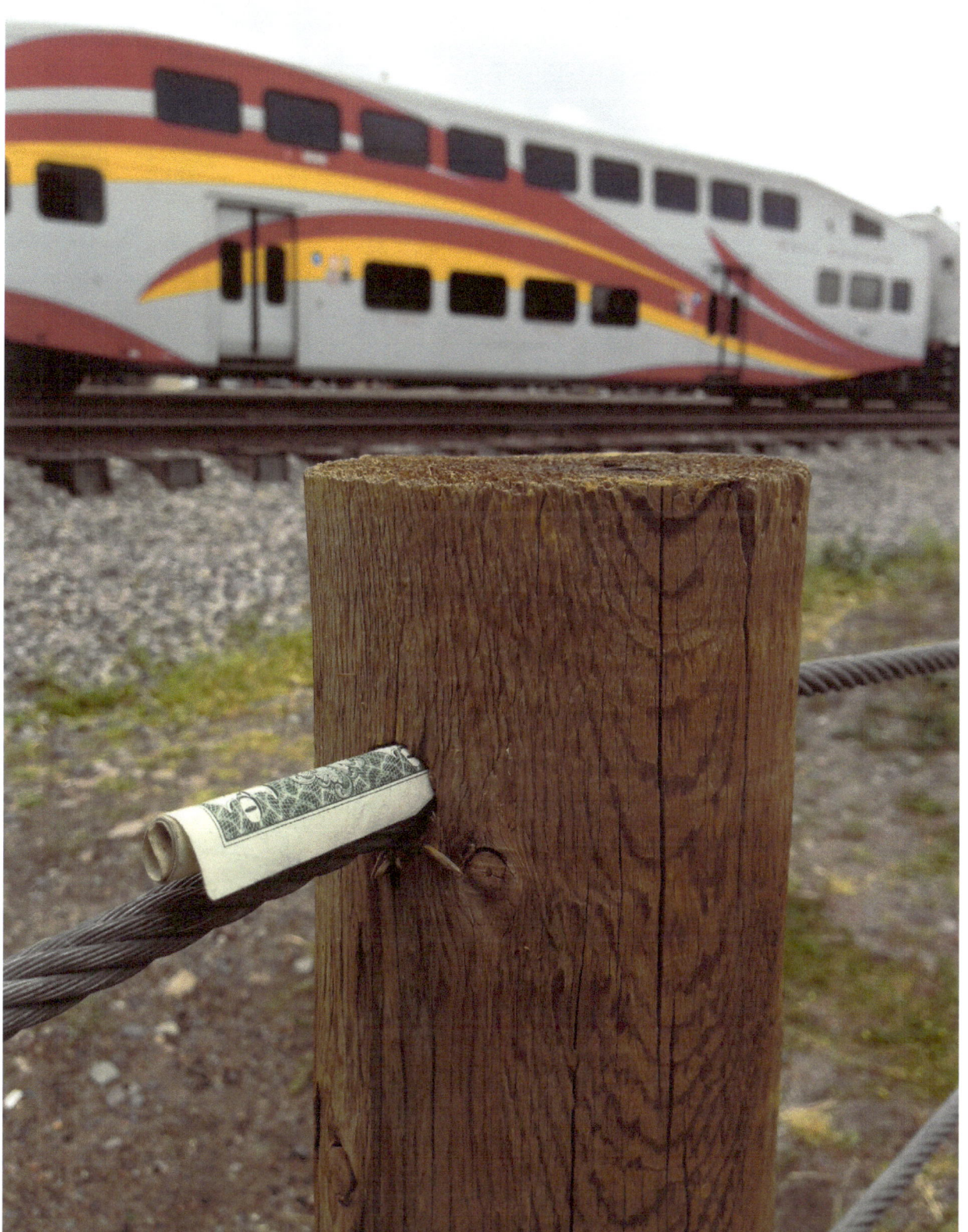

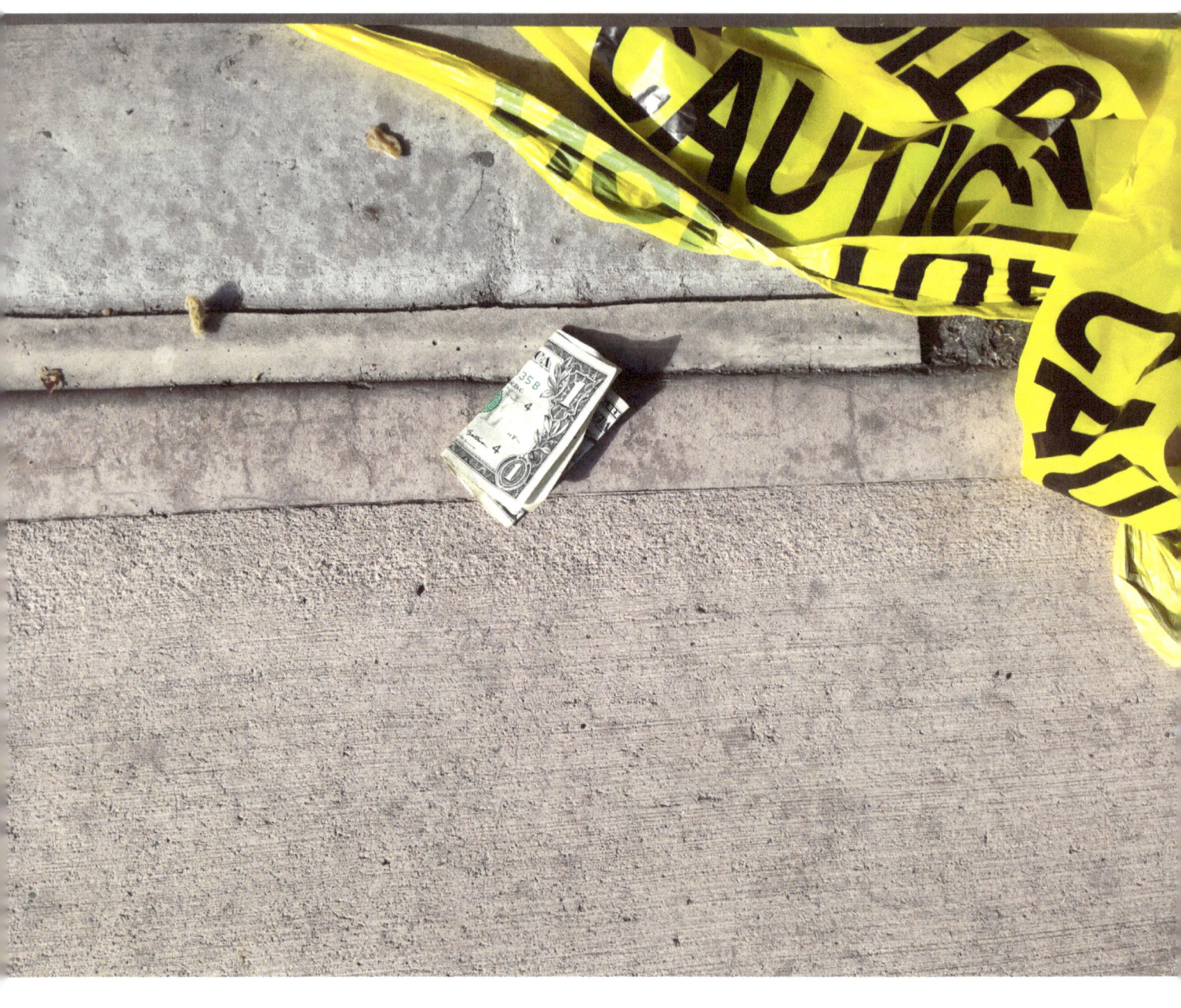

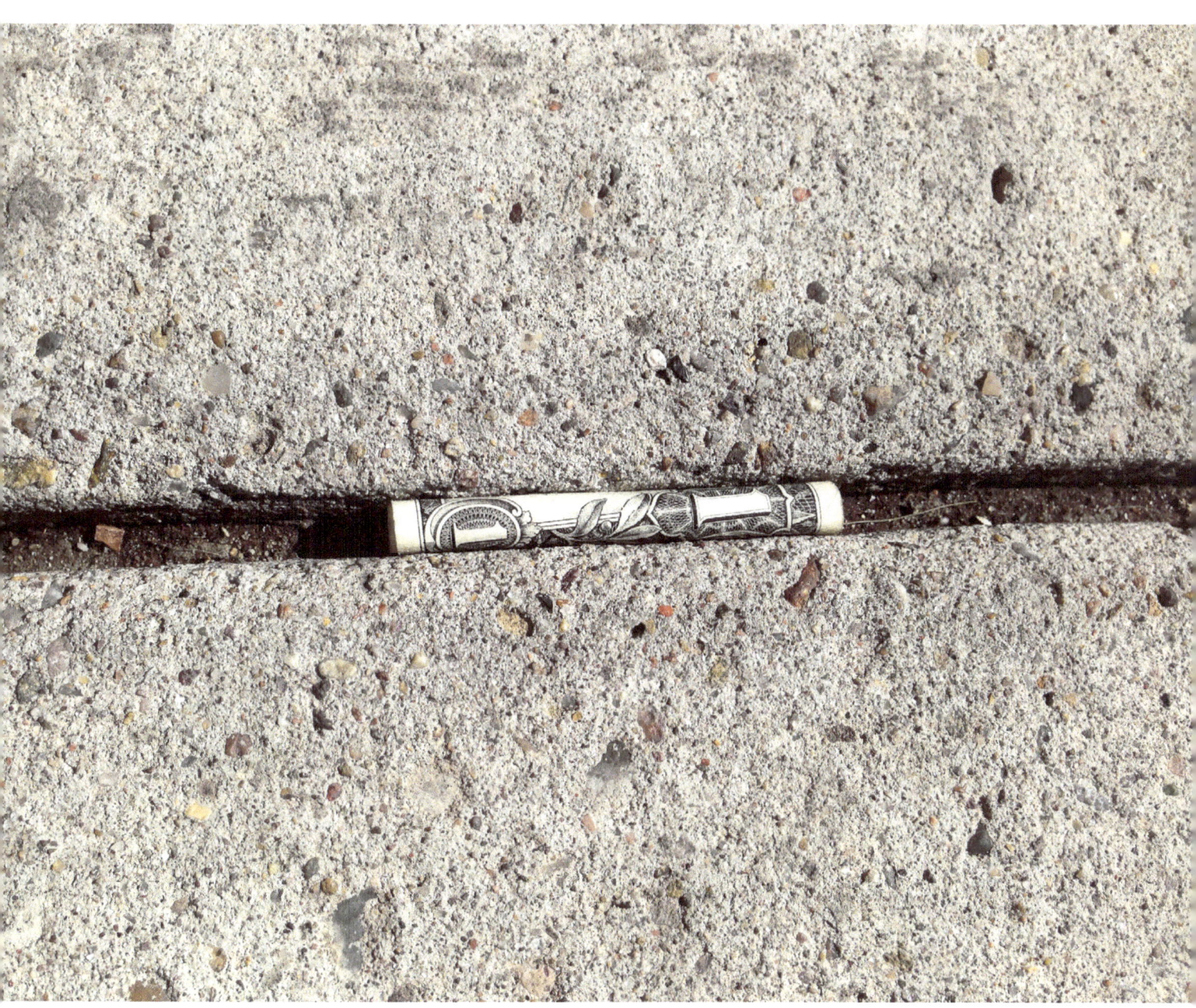

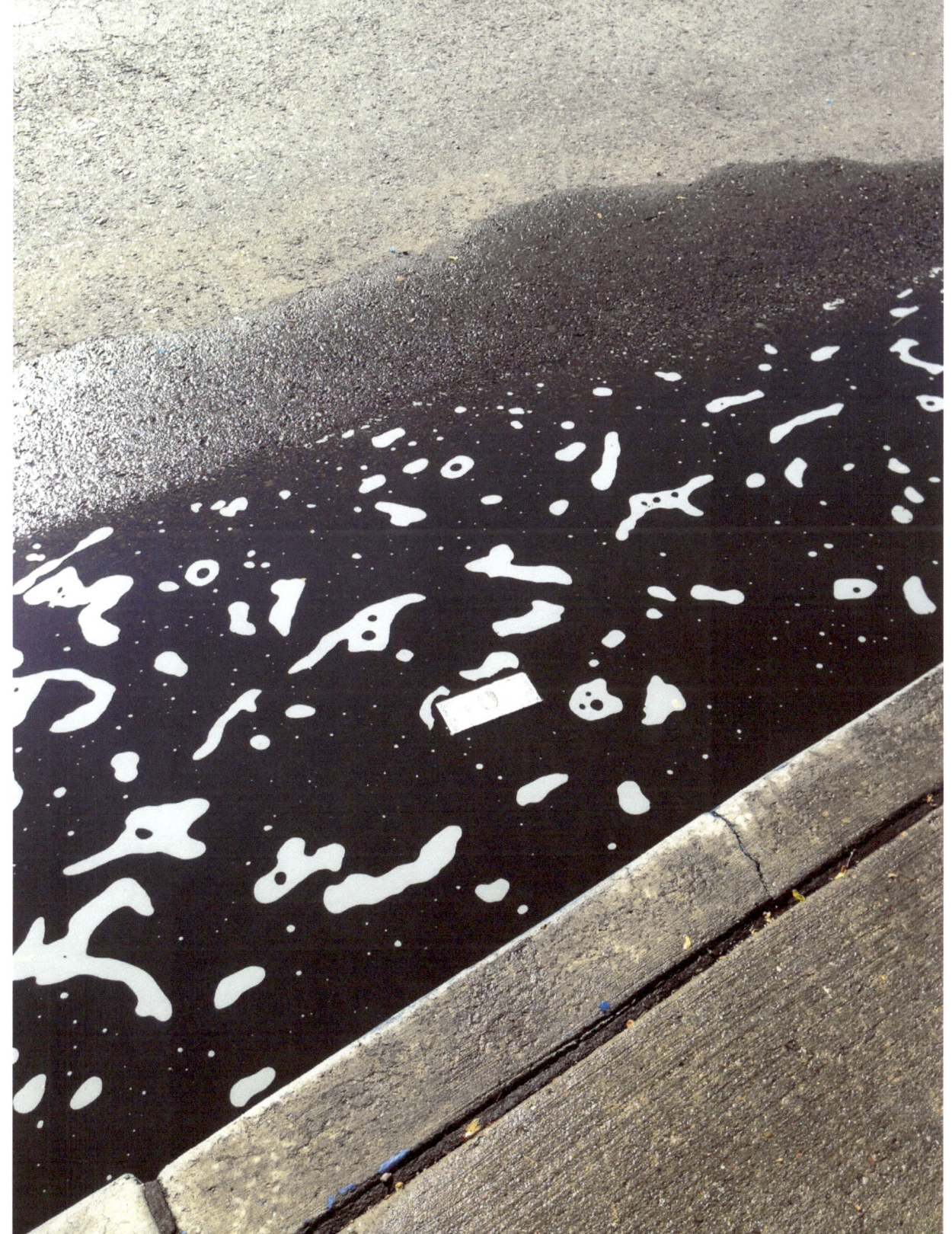

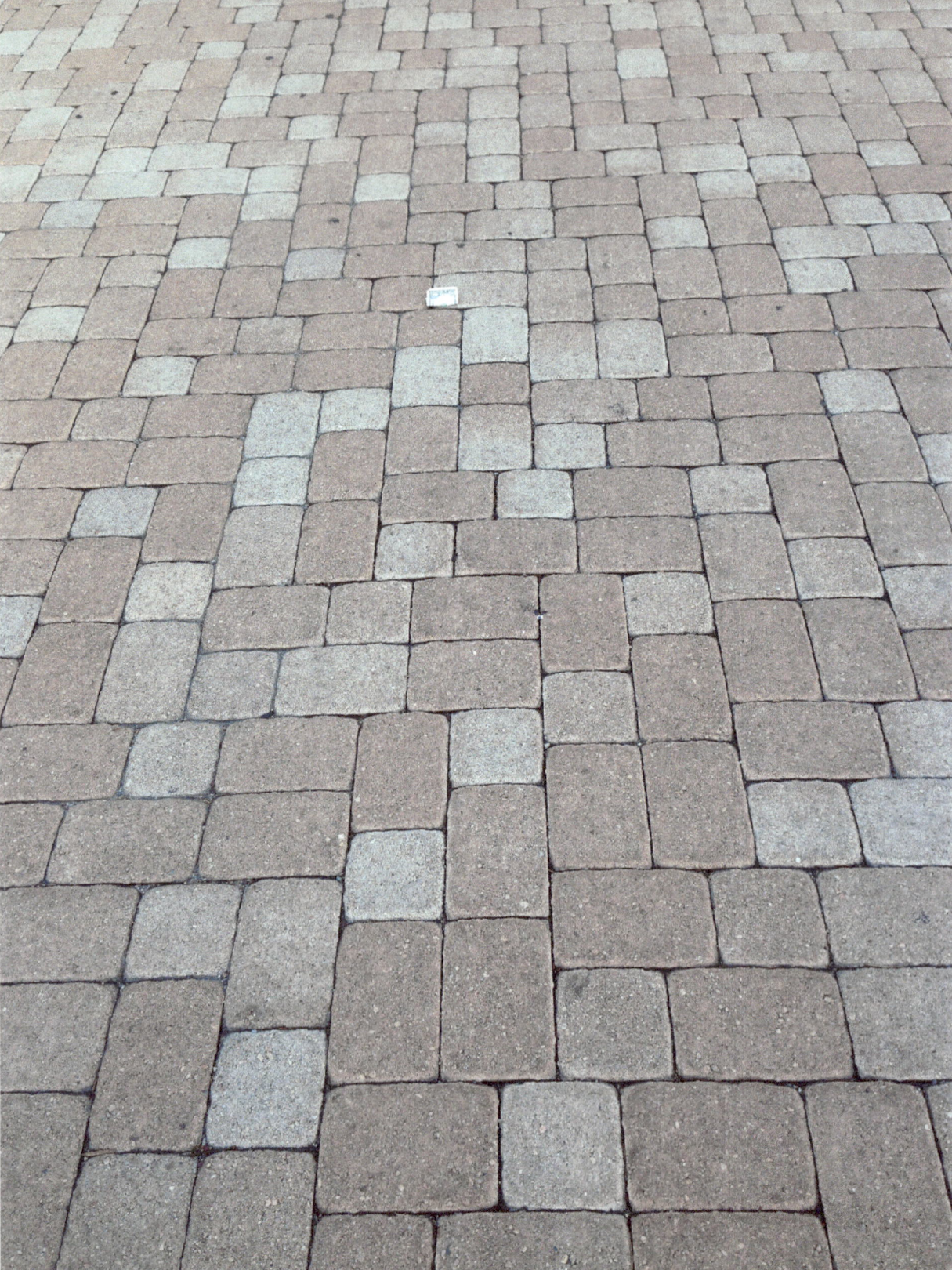

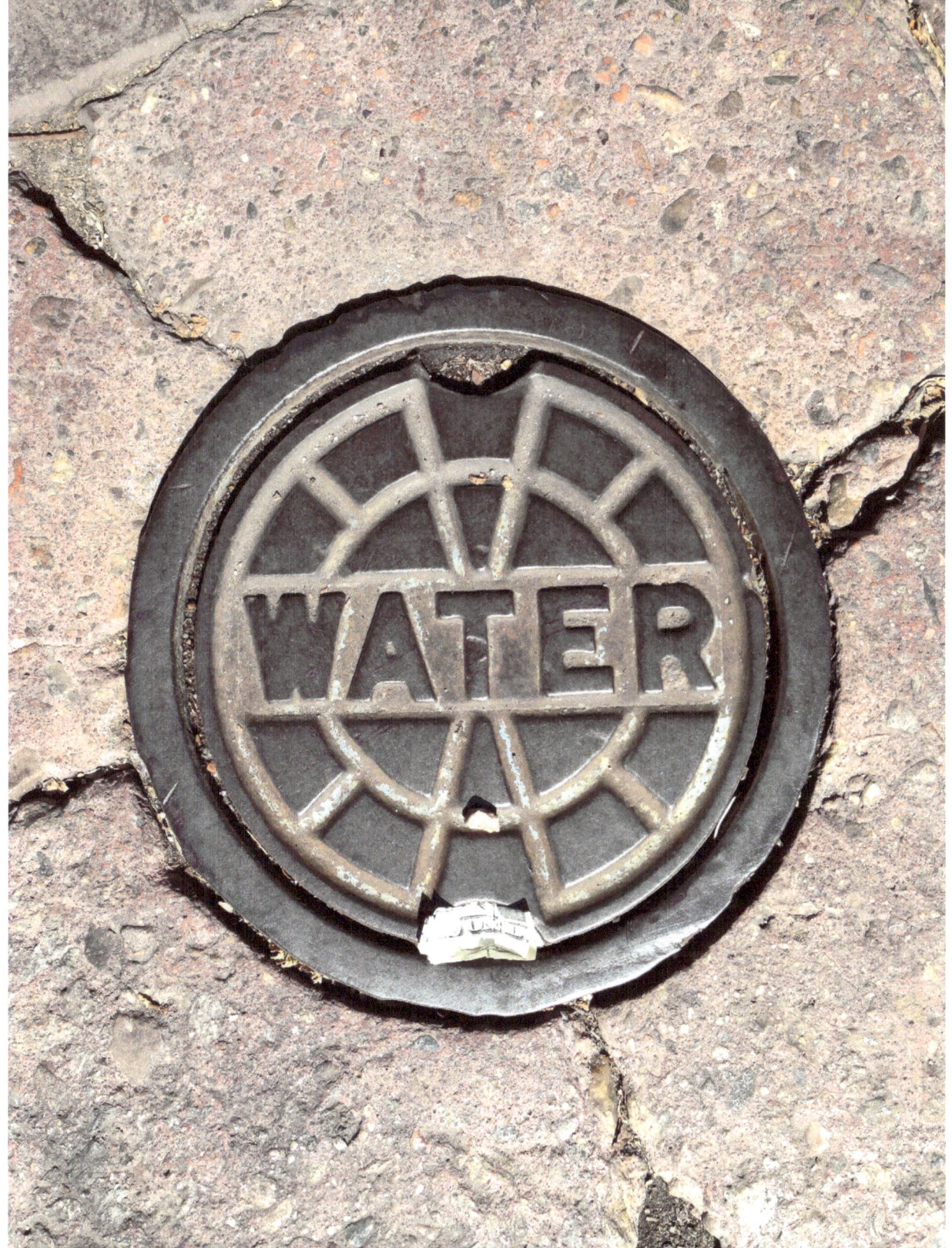

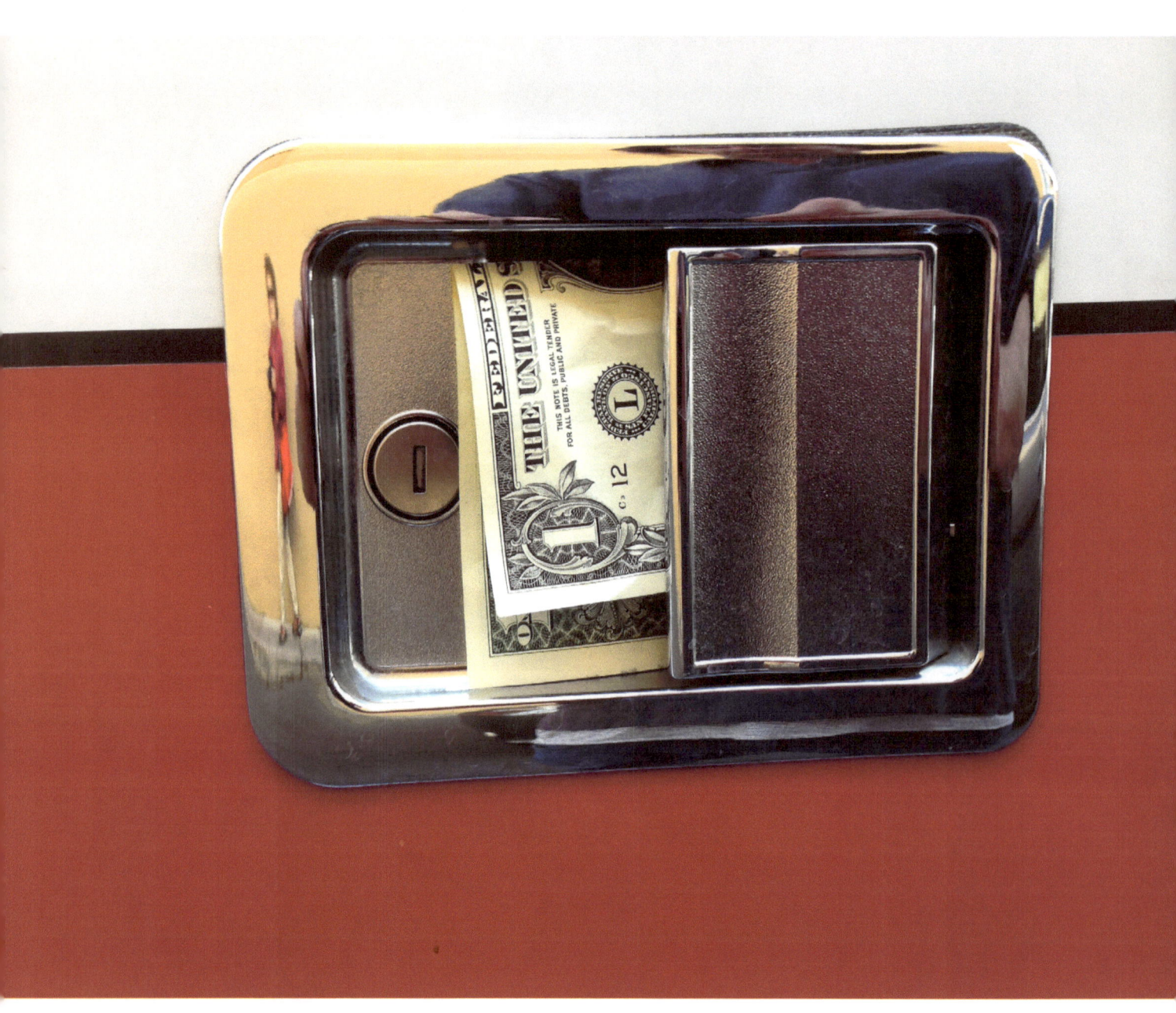

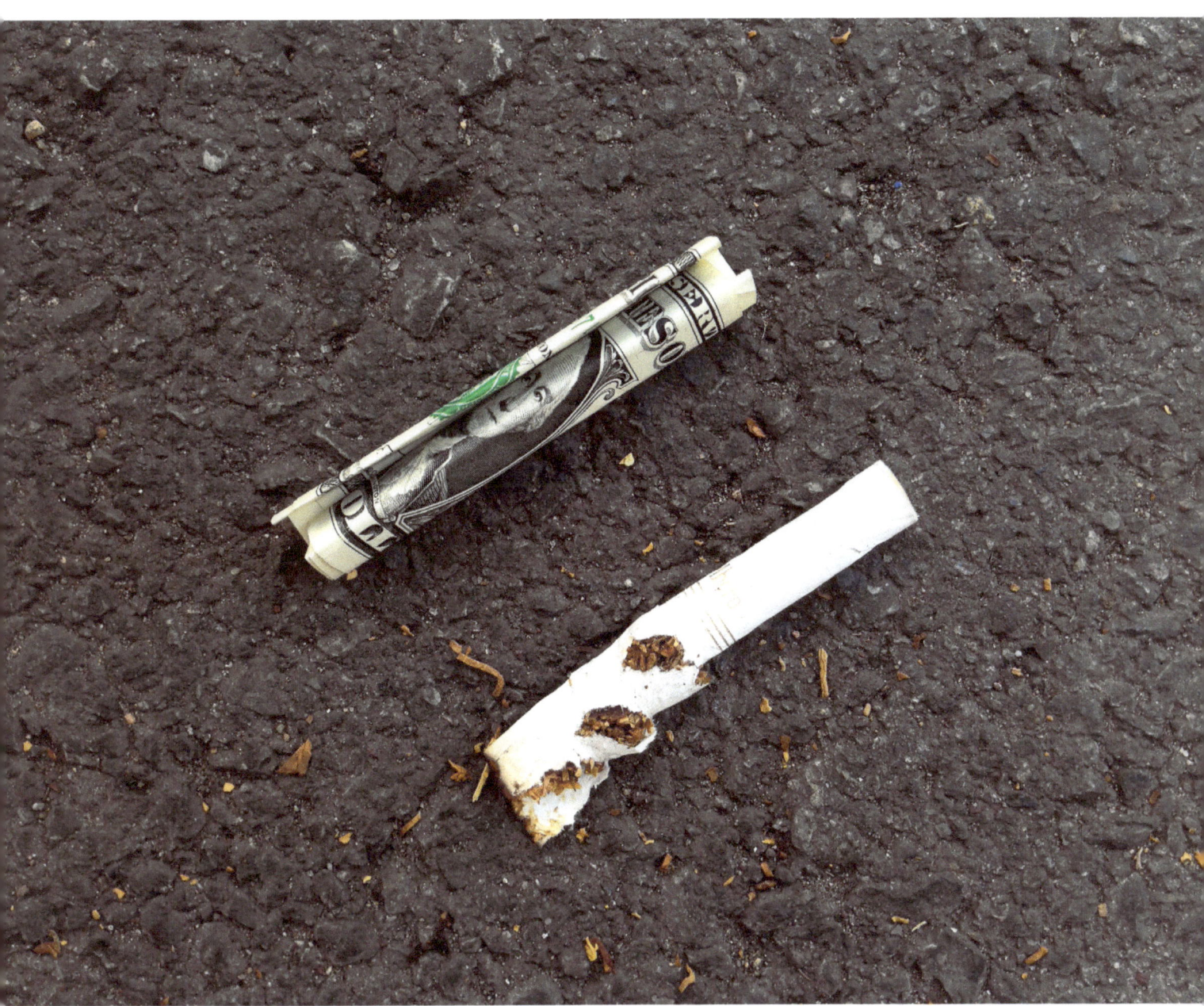

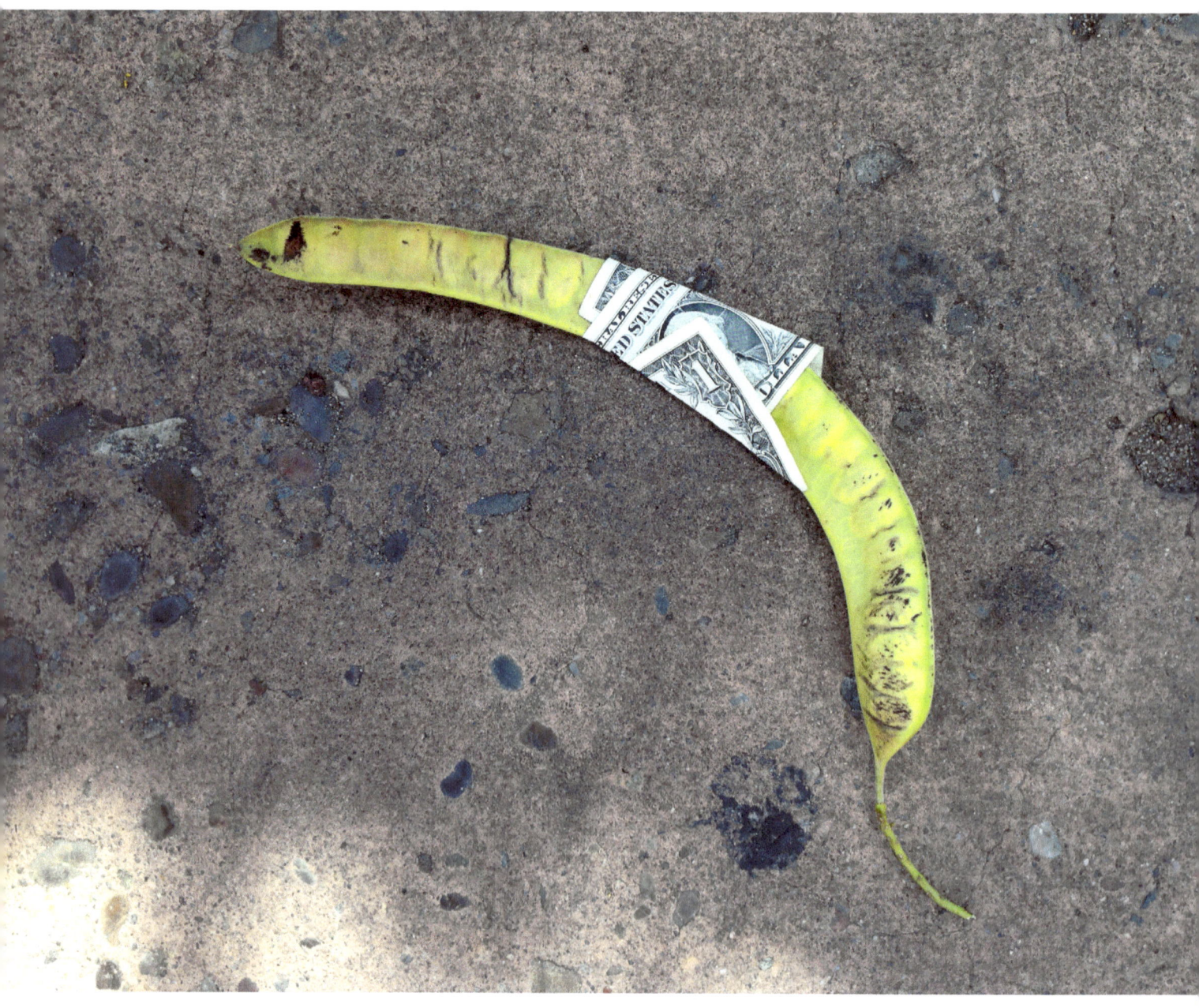

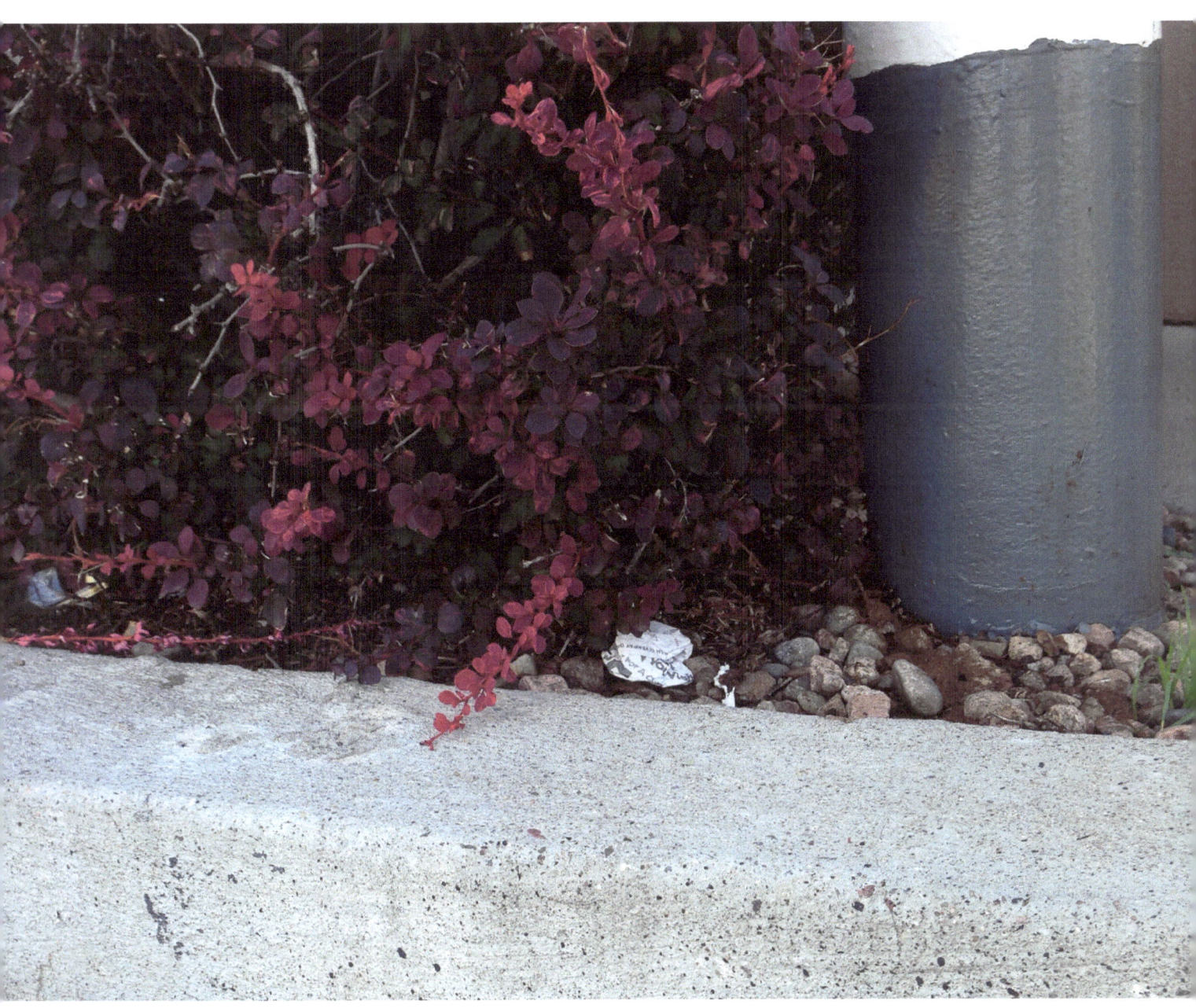

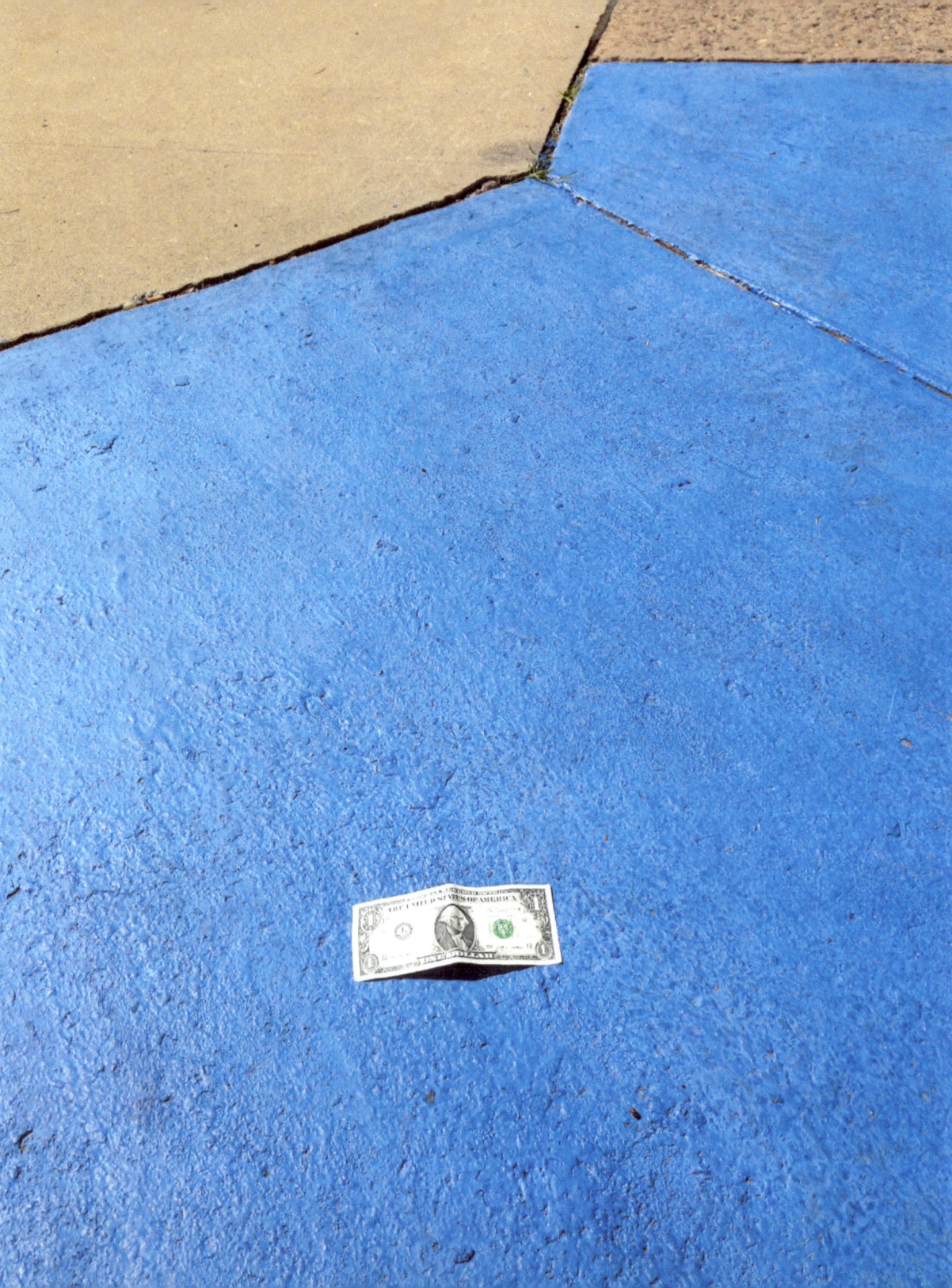

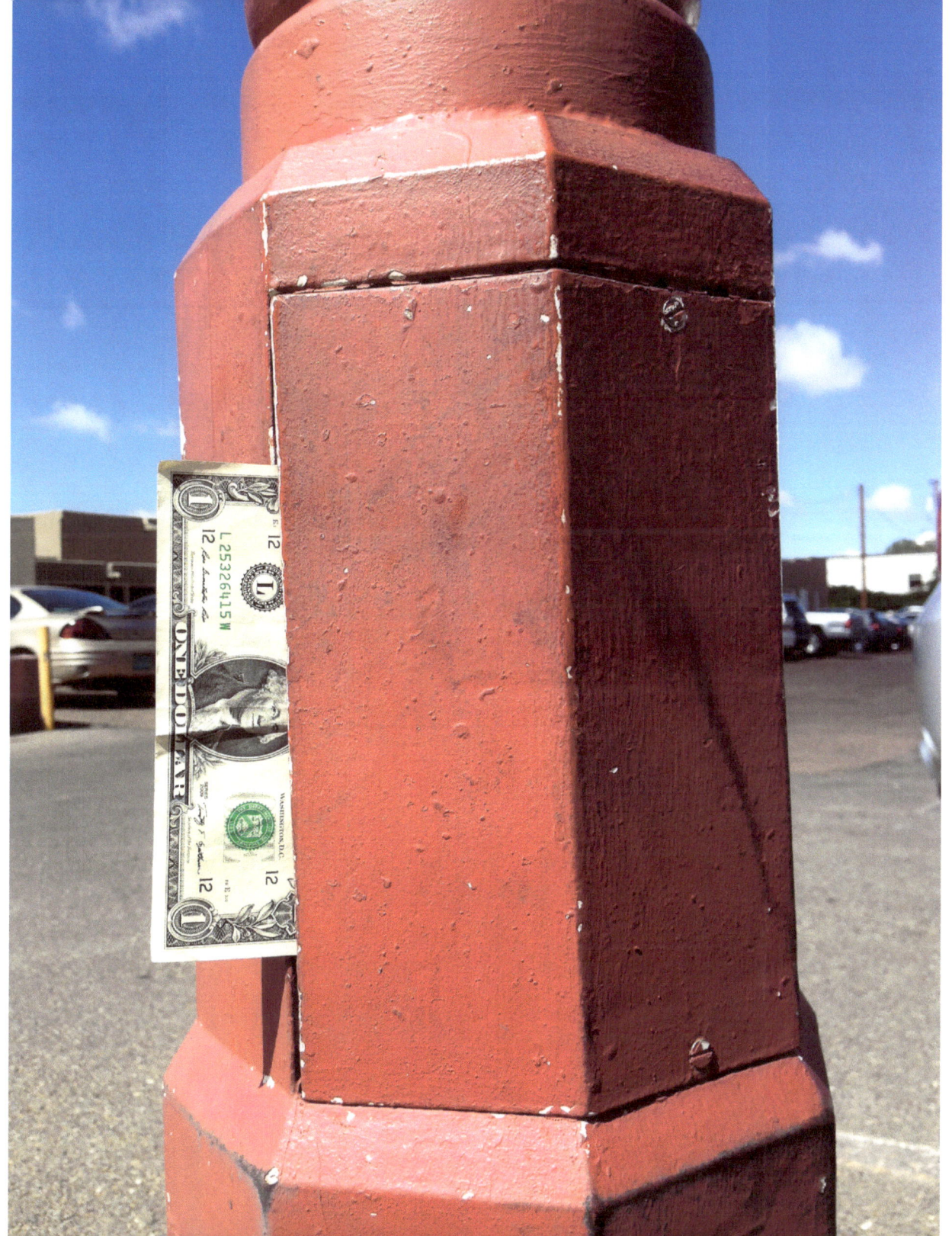

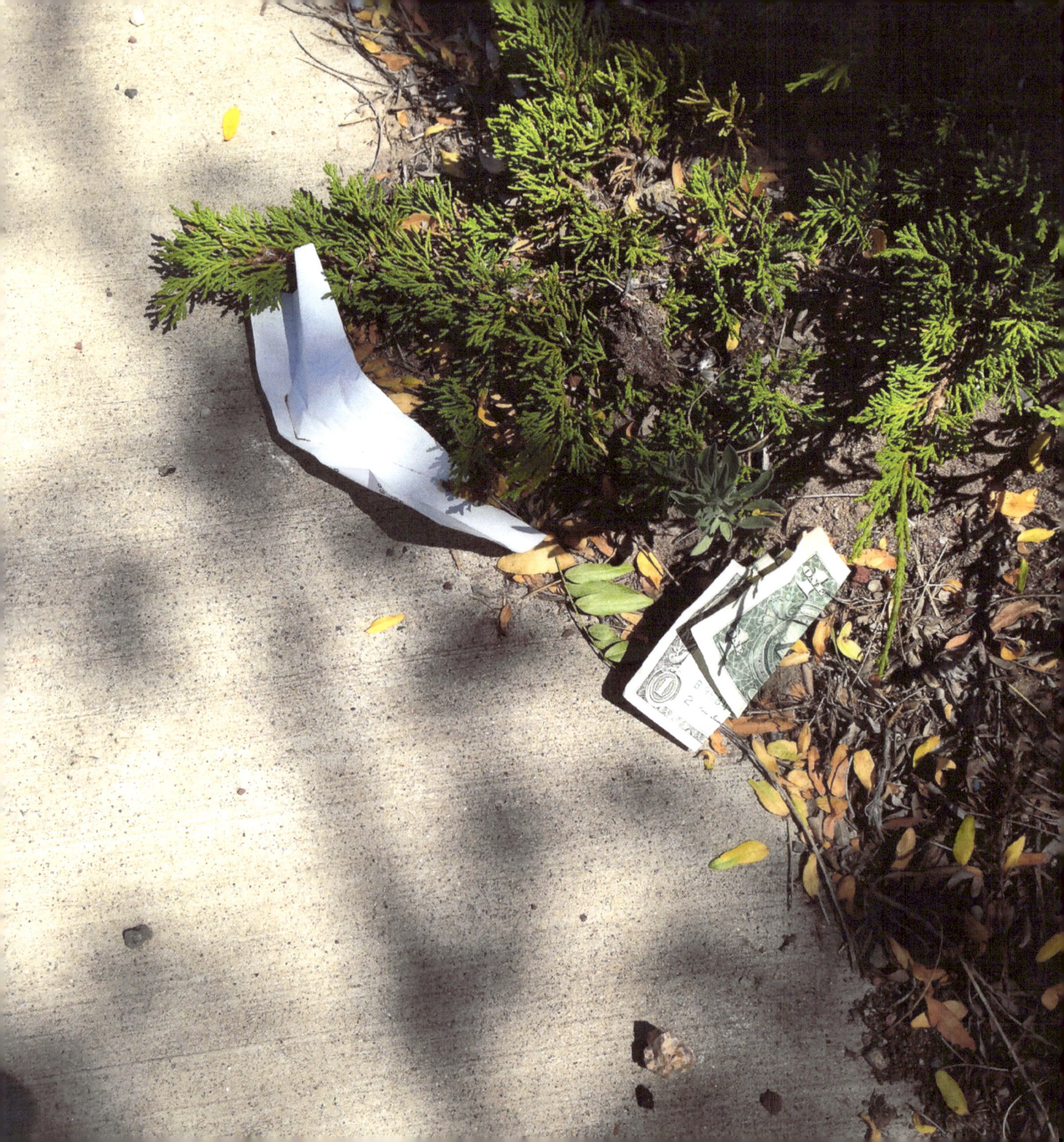

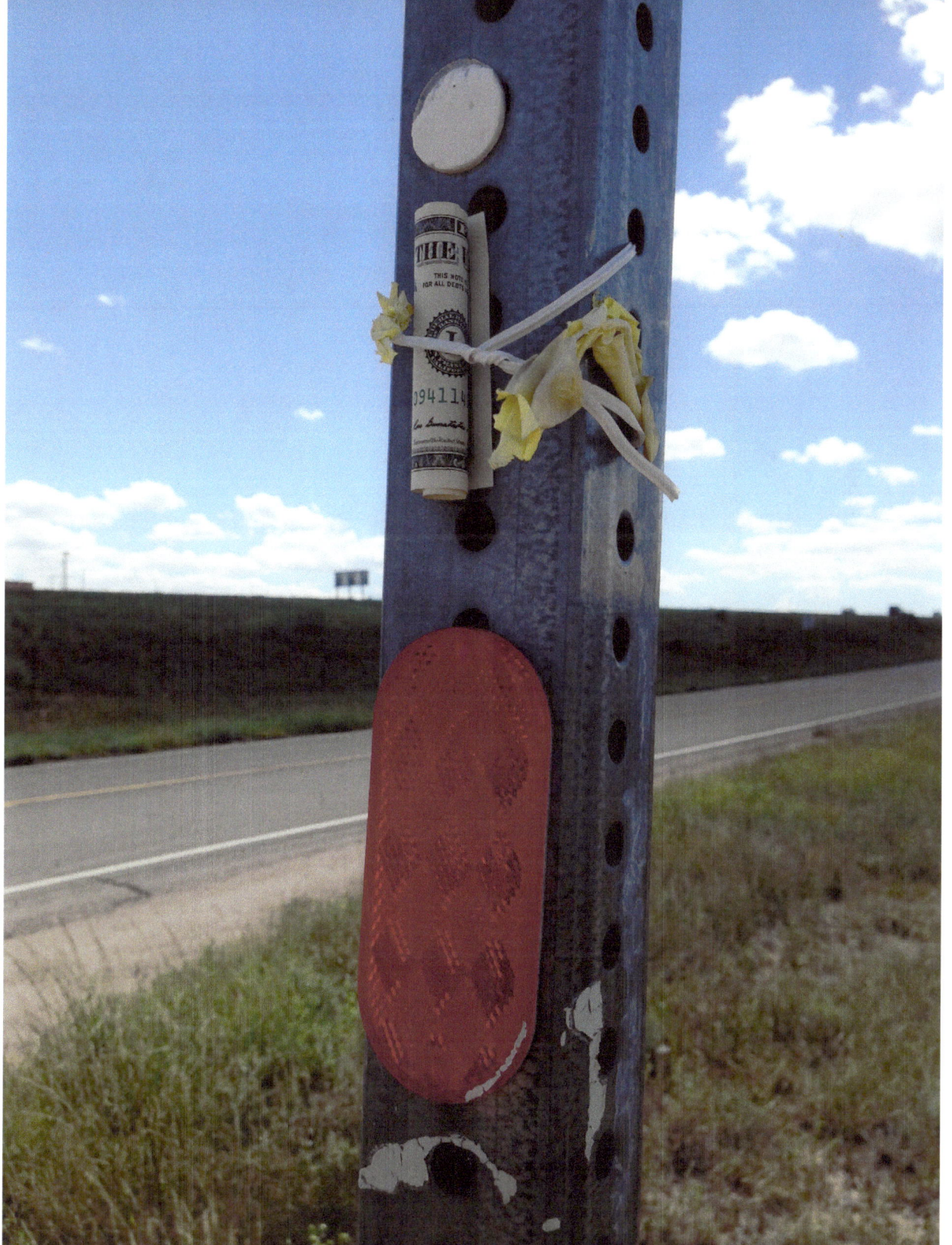

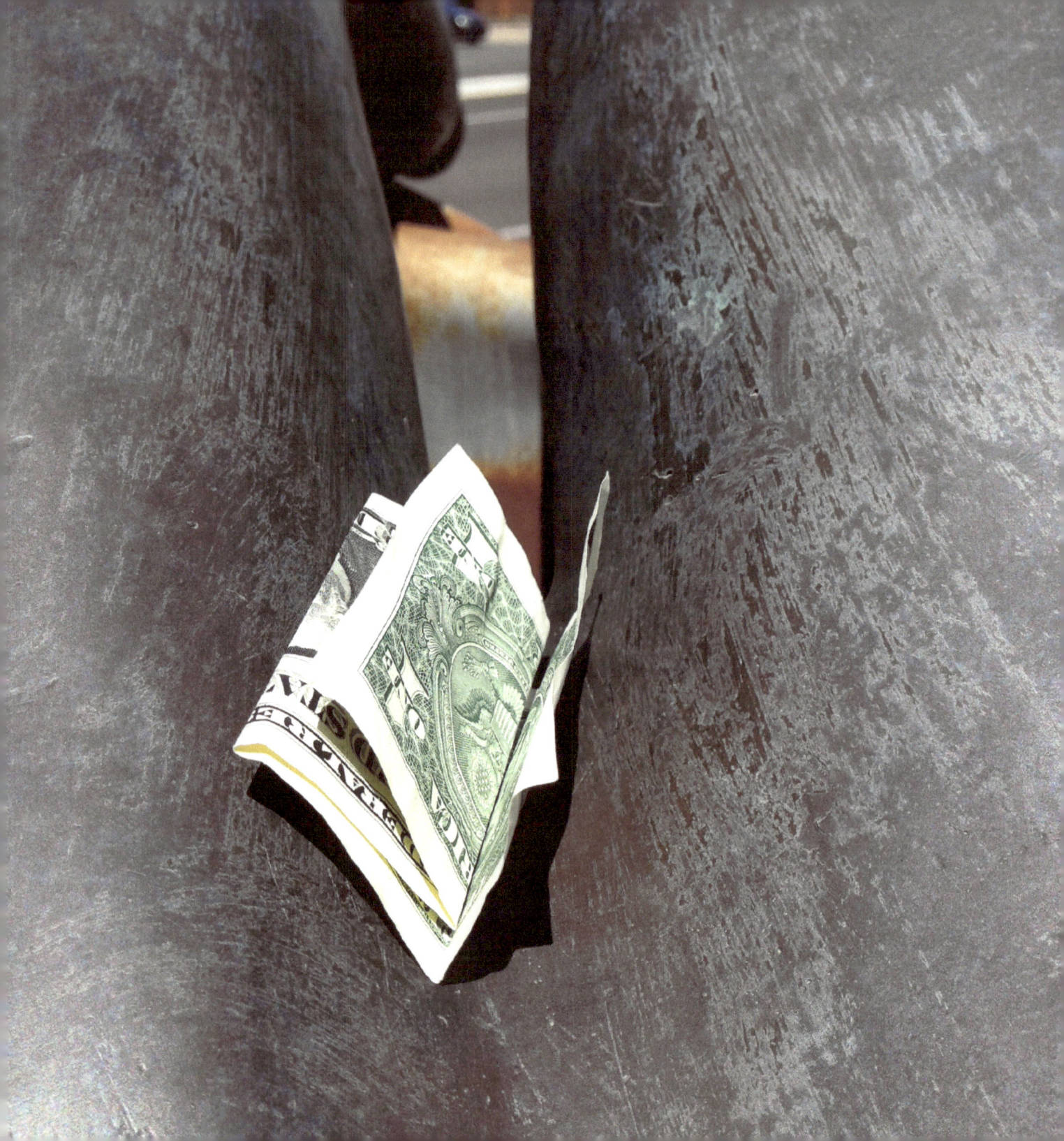

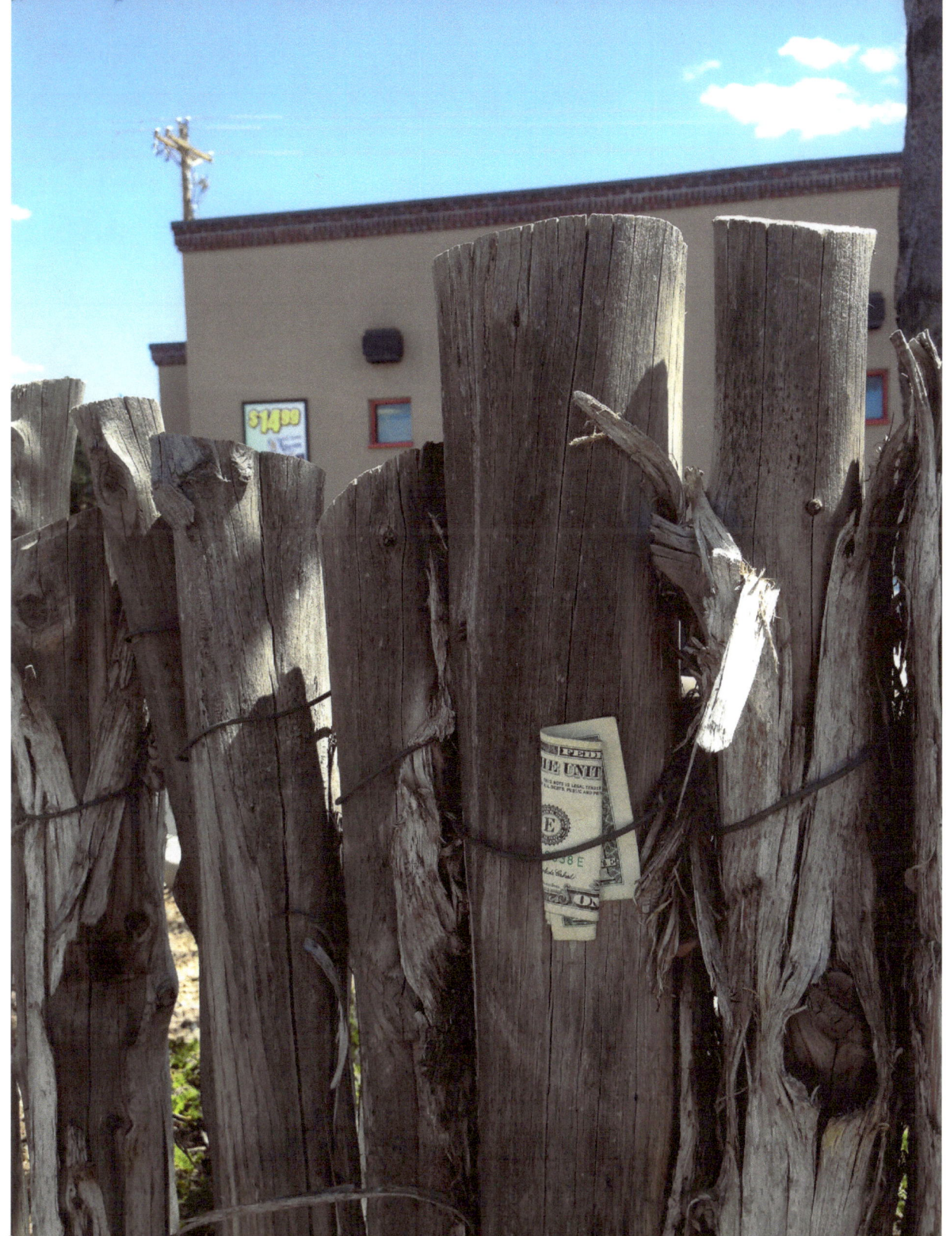

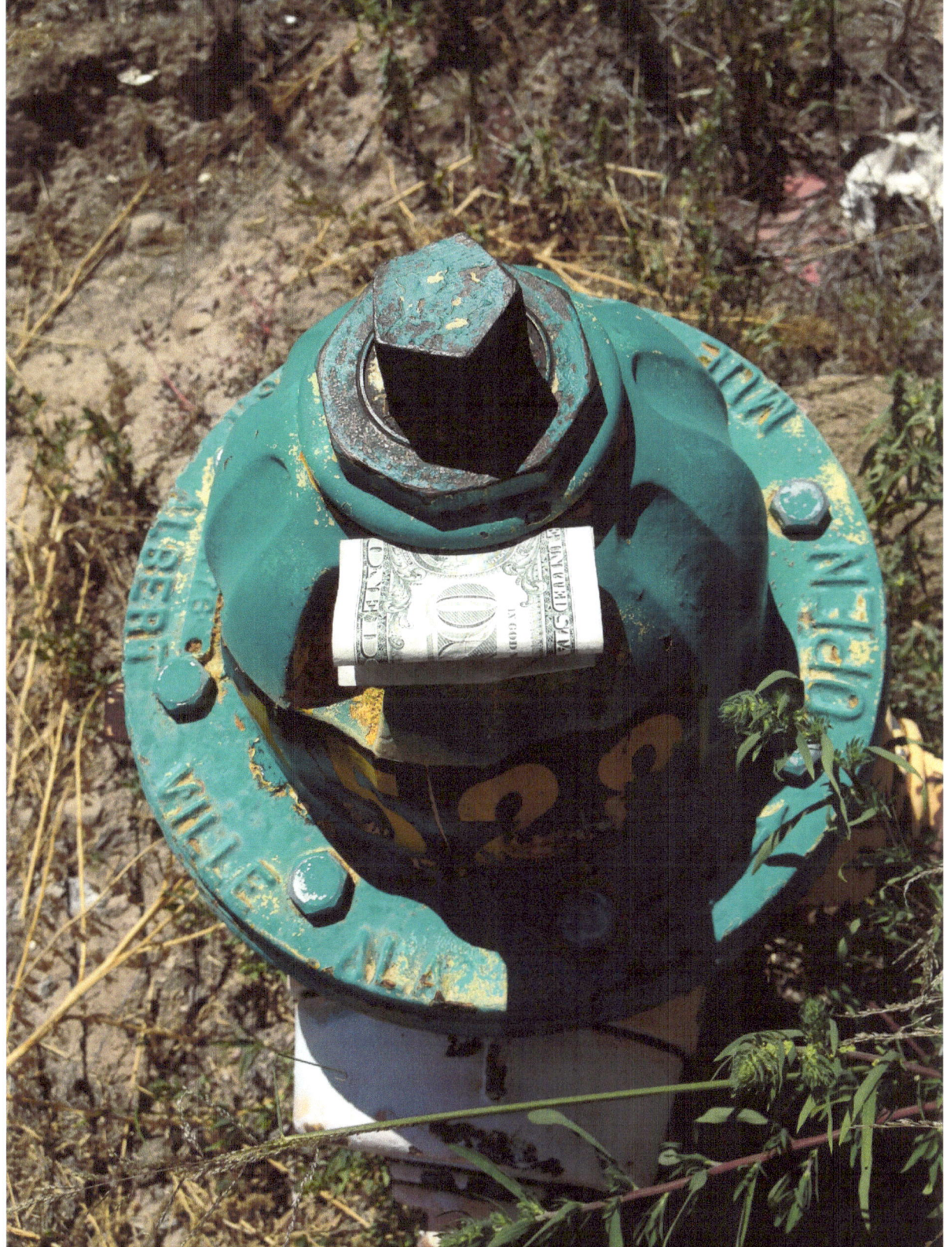

53

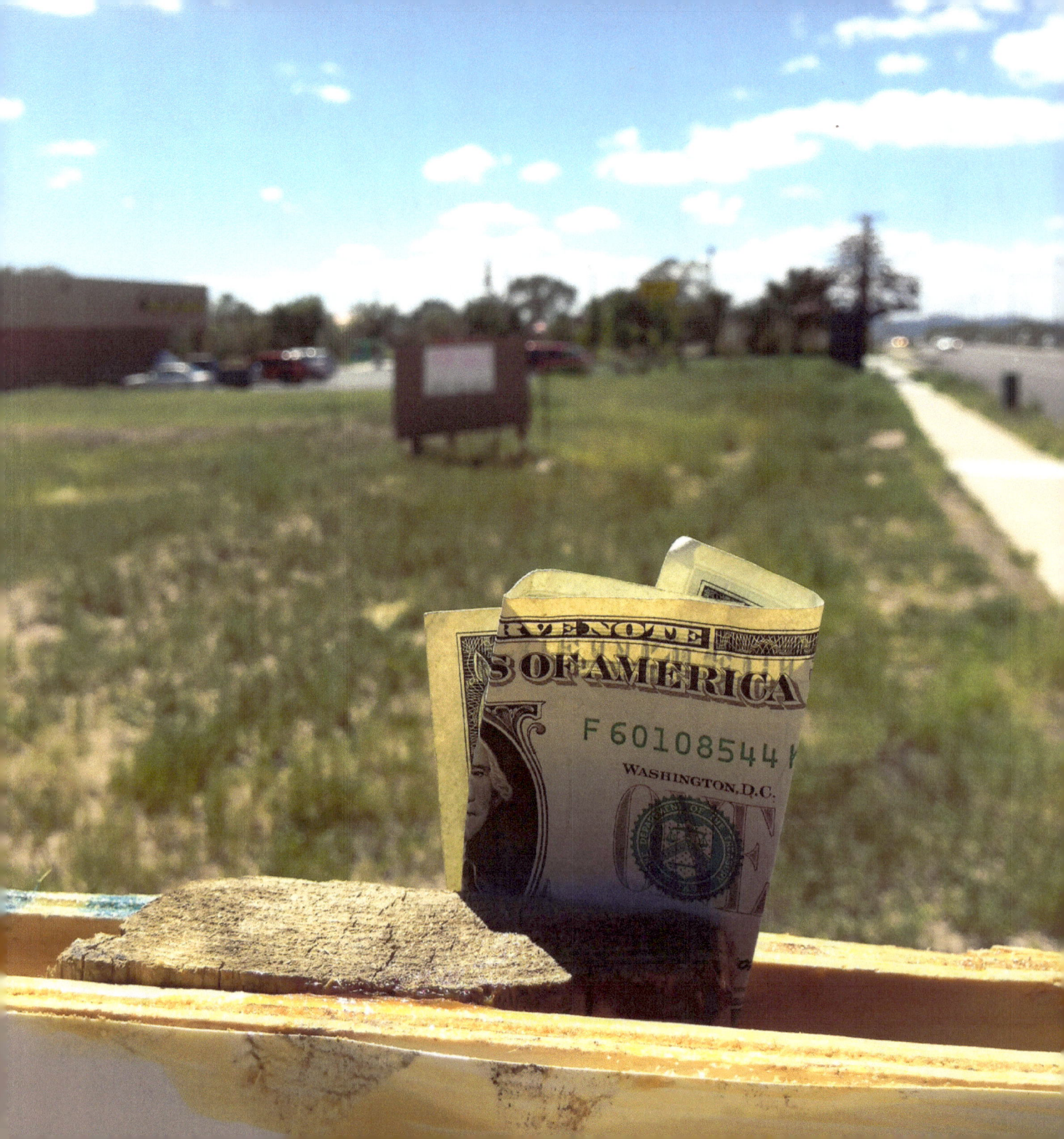

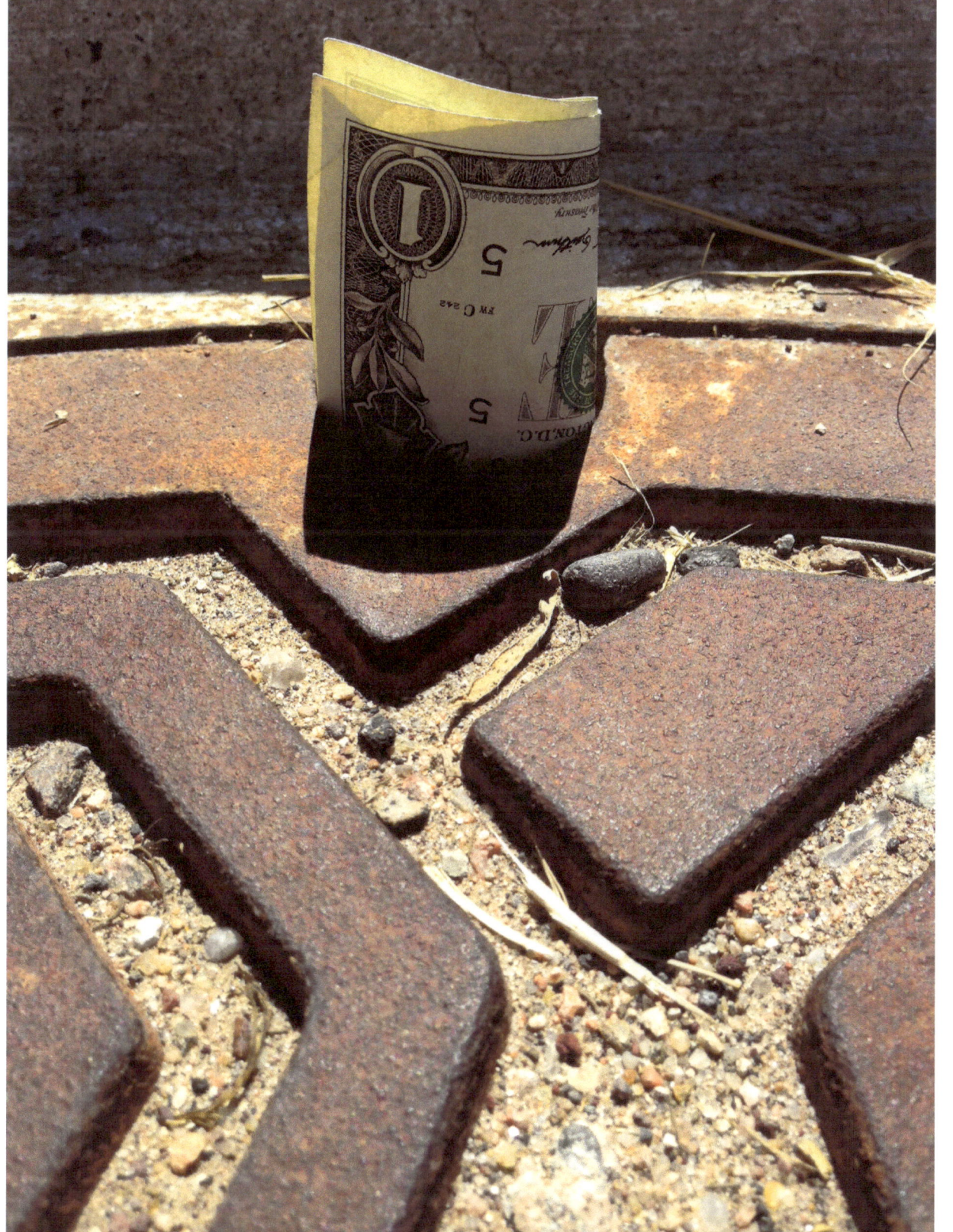

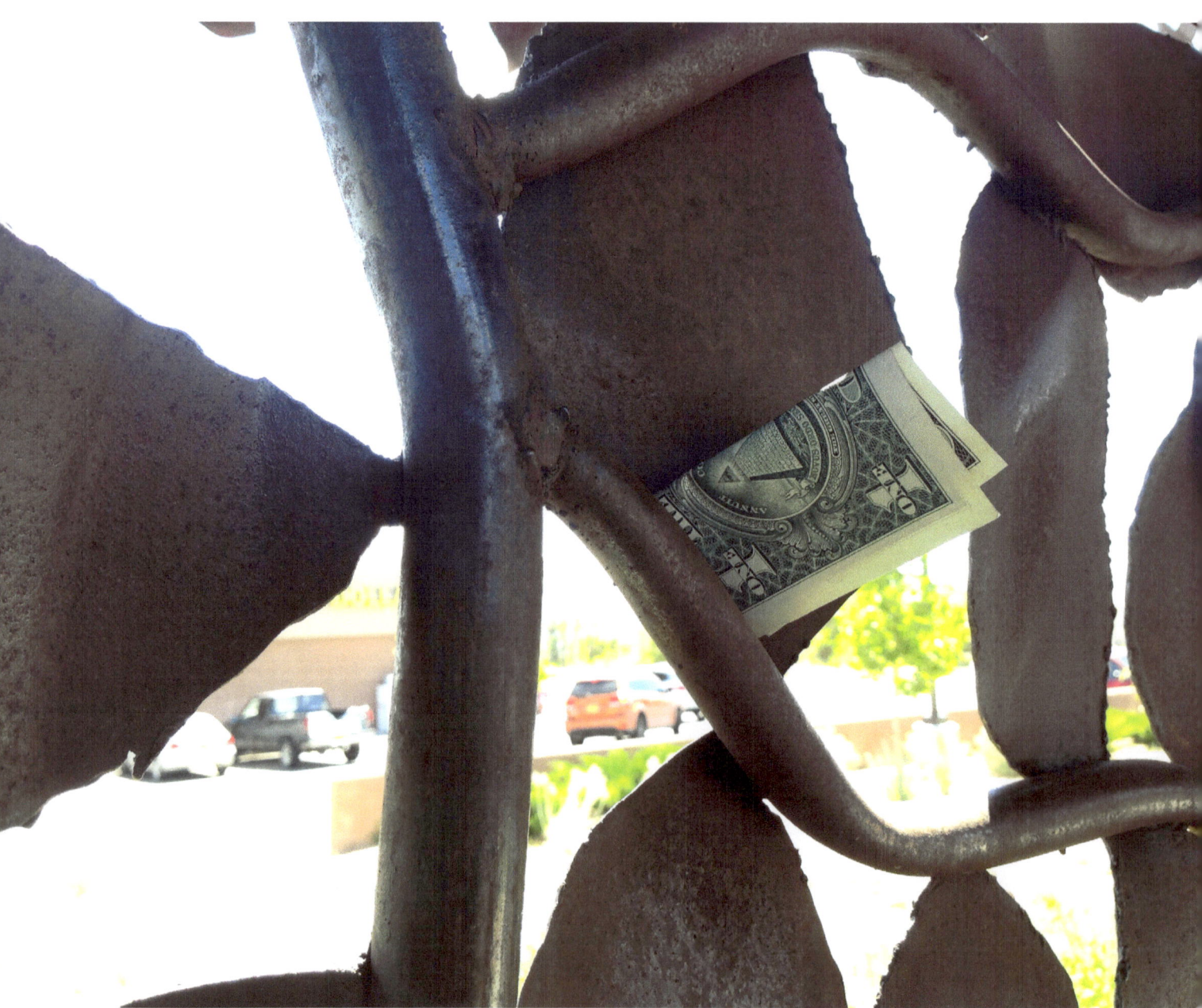

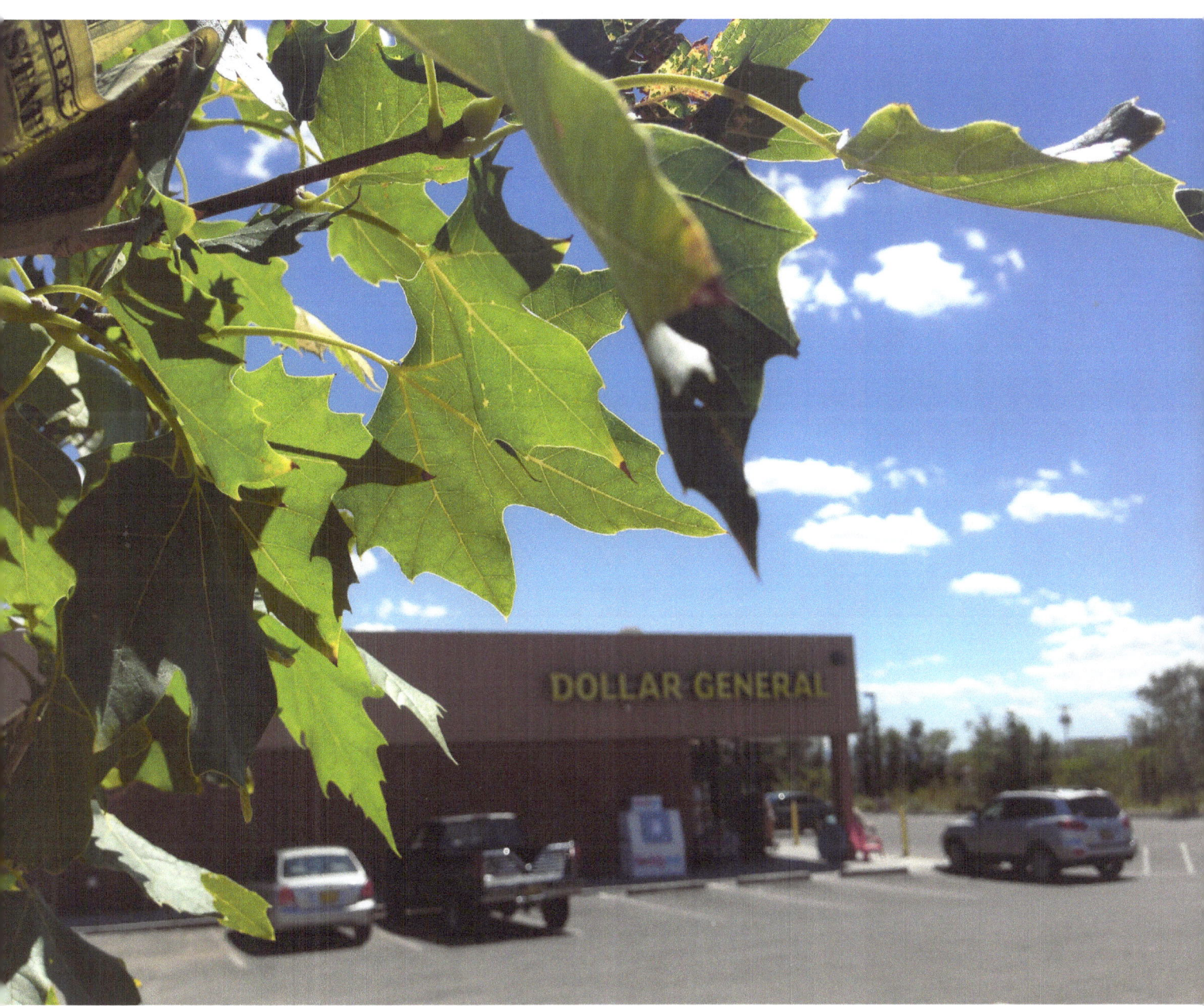

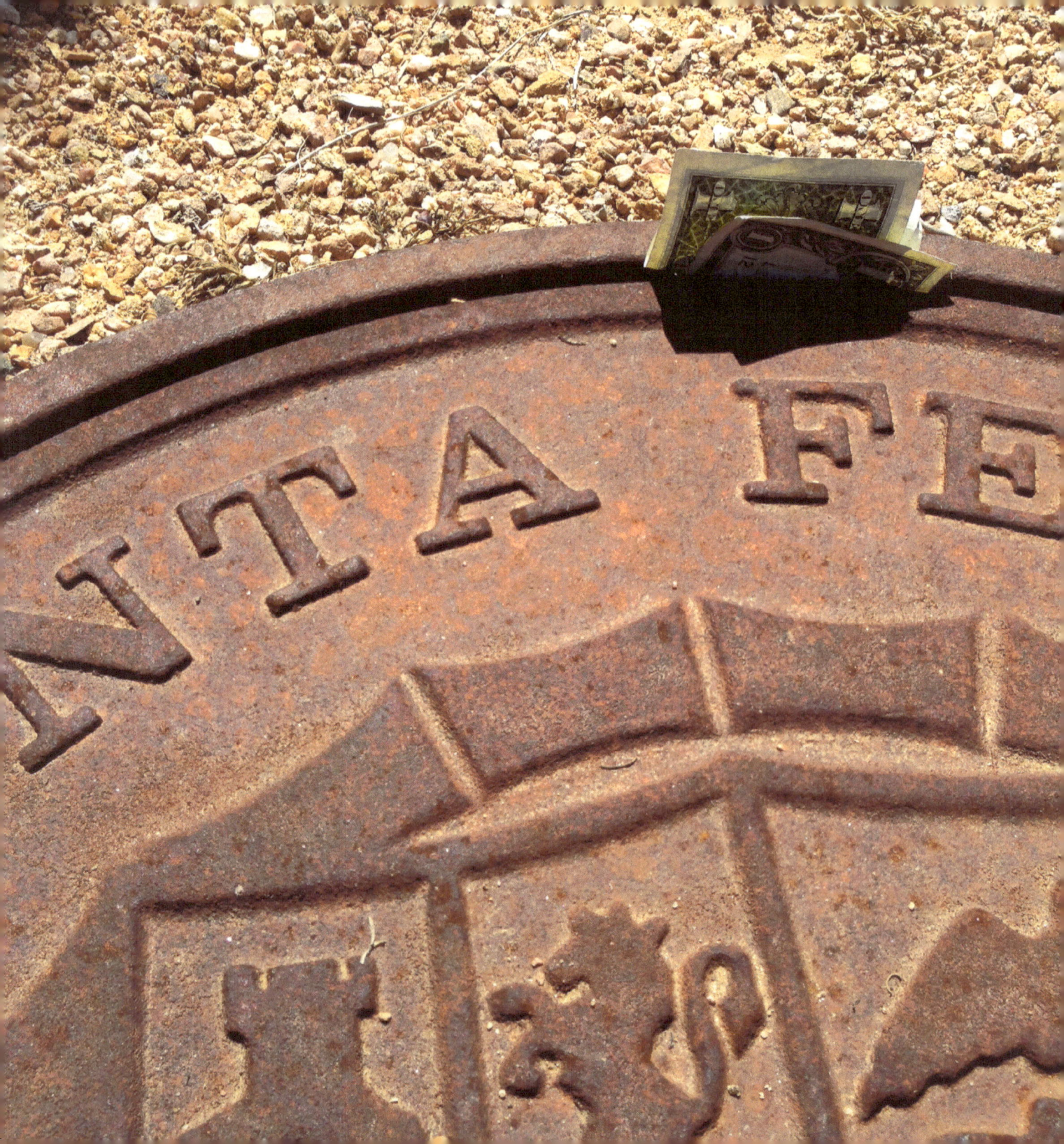

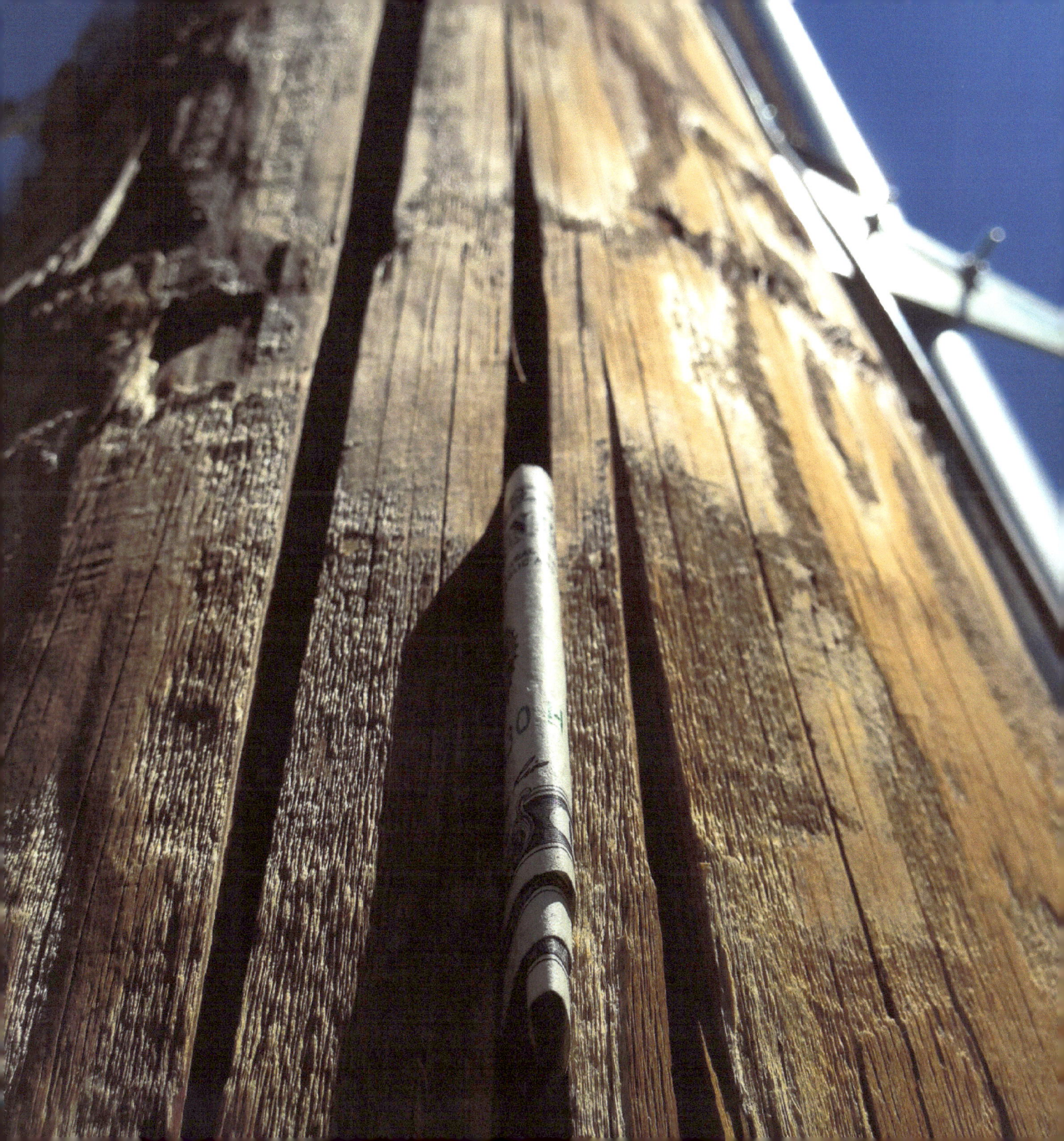

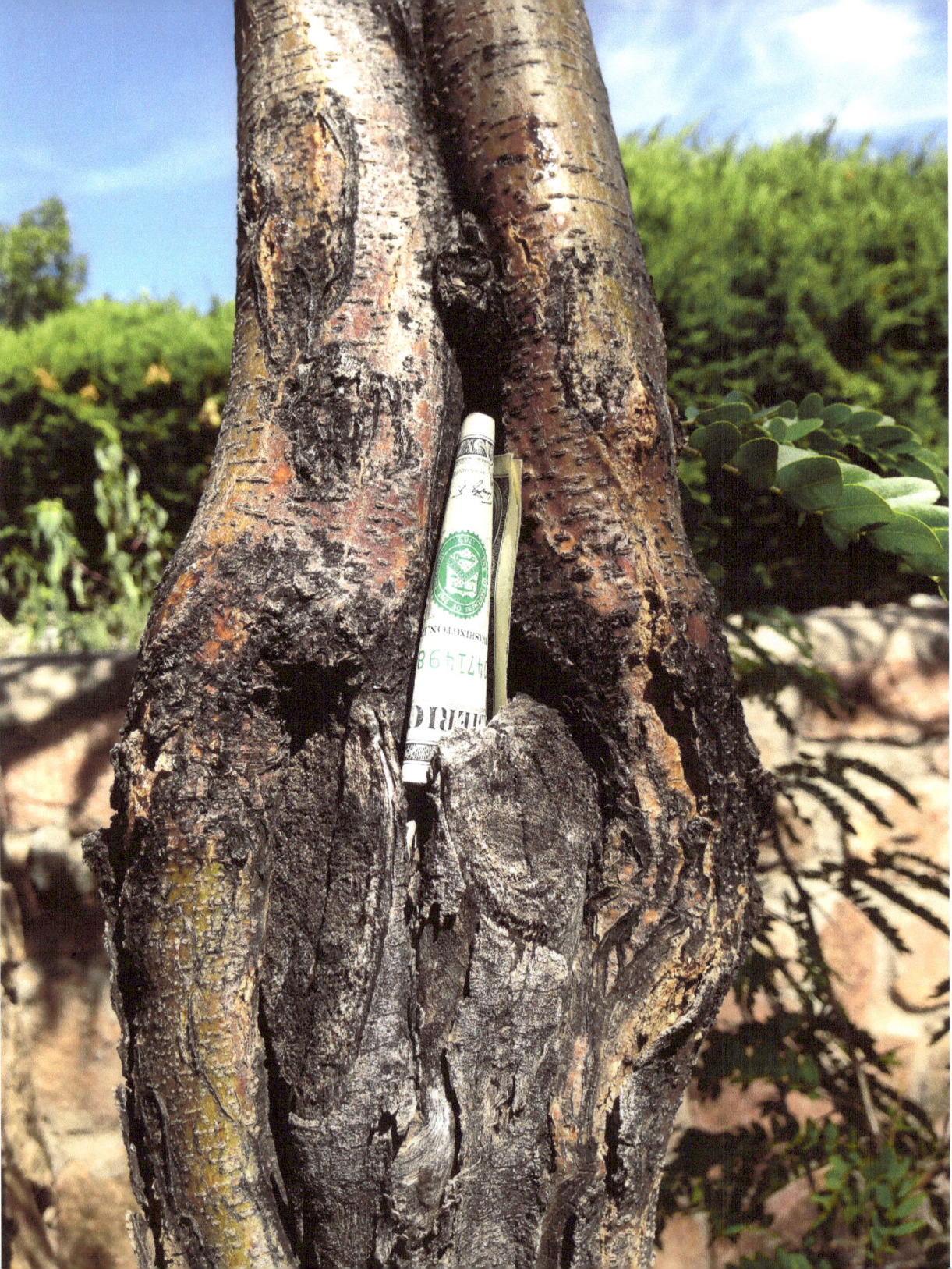

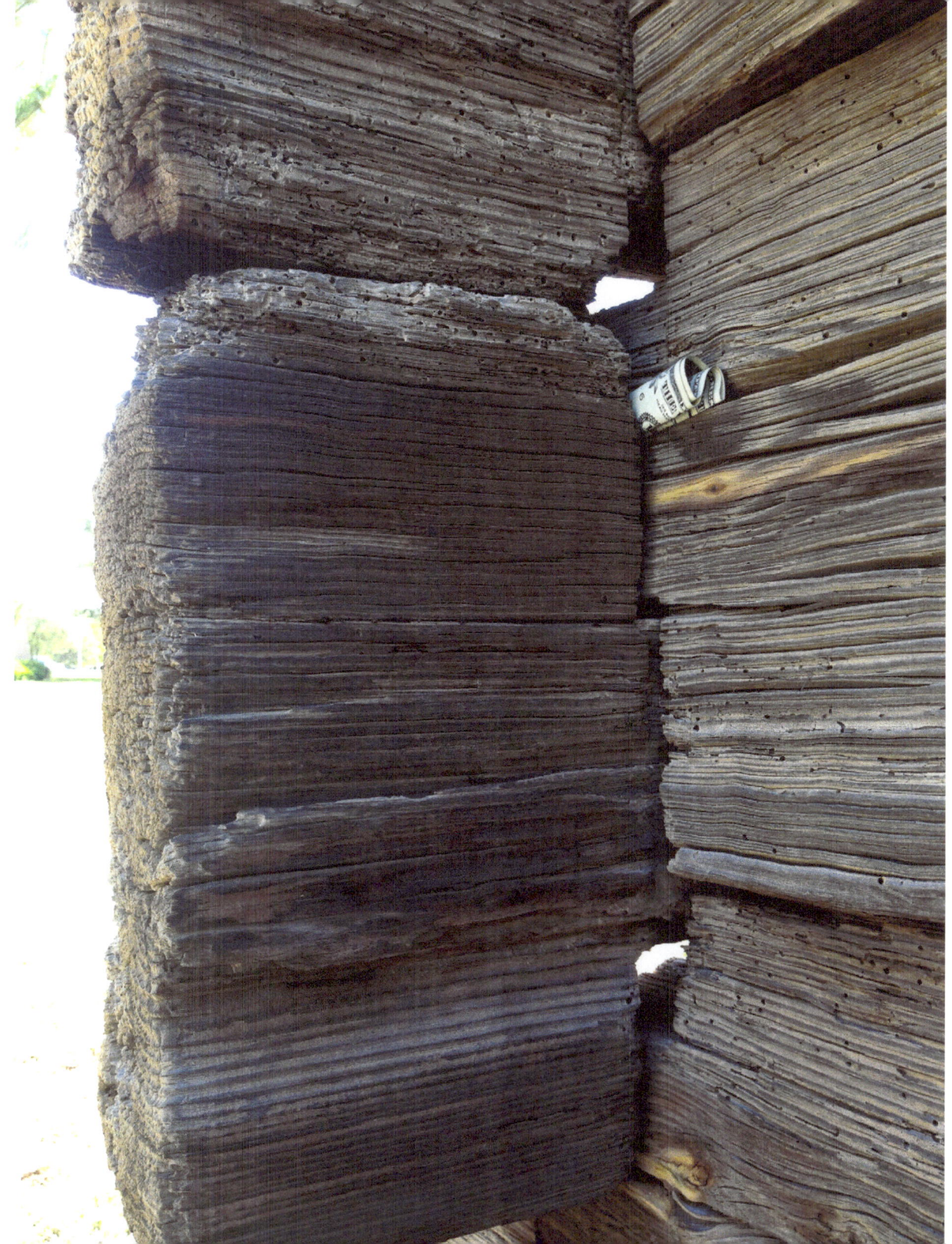

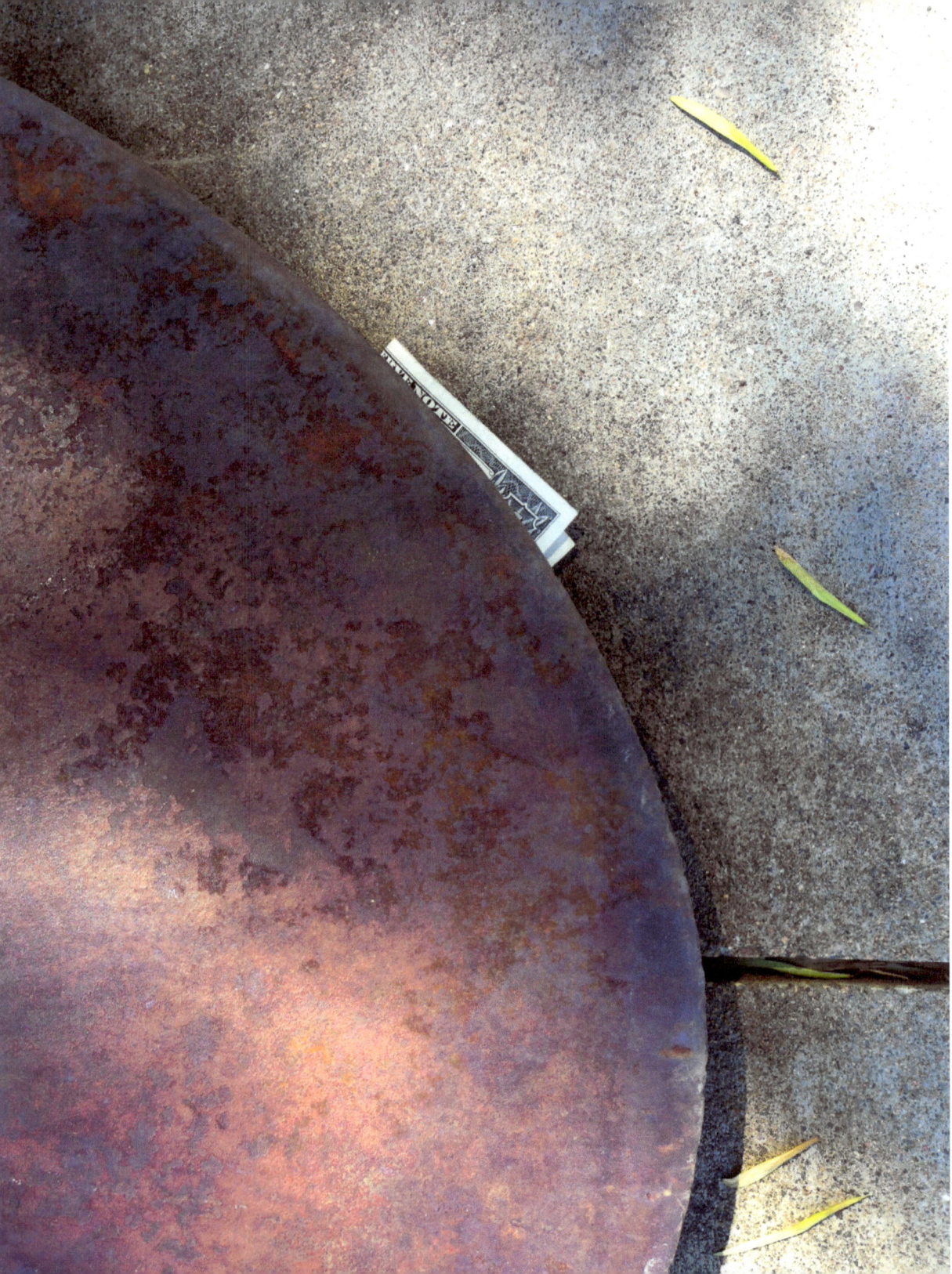

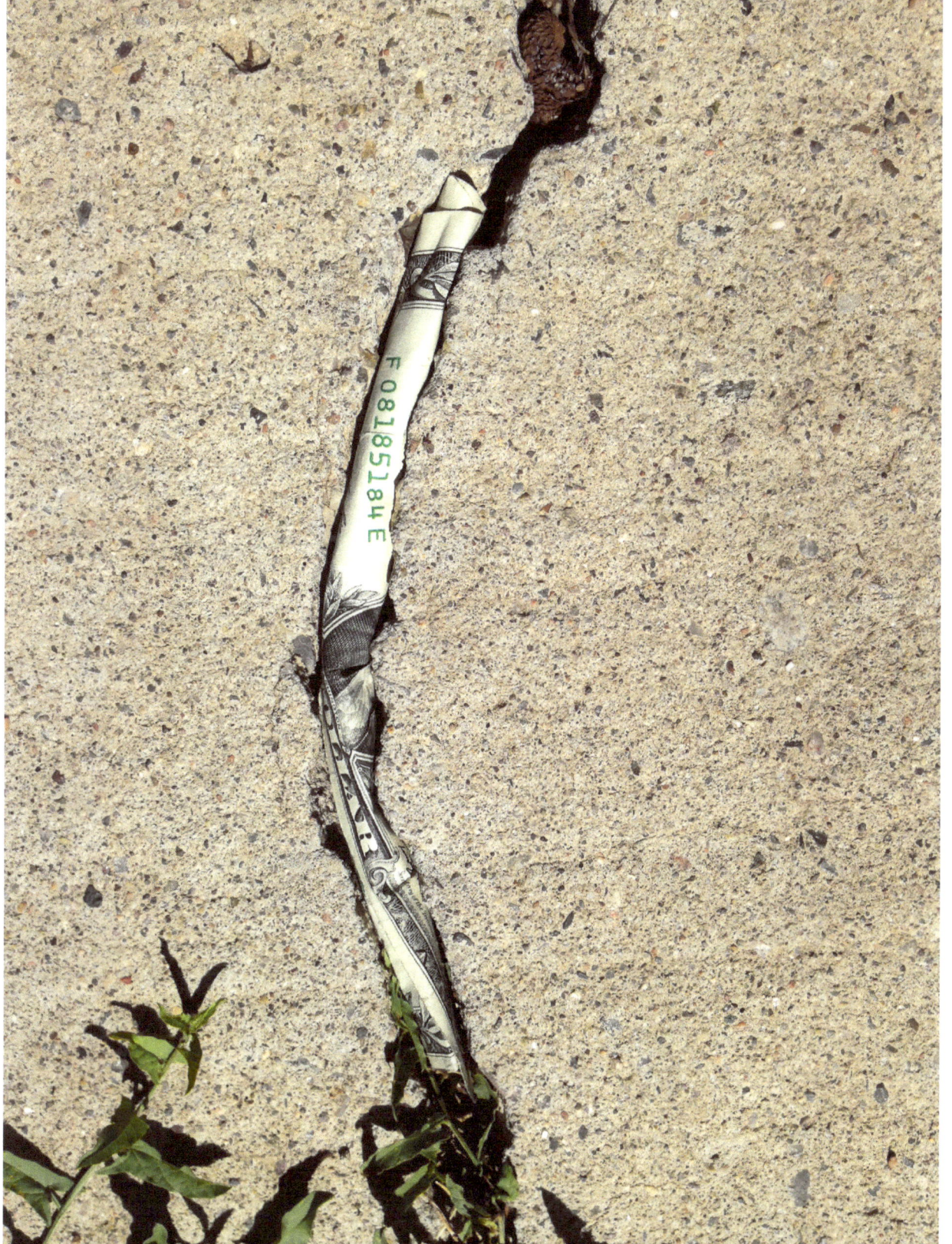

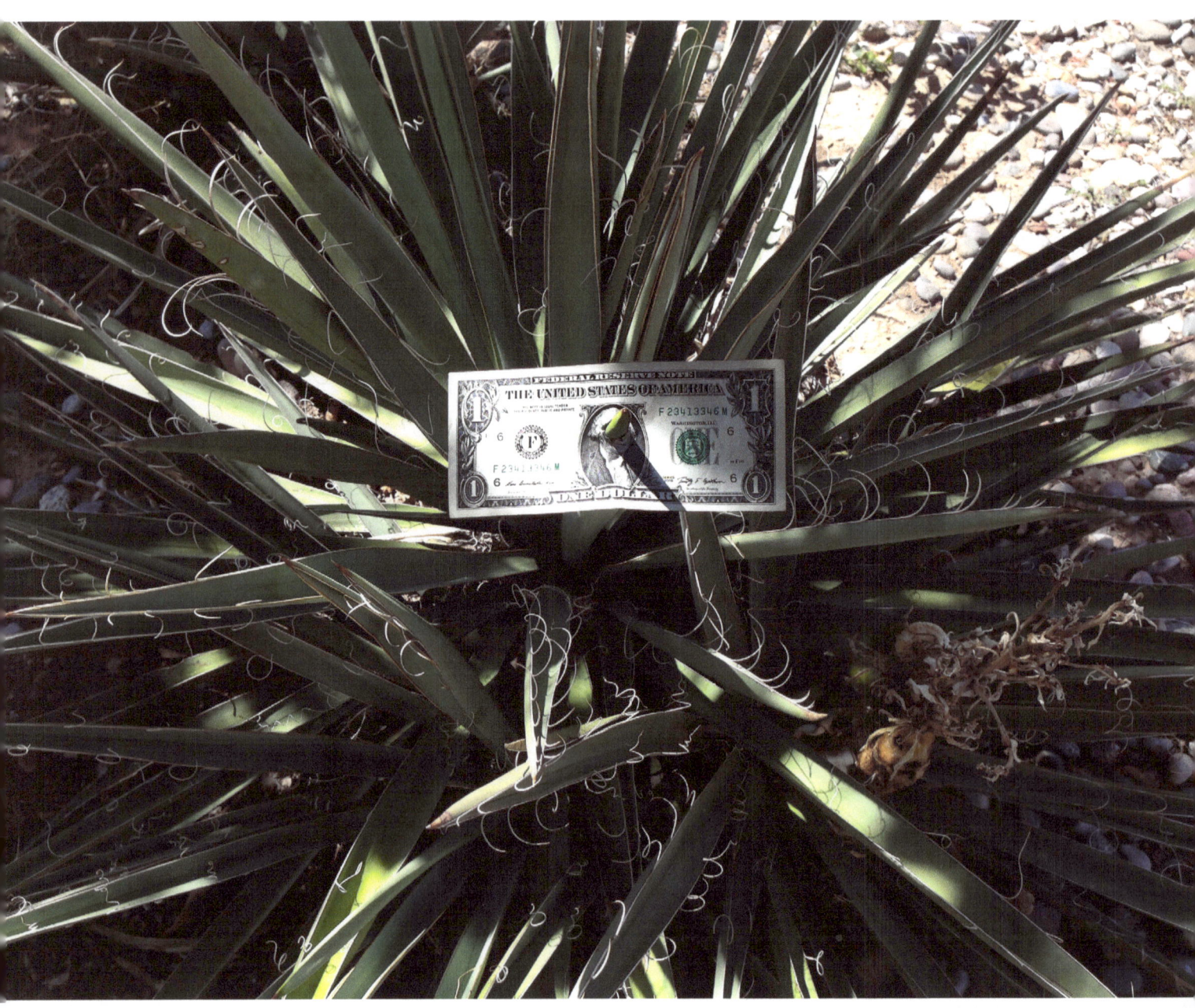

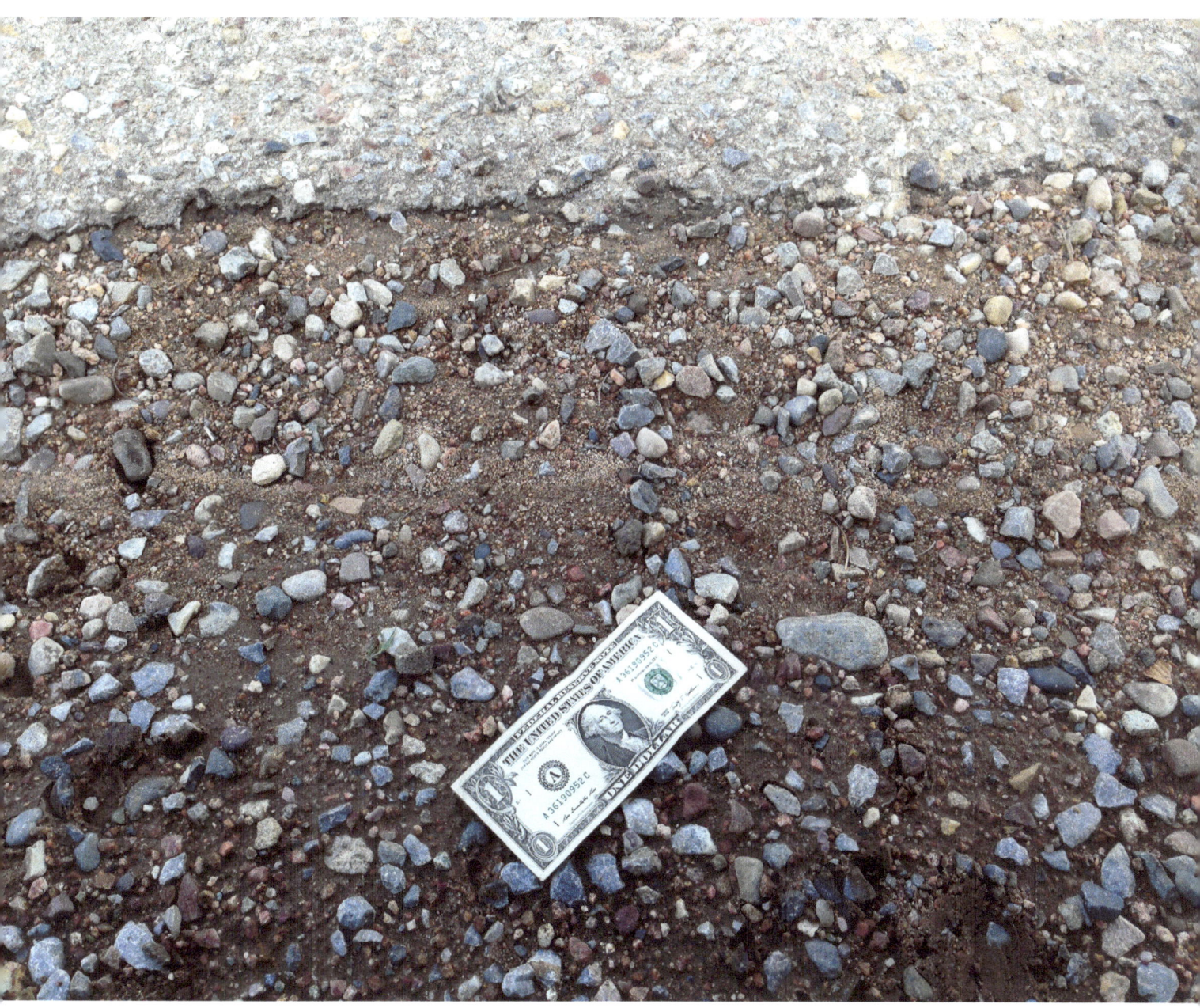

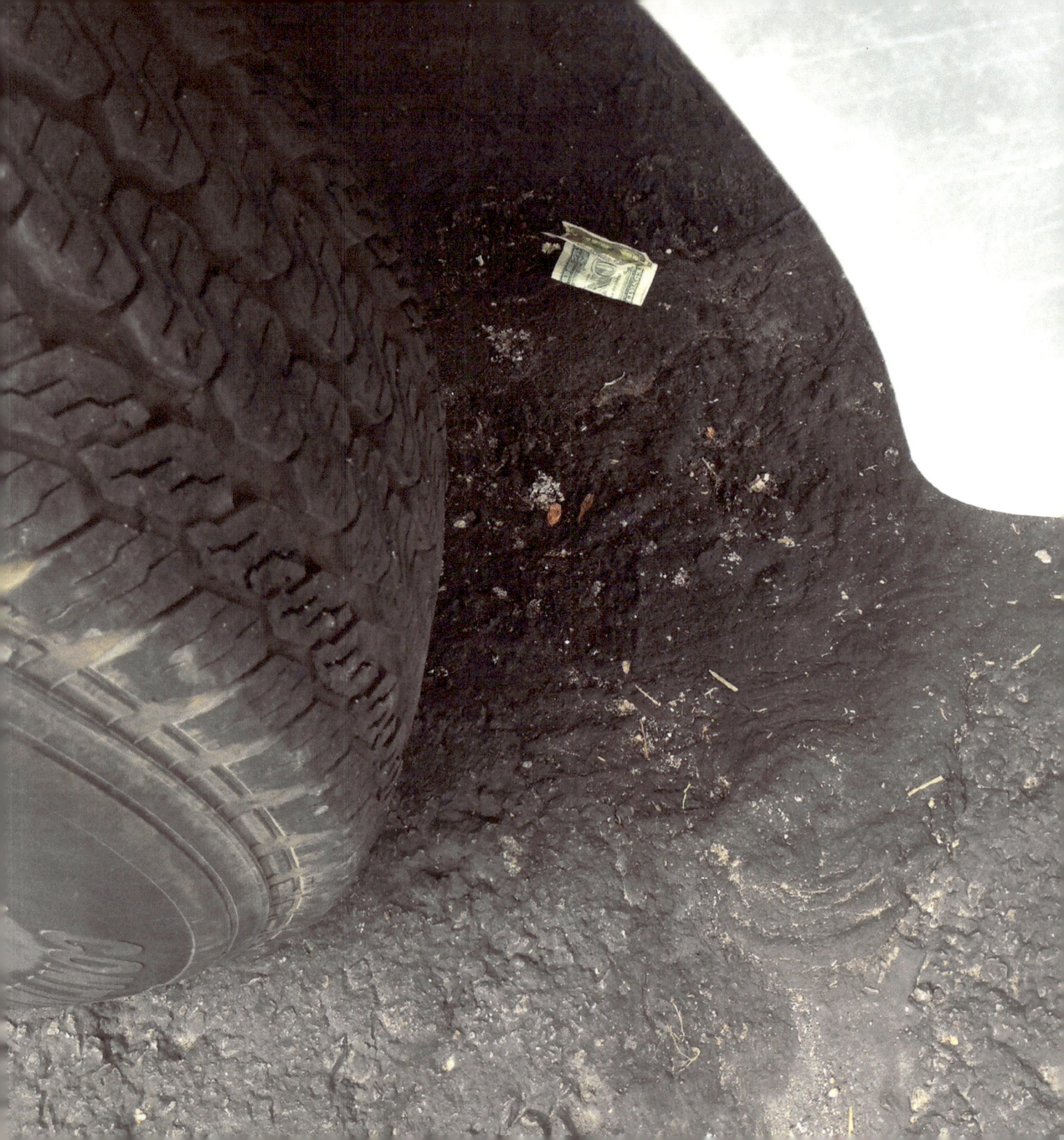

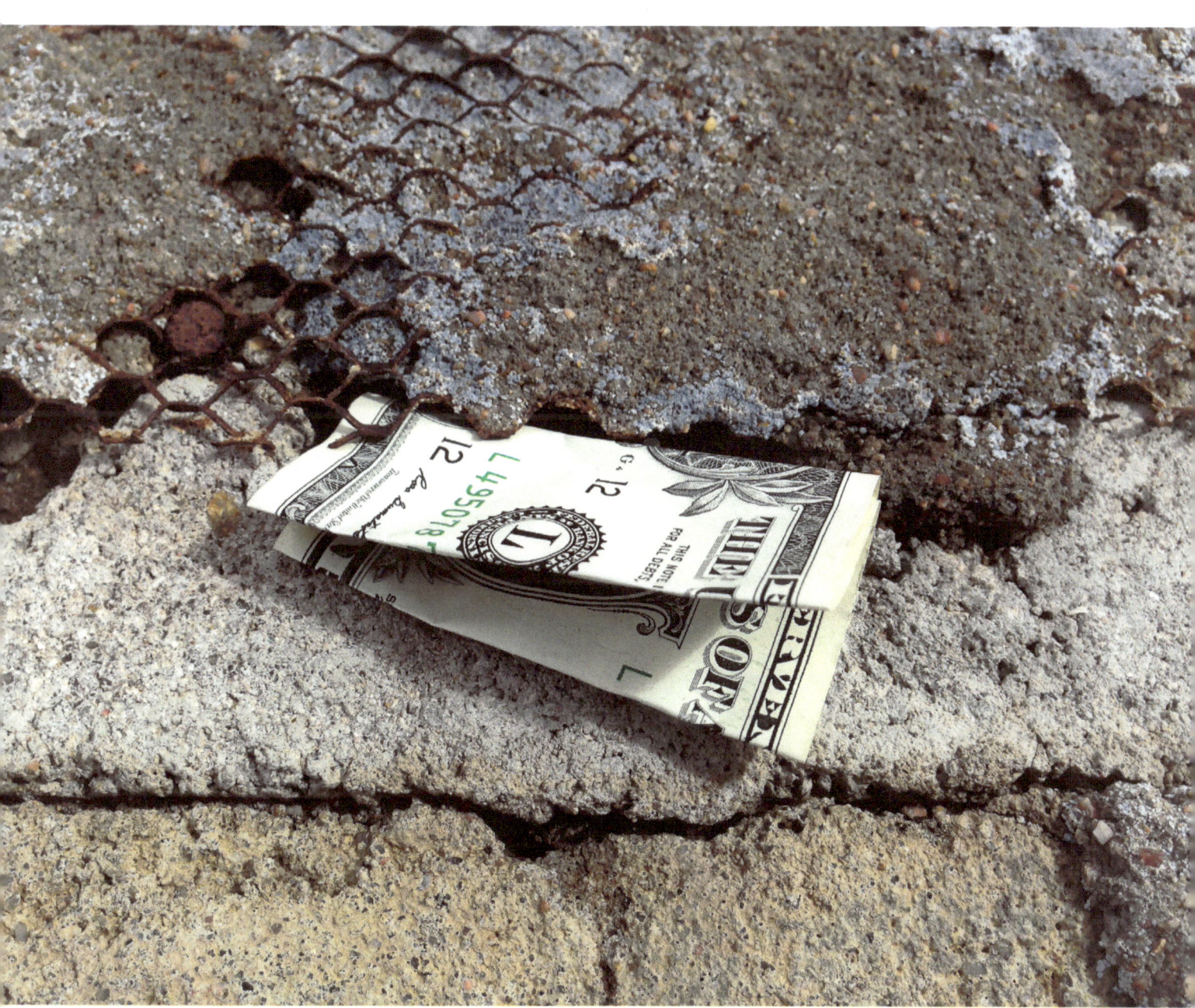

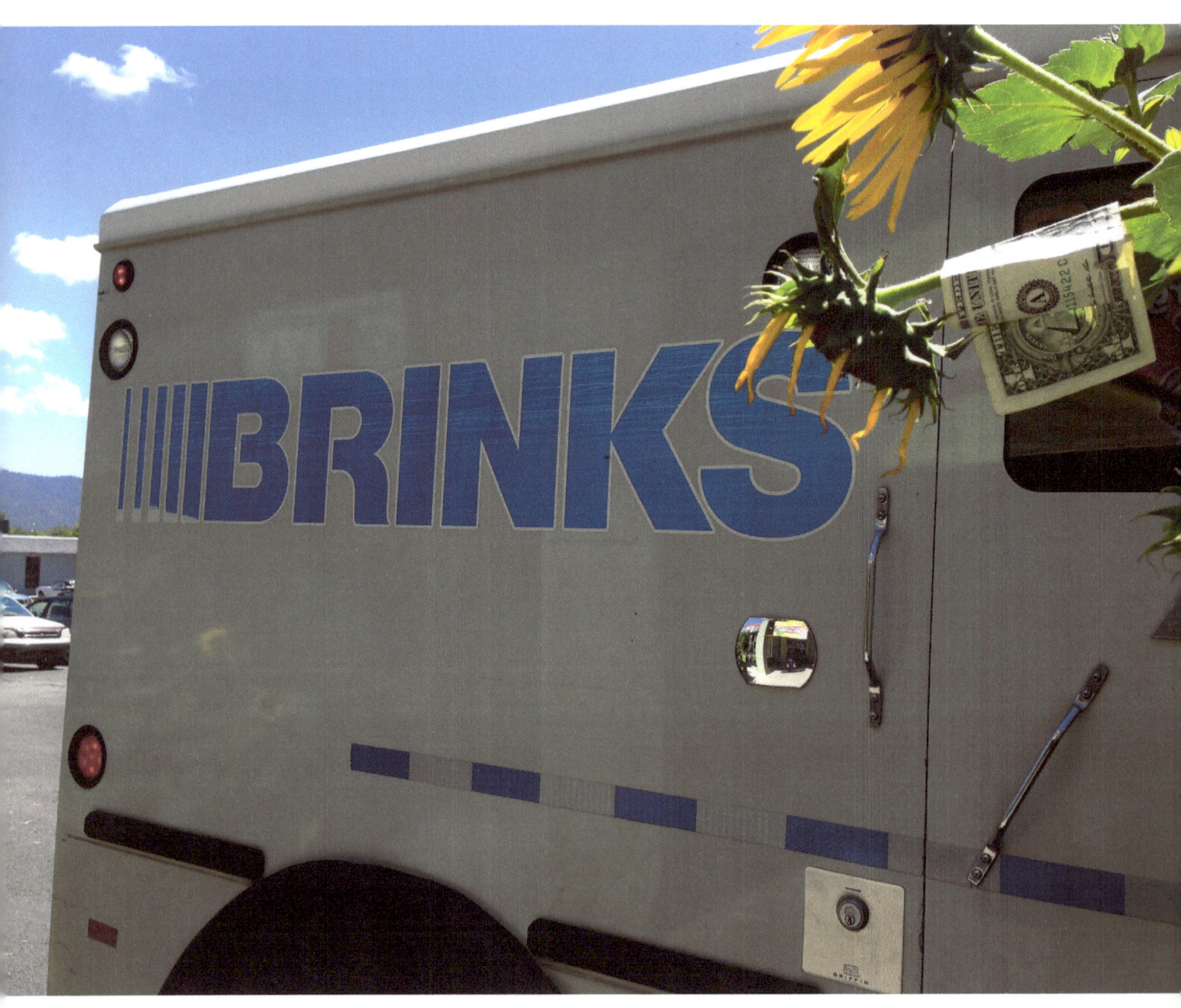

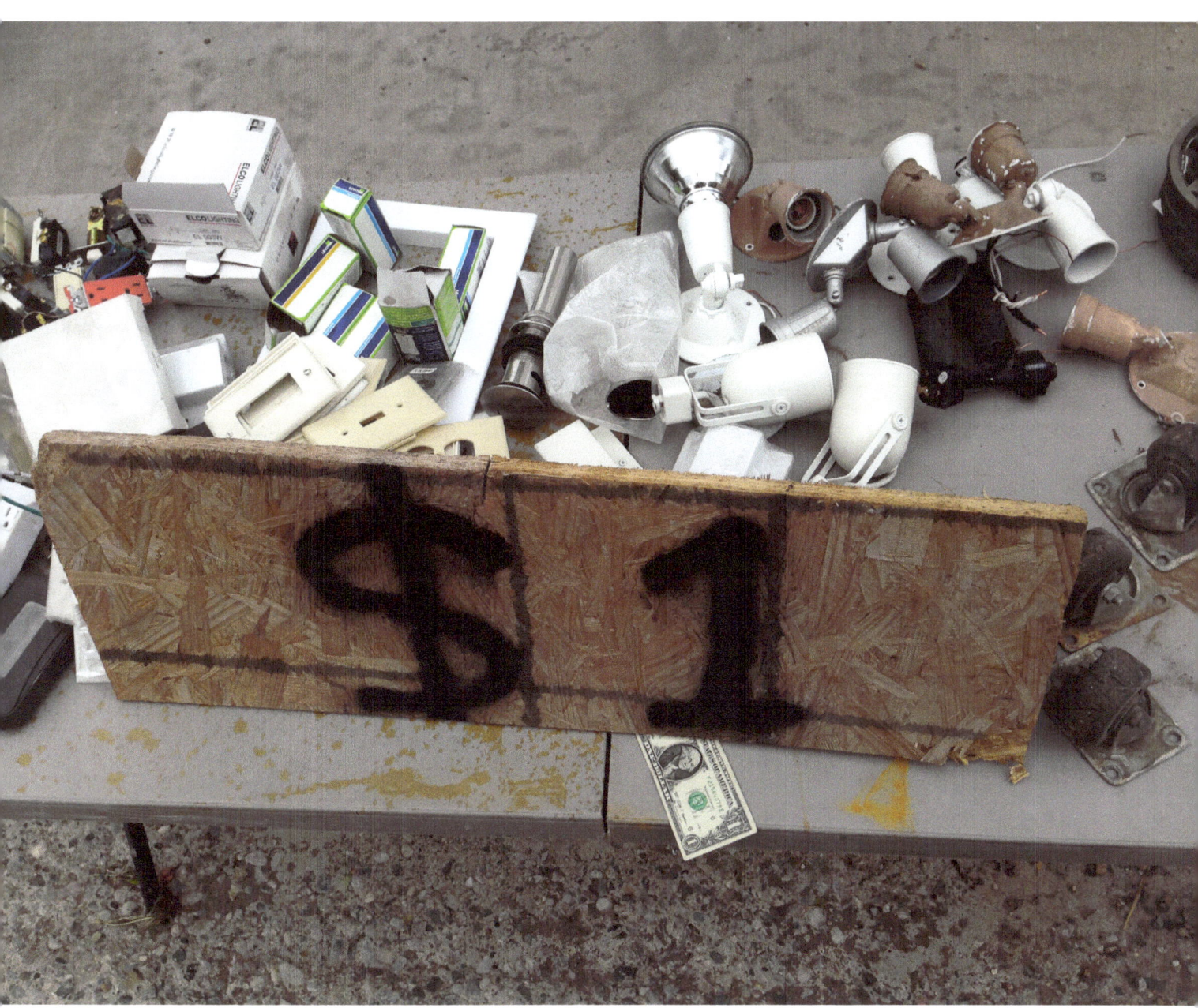

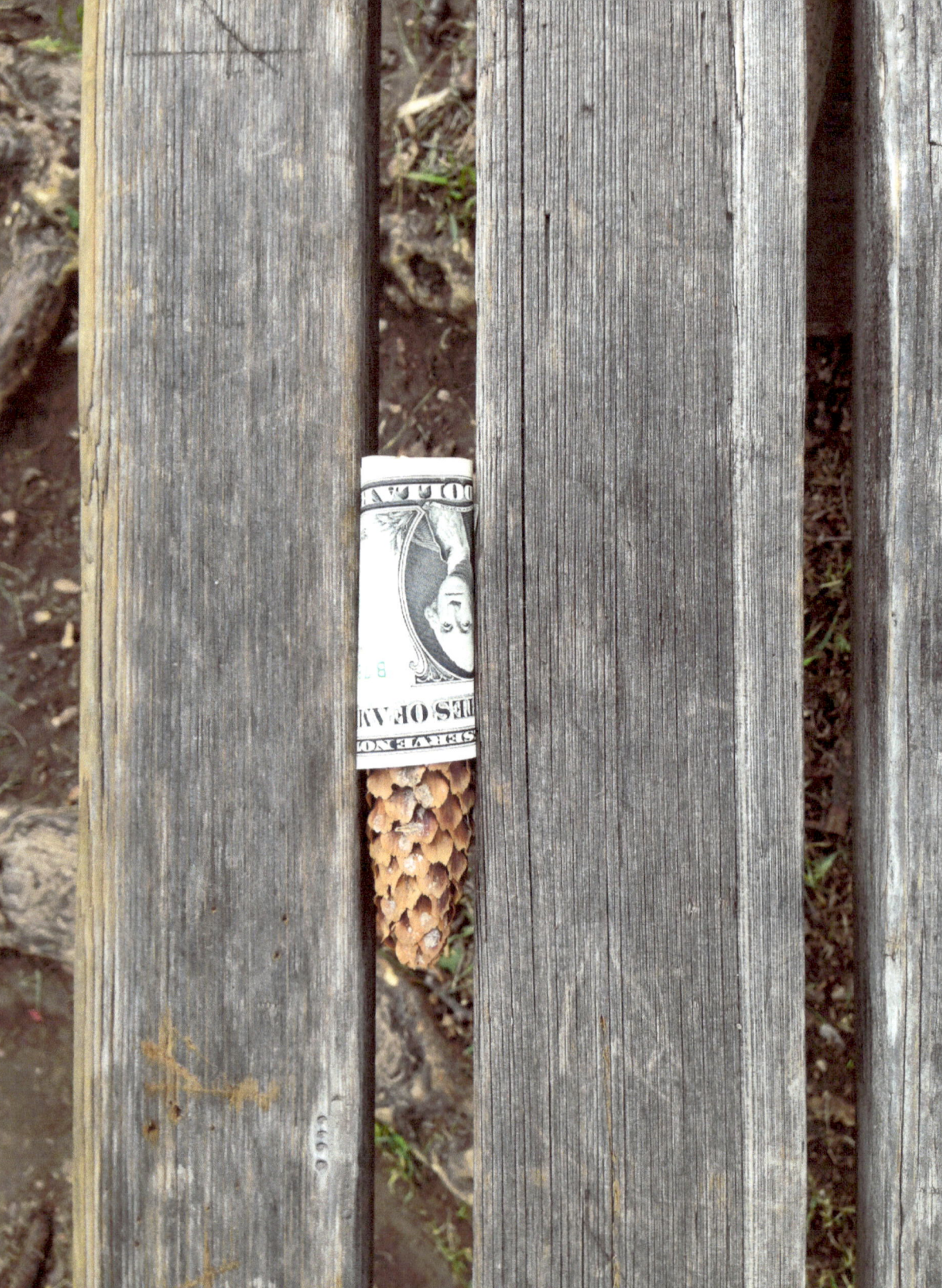

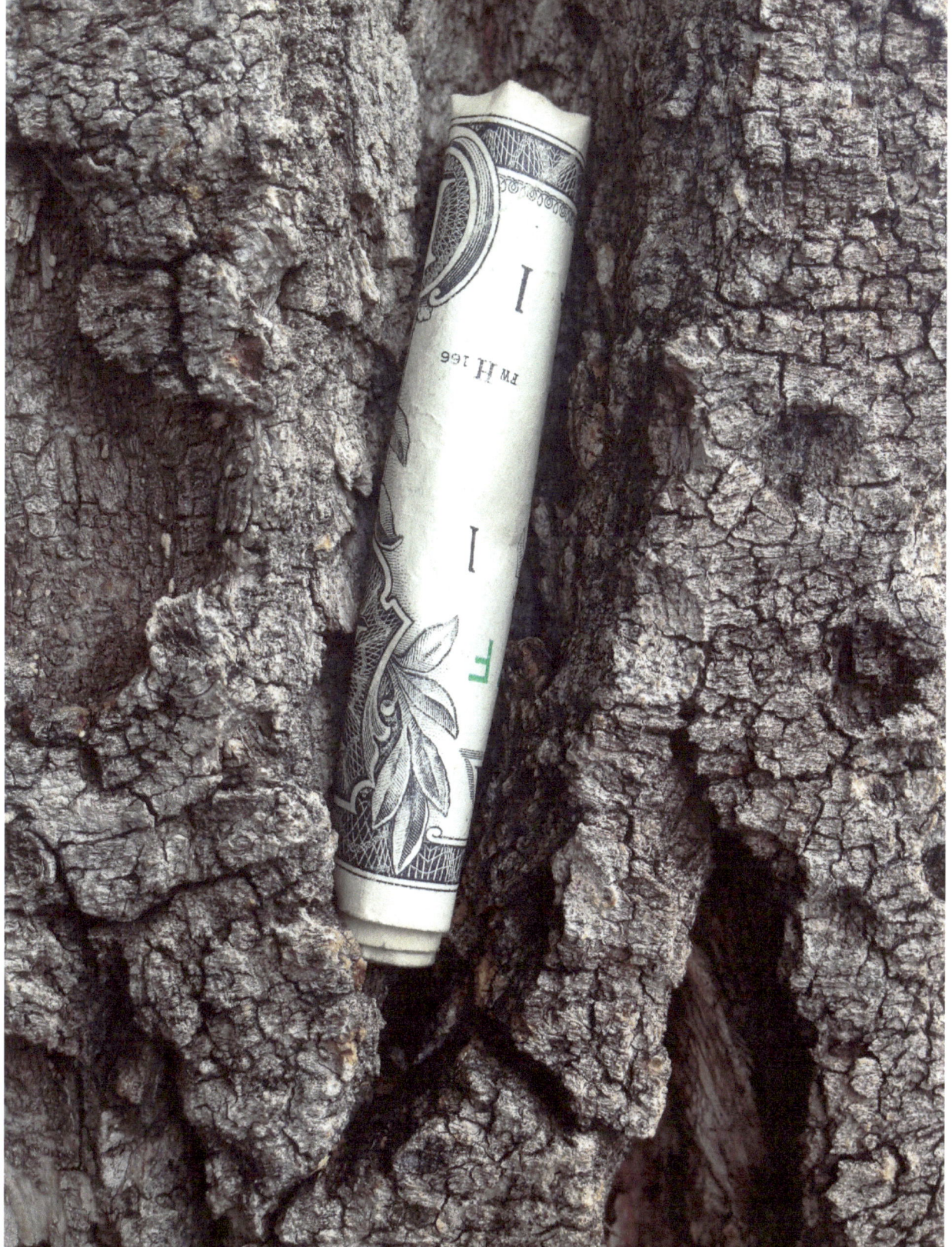

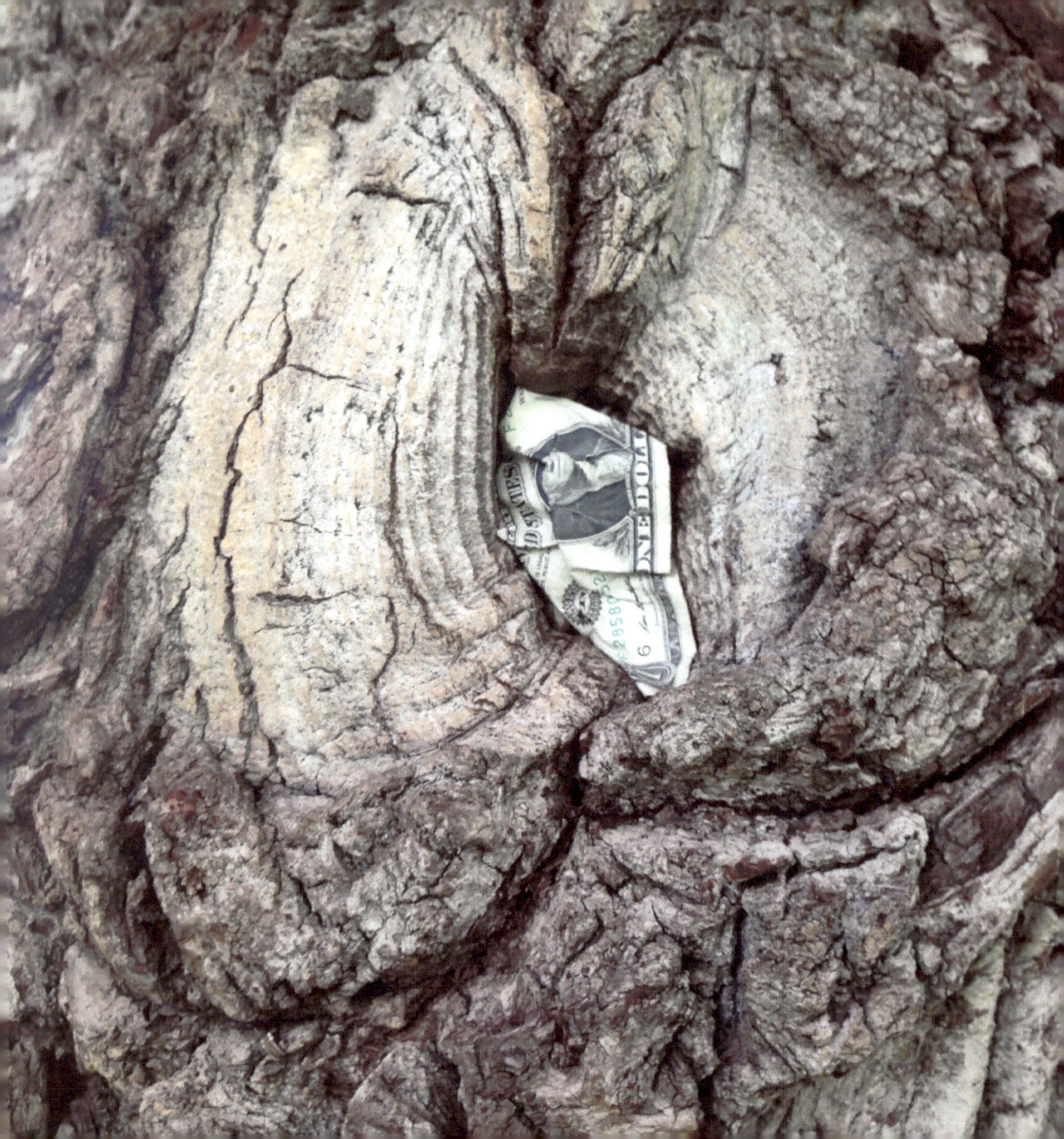

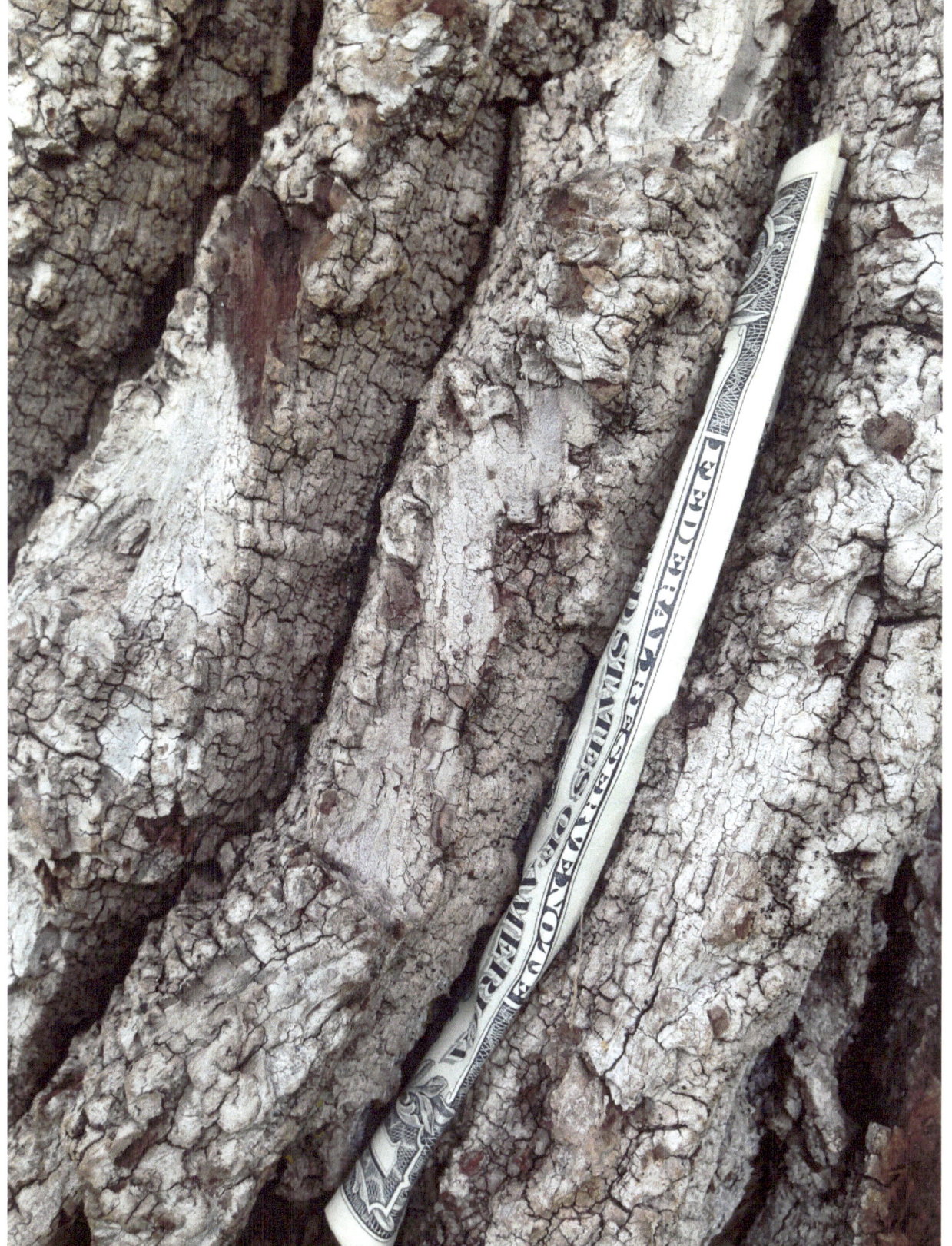

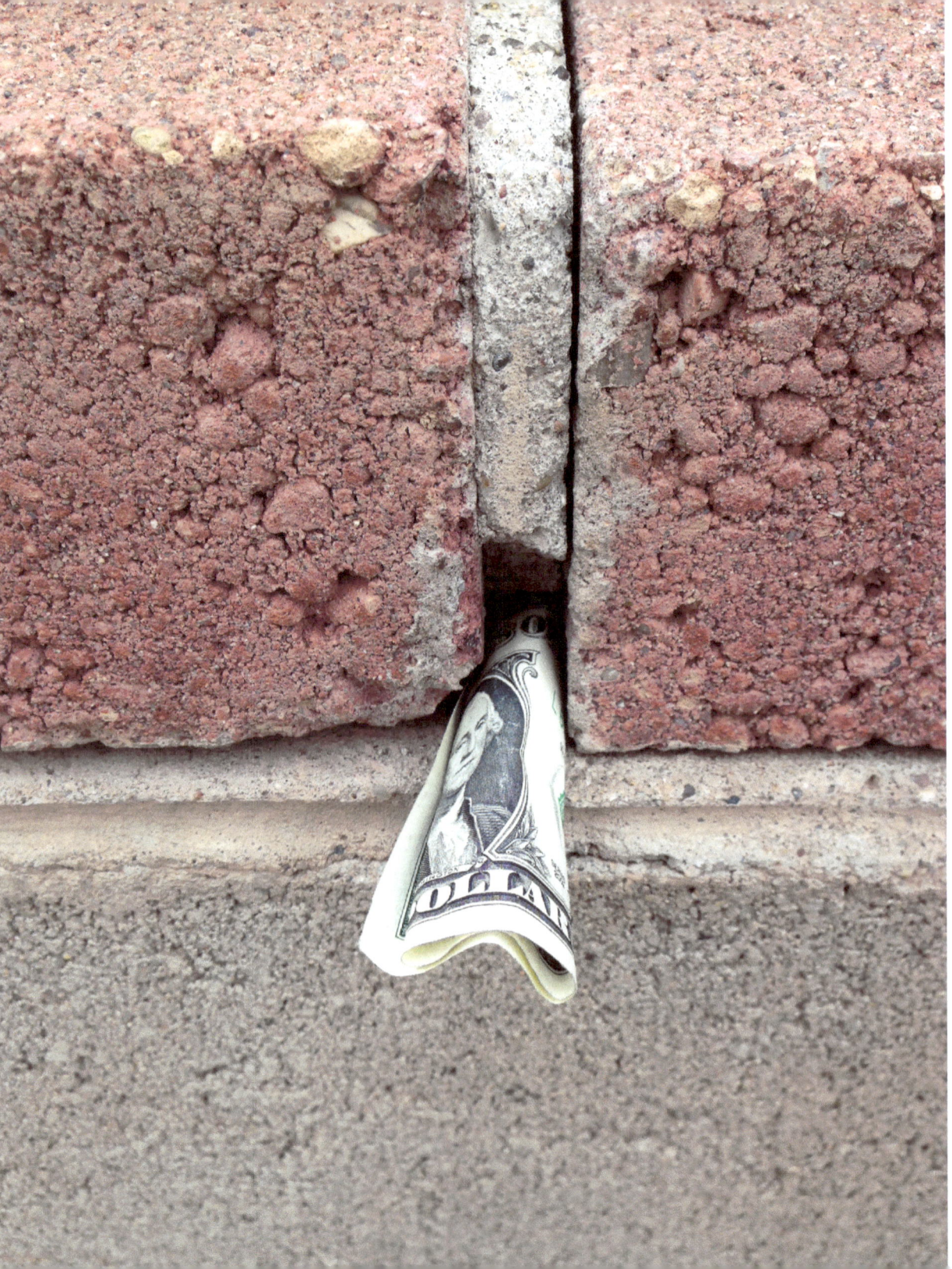

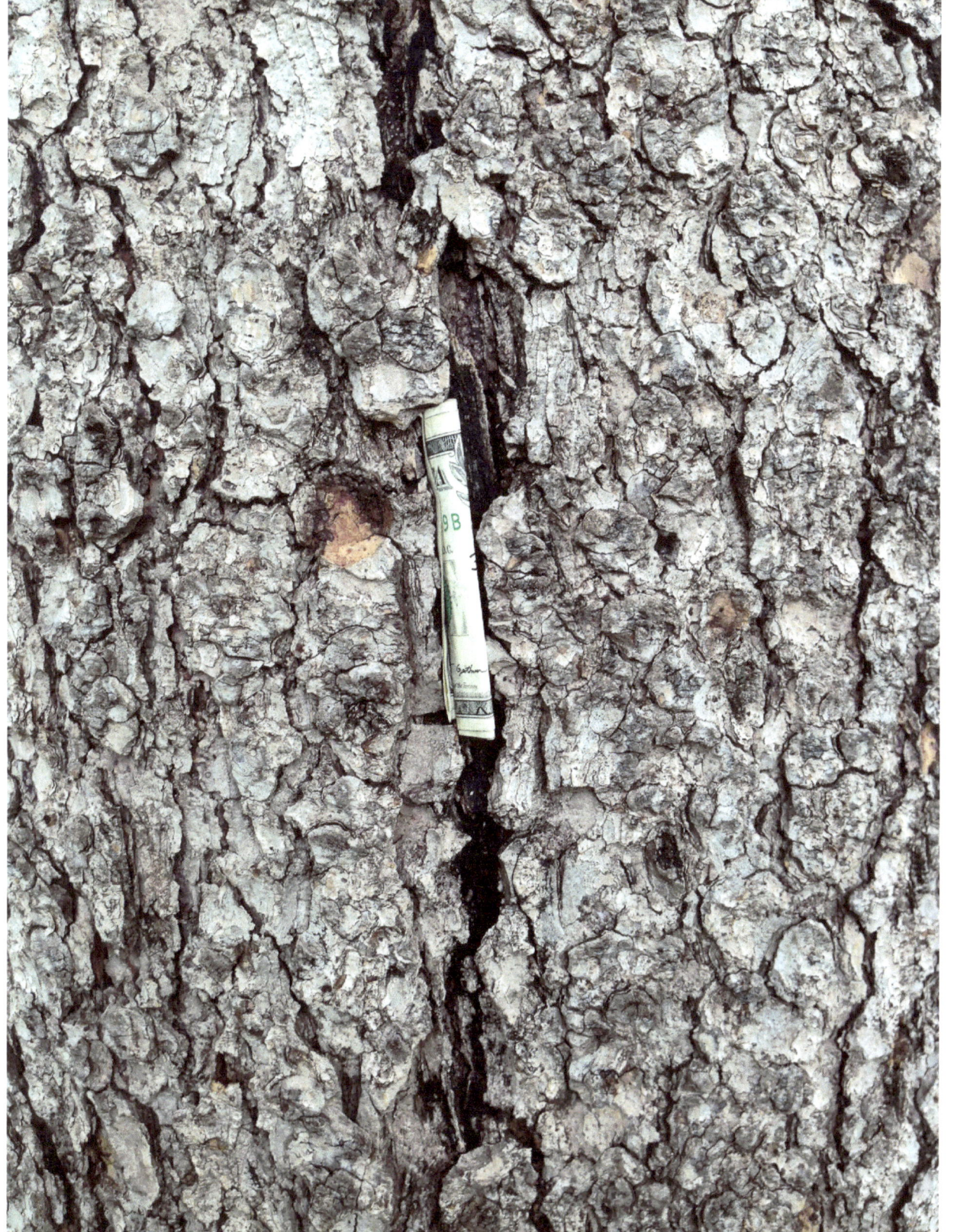

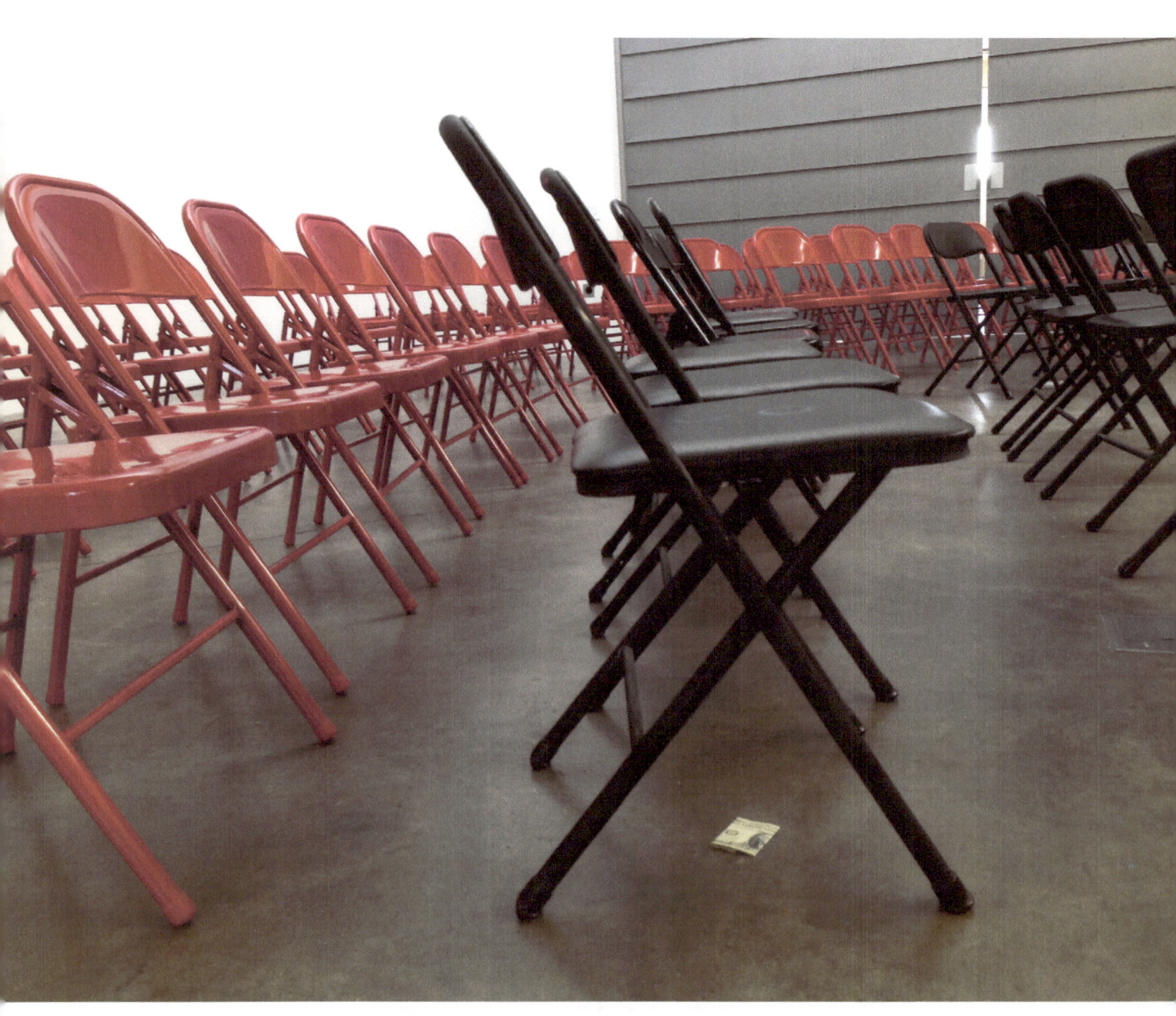

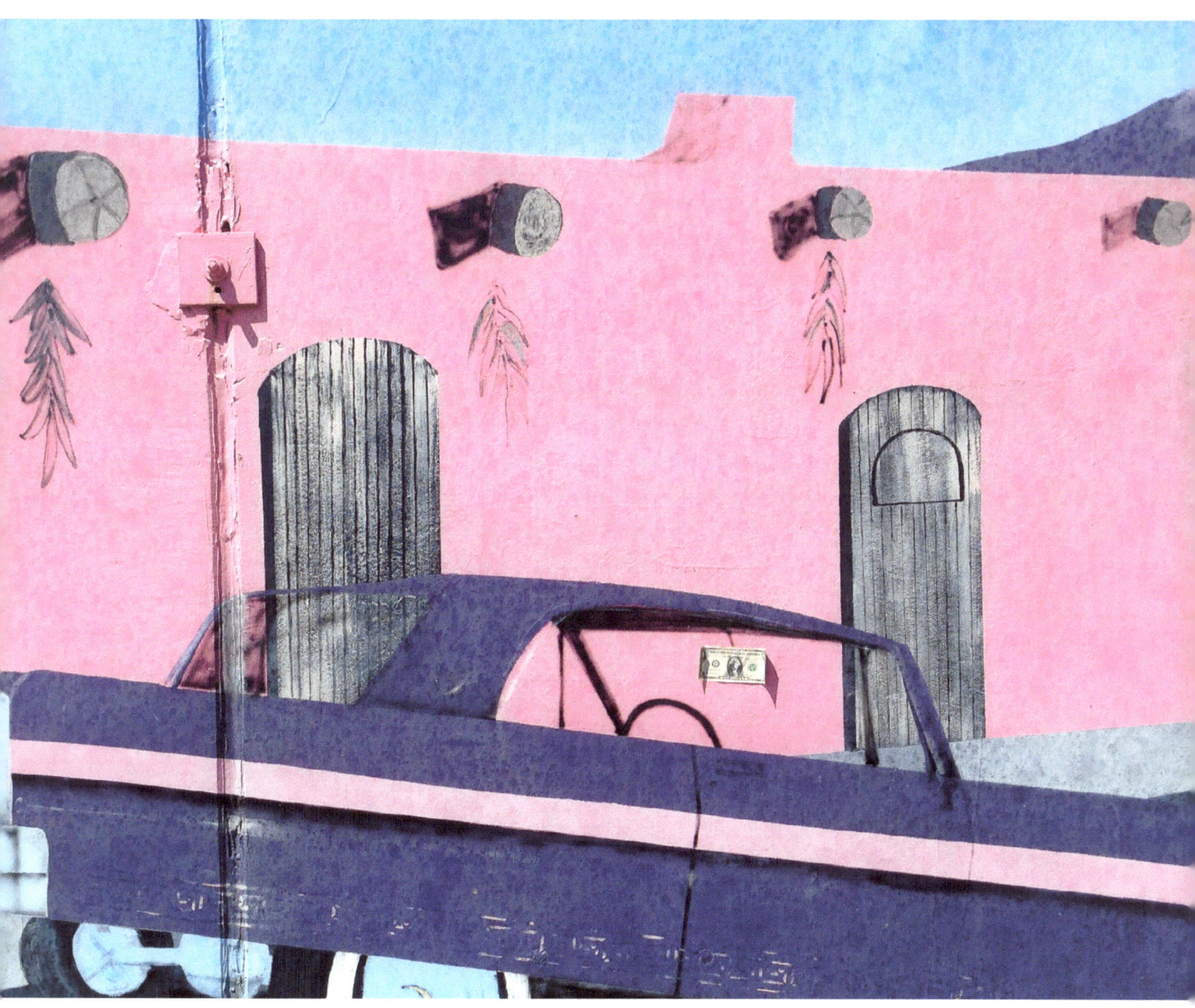

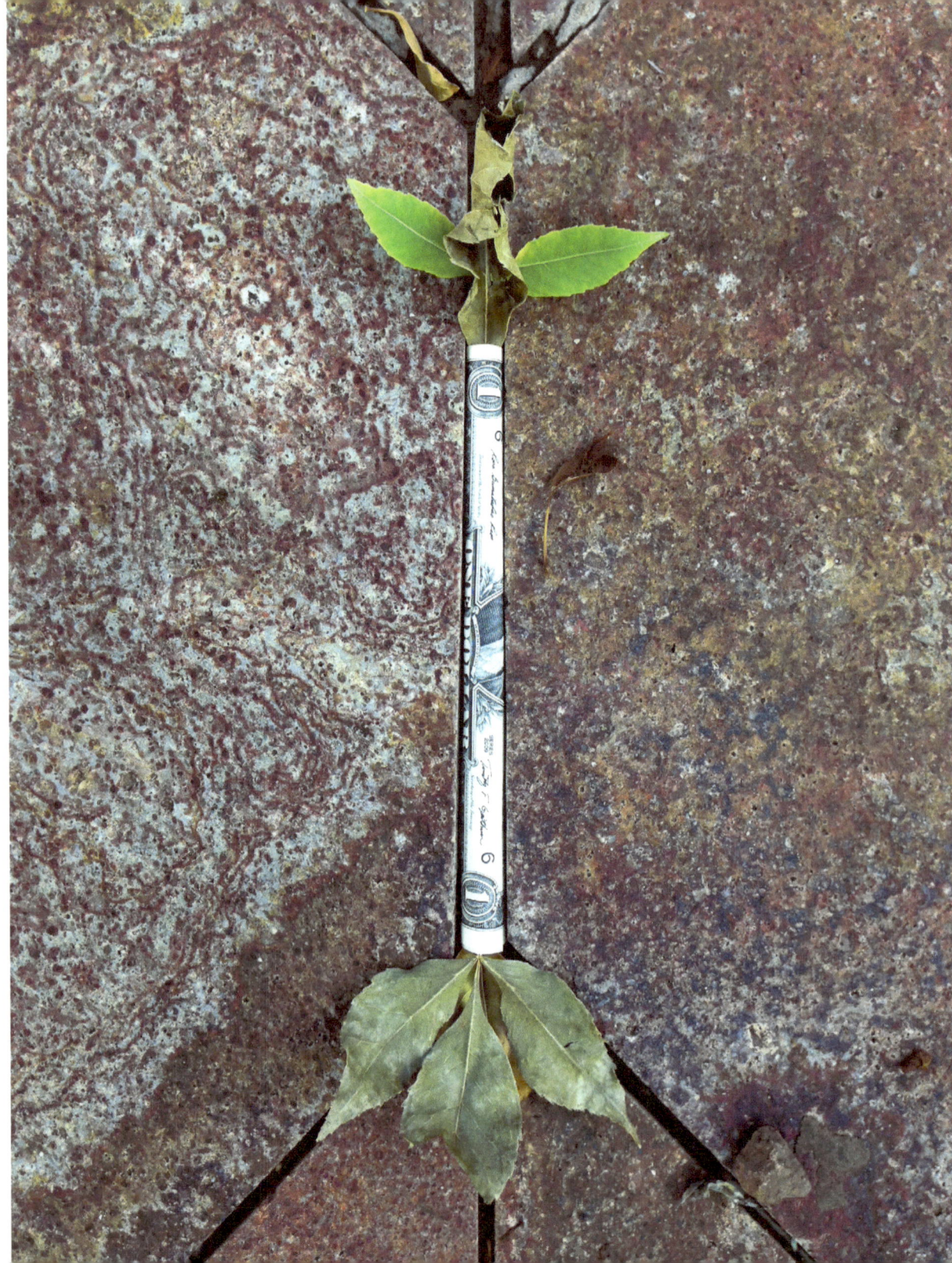

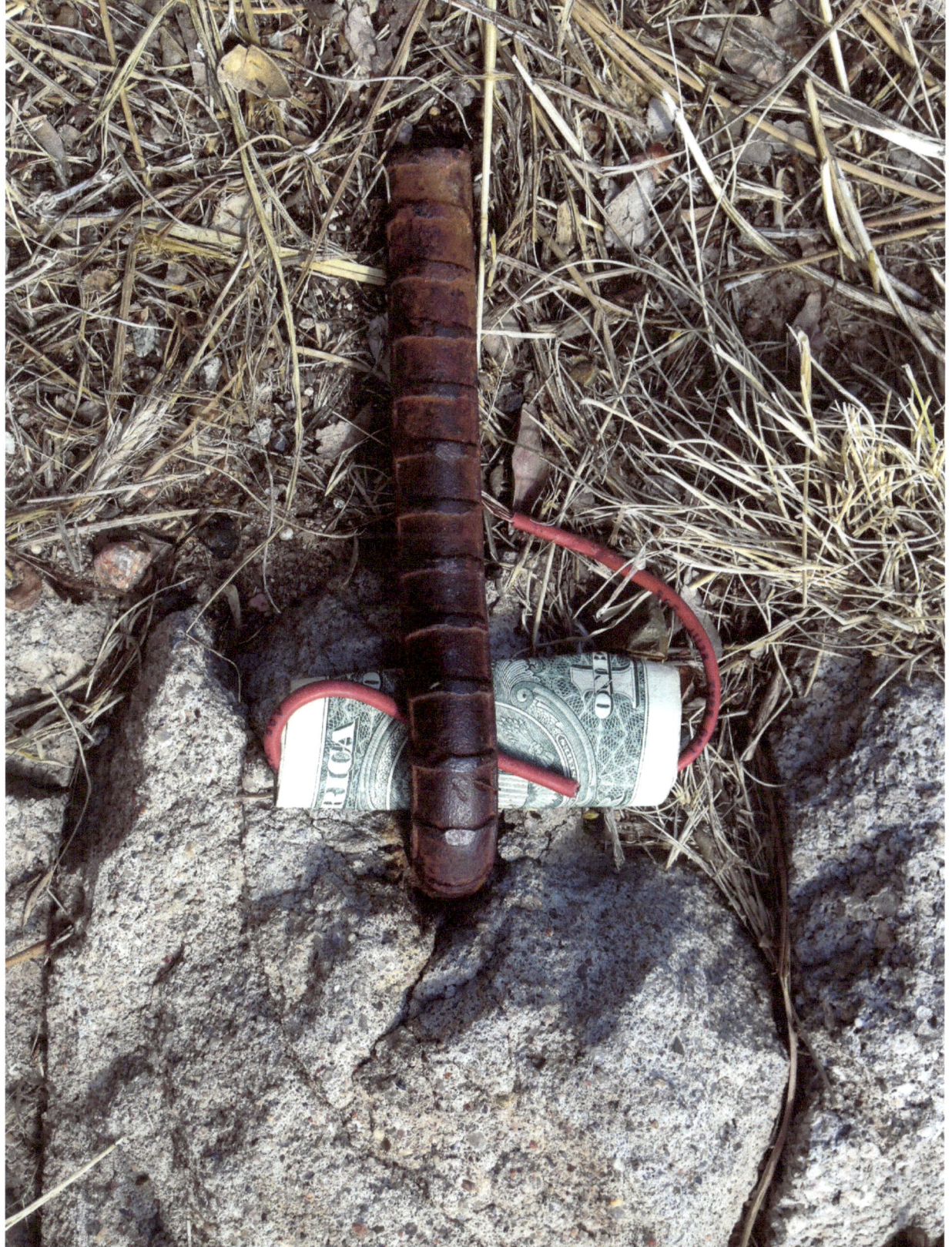

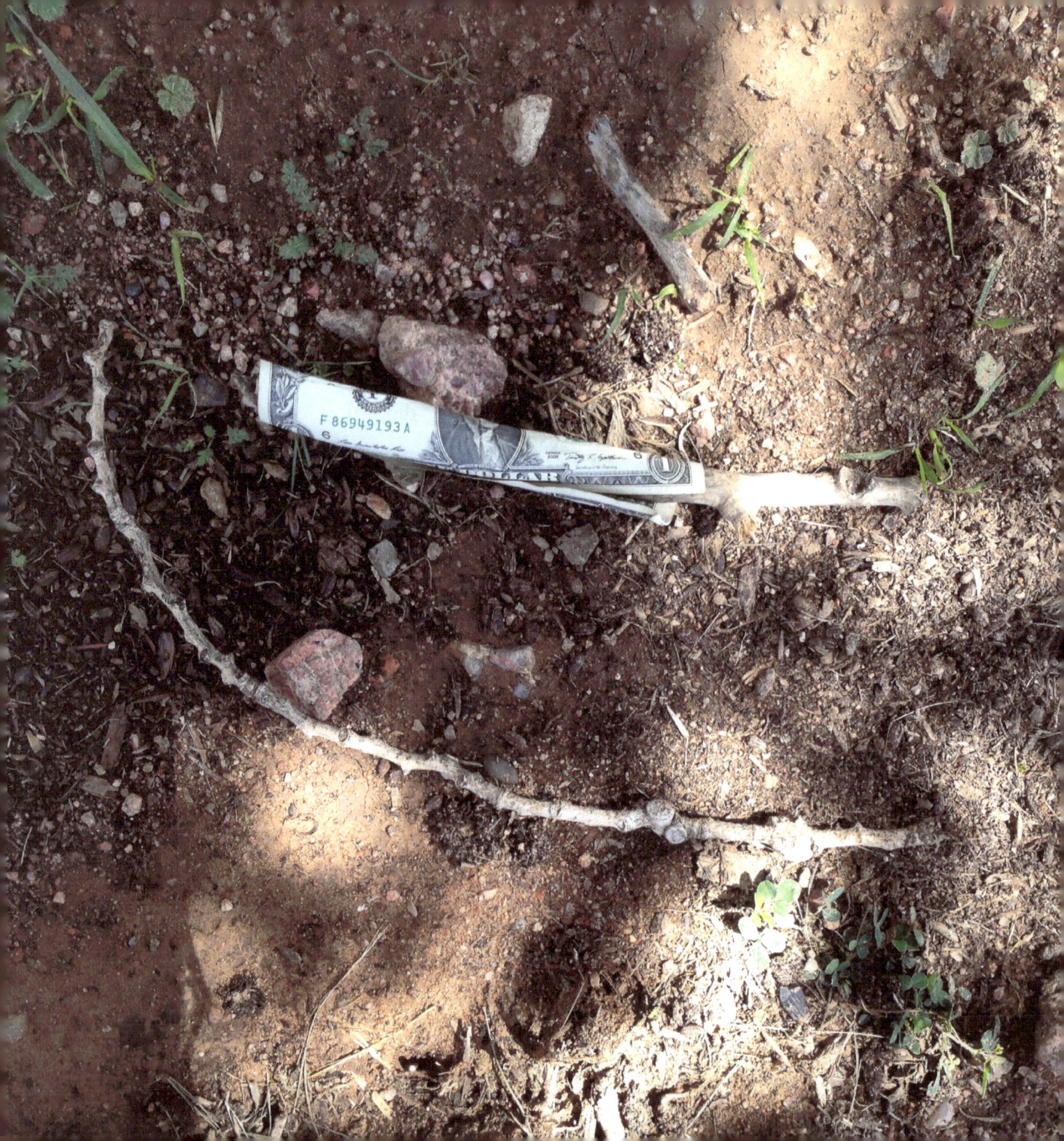

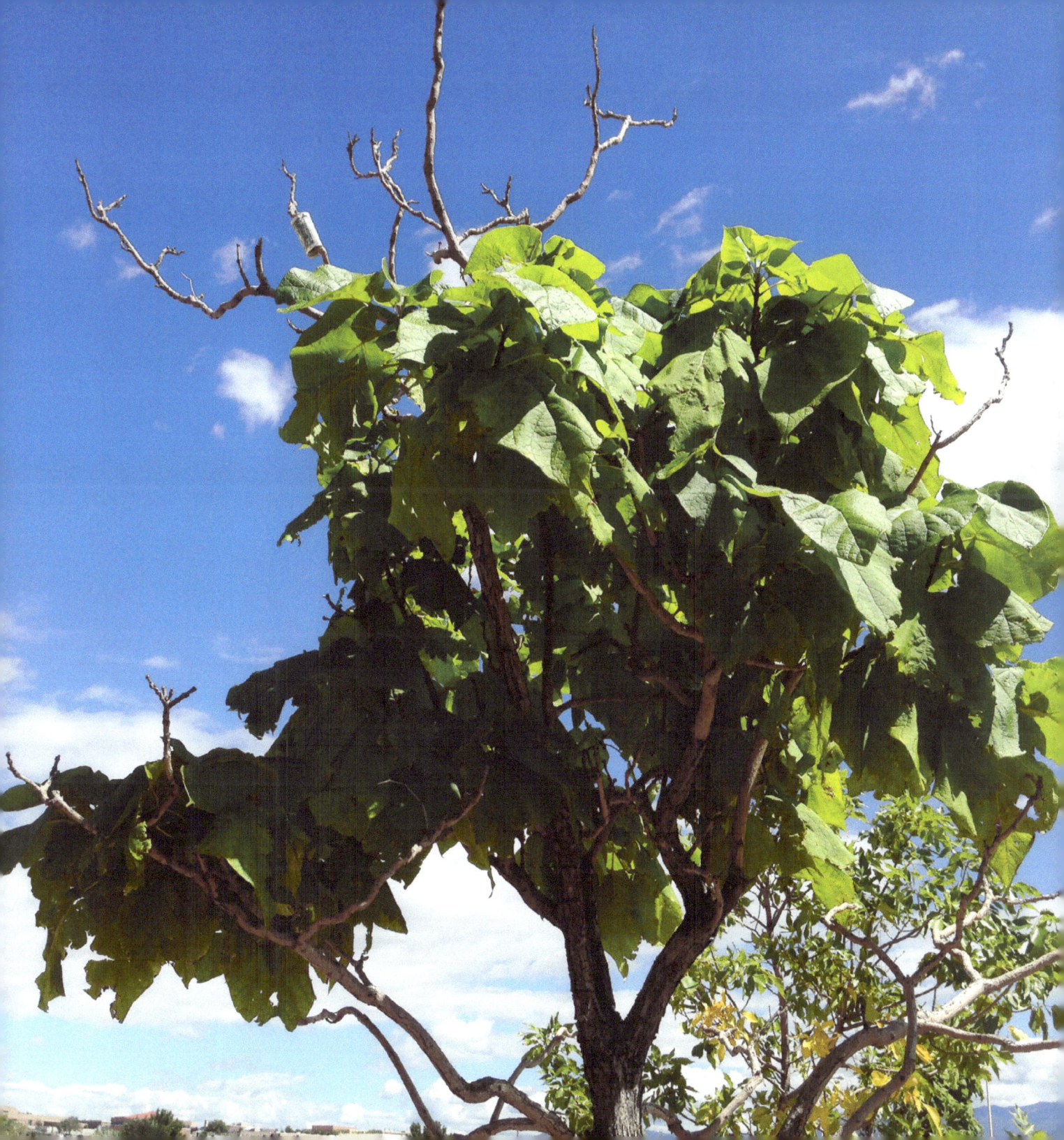

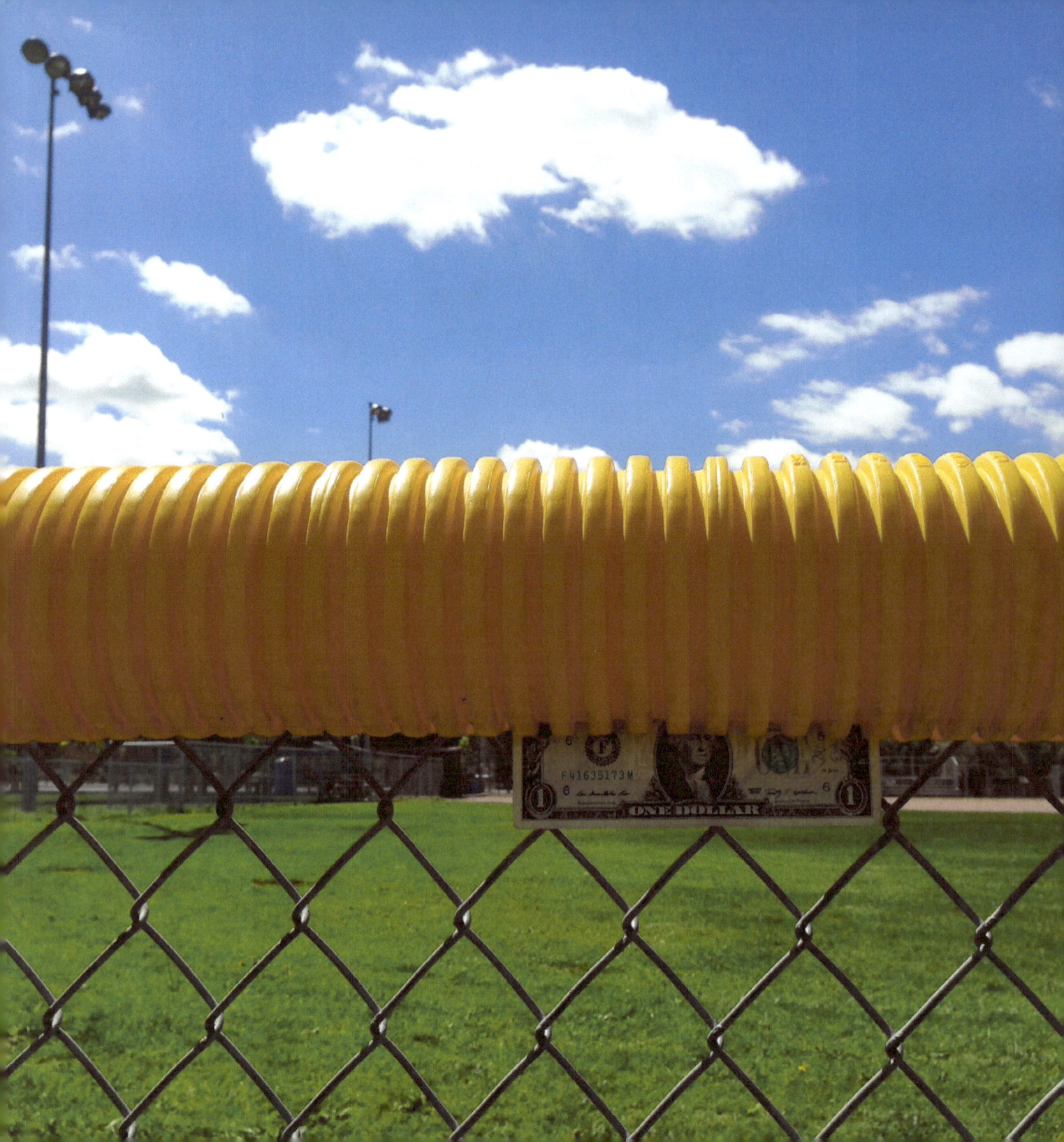

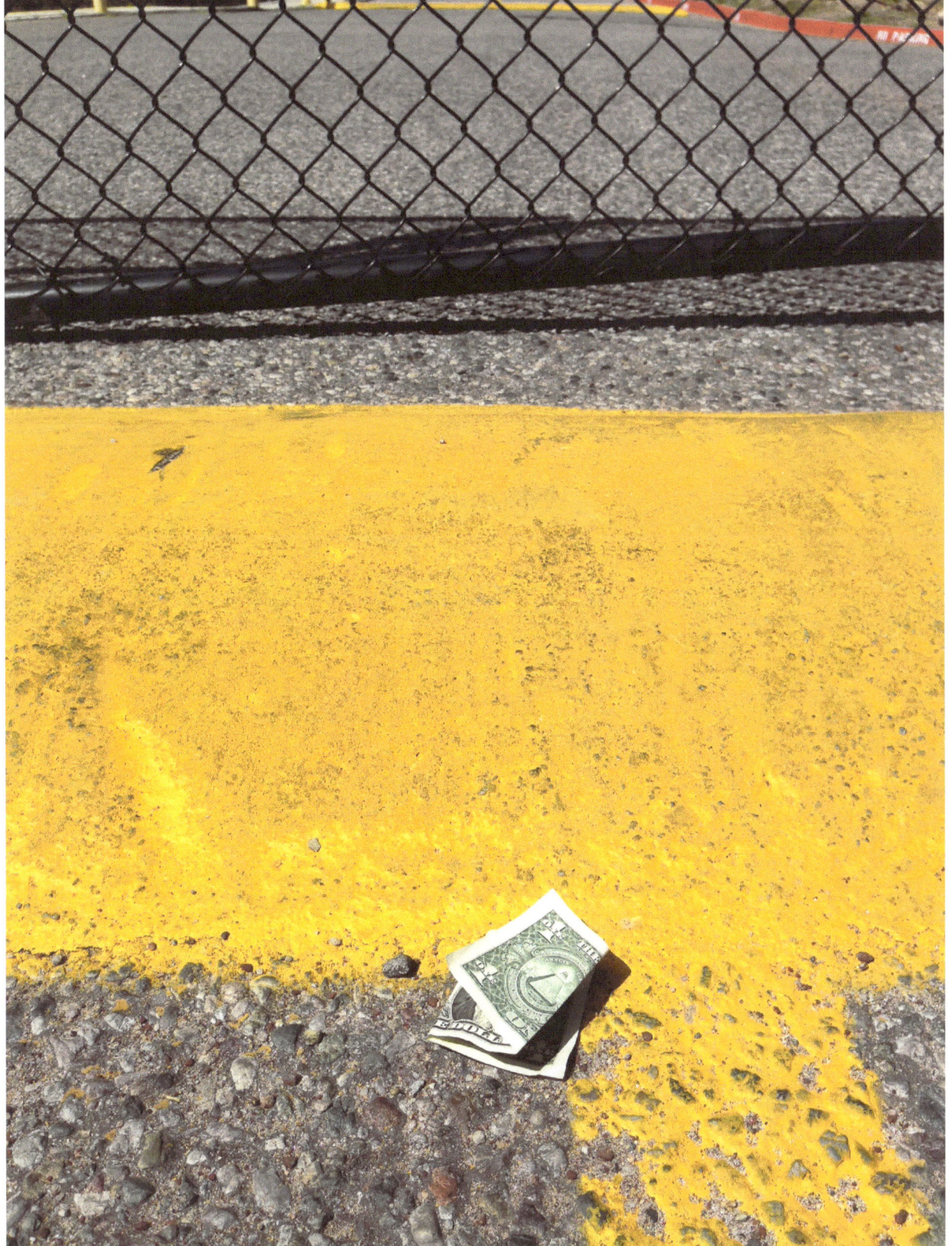

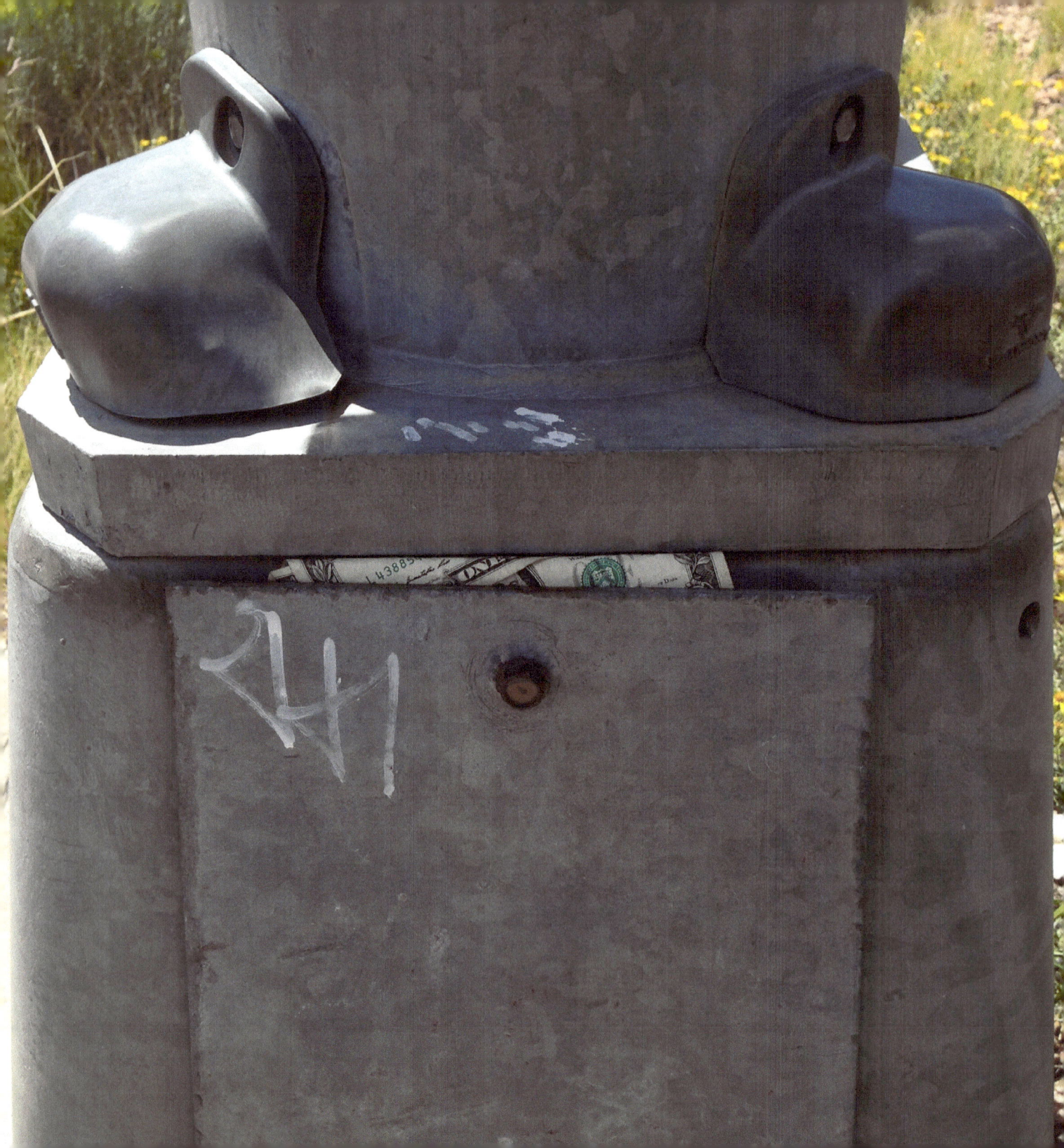

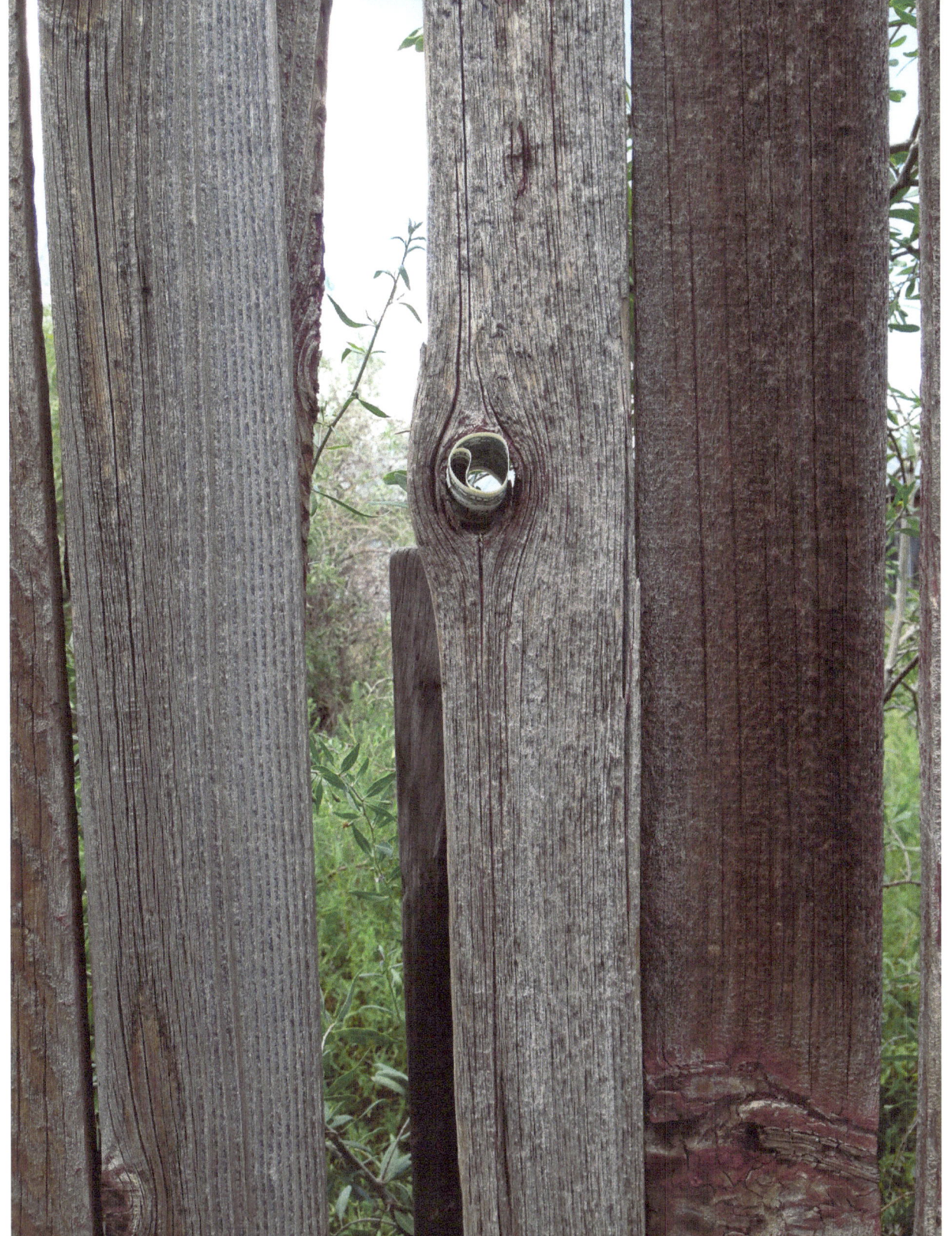

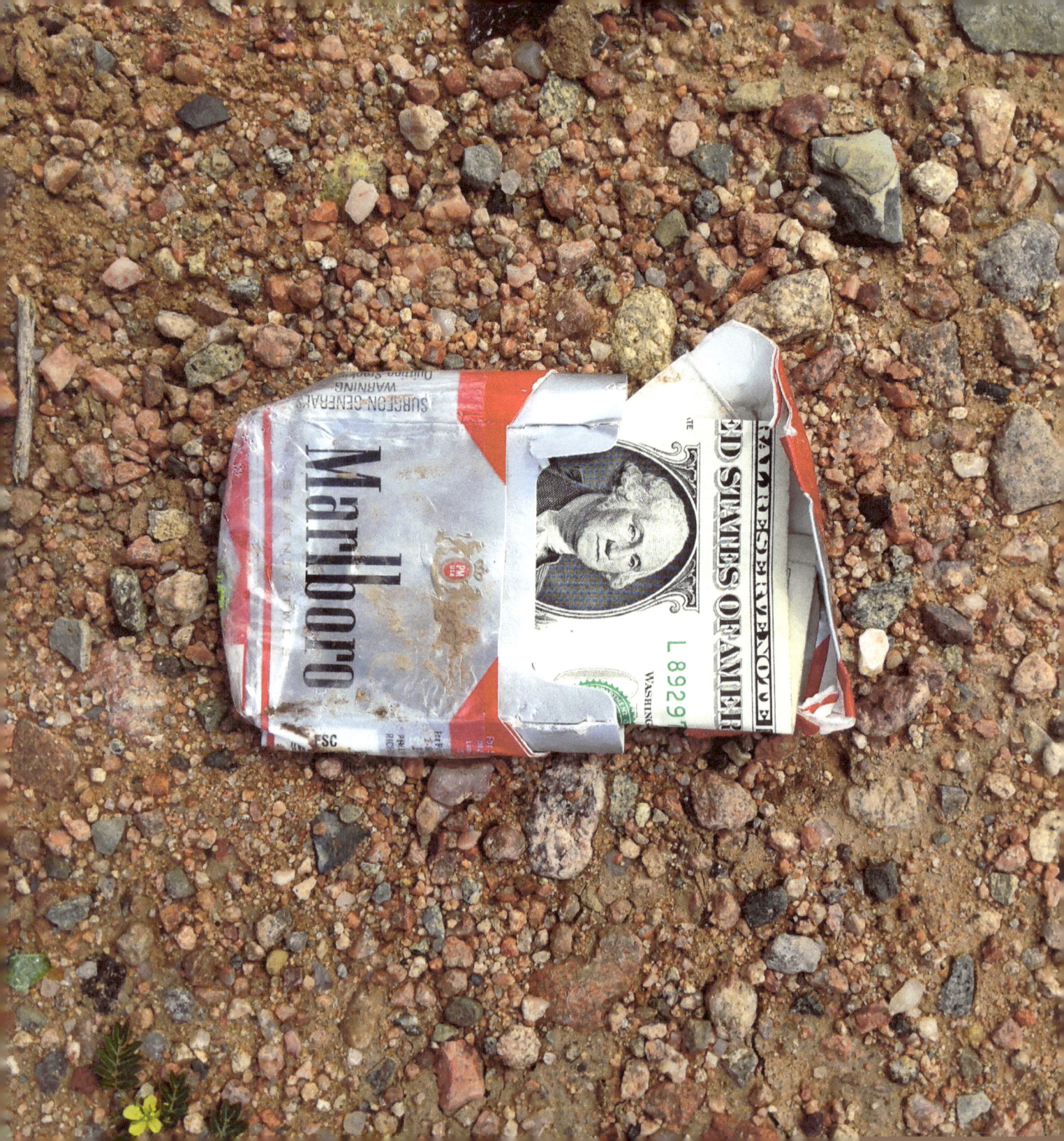

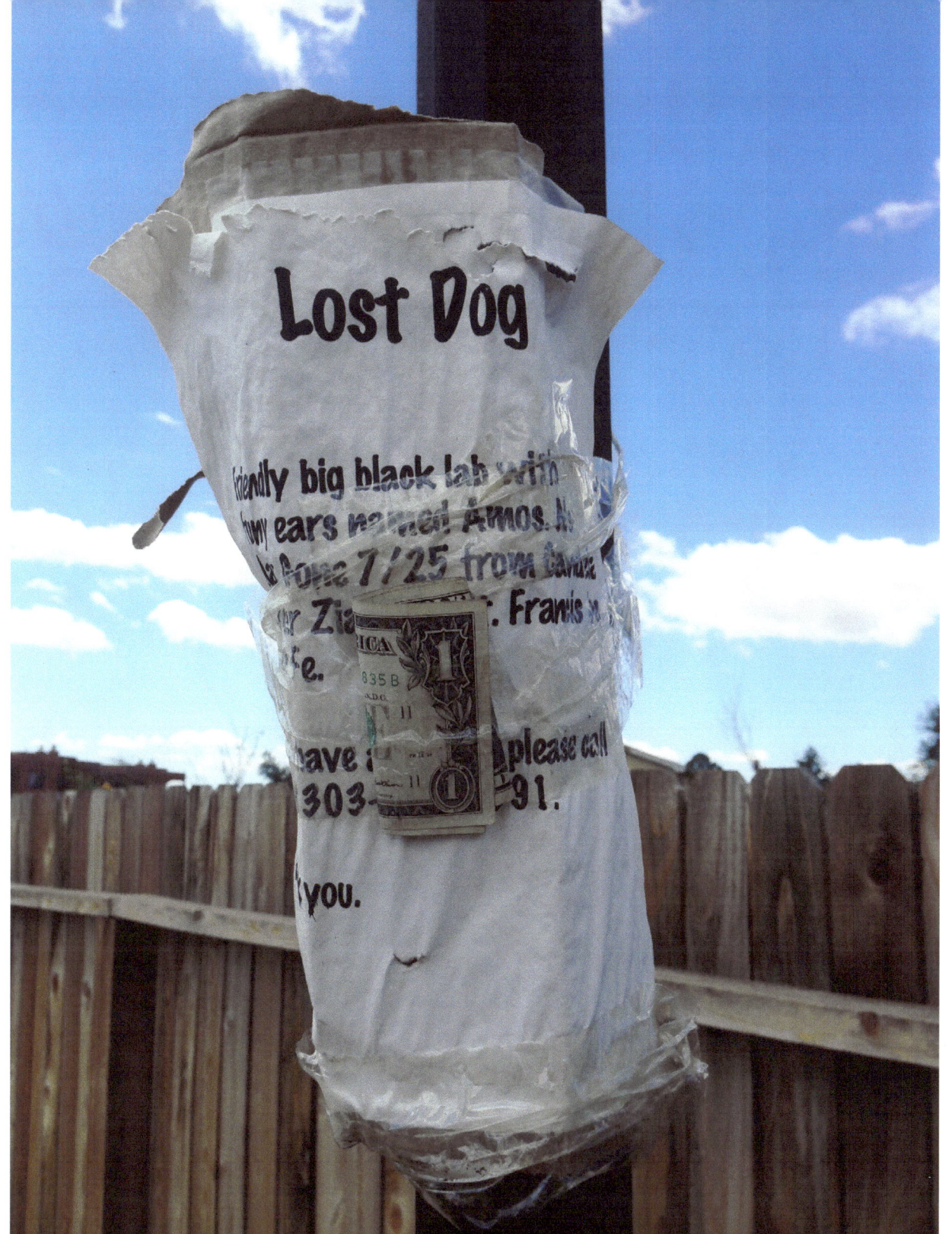

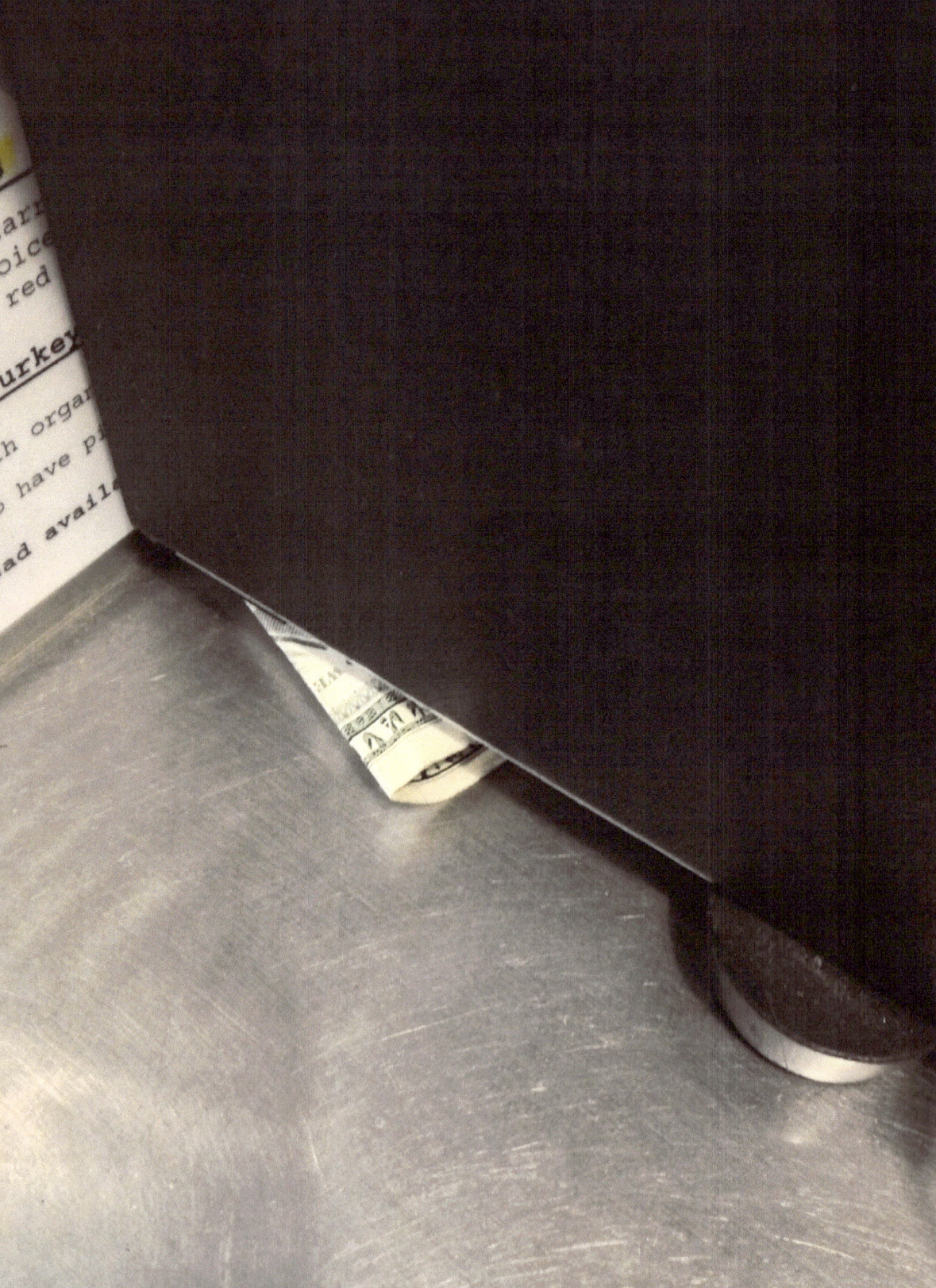

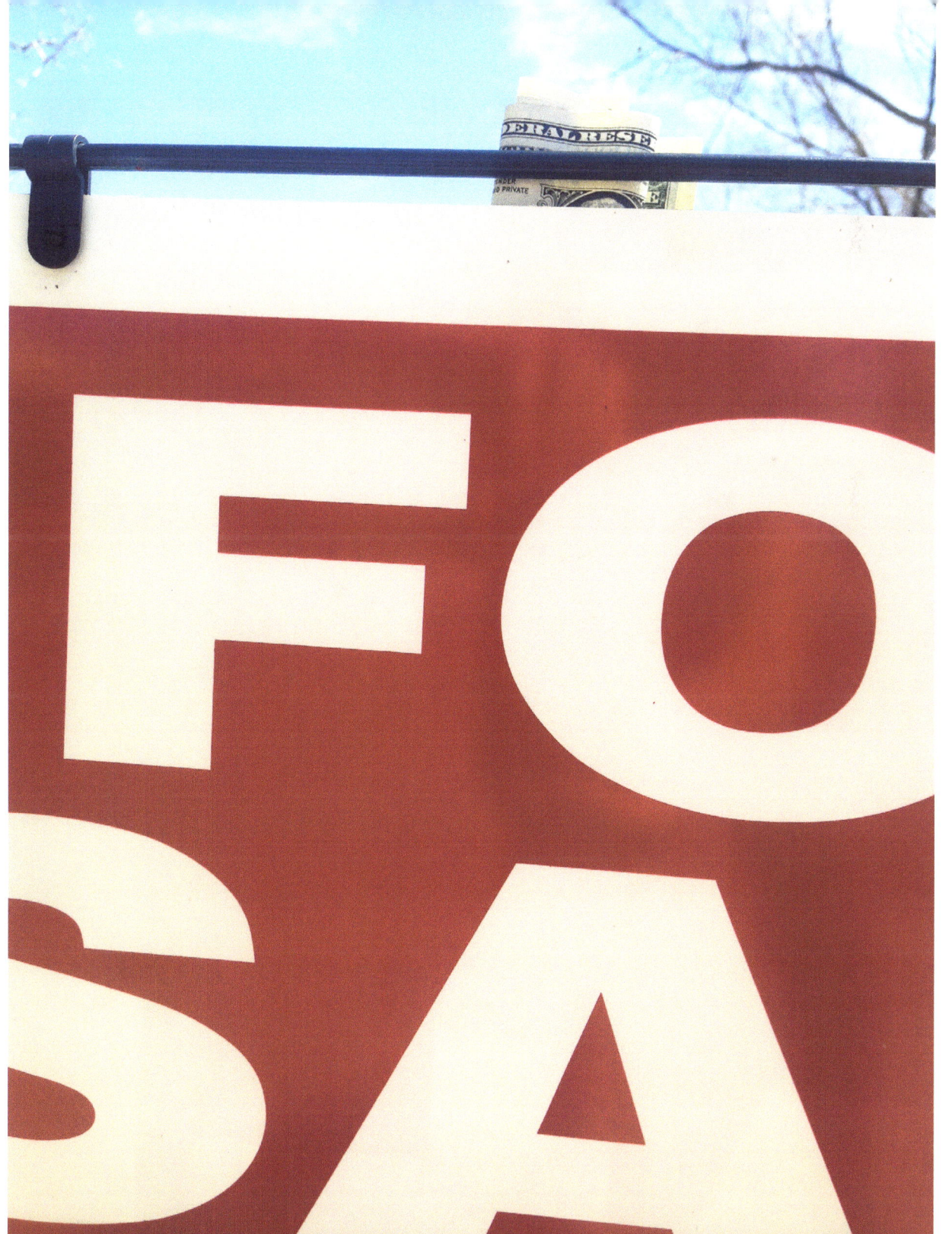

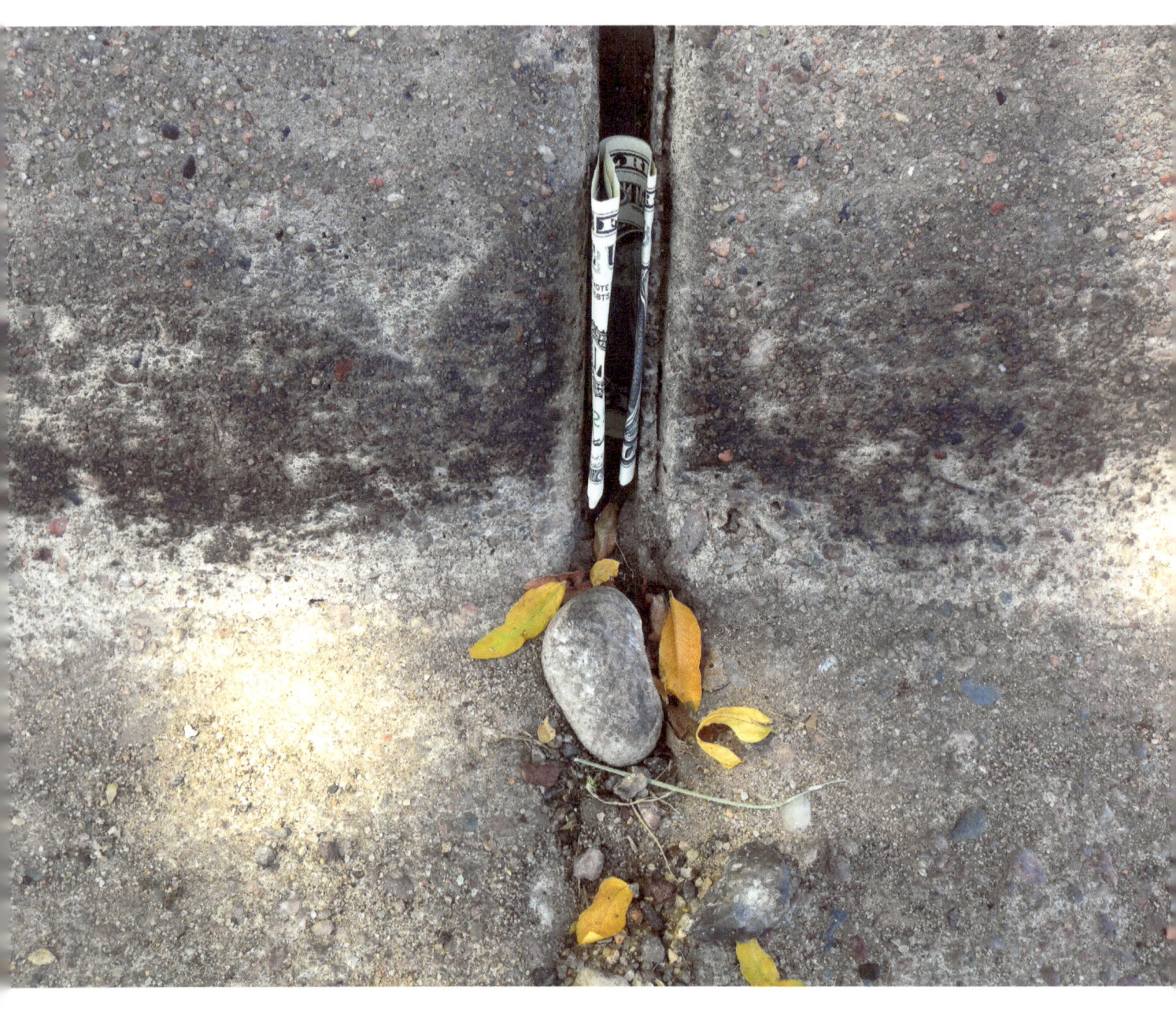

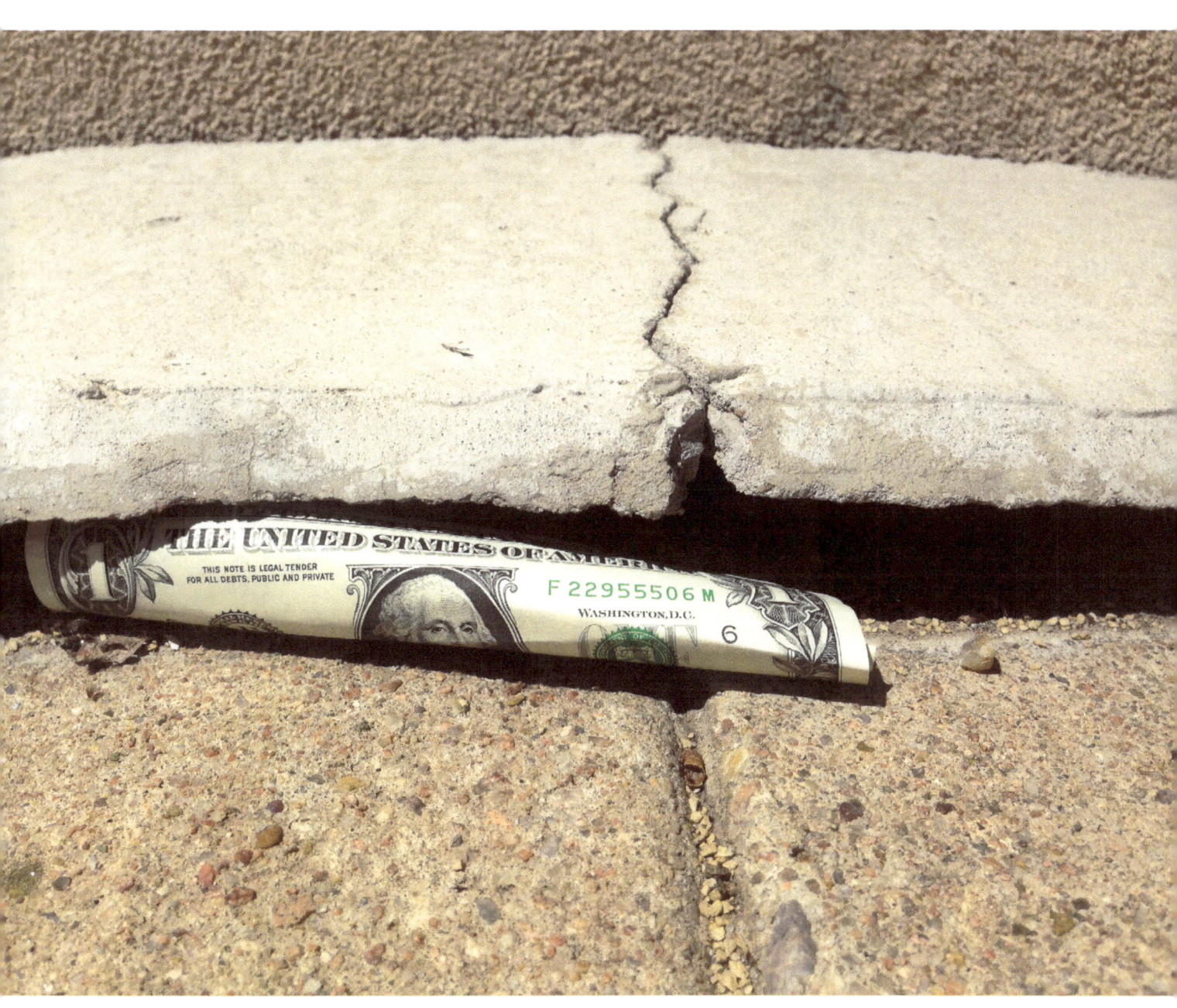

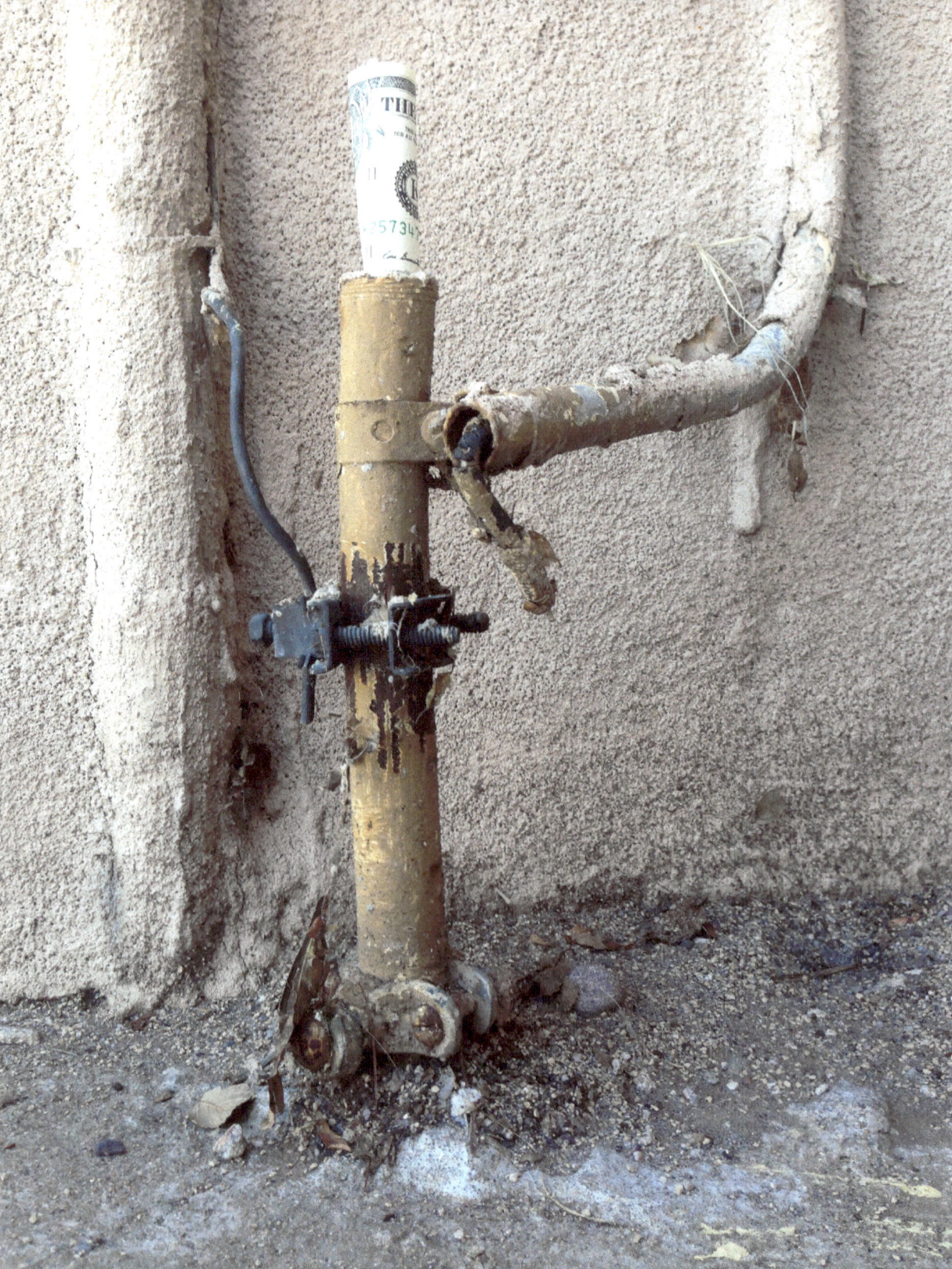

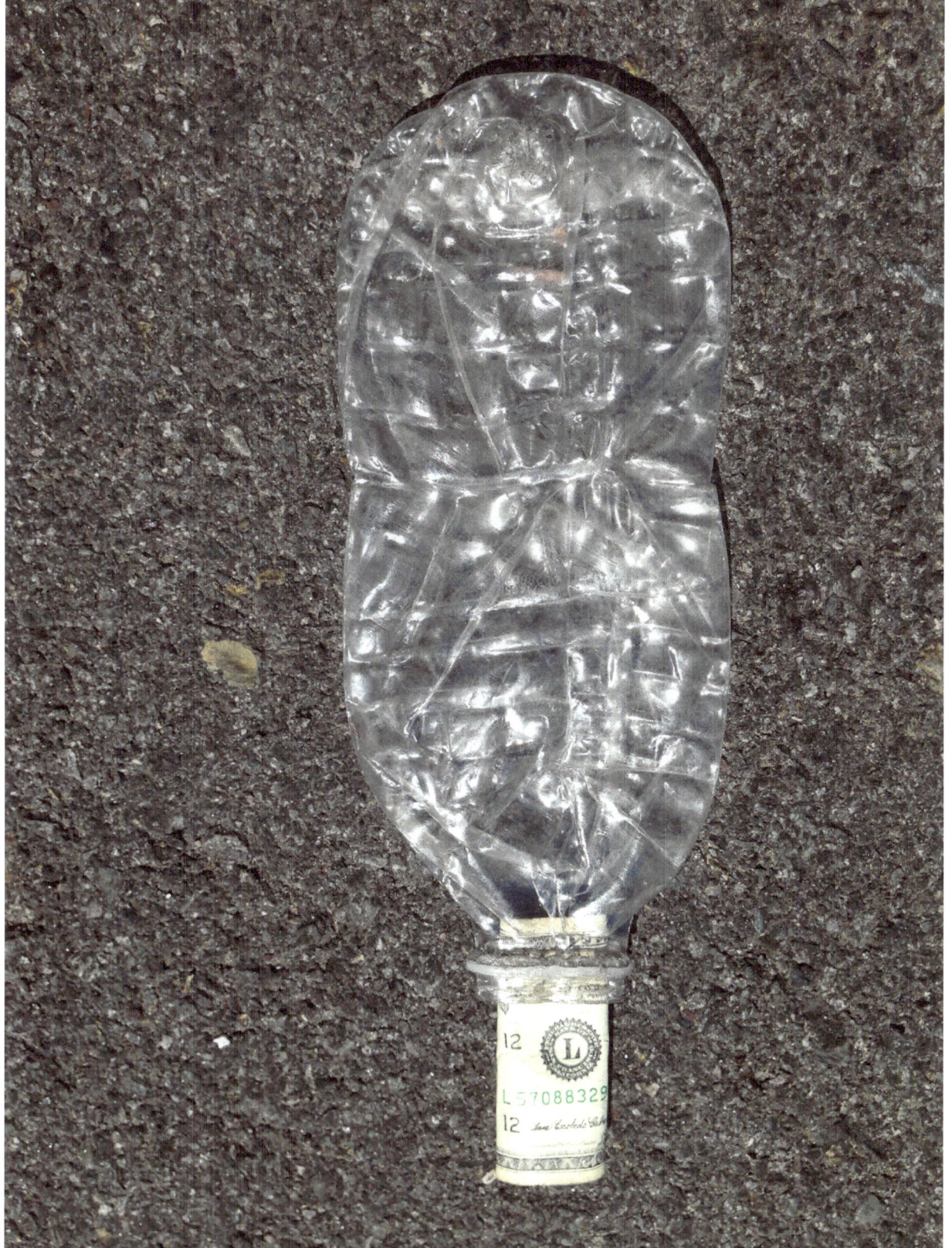

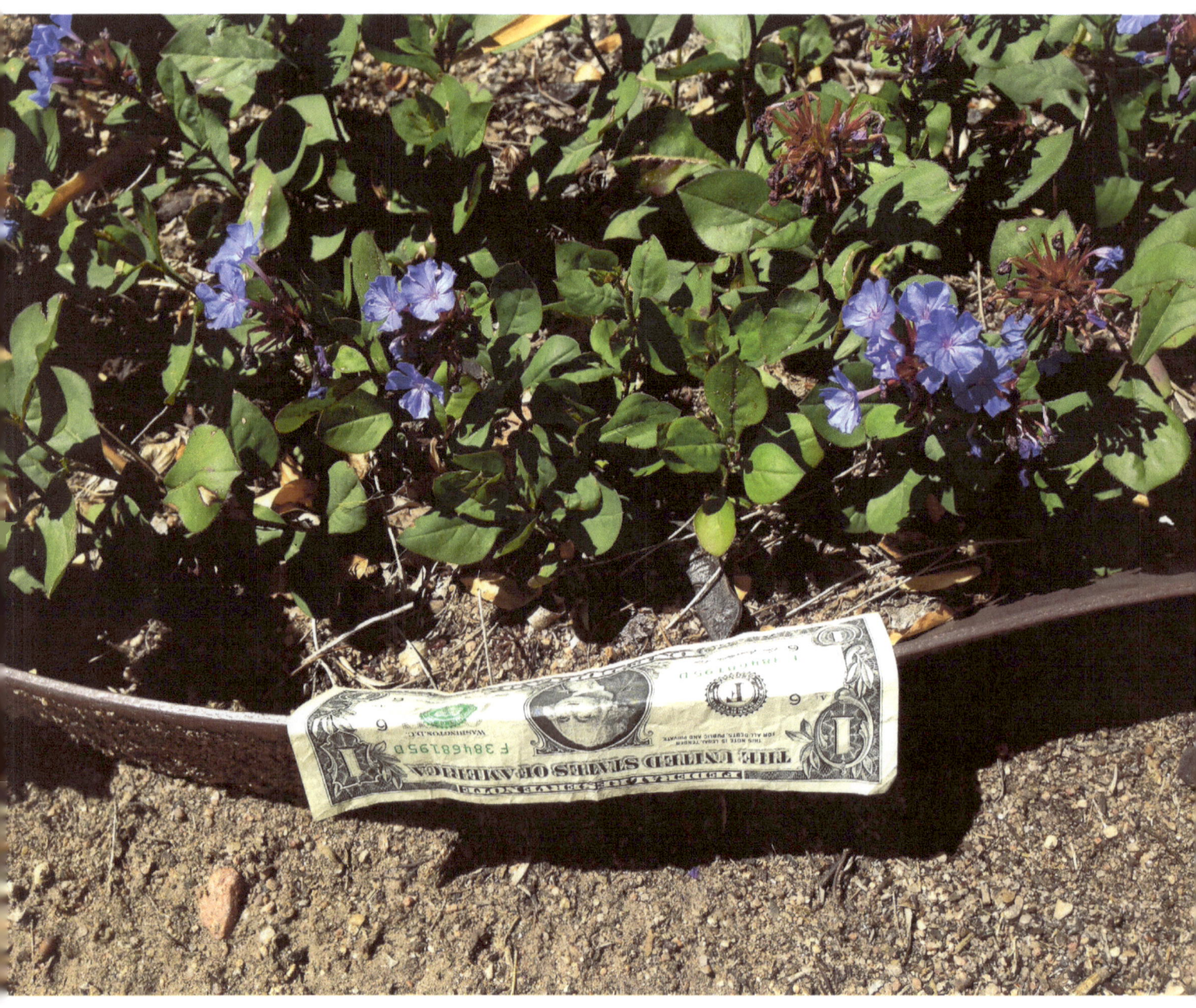

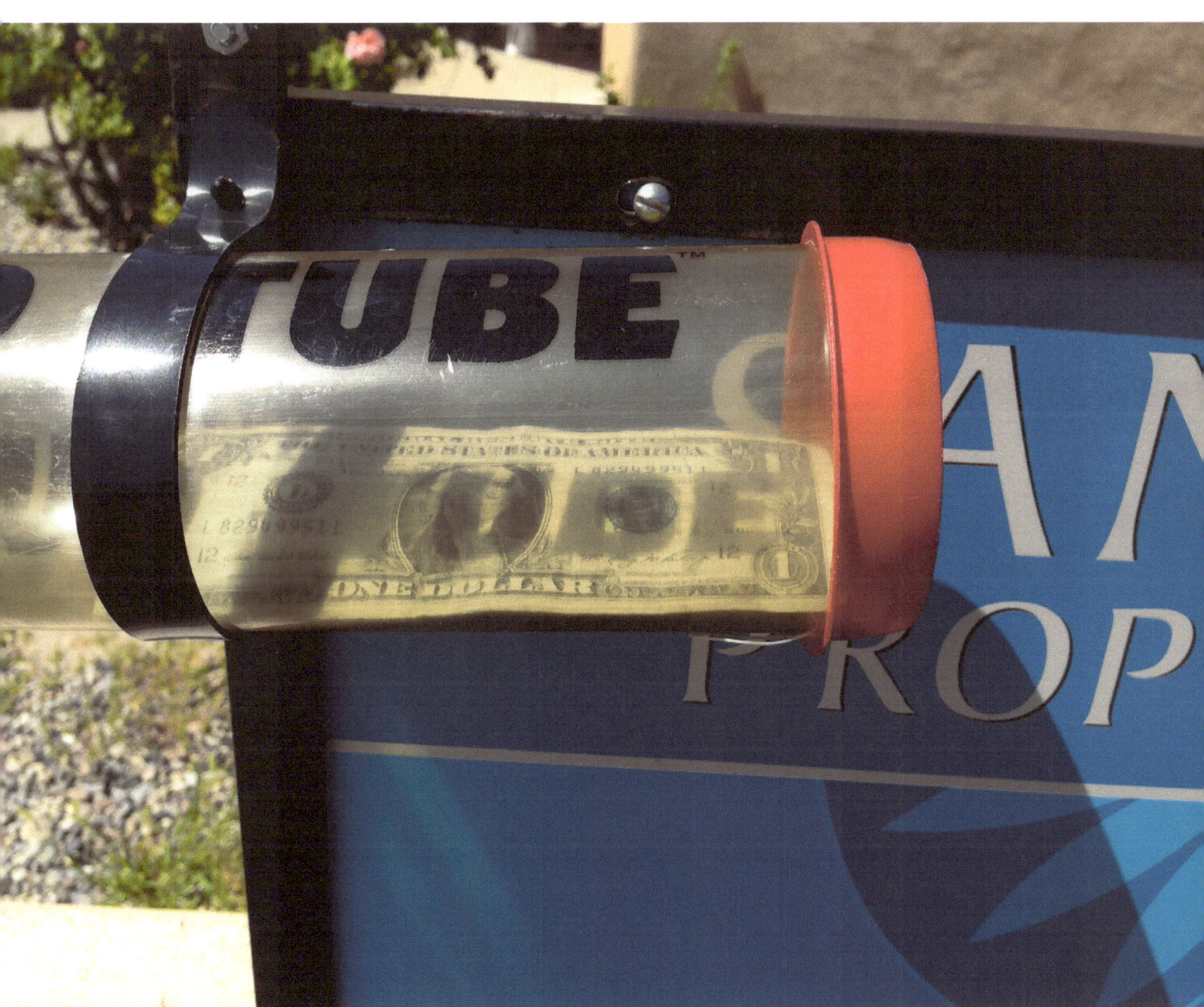

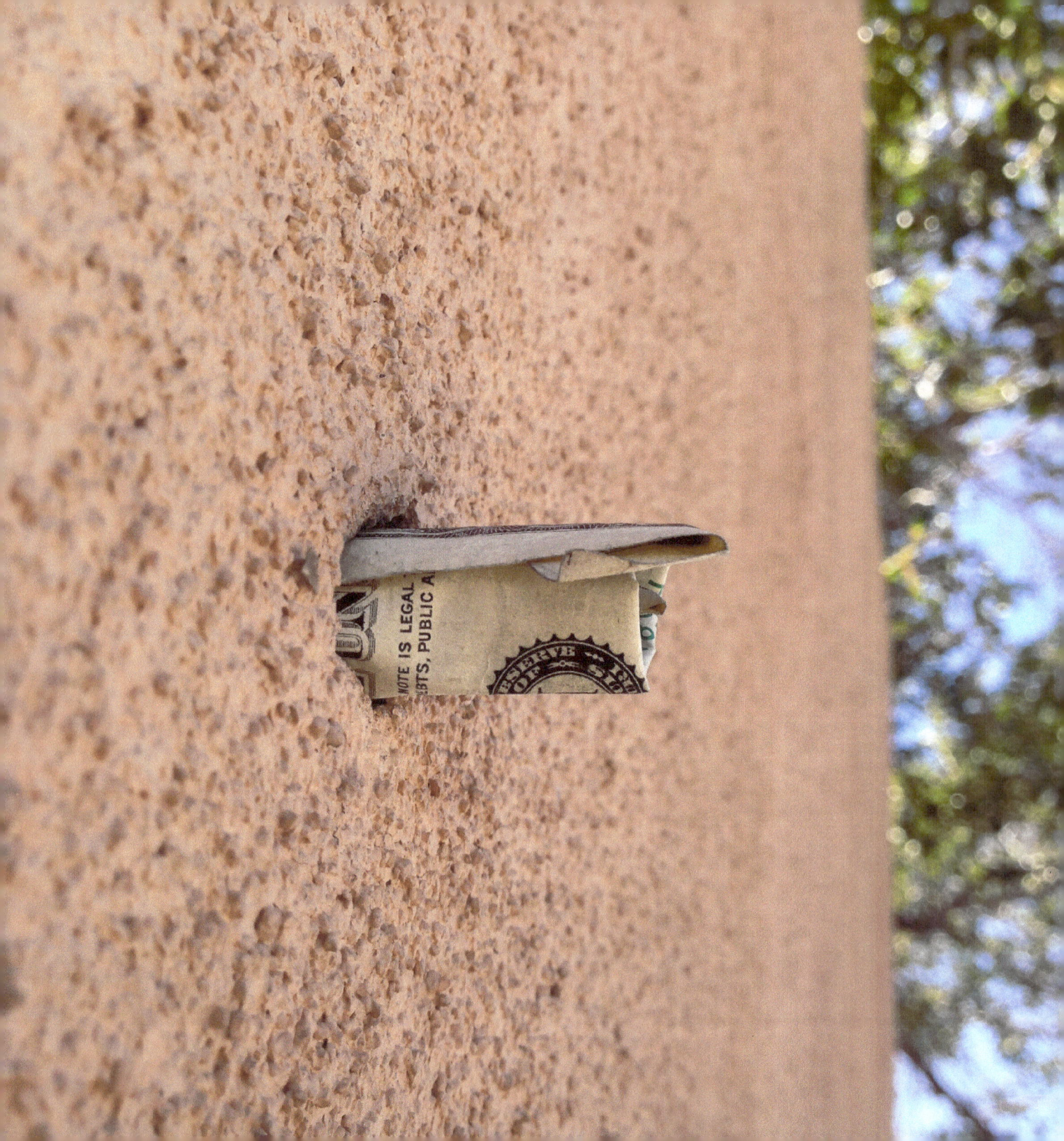

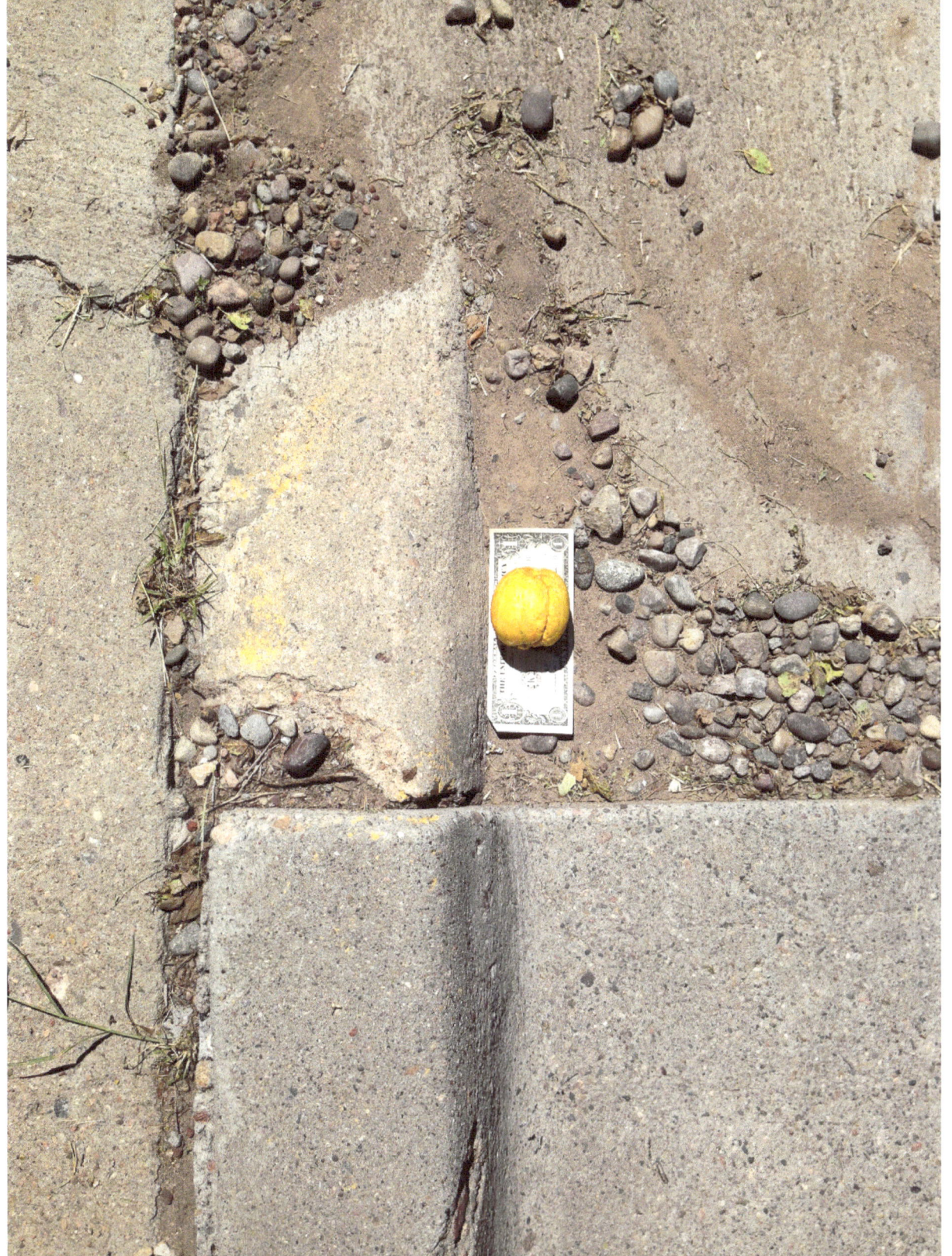

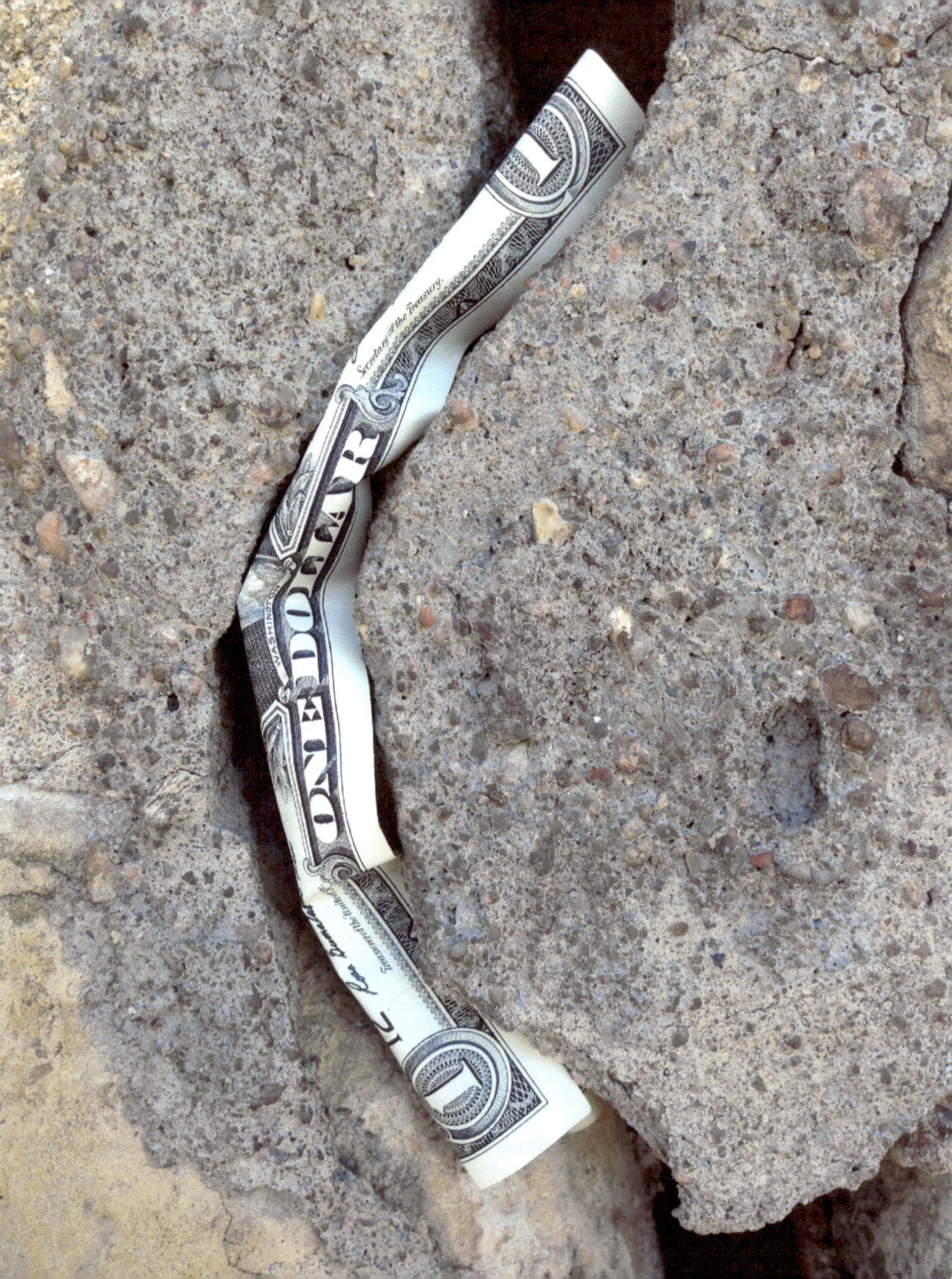

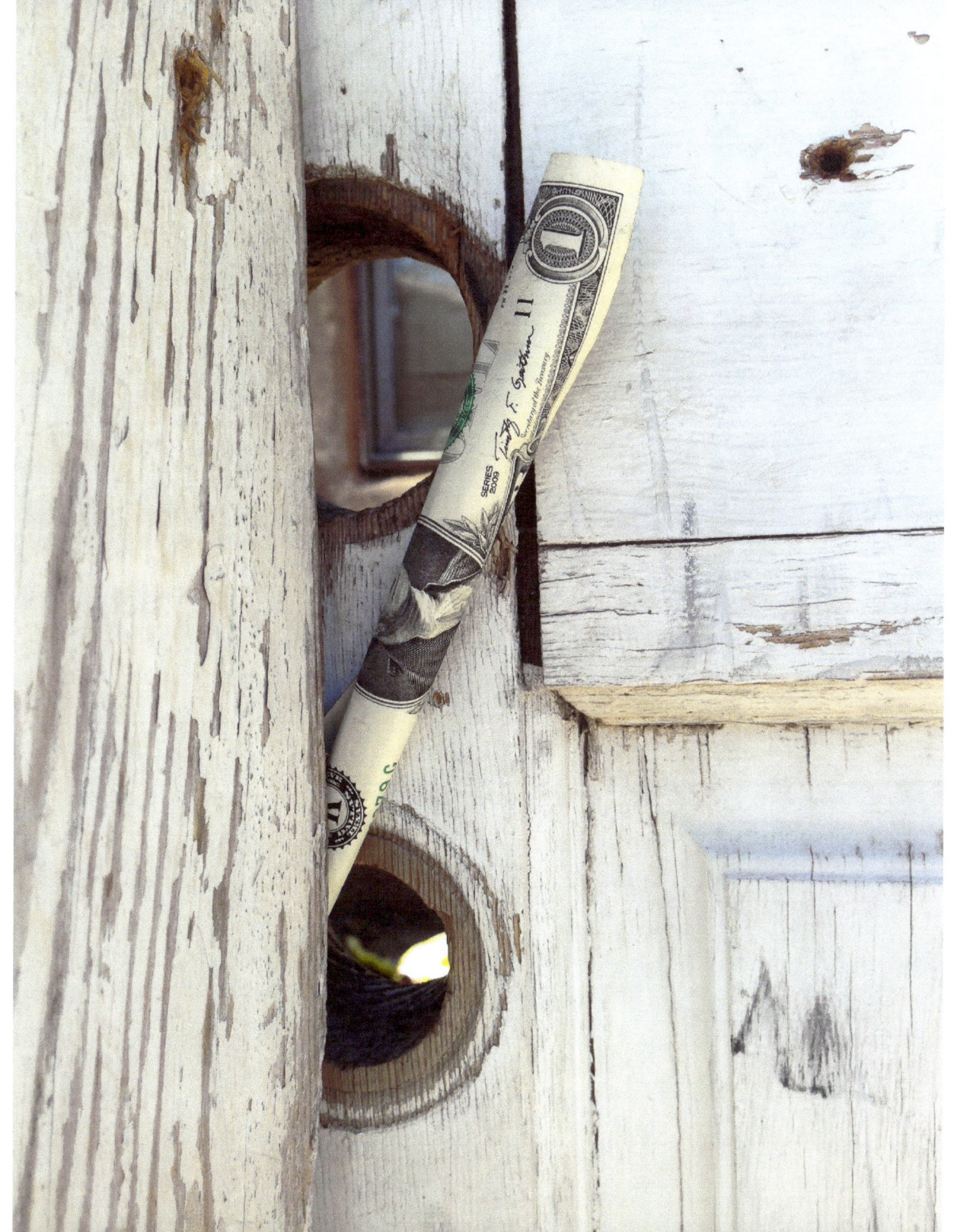

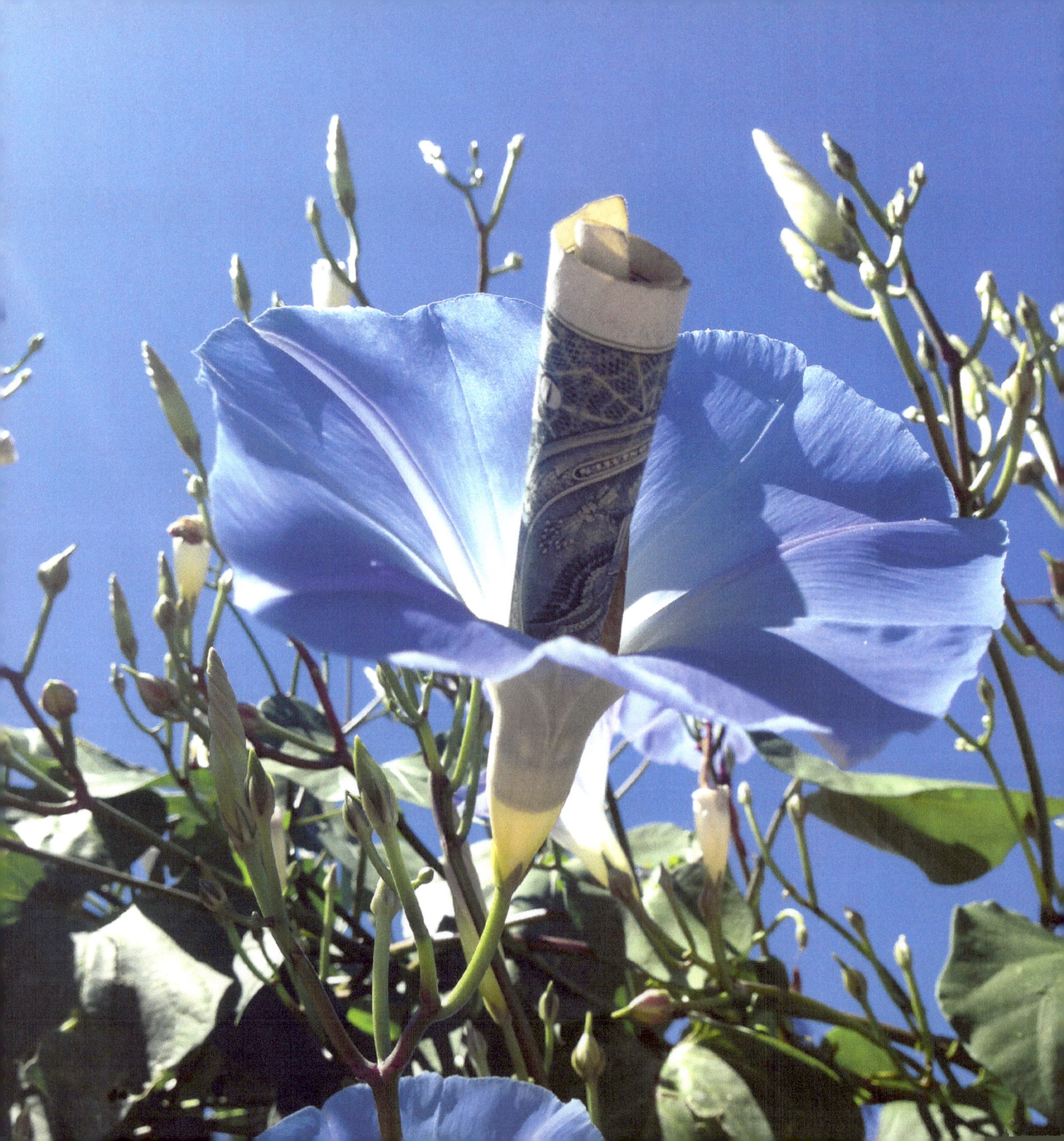

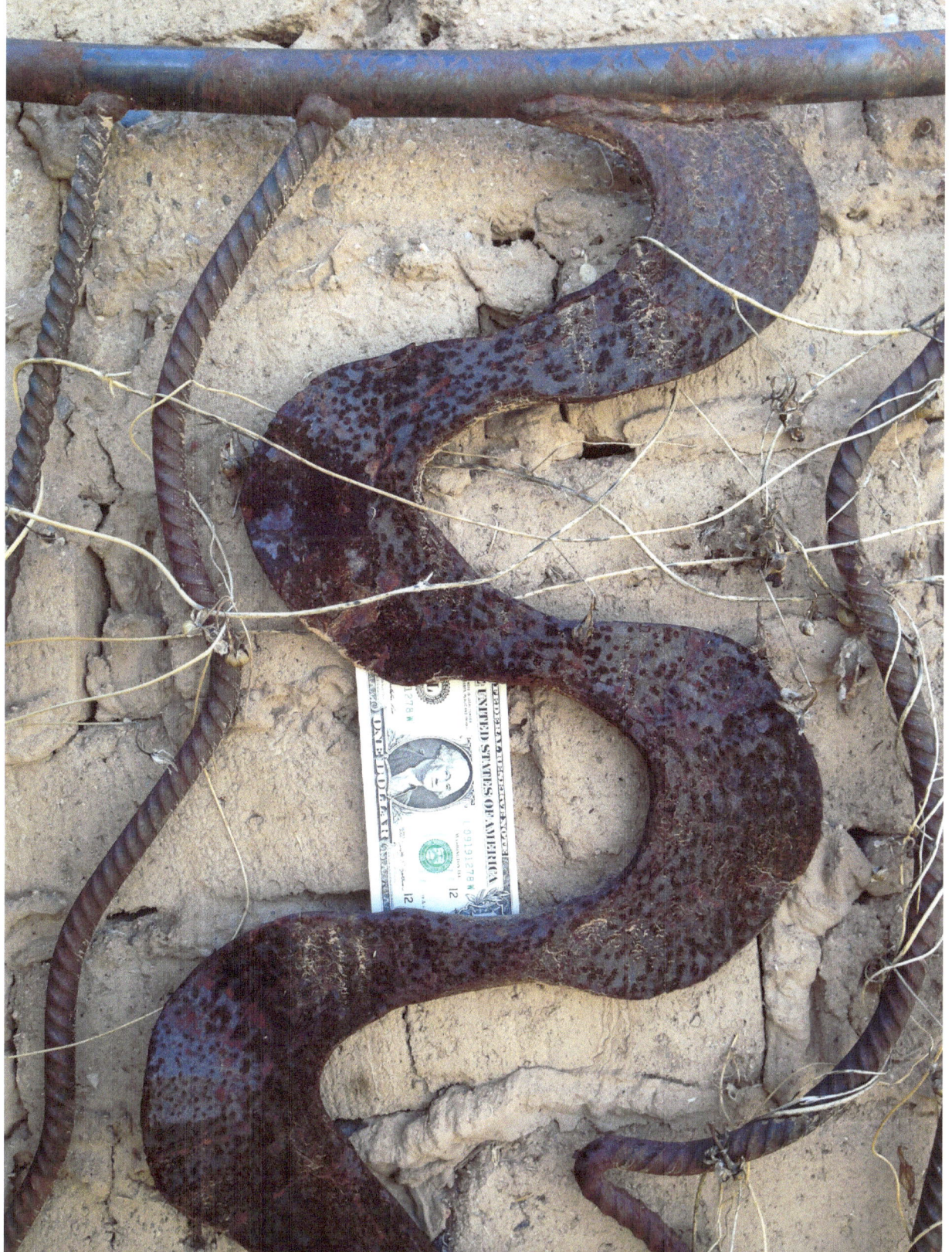

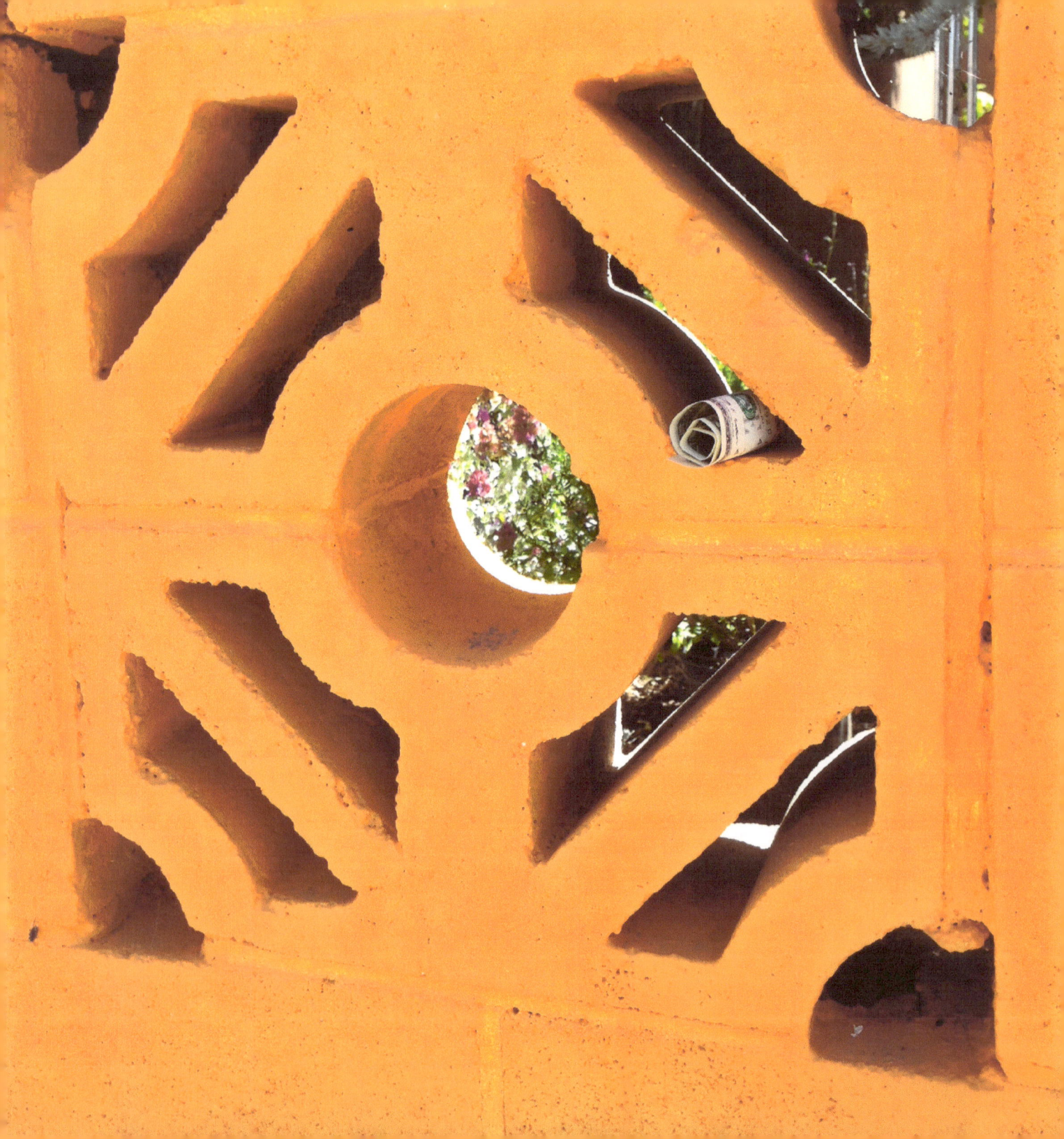

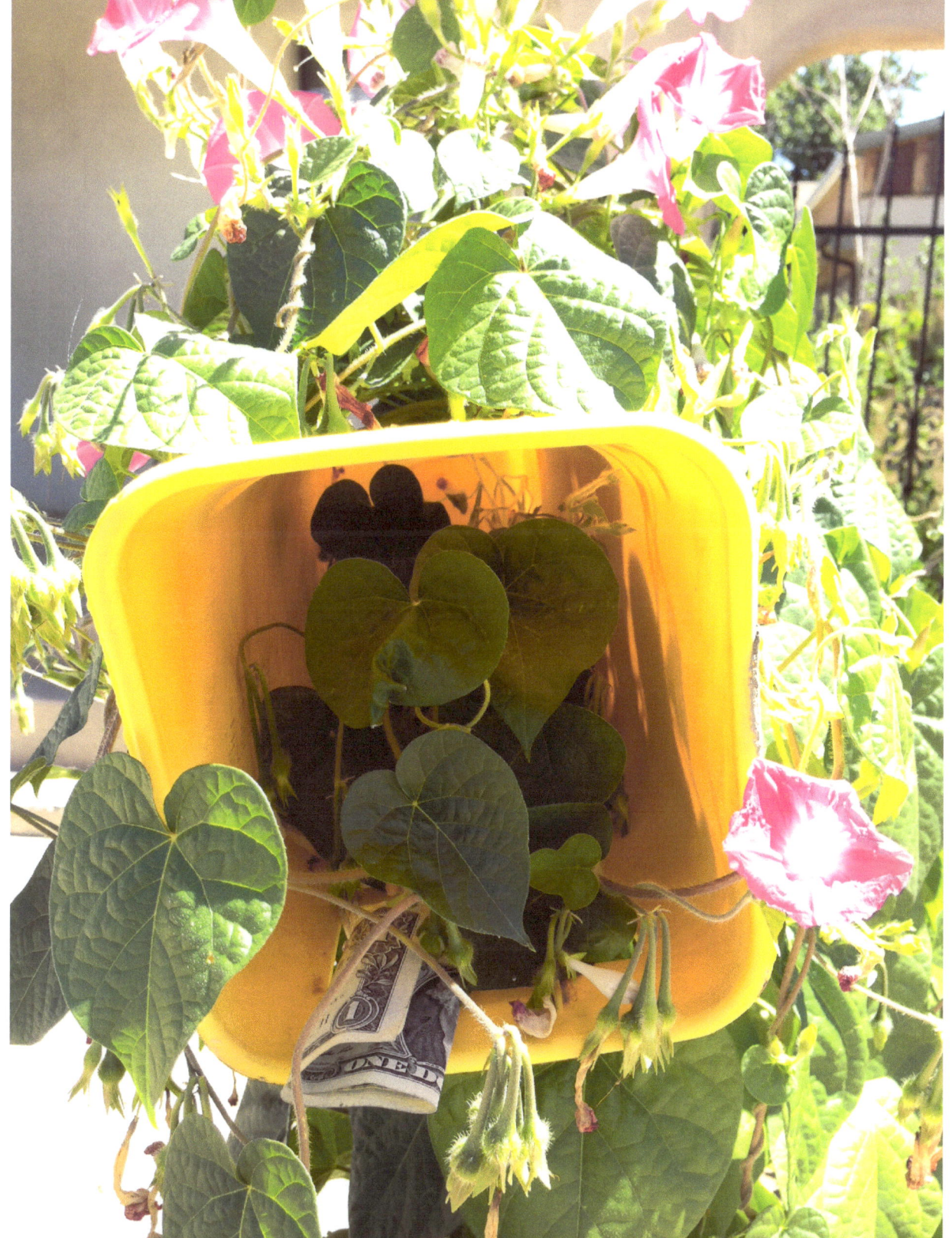

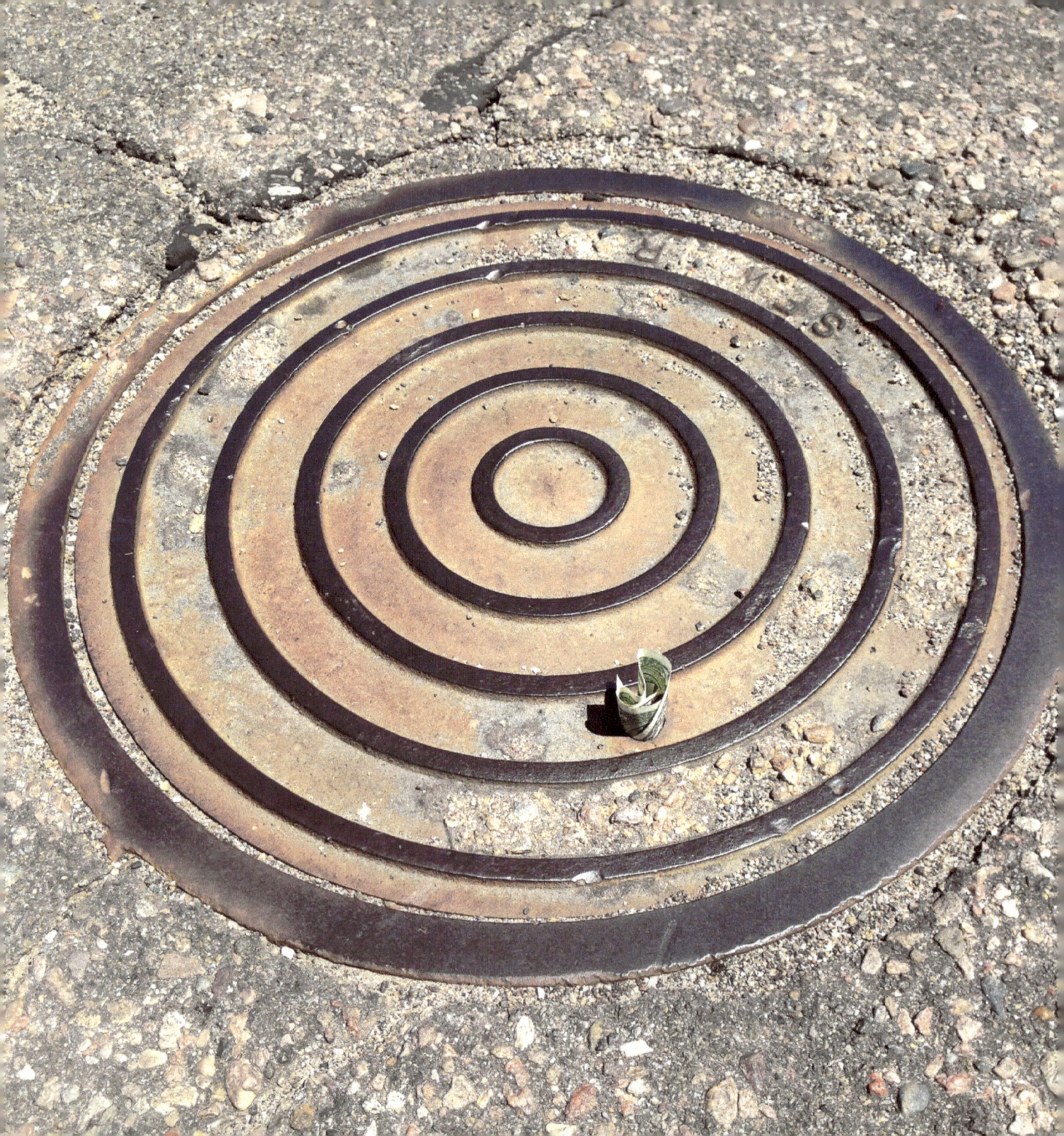

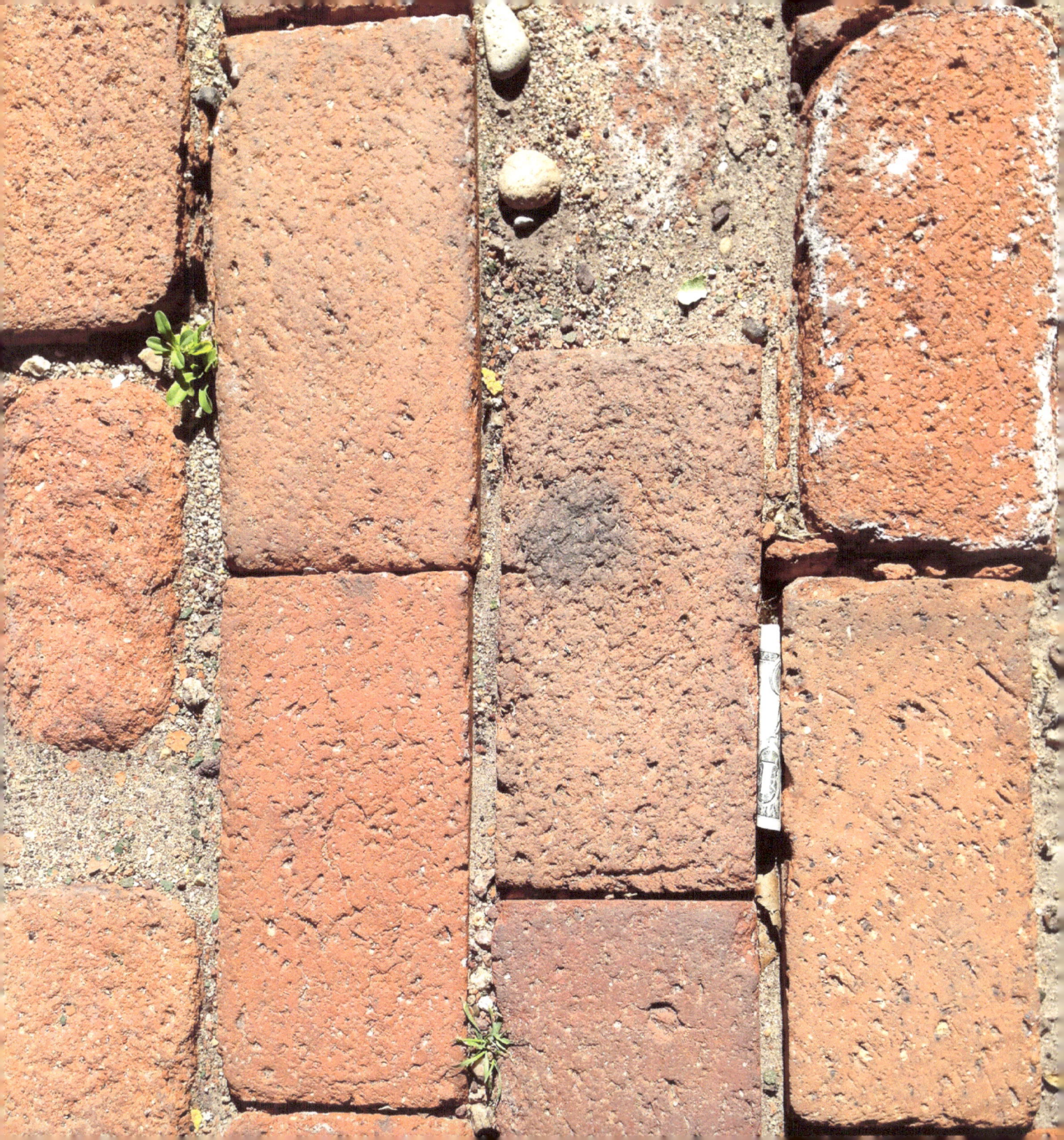

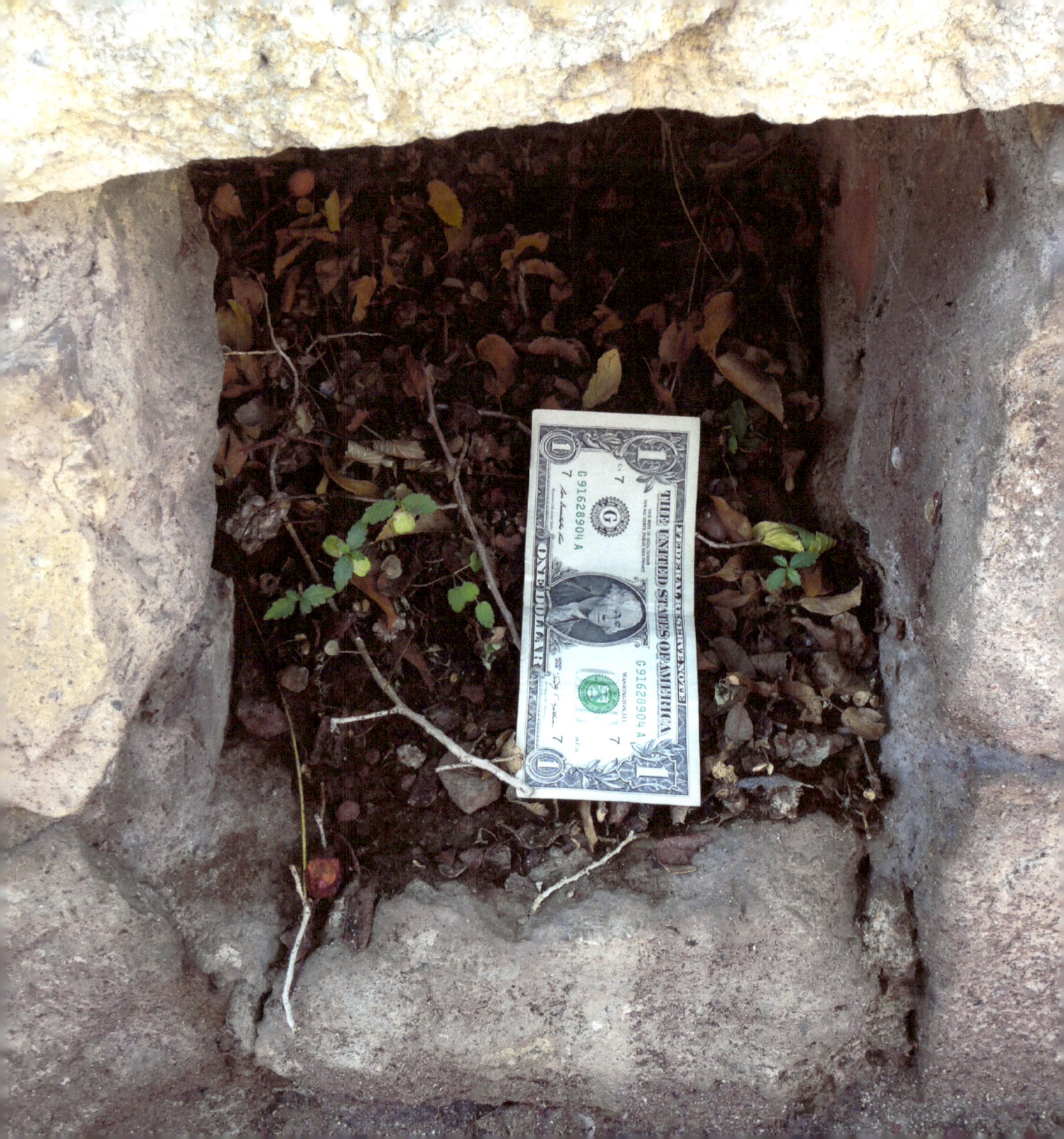

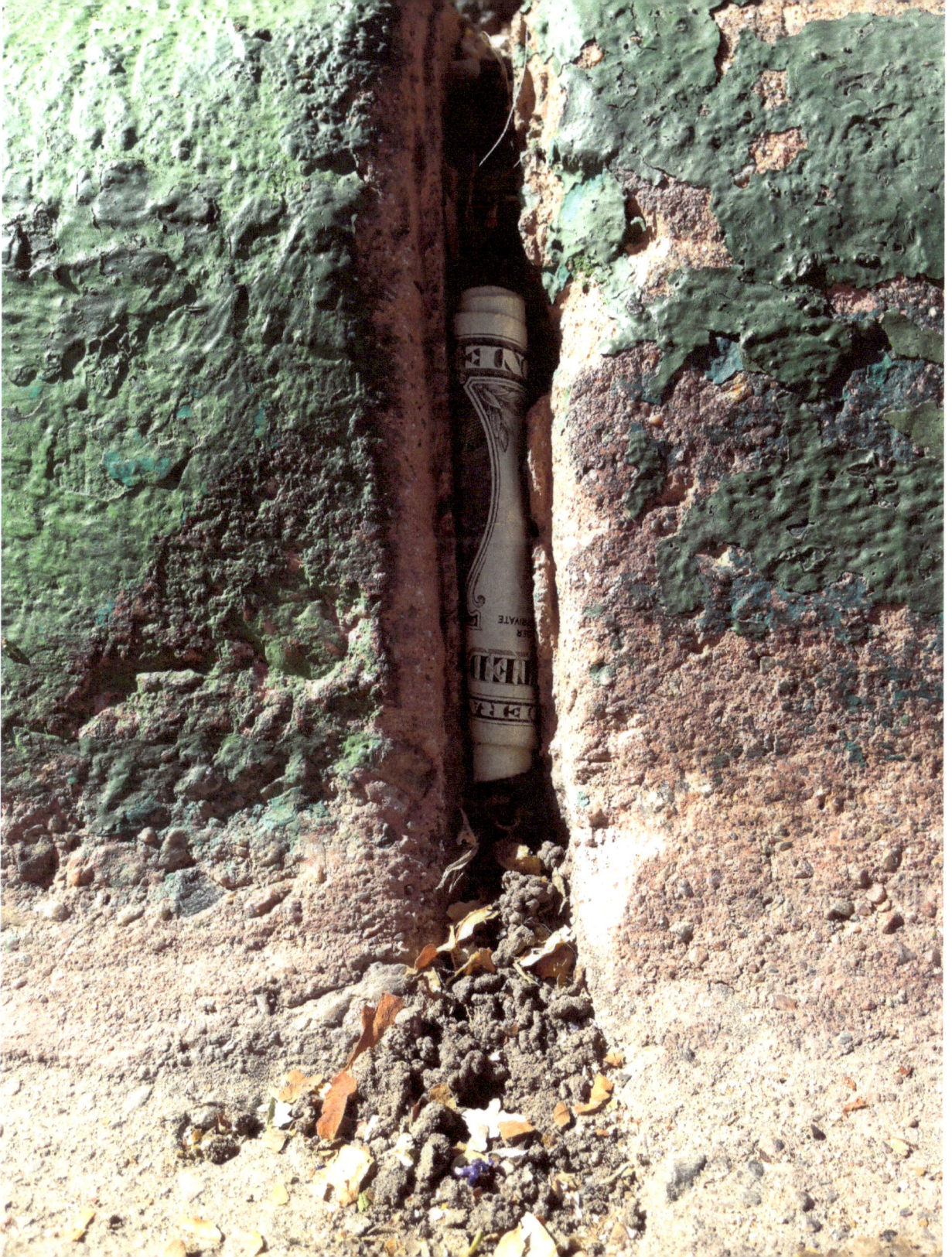

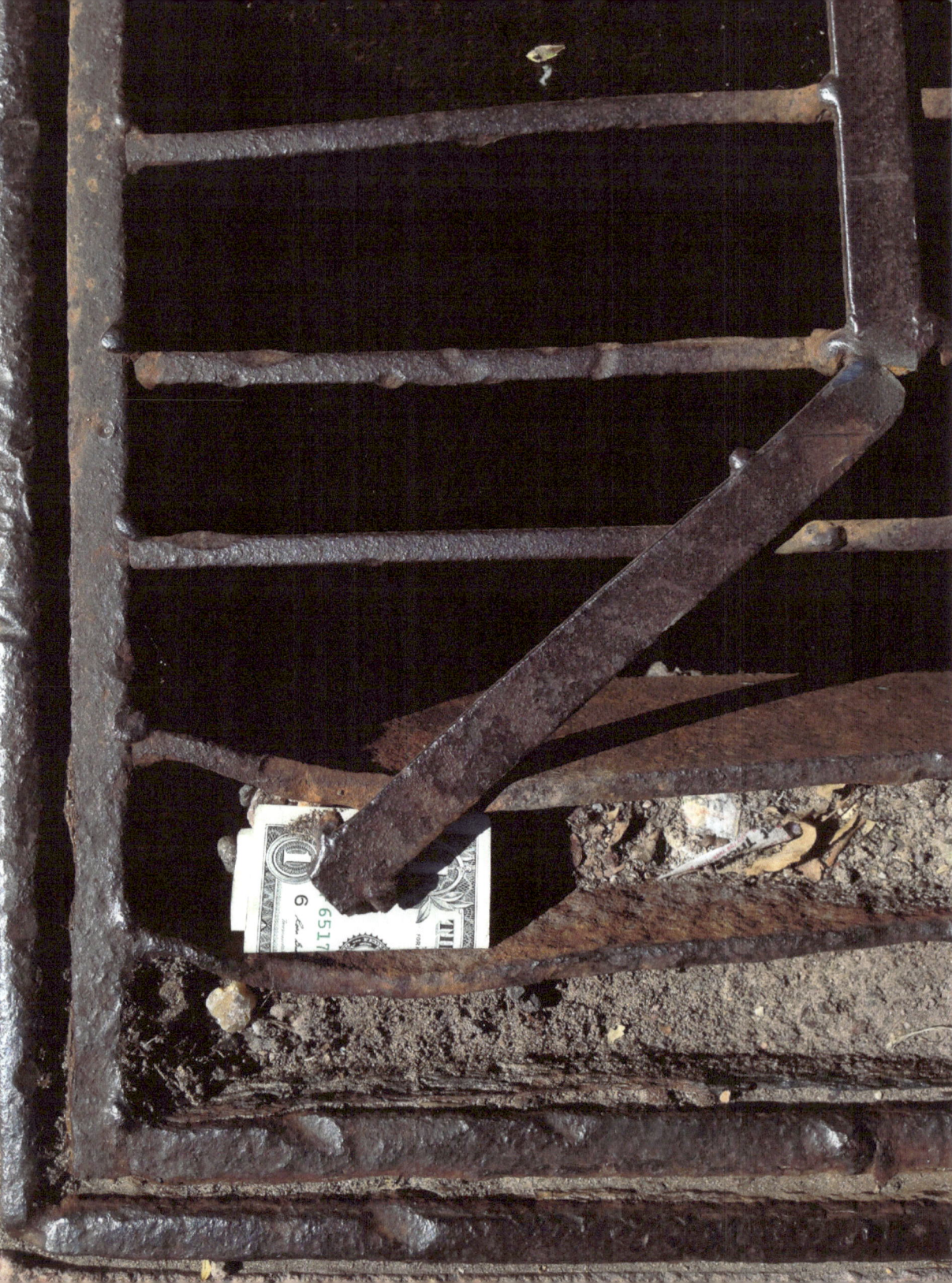

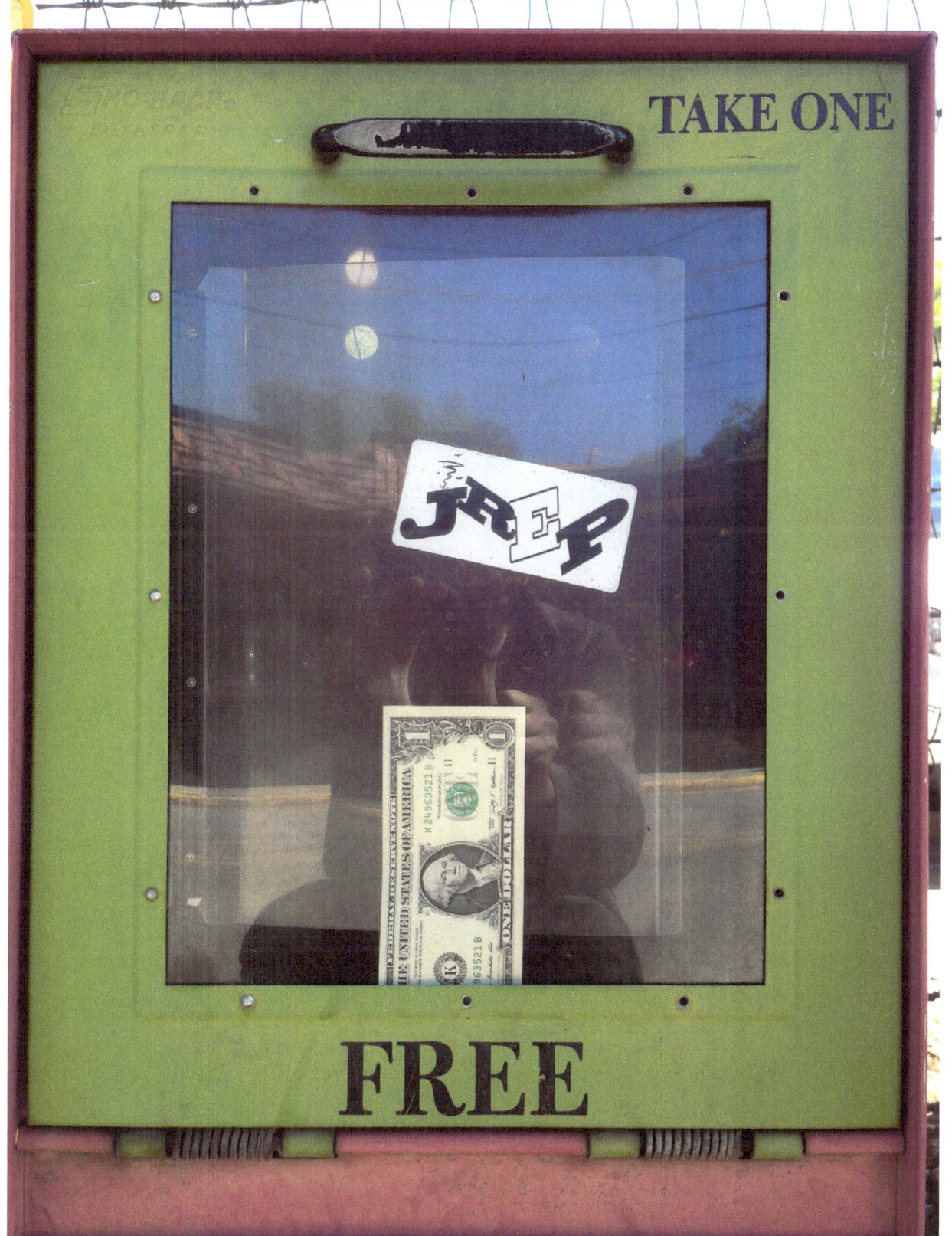

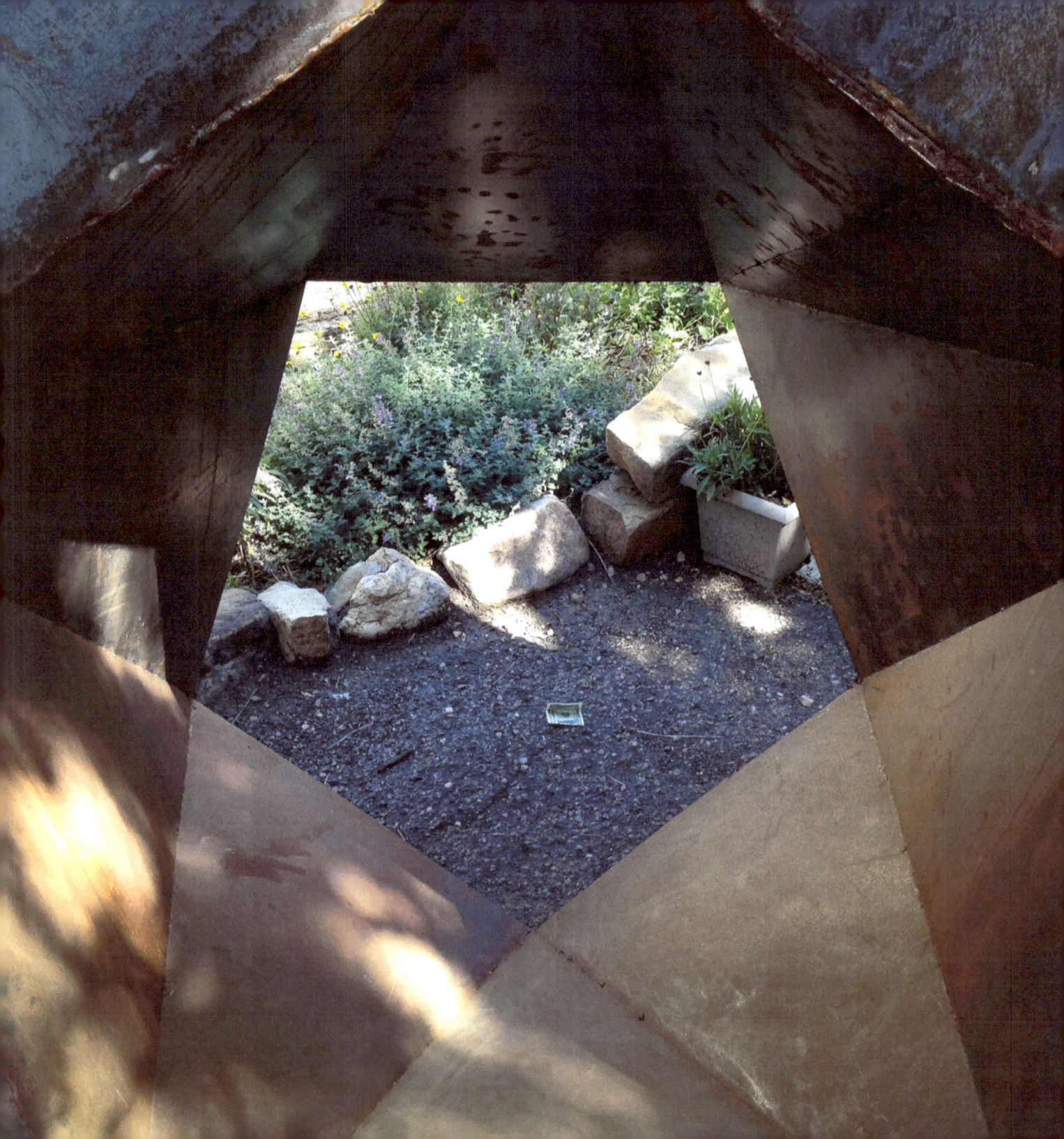

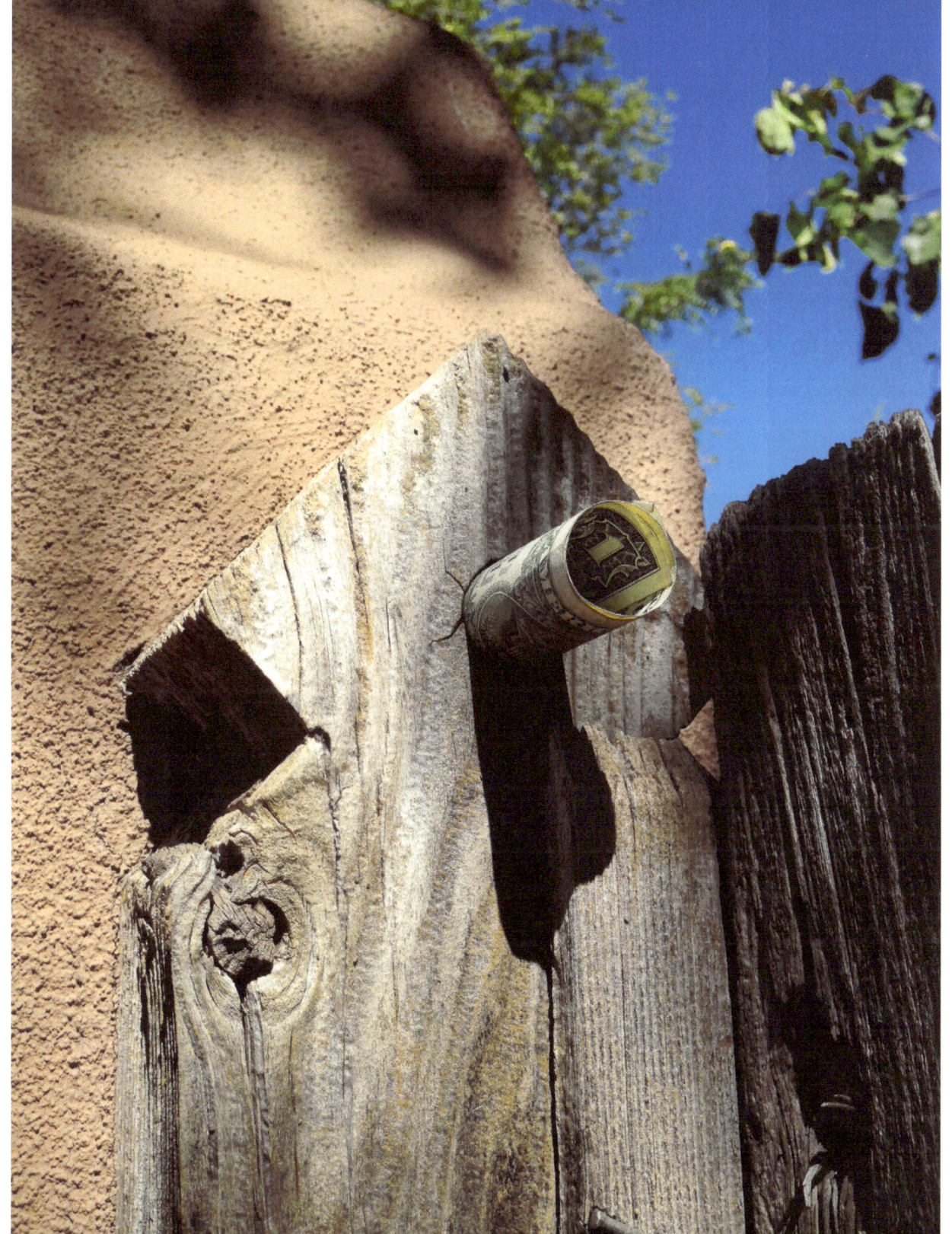

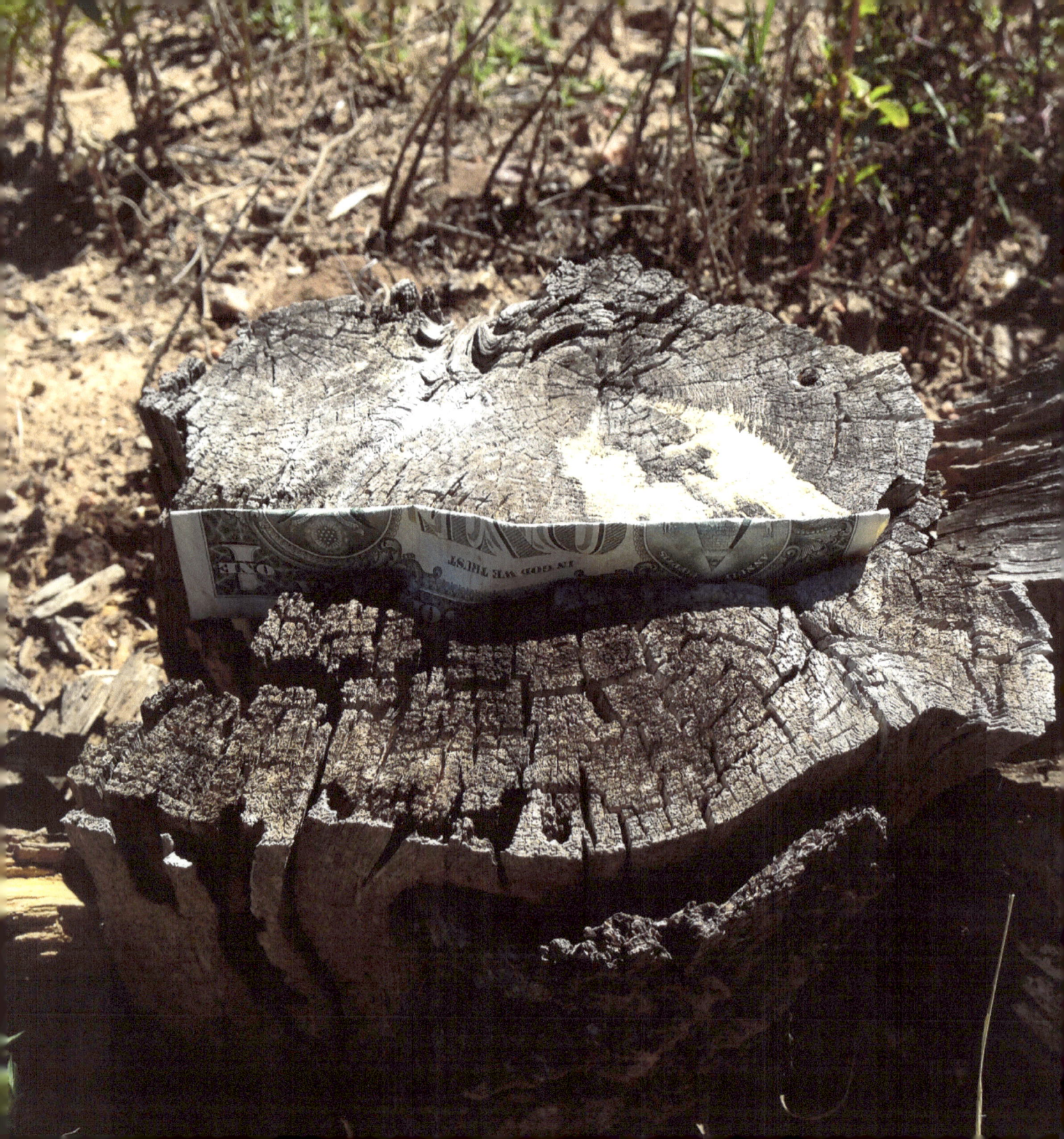

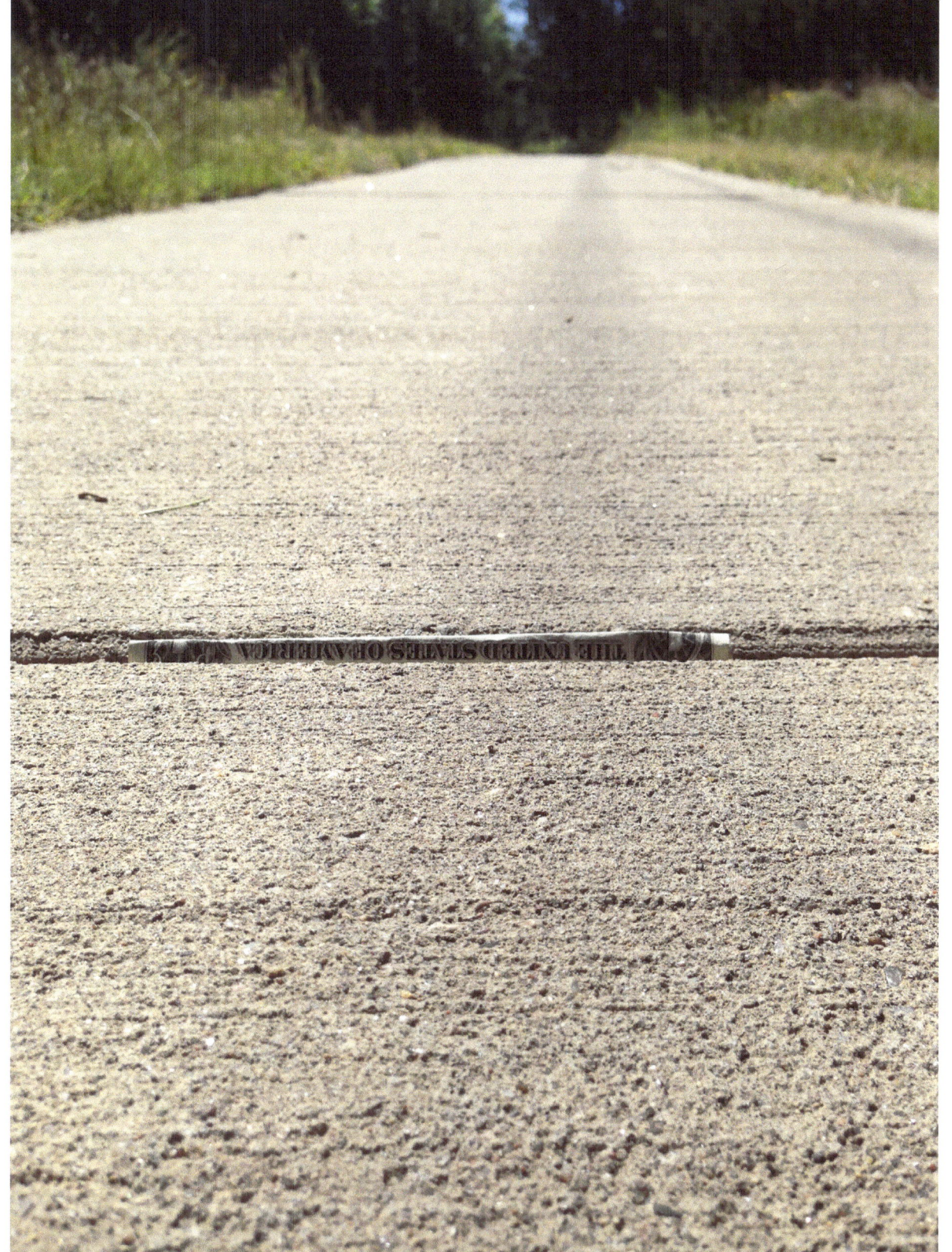

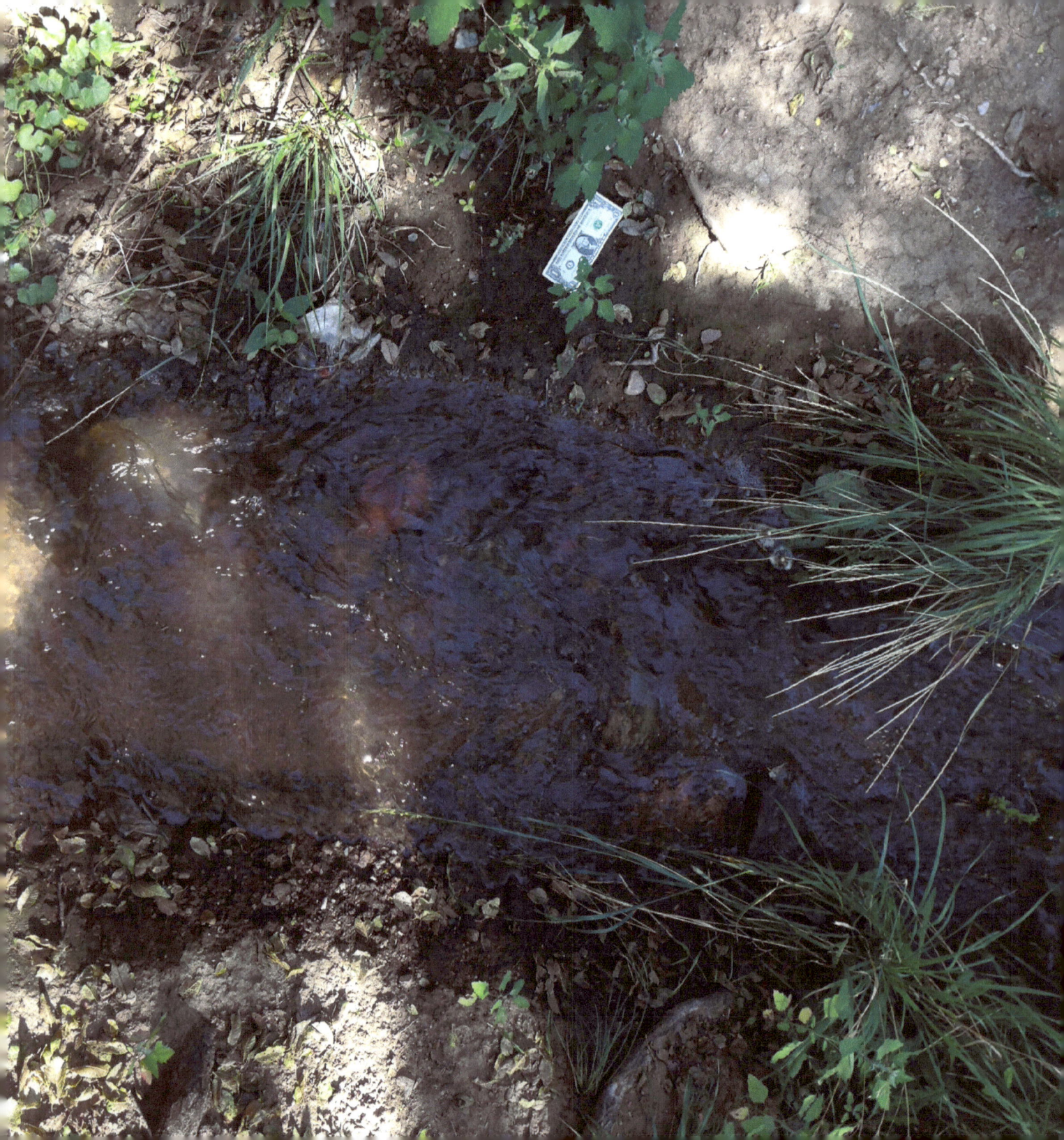

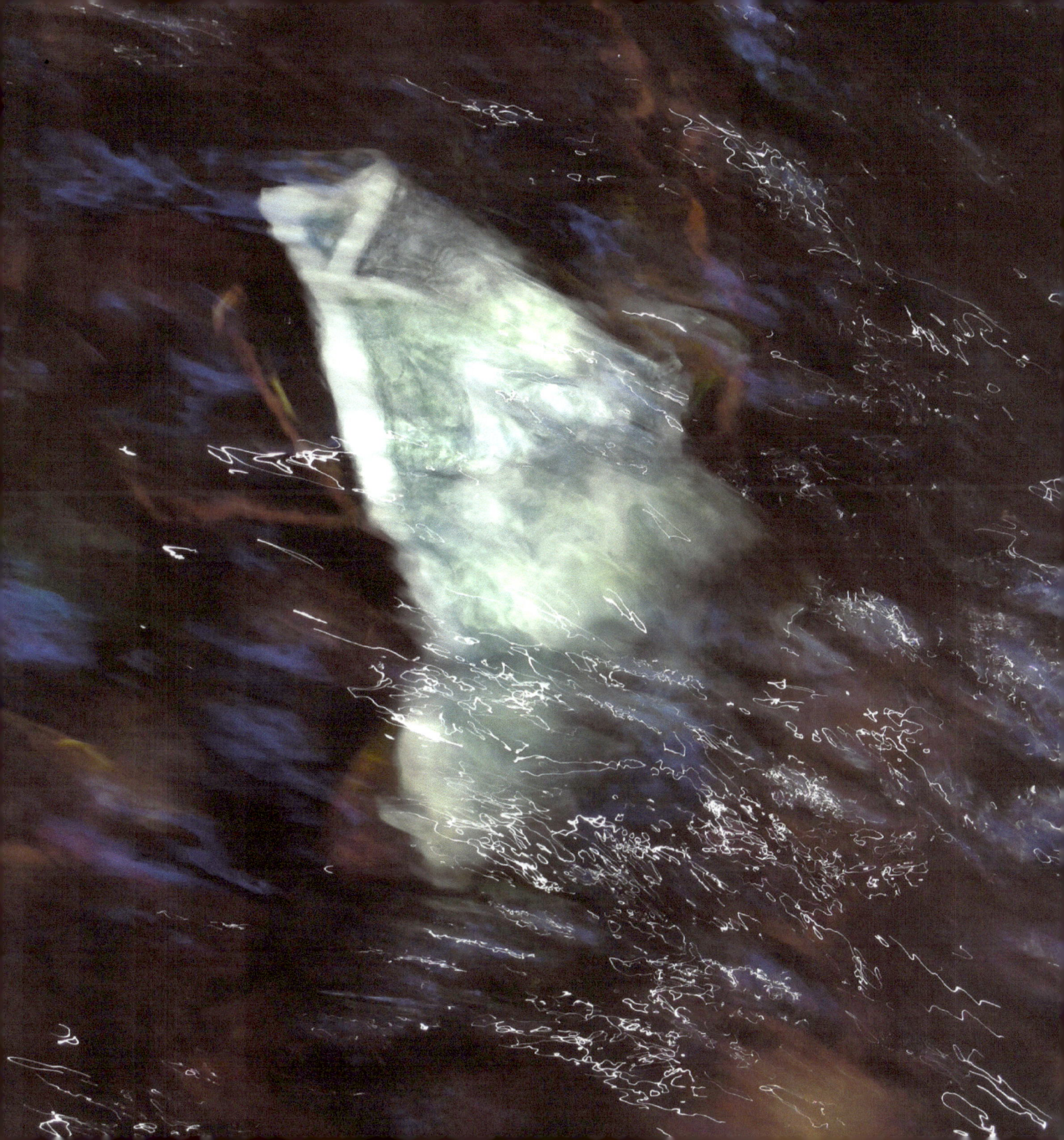

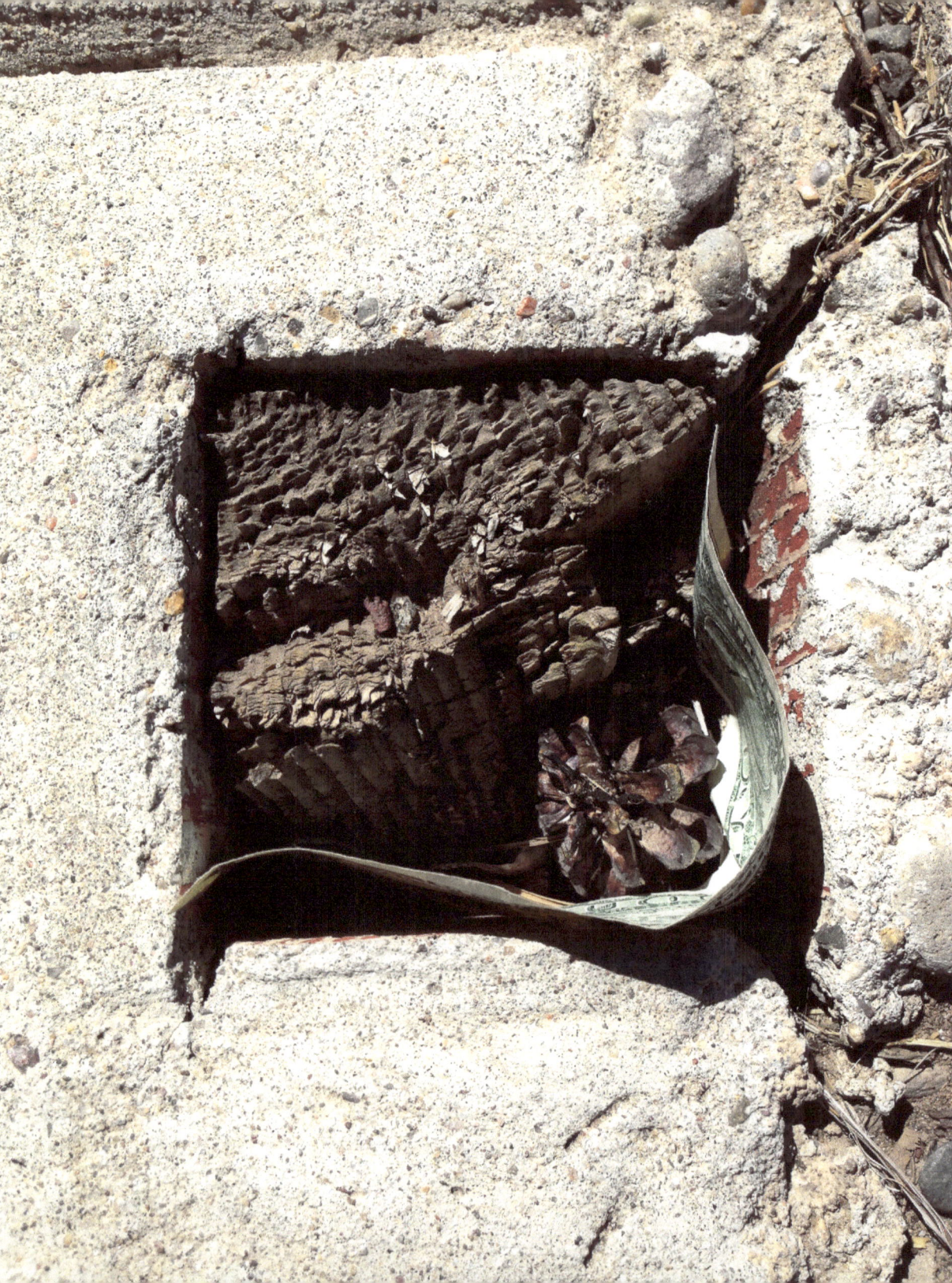

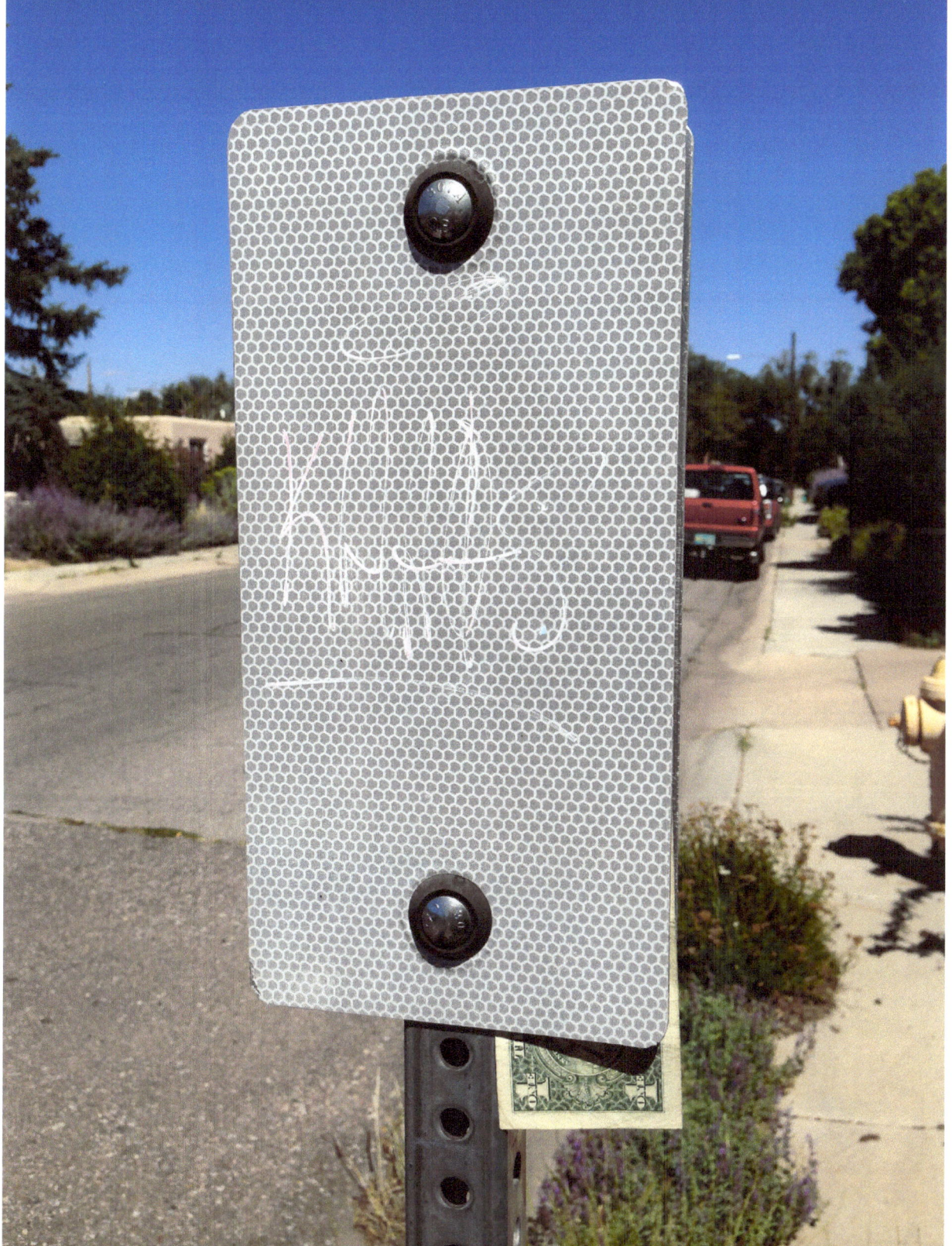

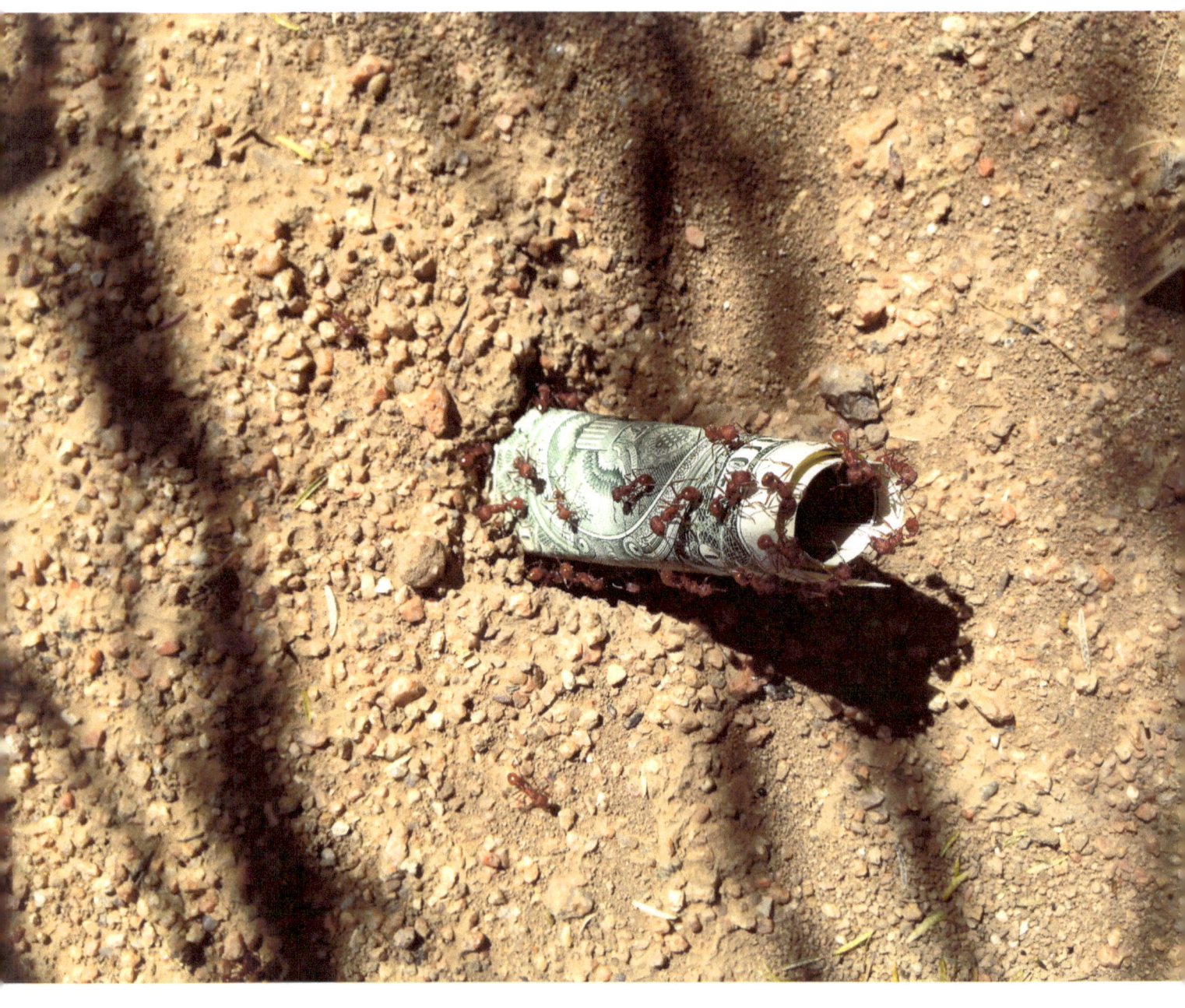

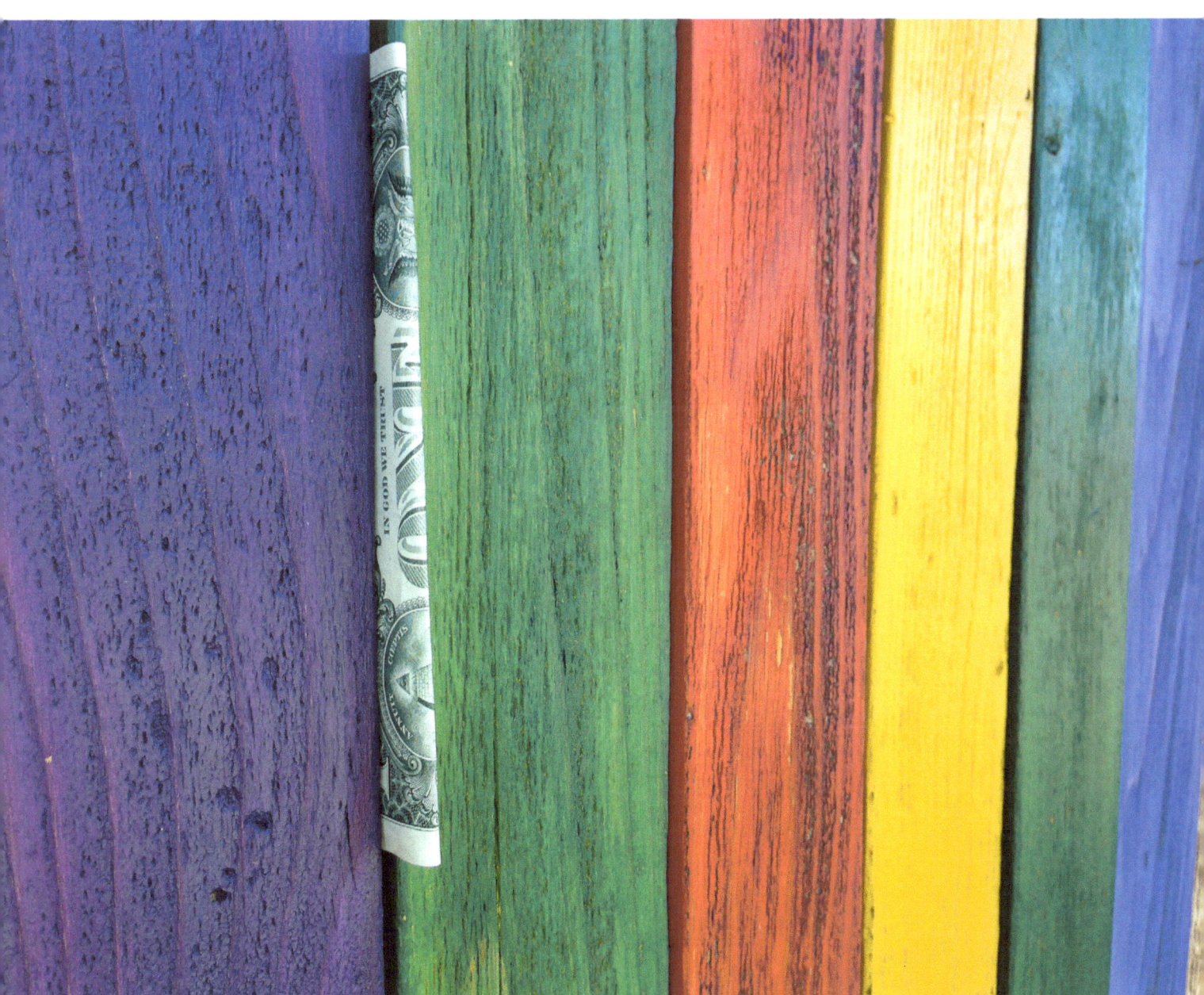

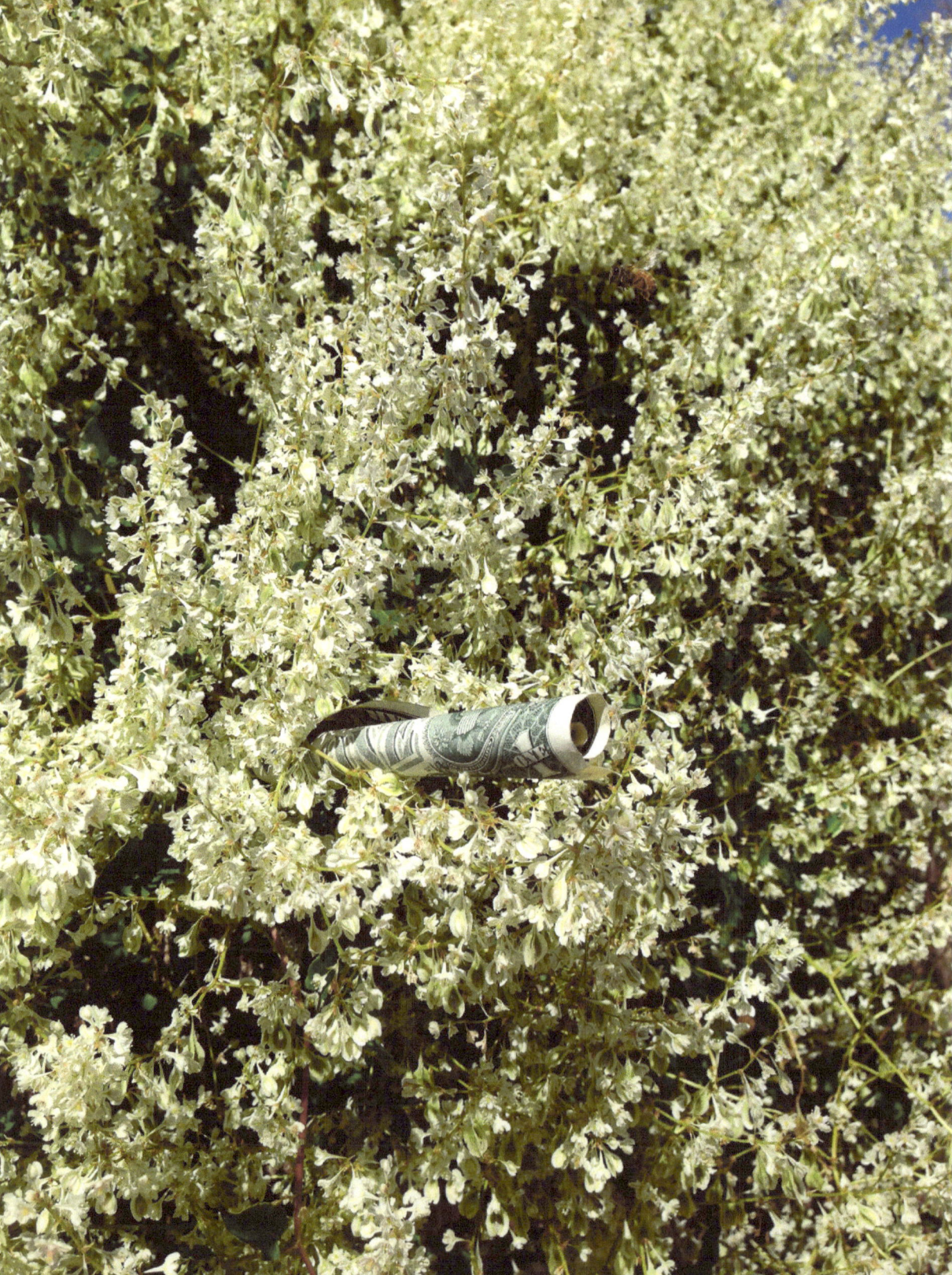

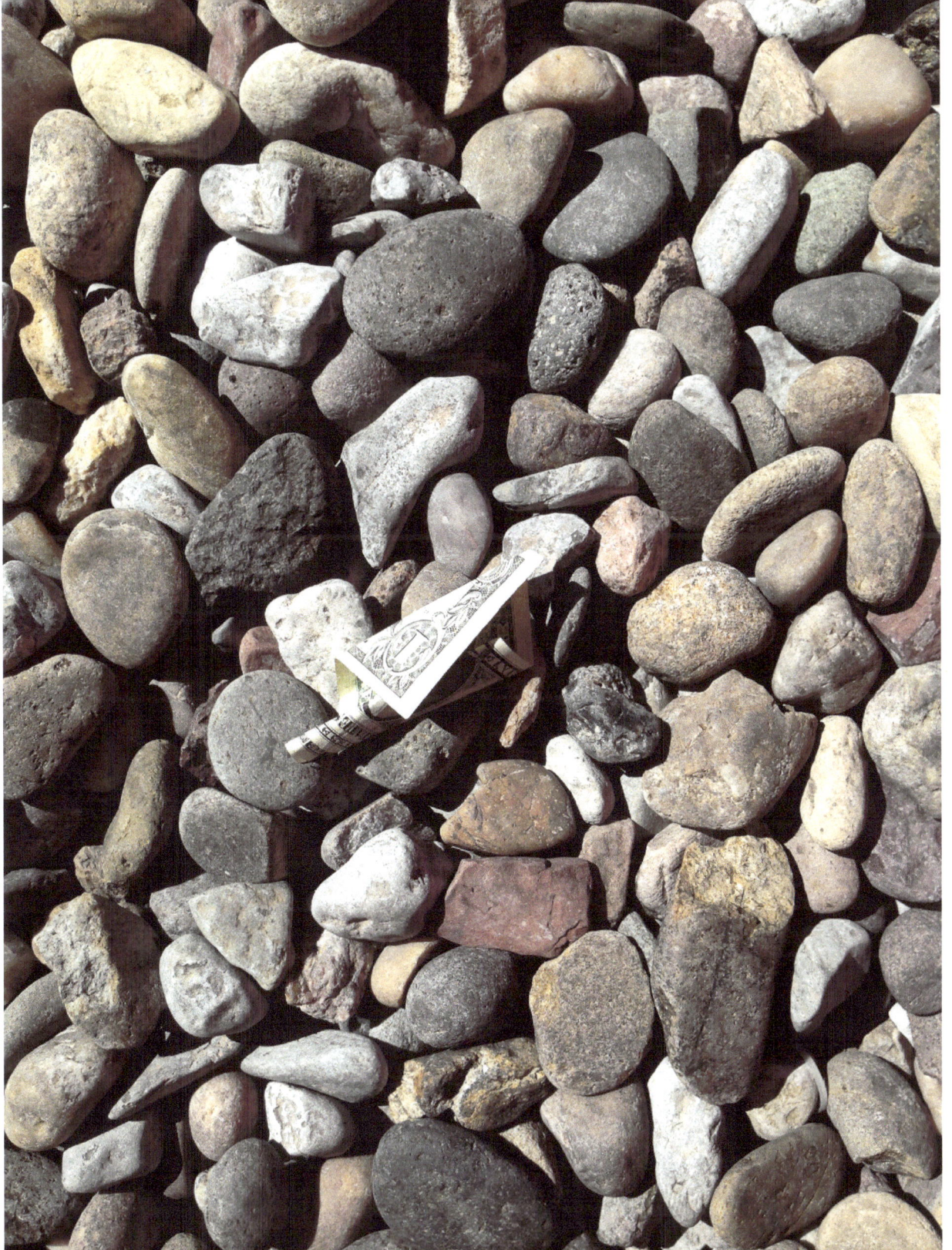

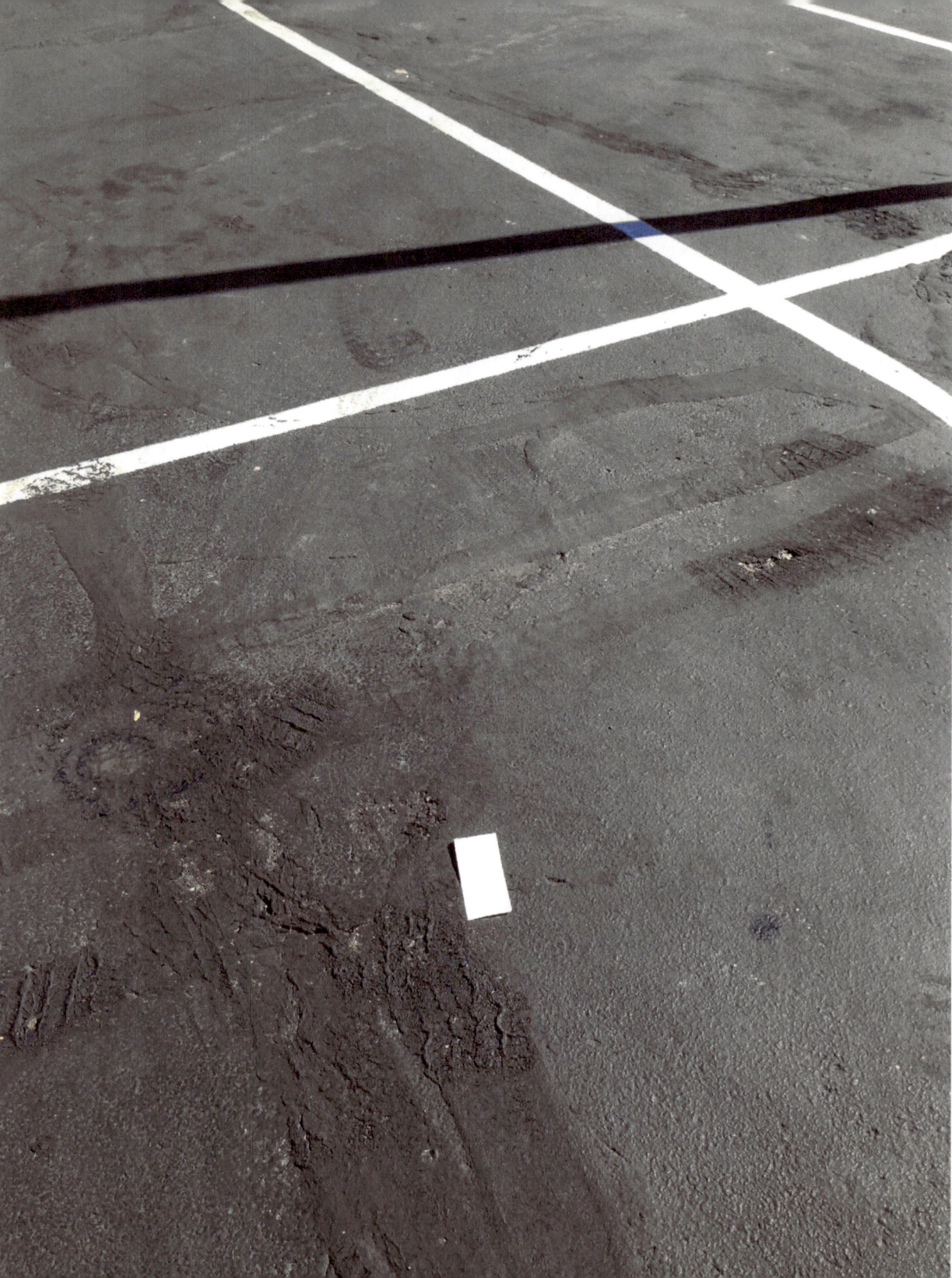

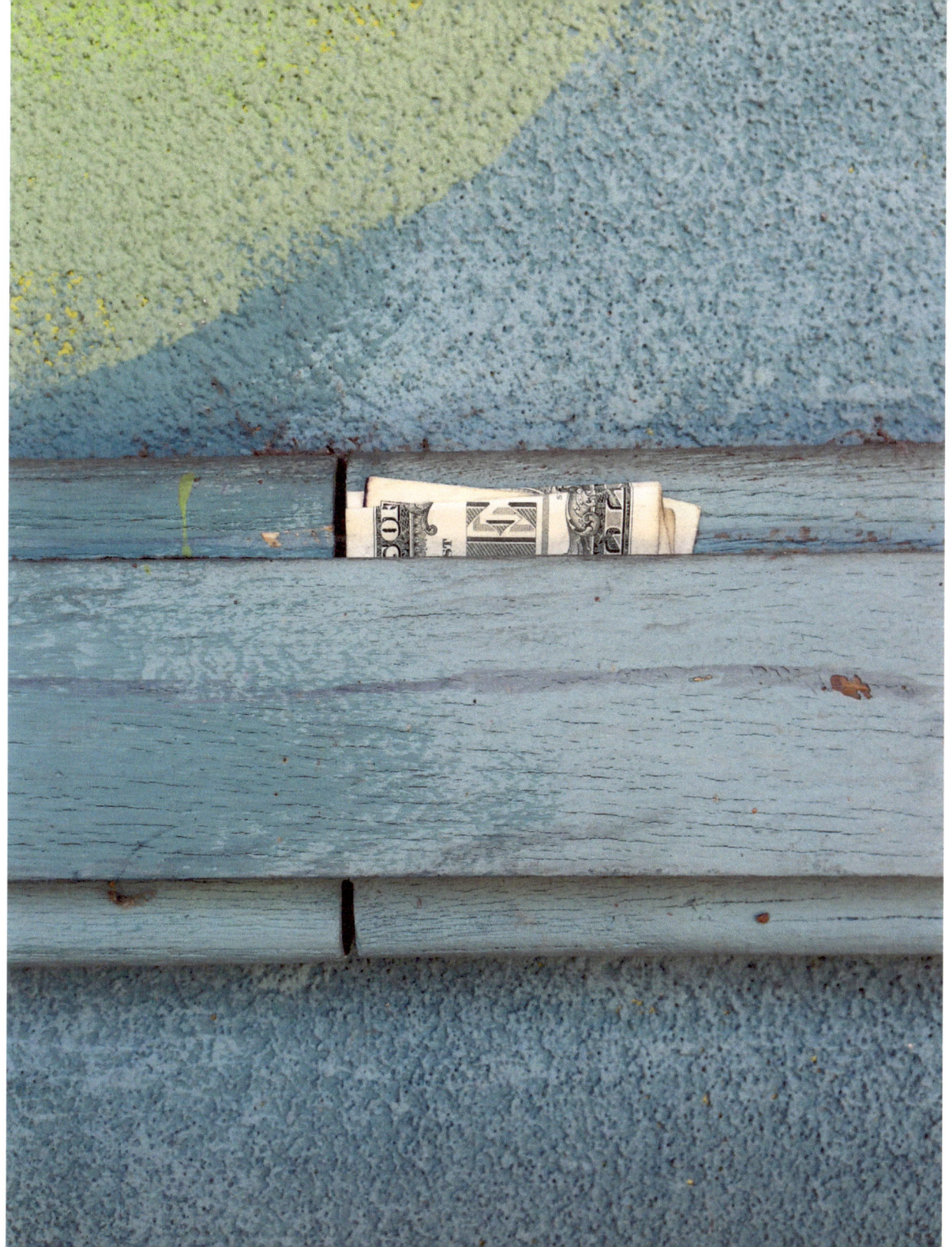

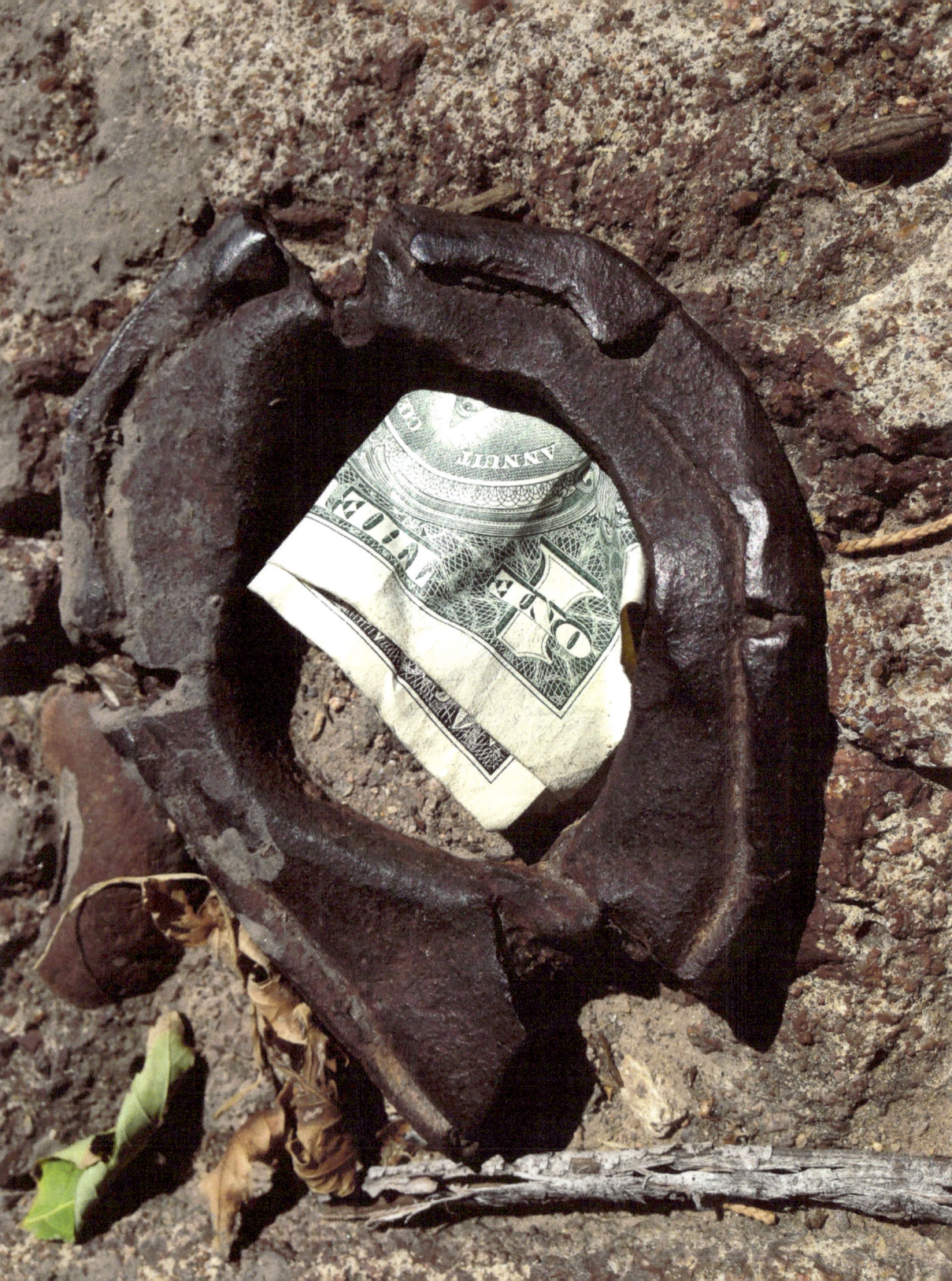

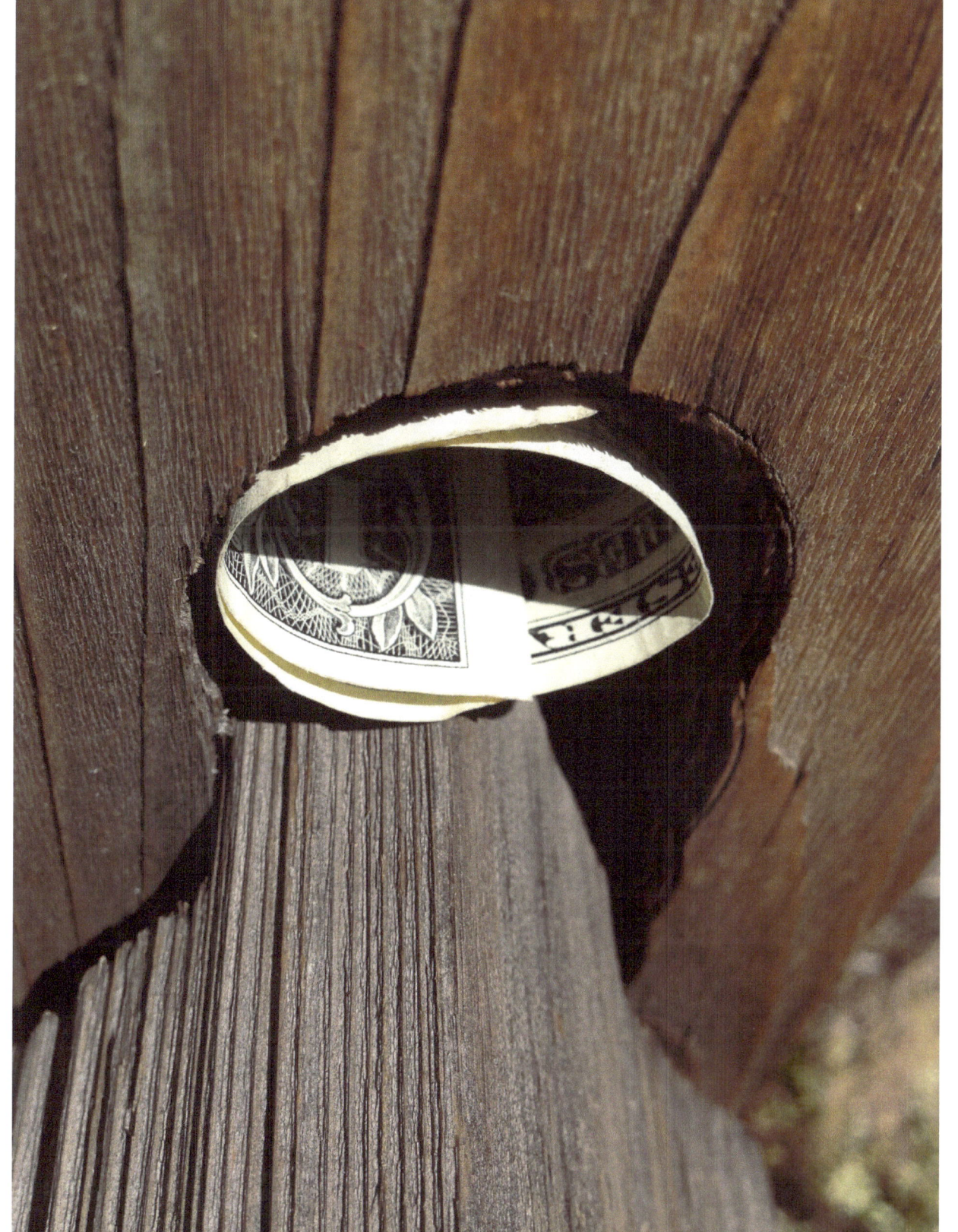

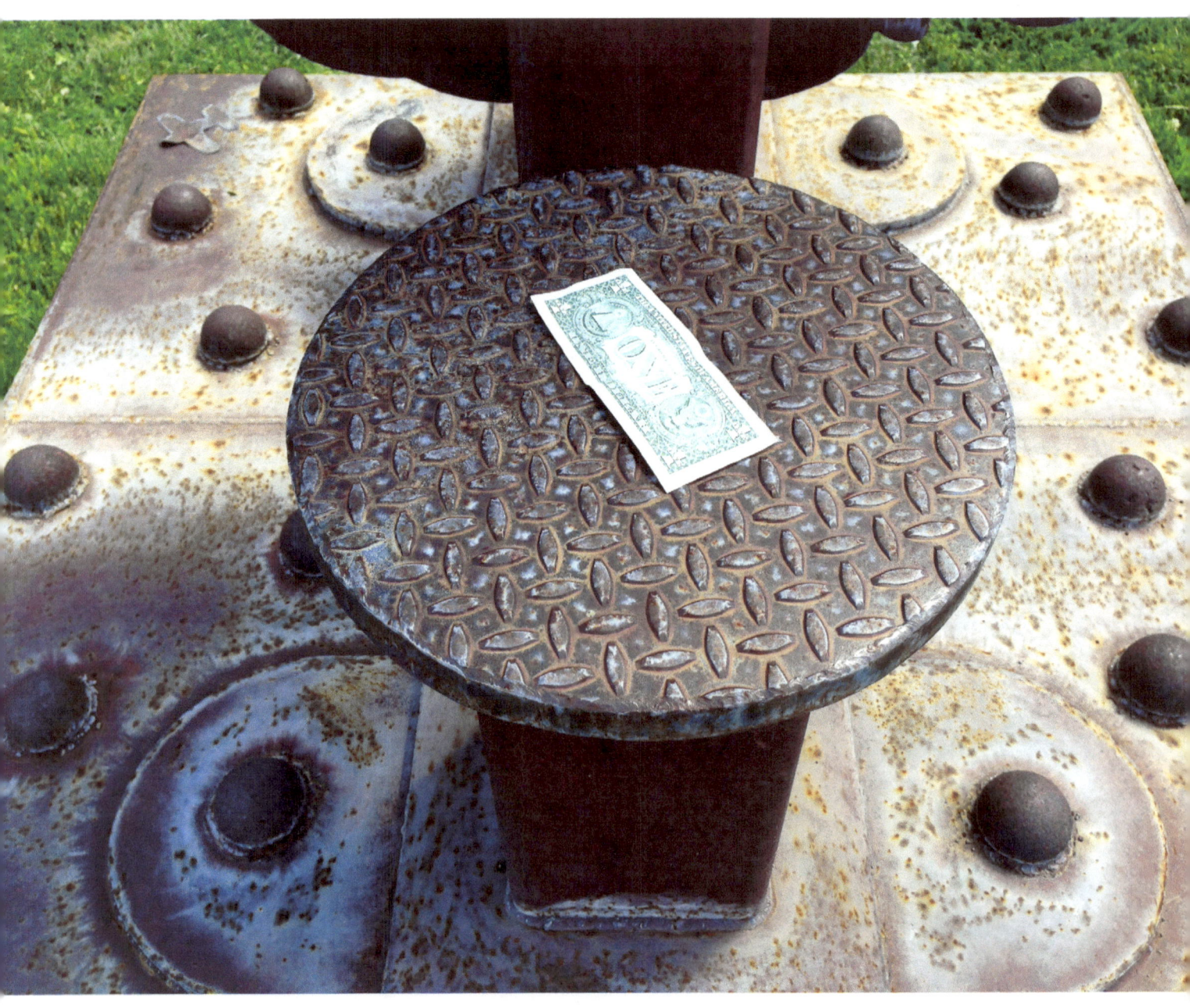

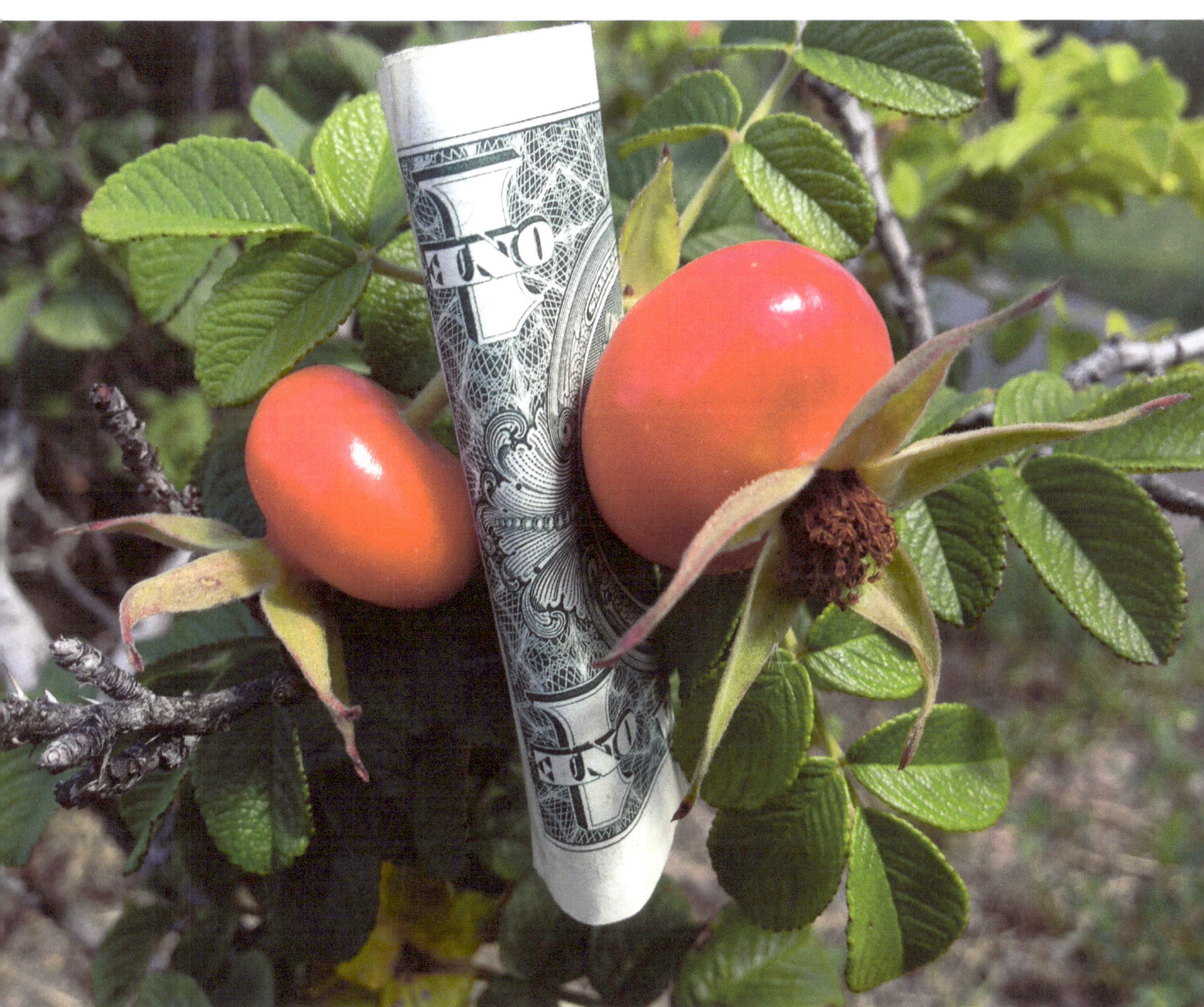

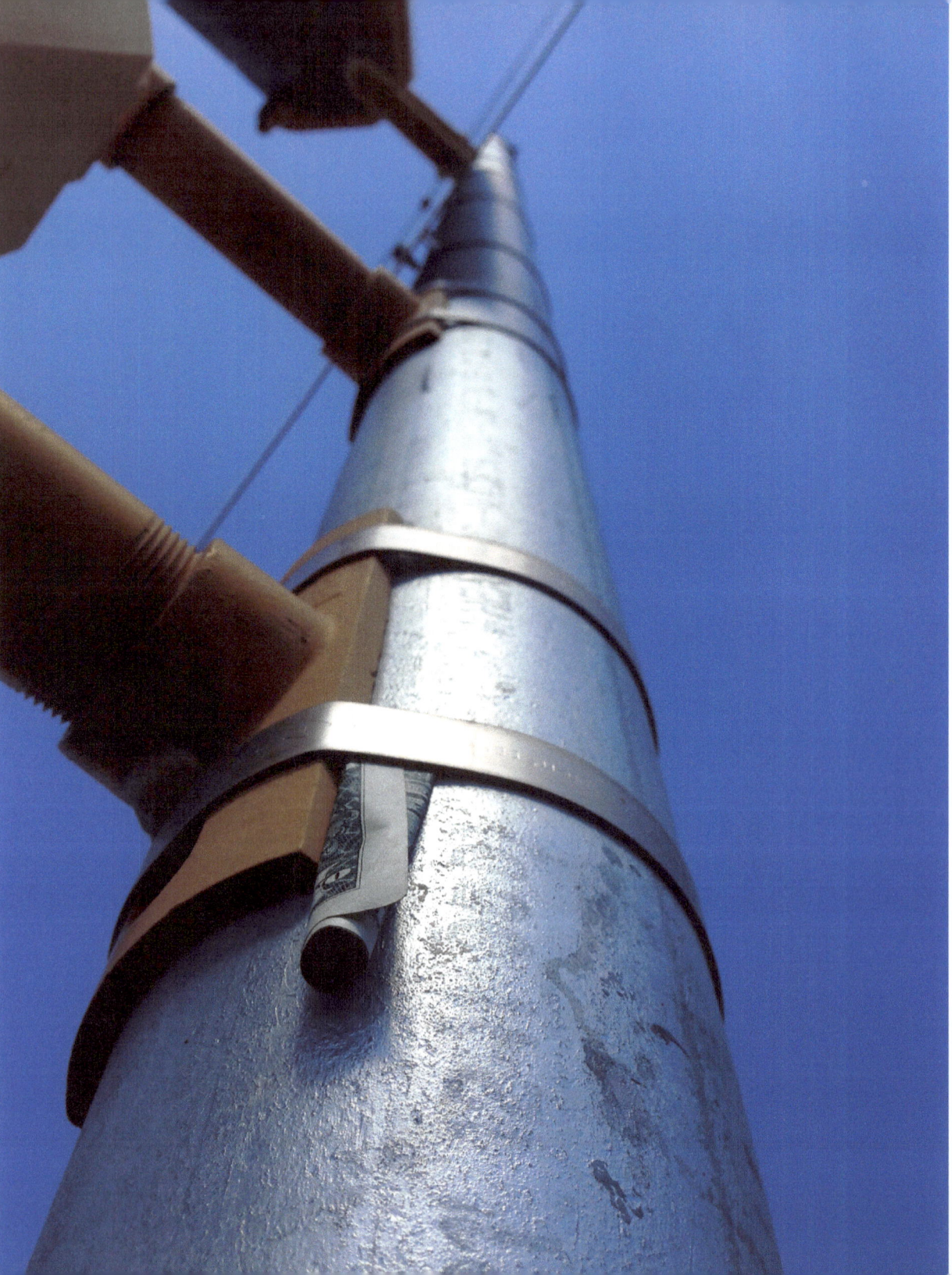

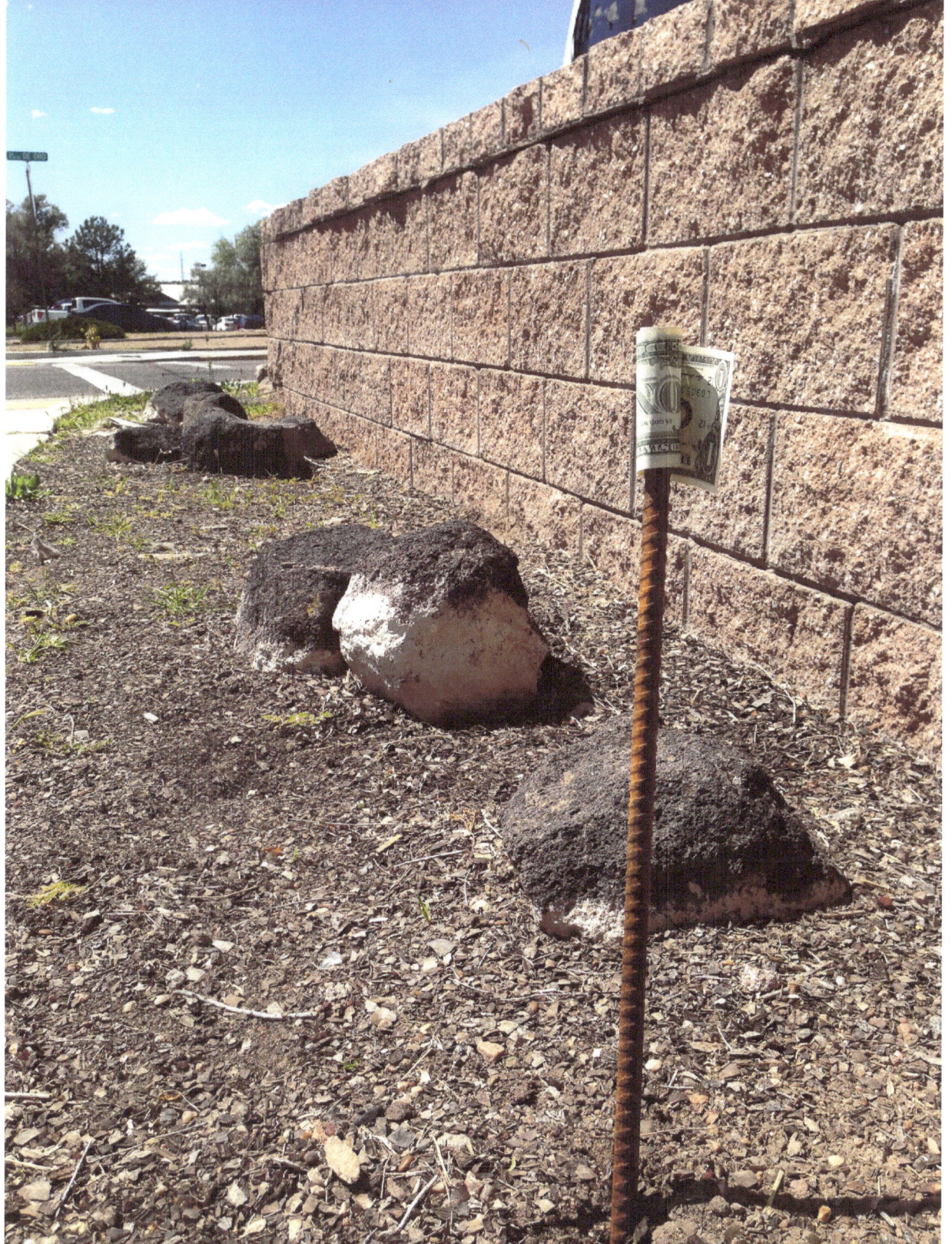

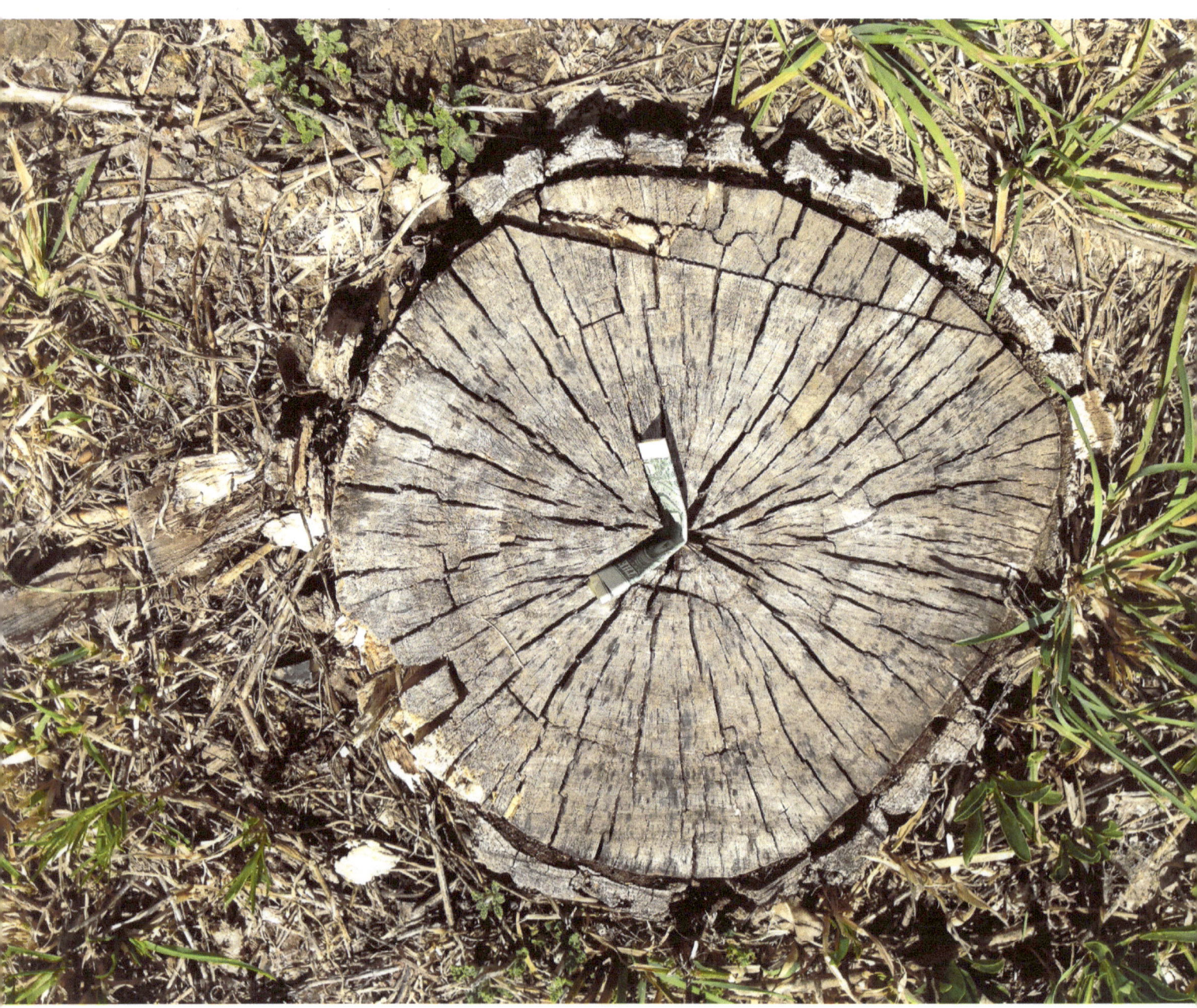

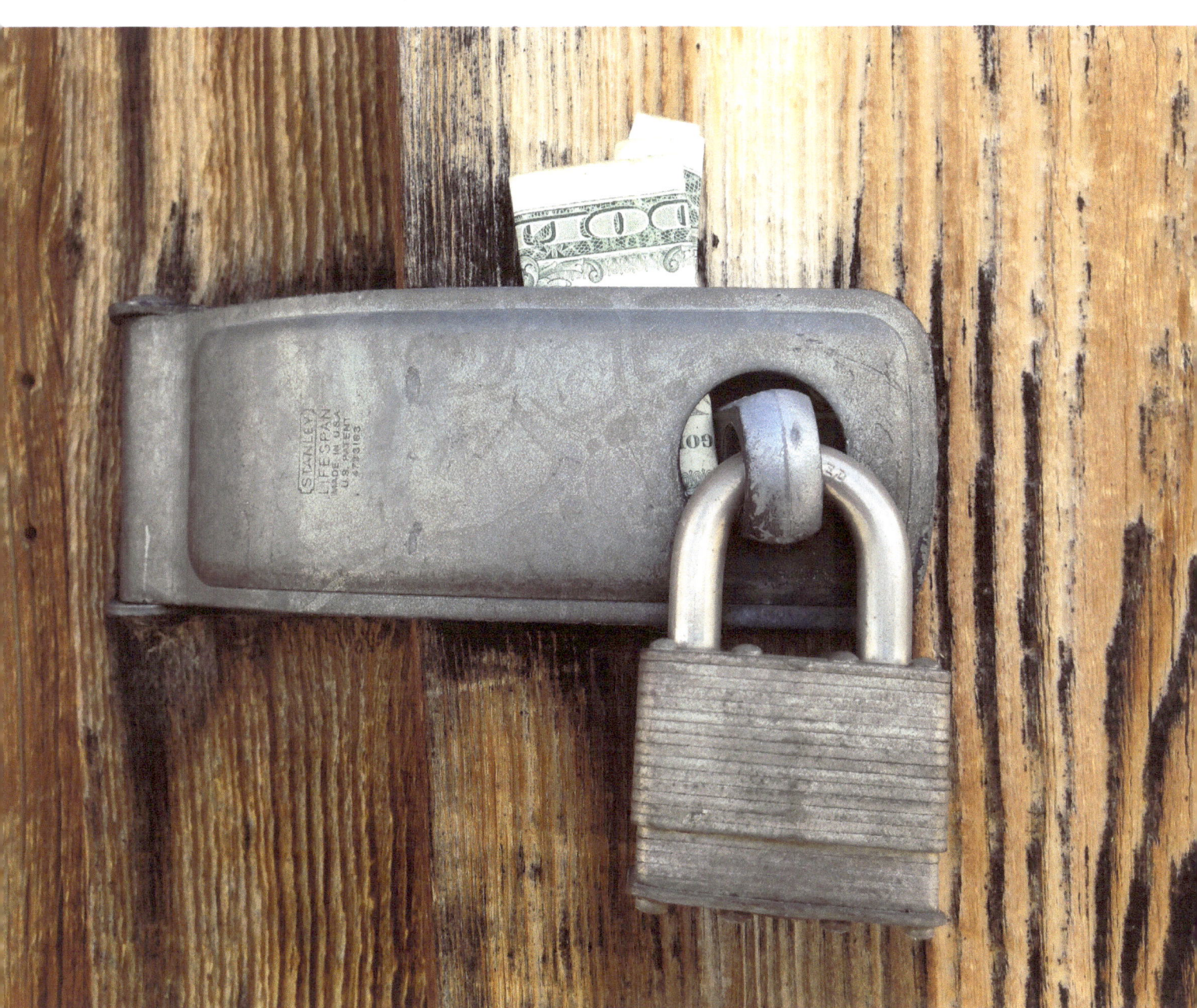

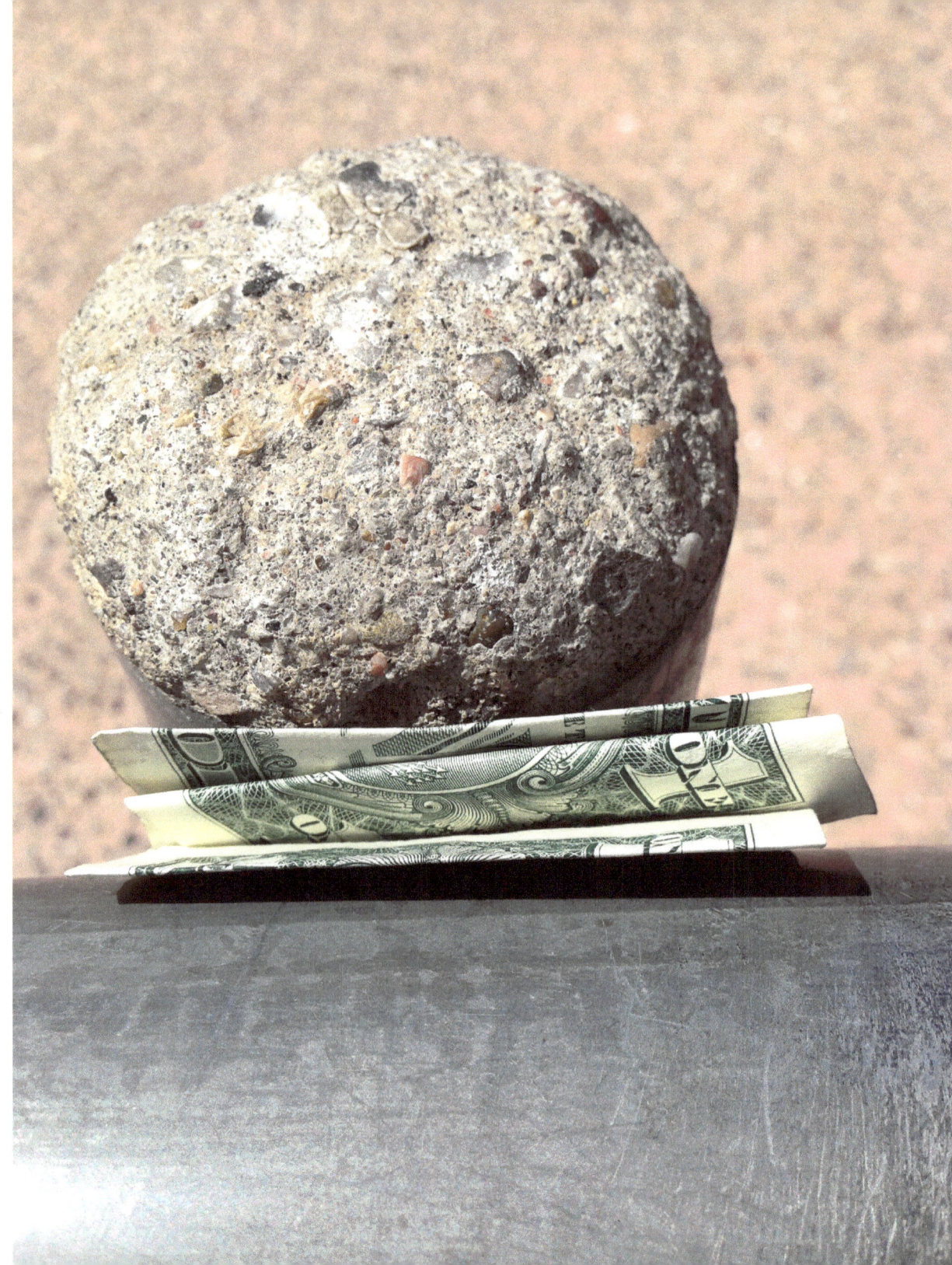

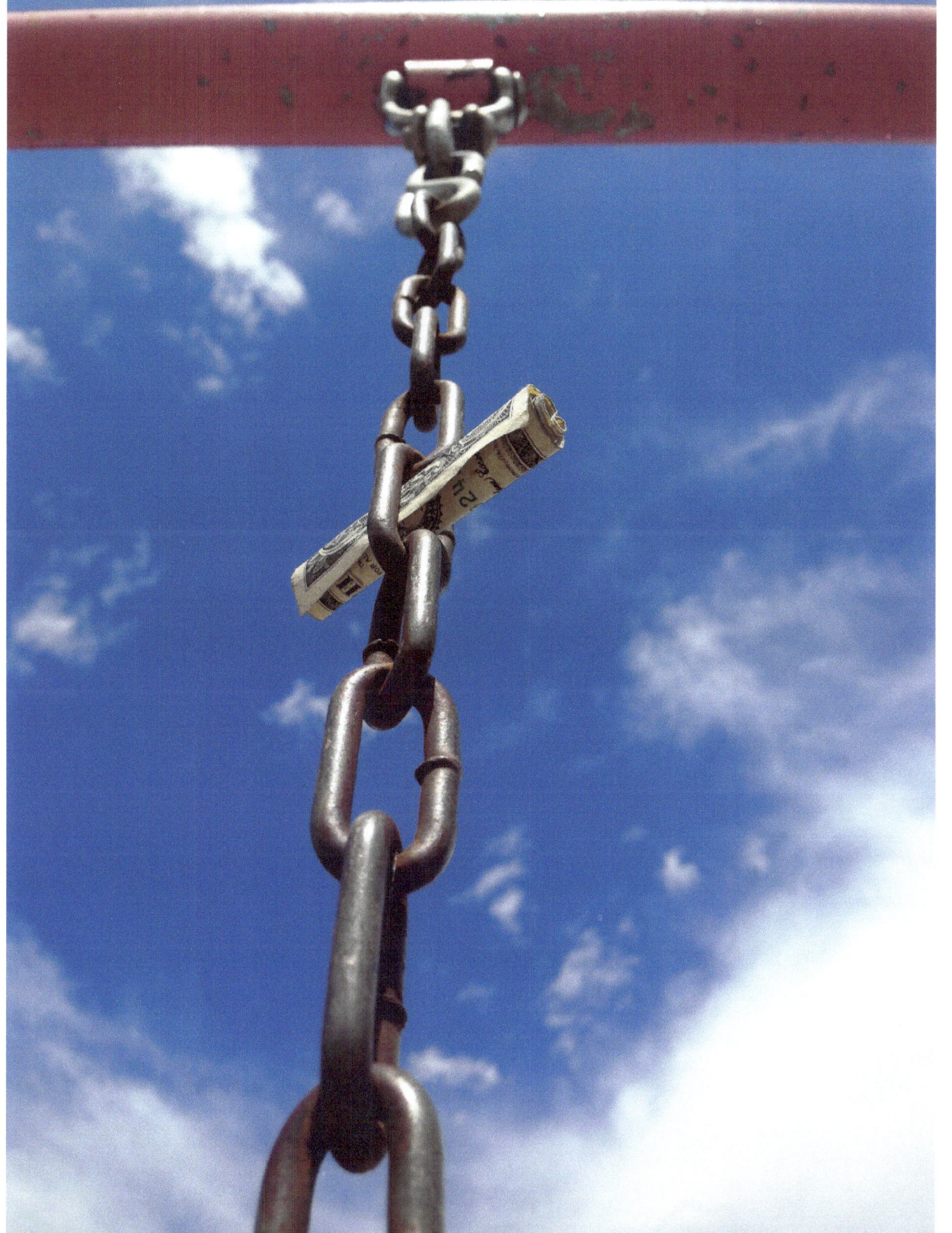

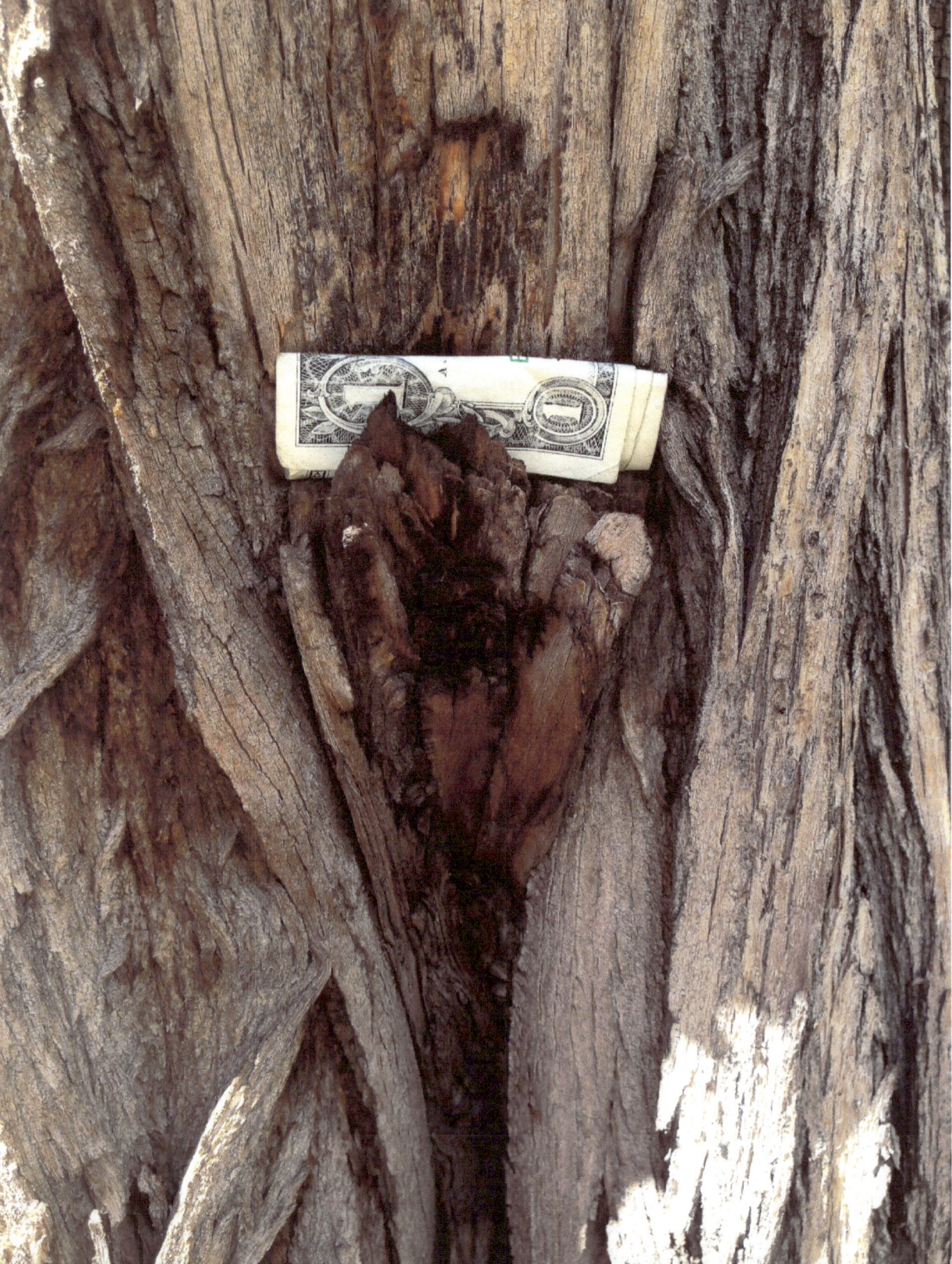

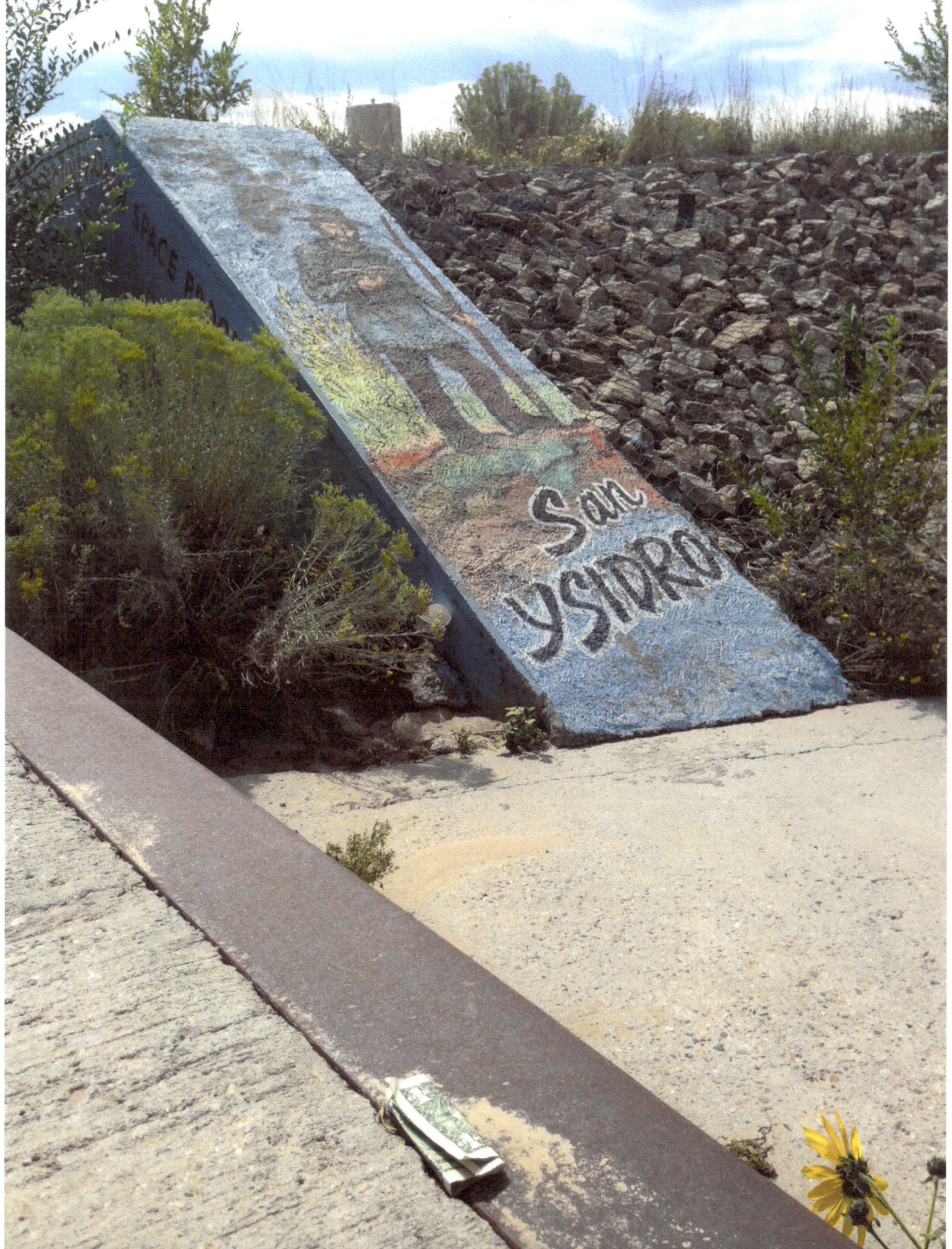

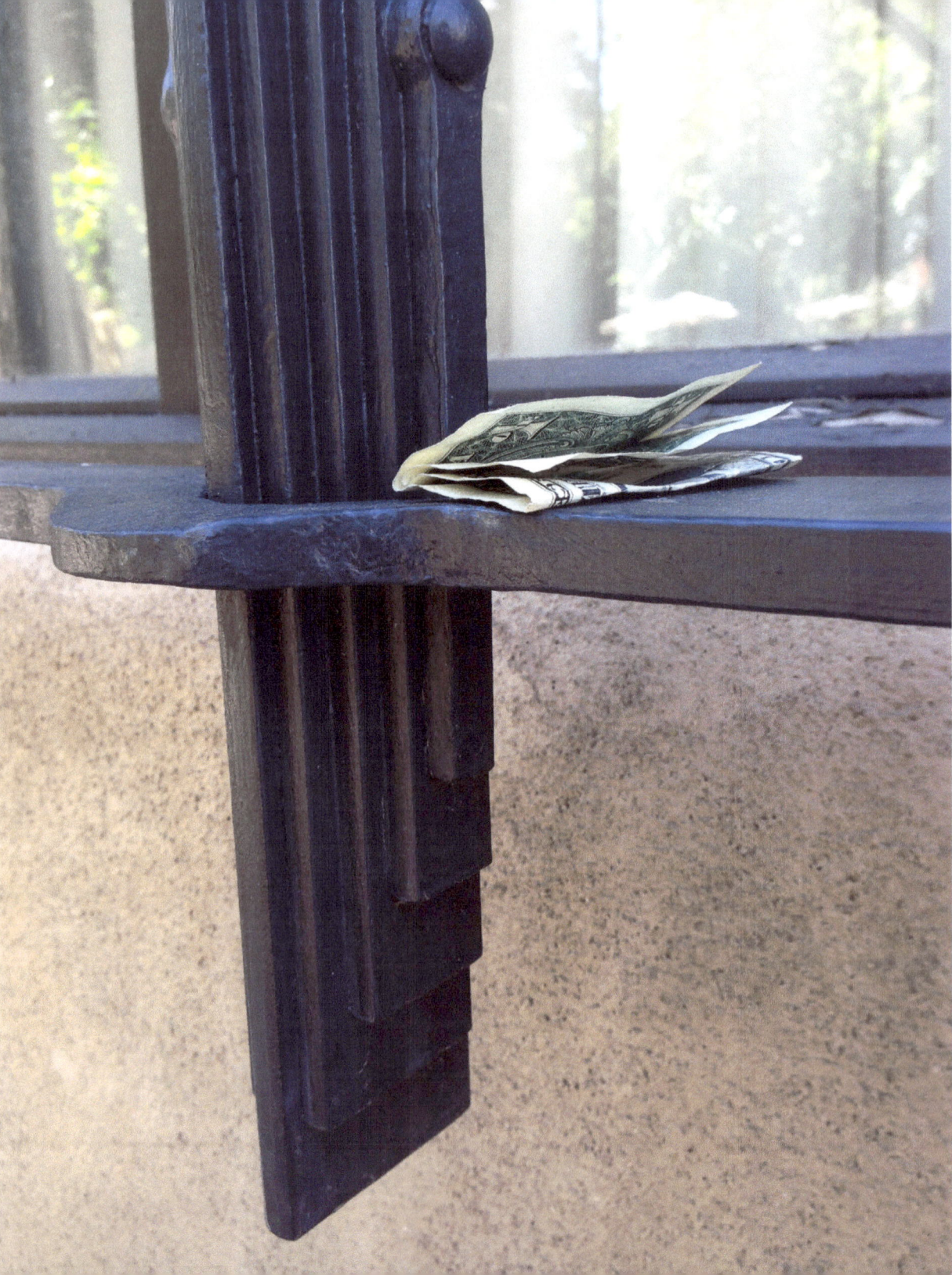

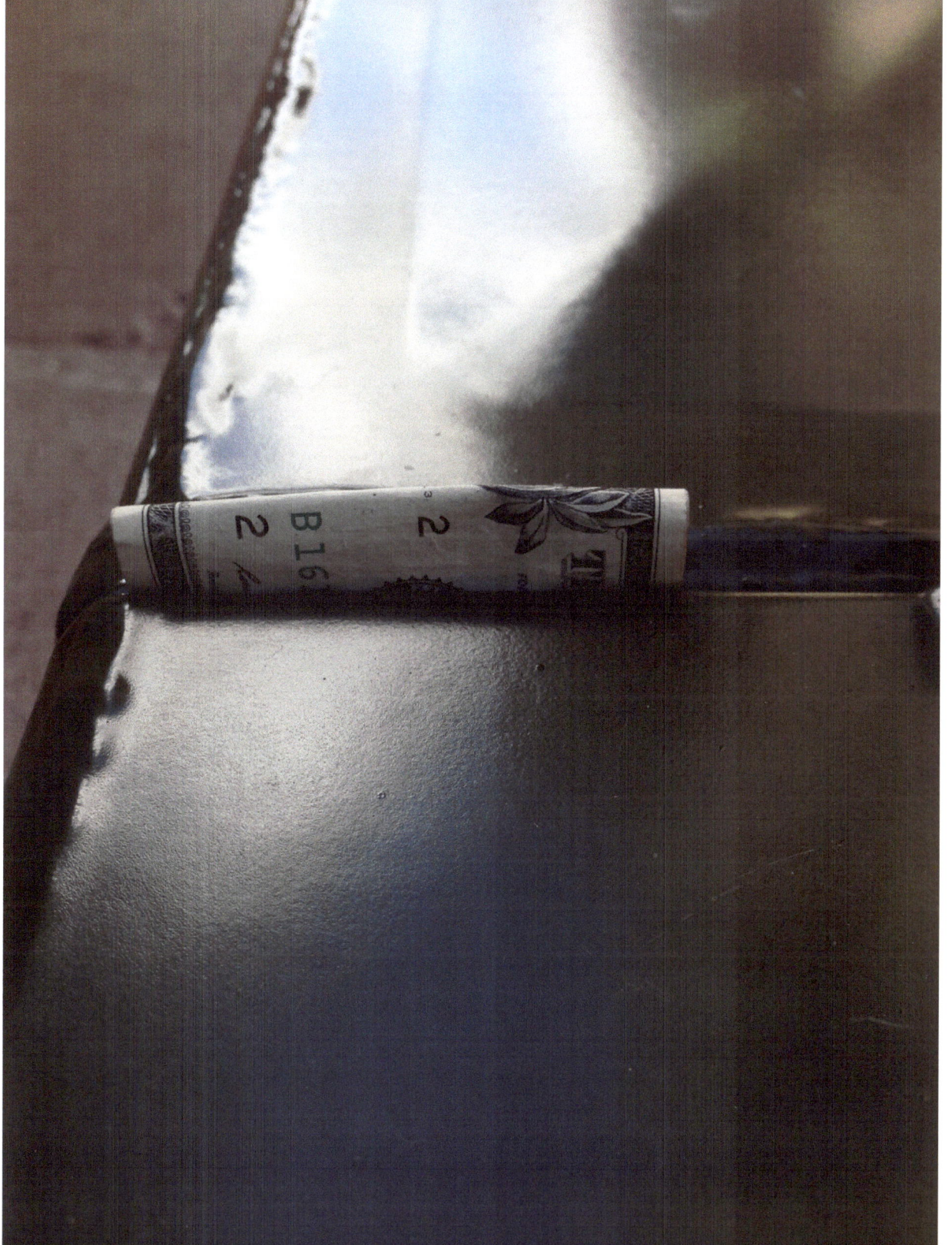

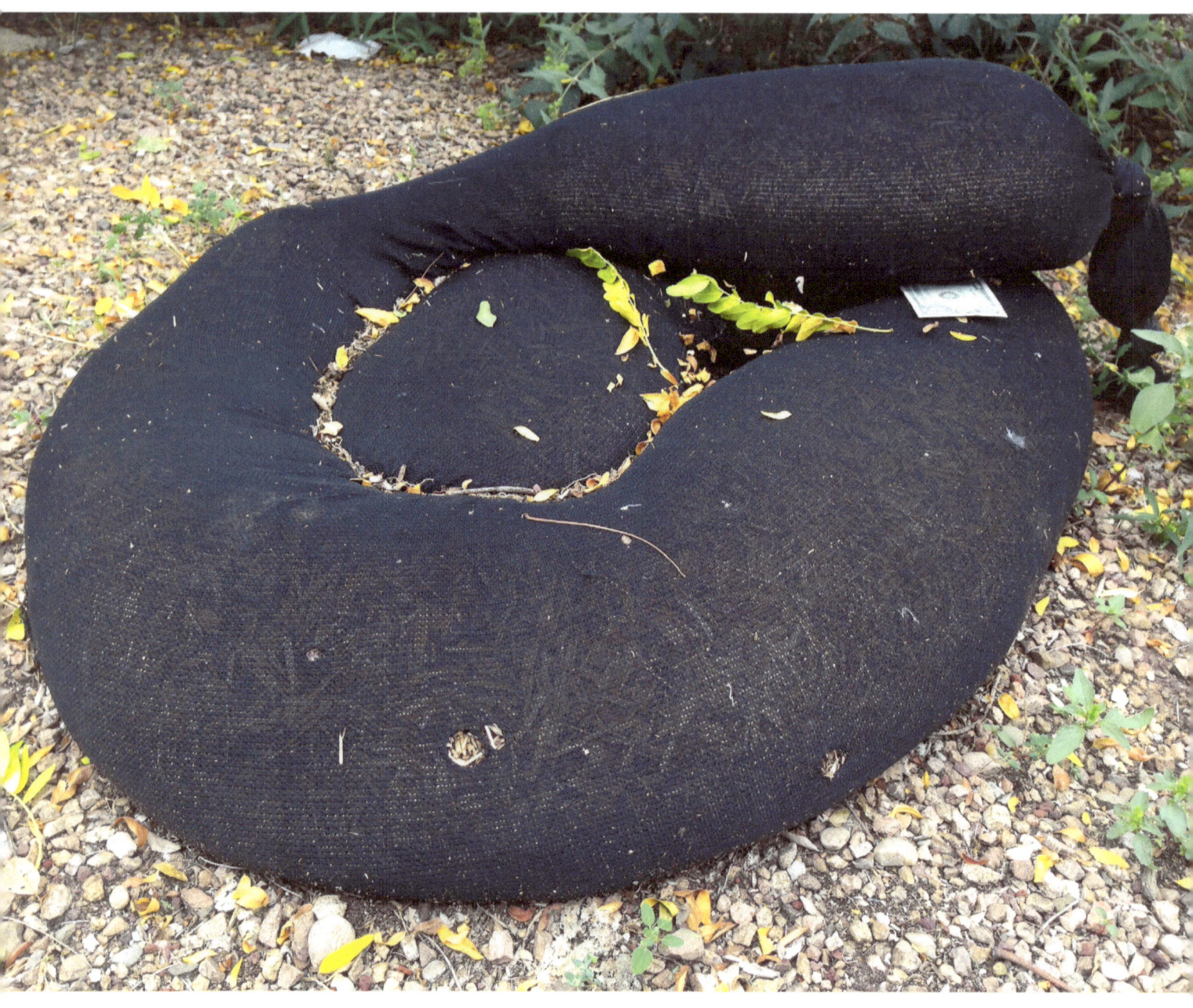

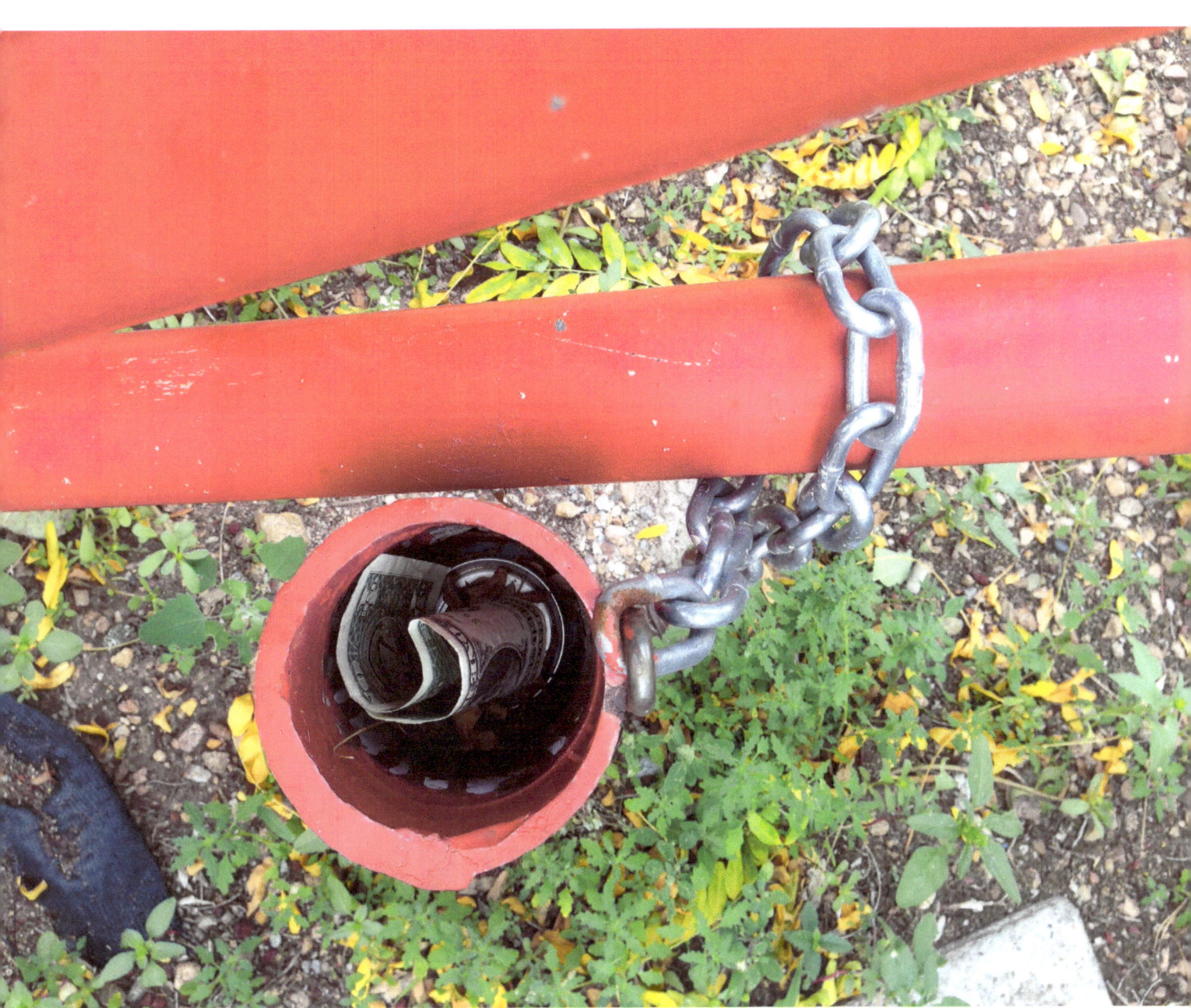

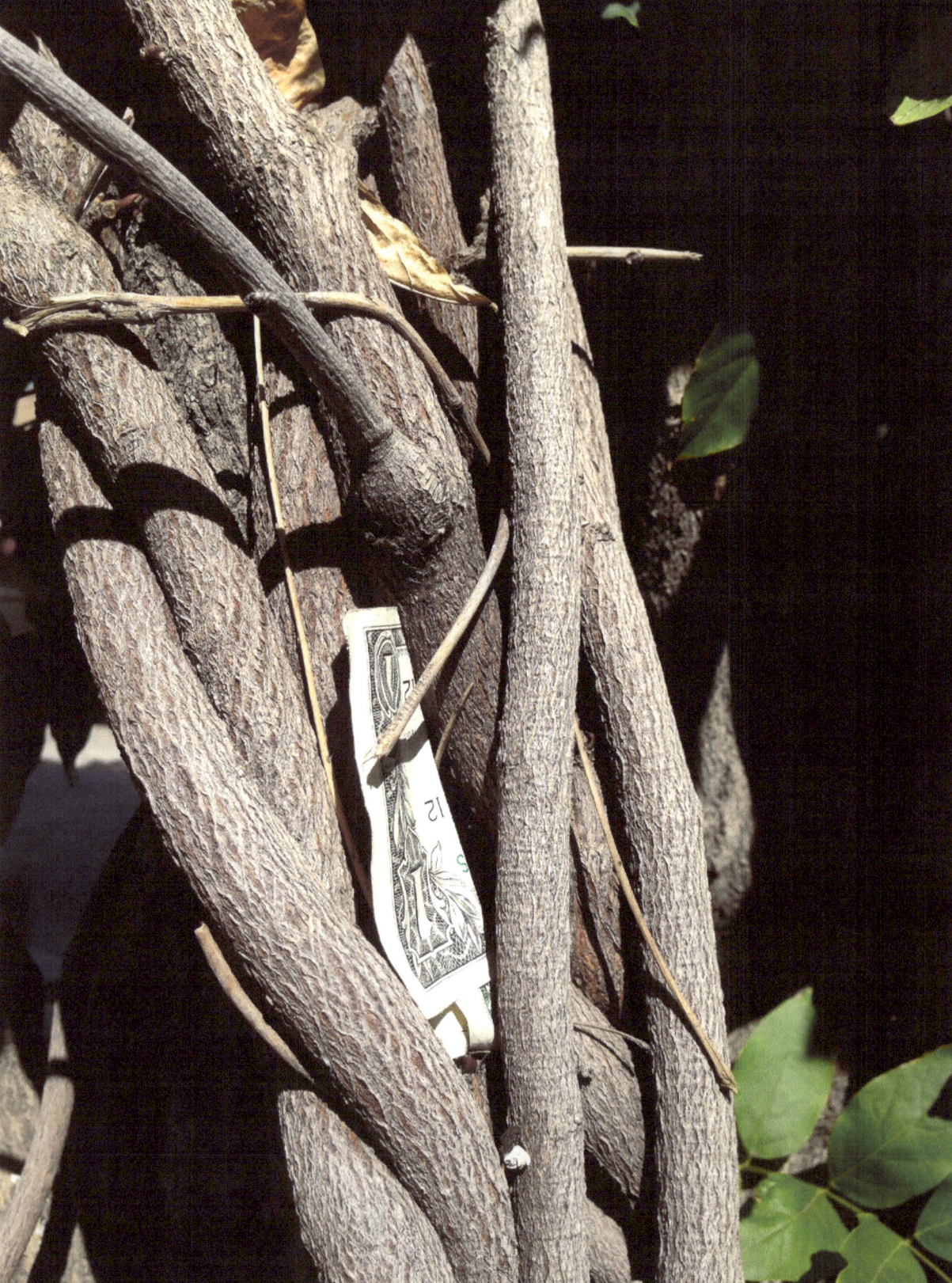

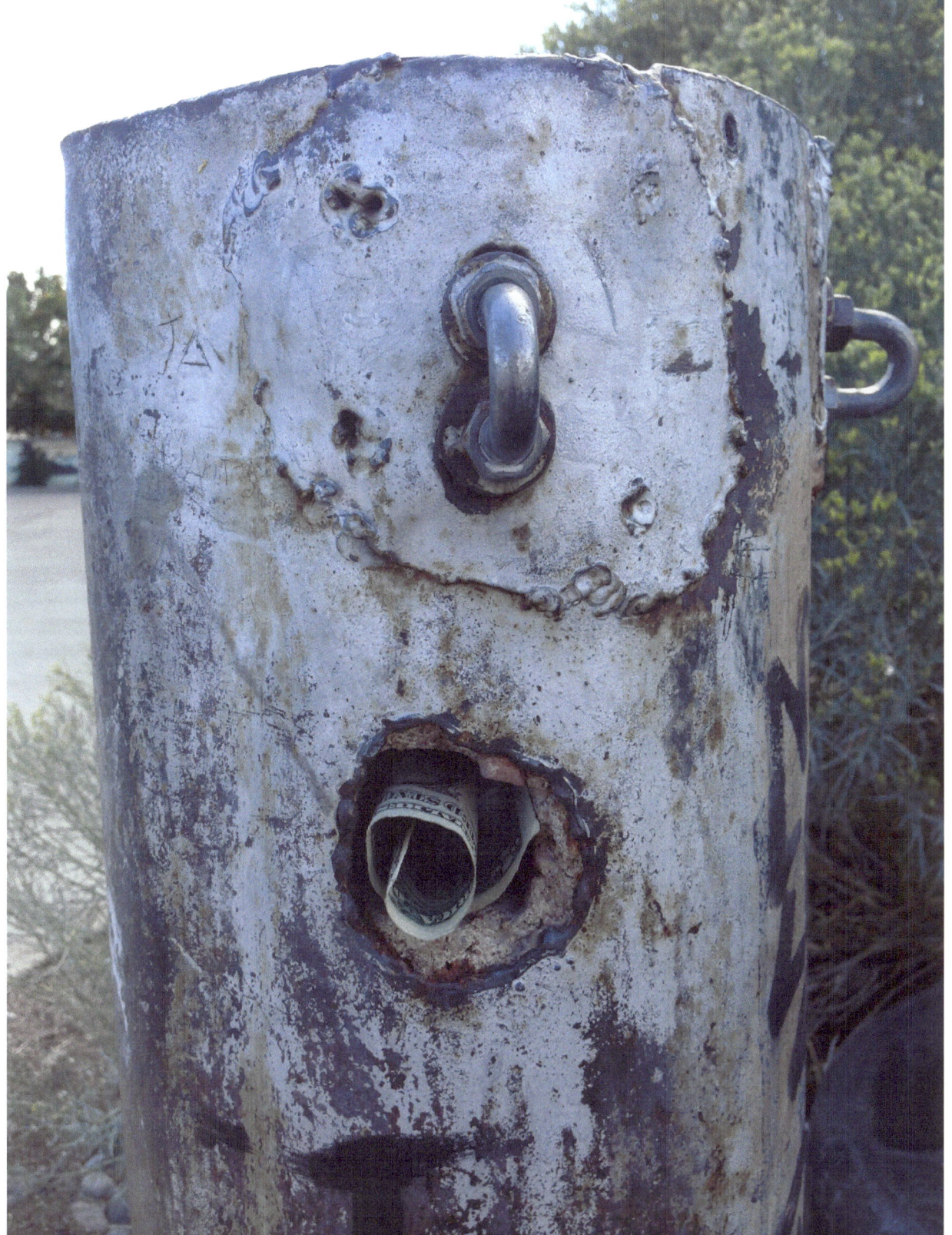

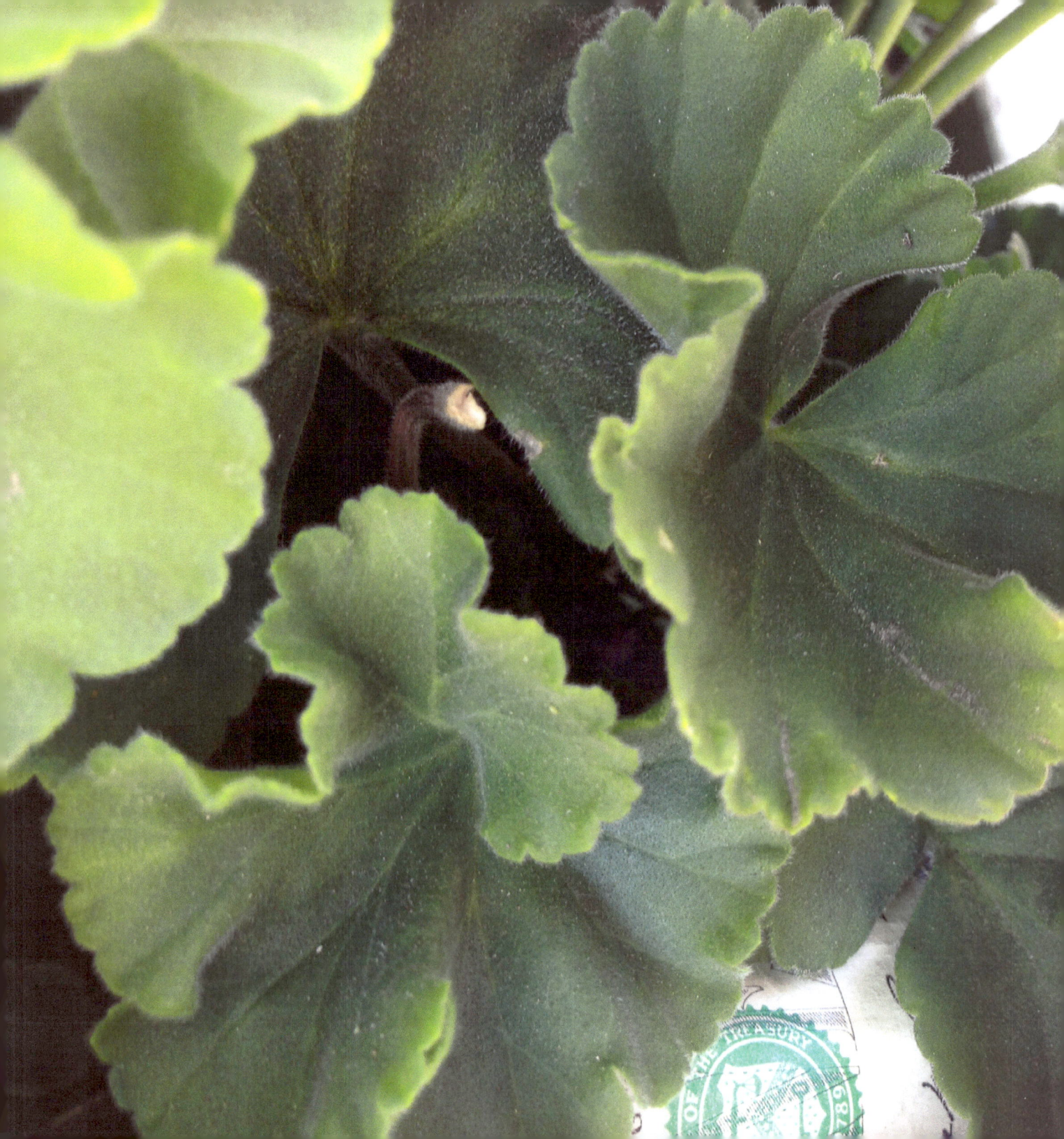

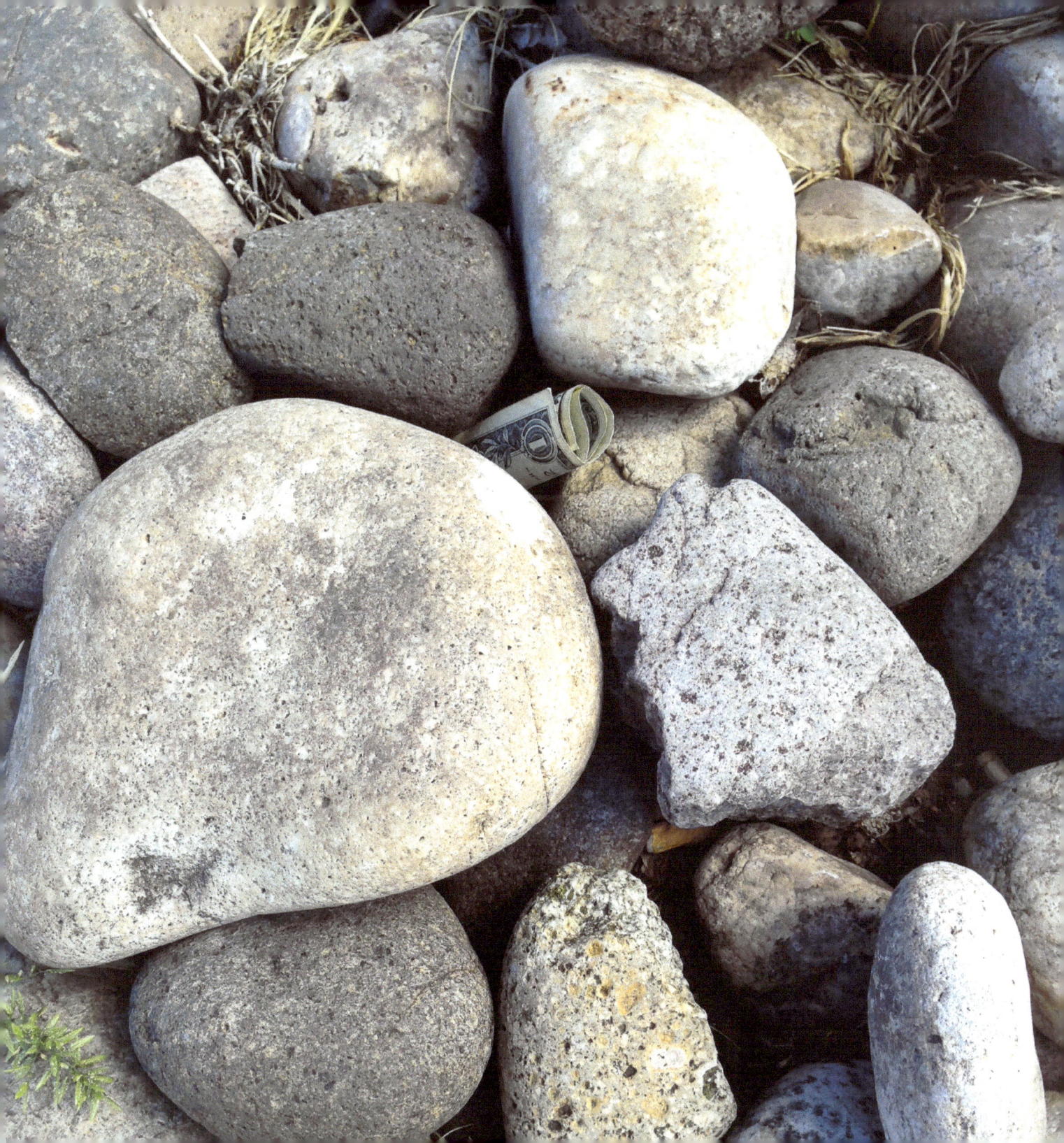

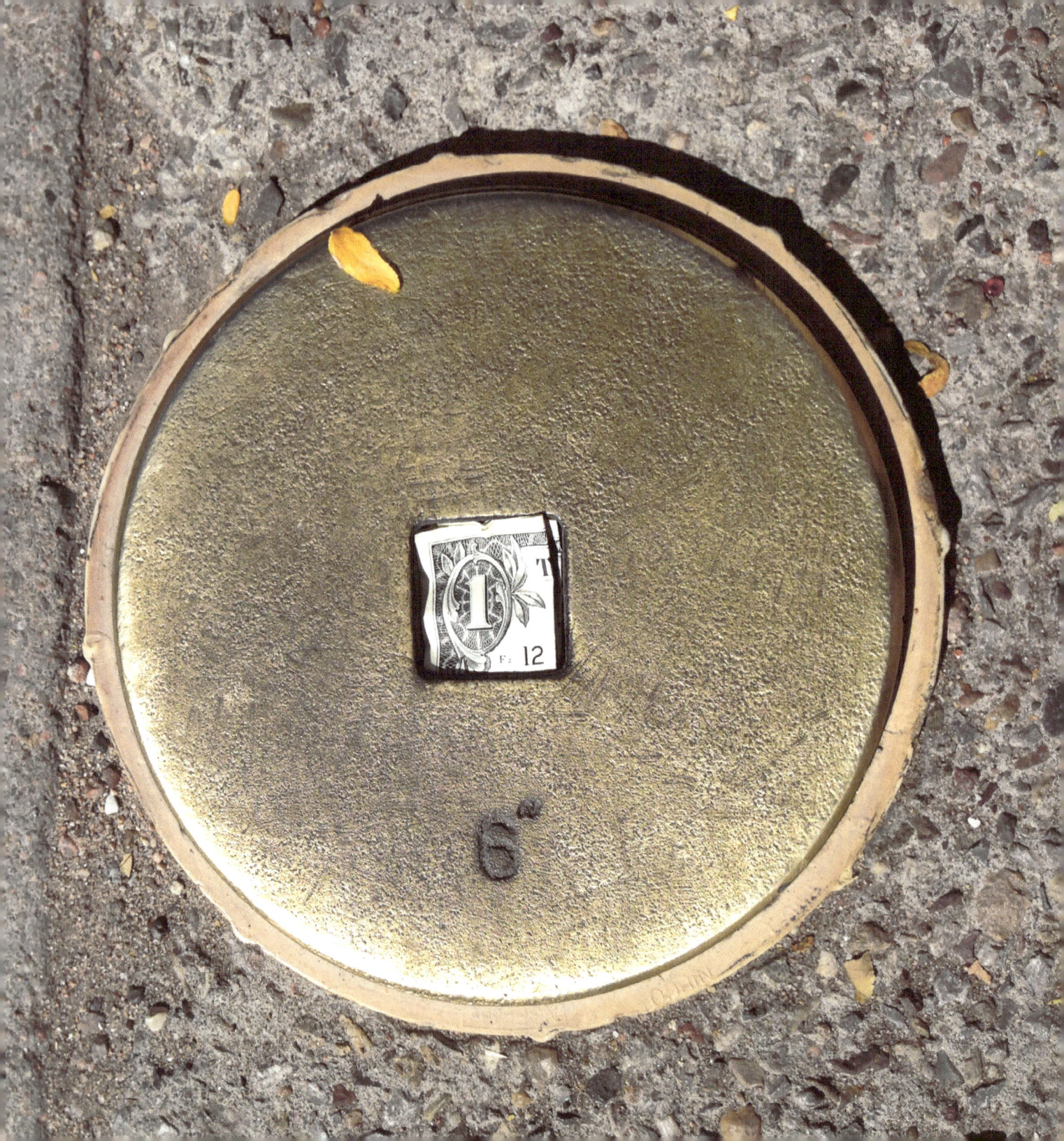

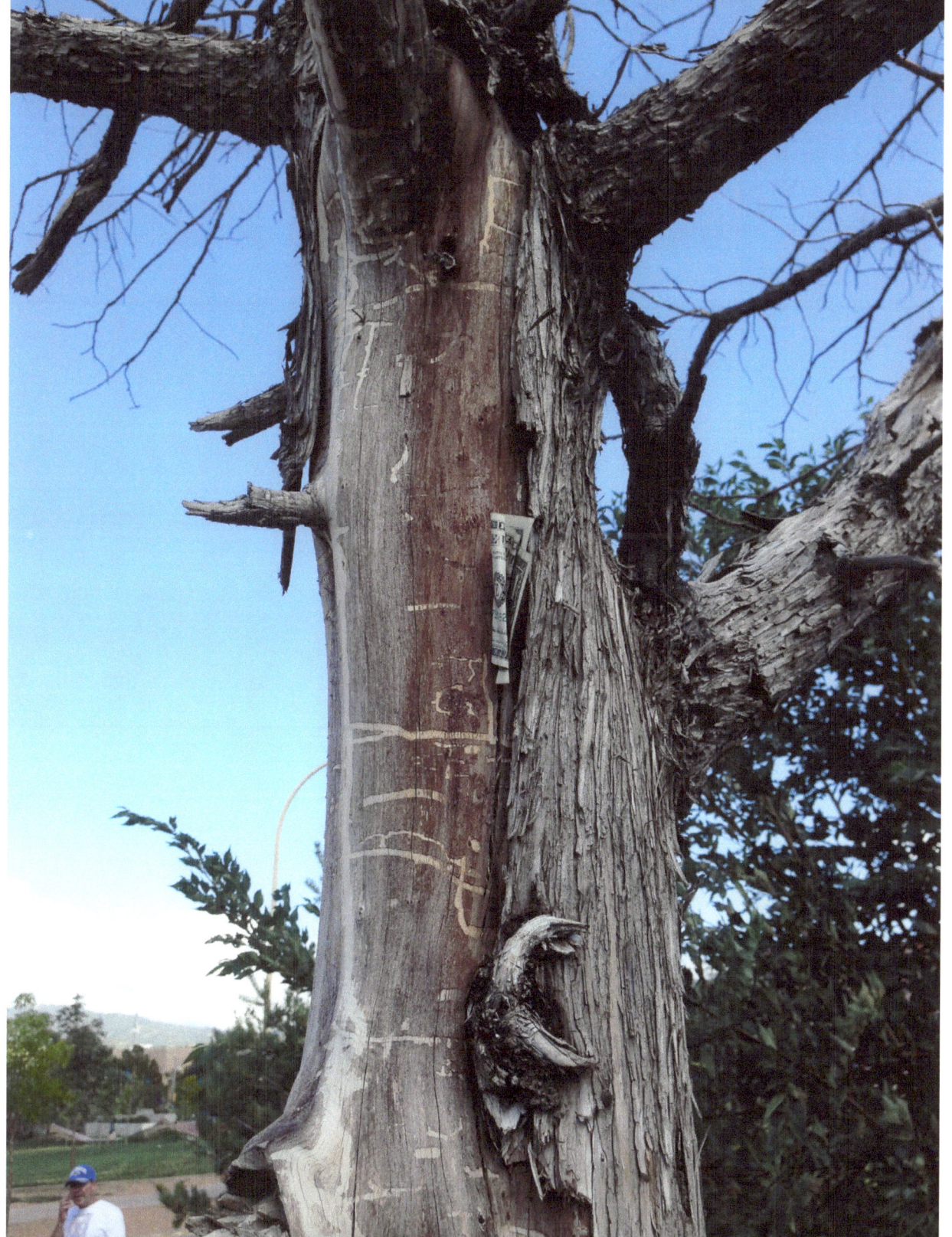

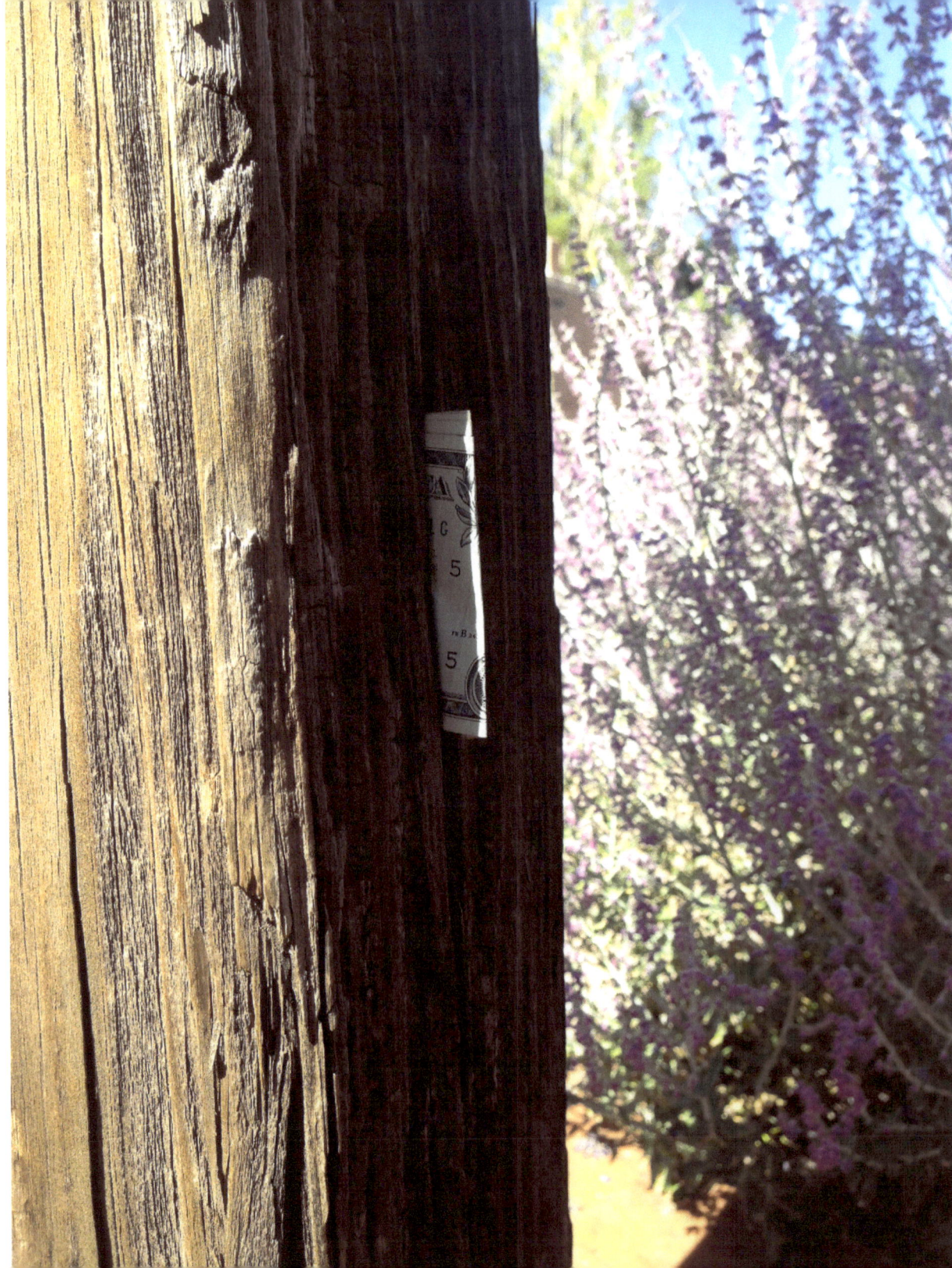

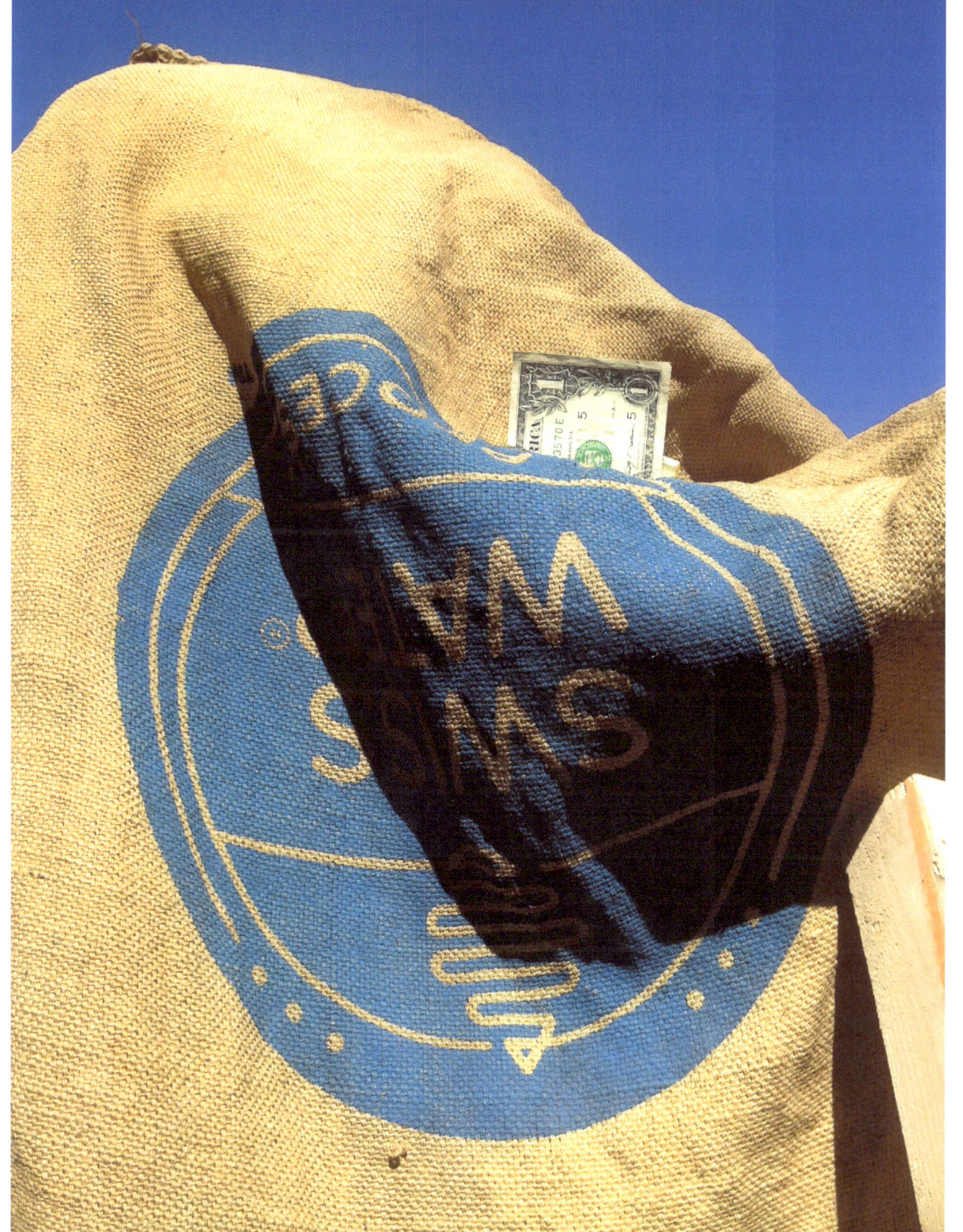

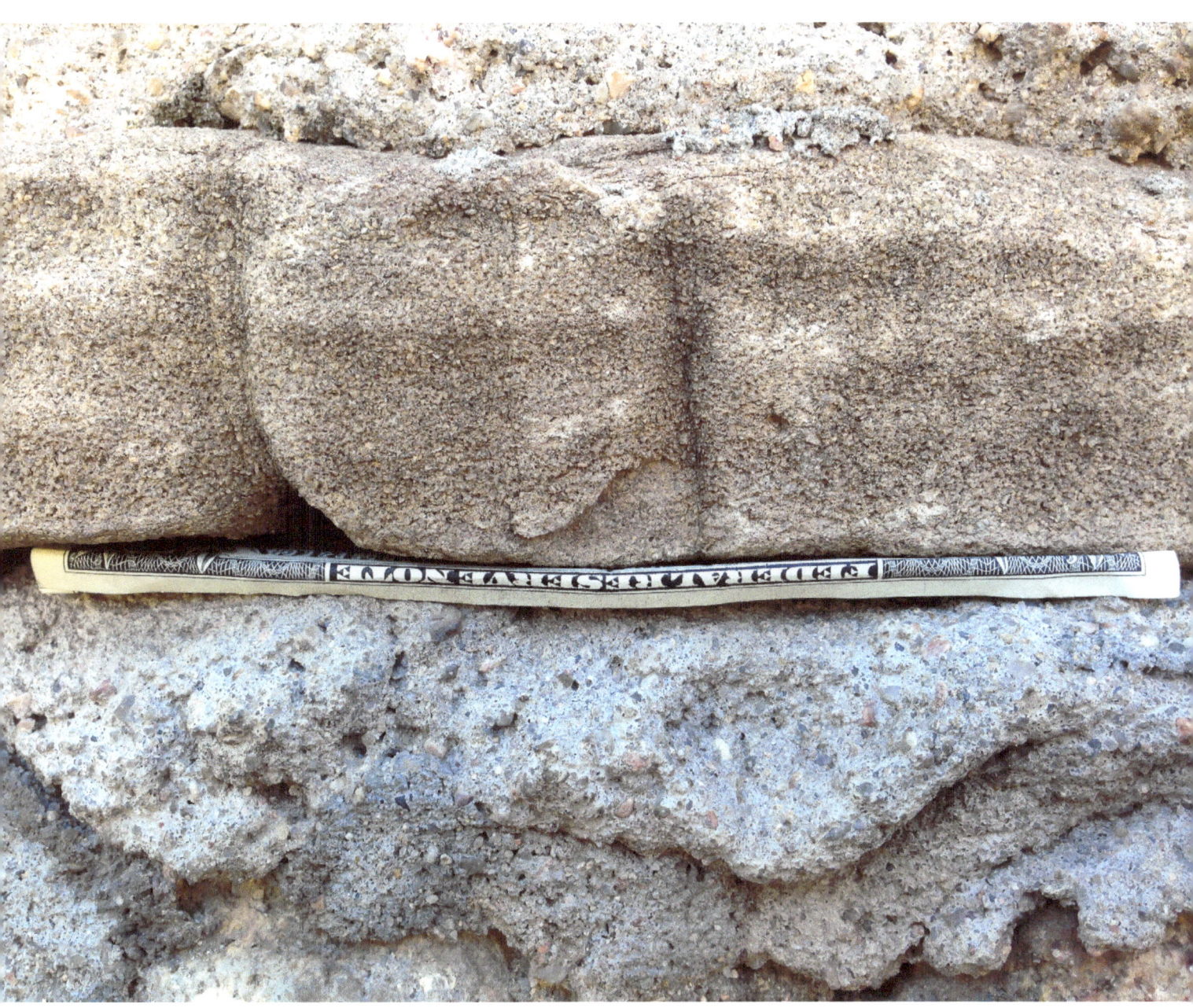

149

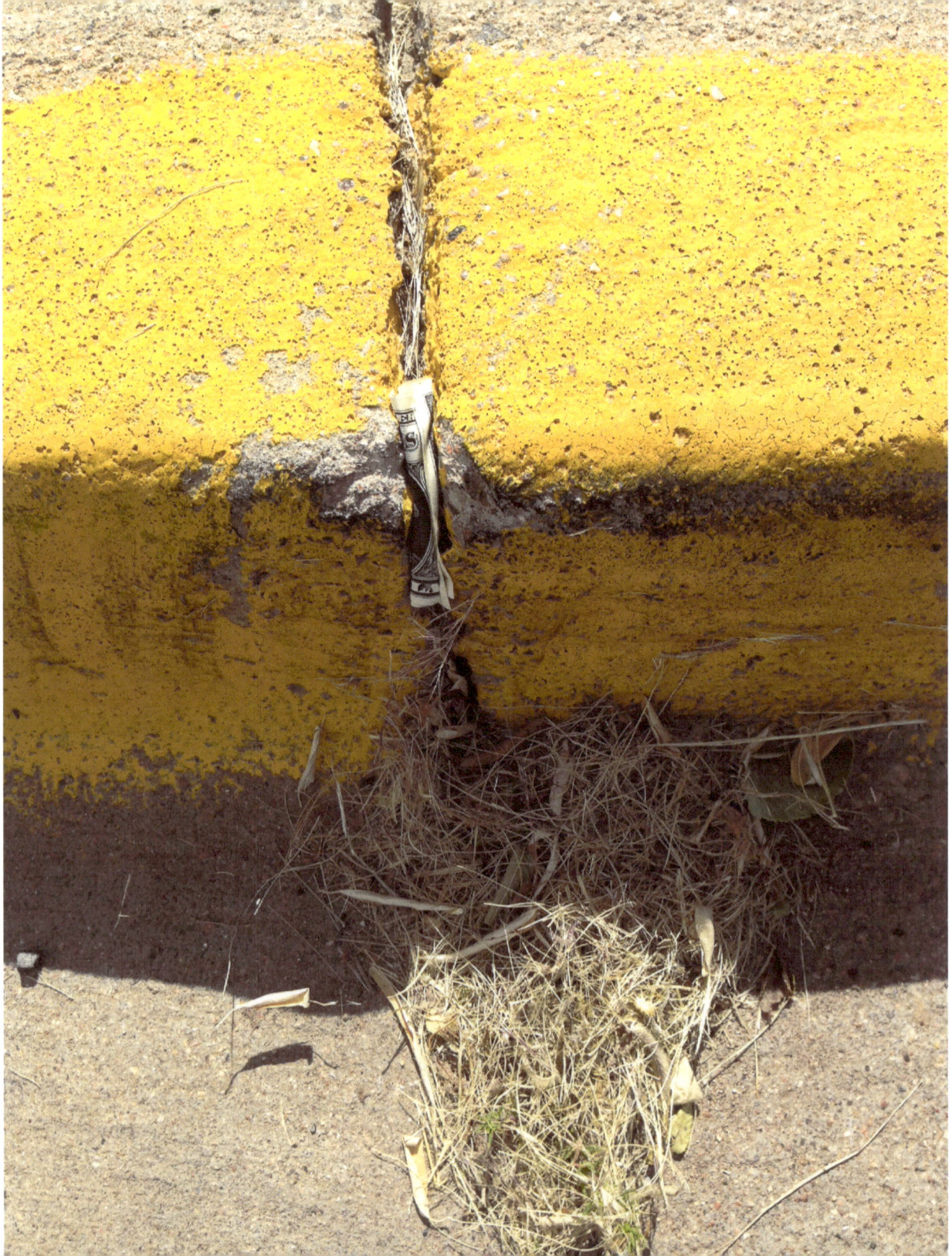

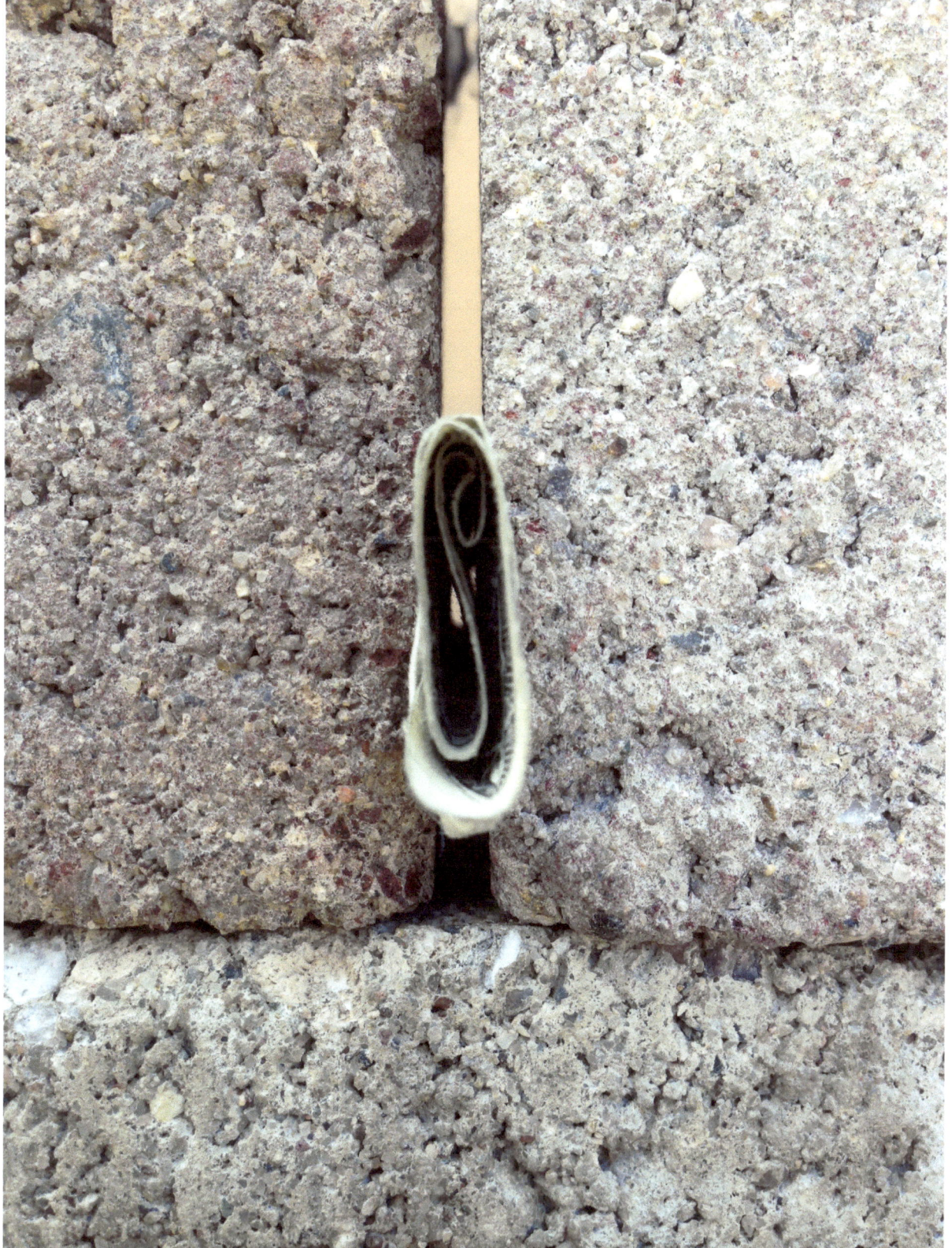

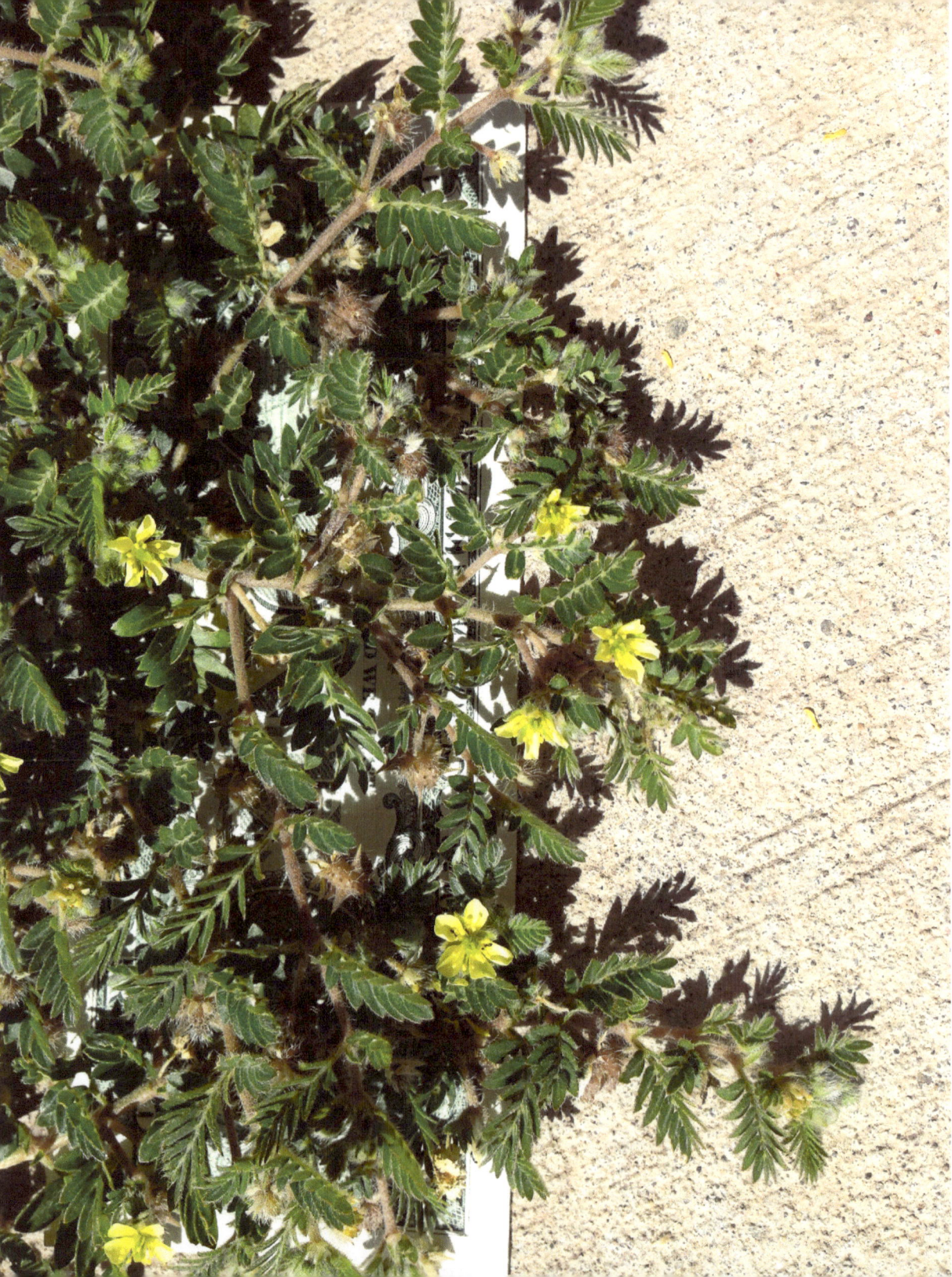

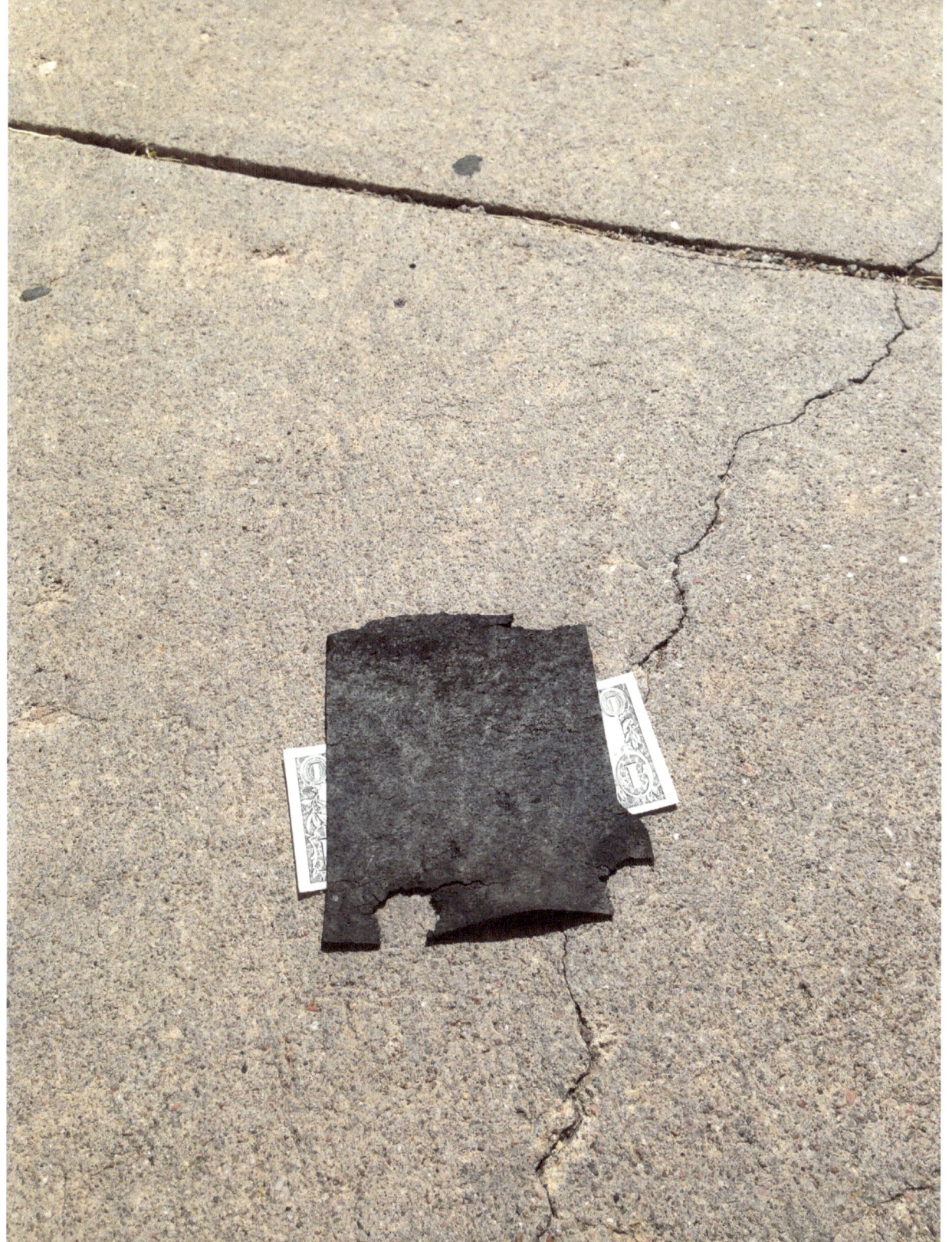

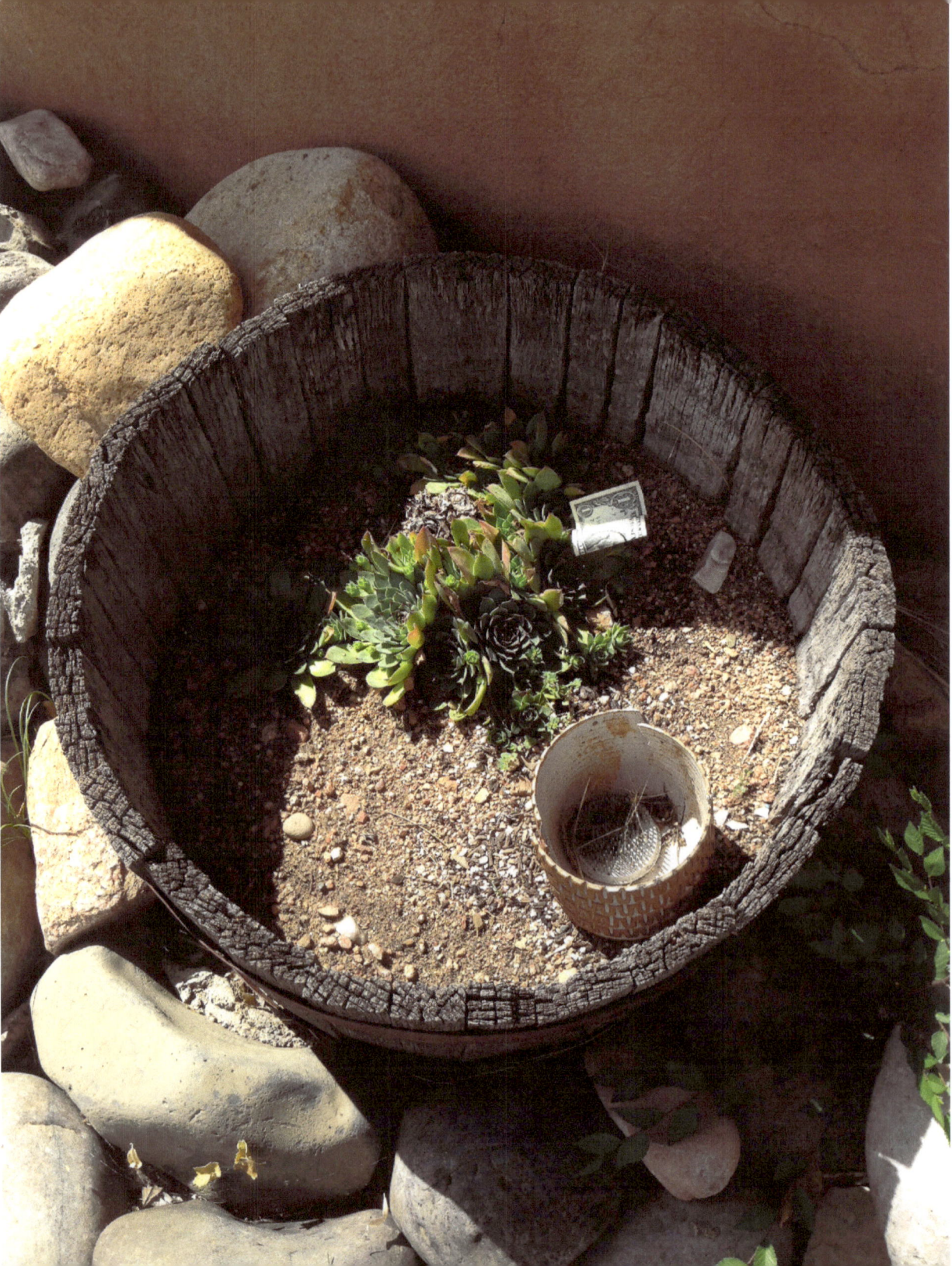

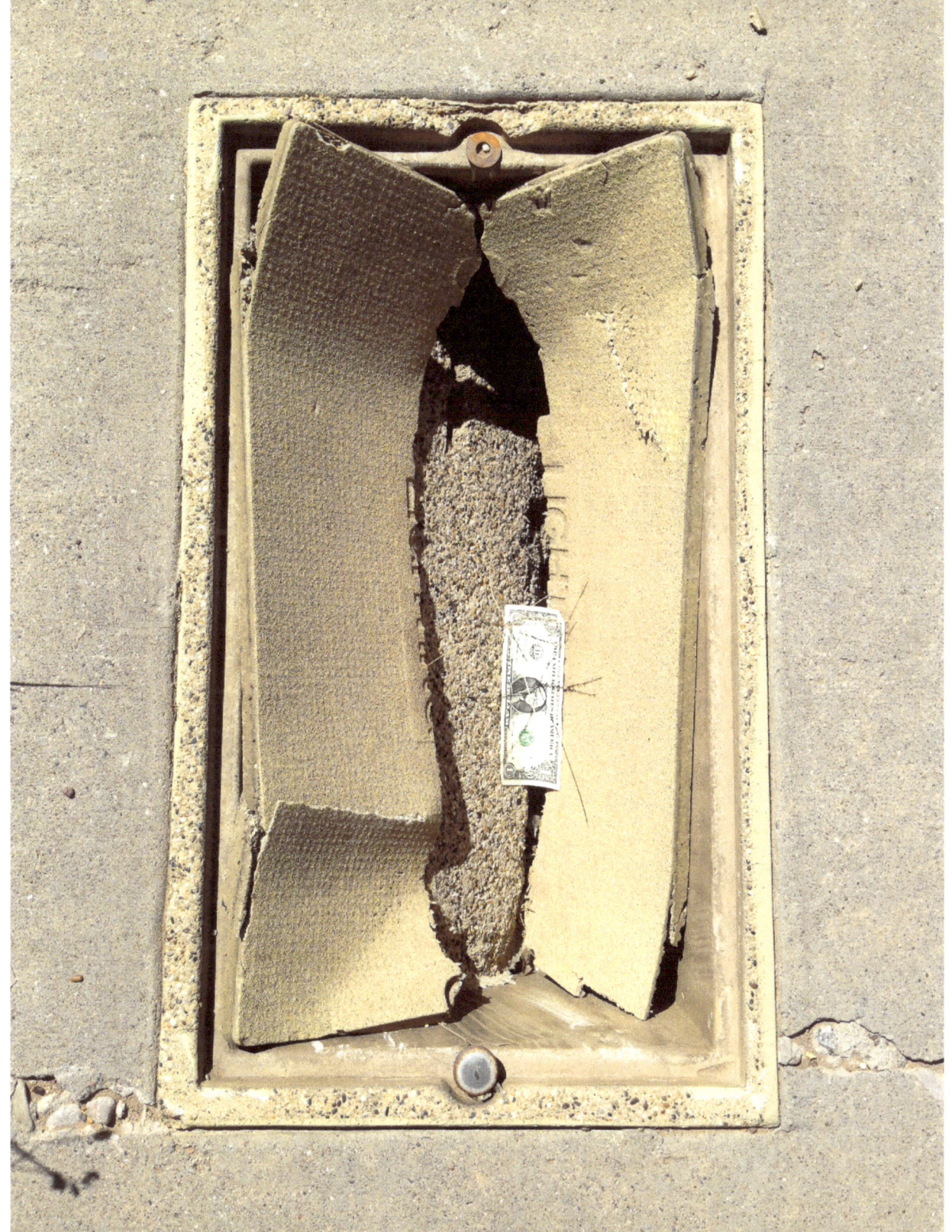

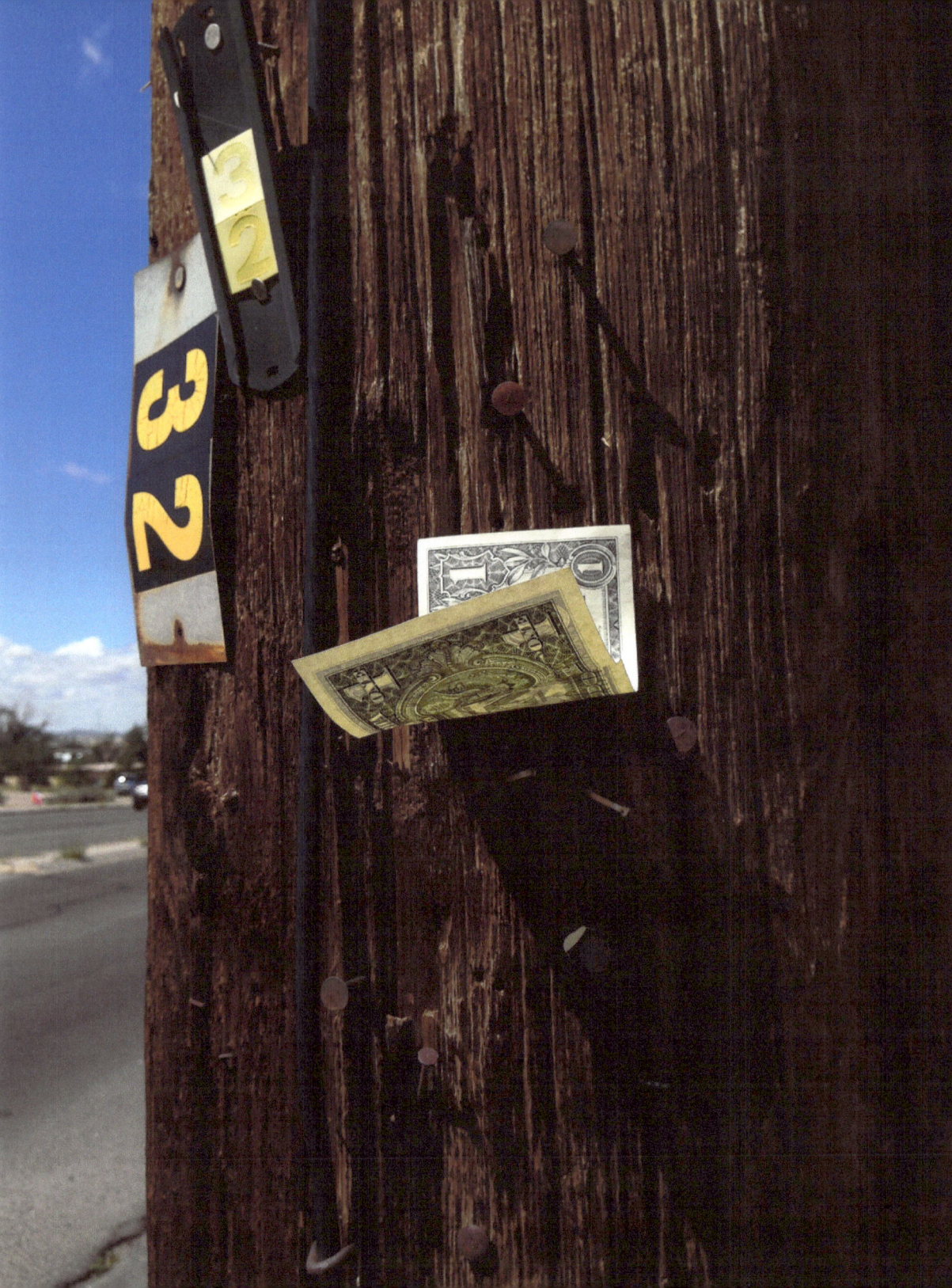

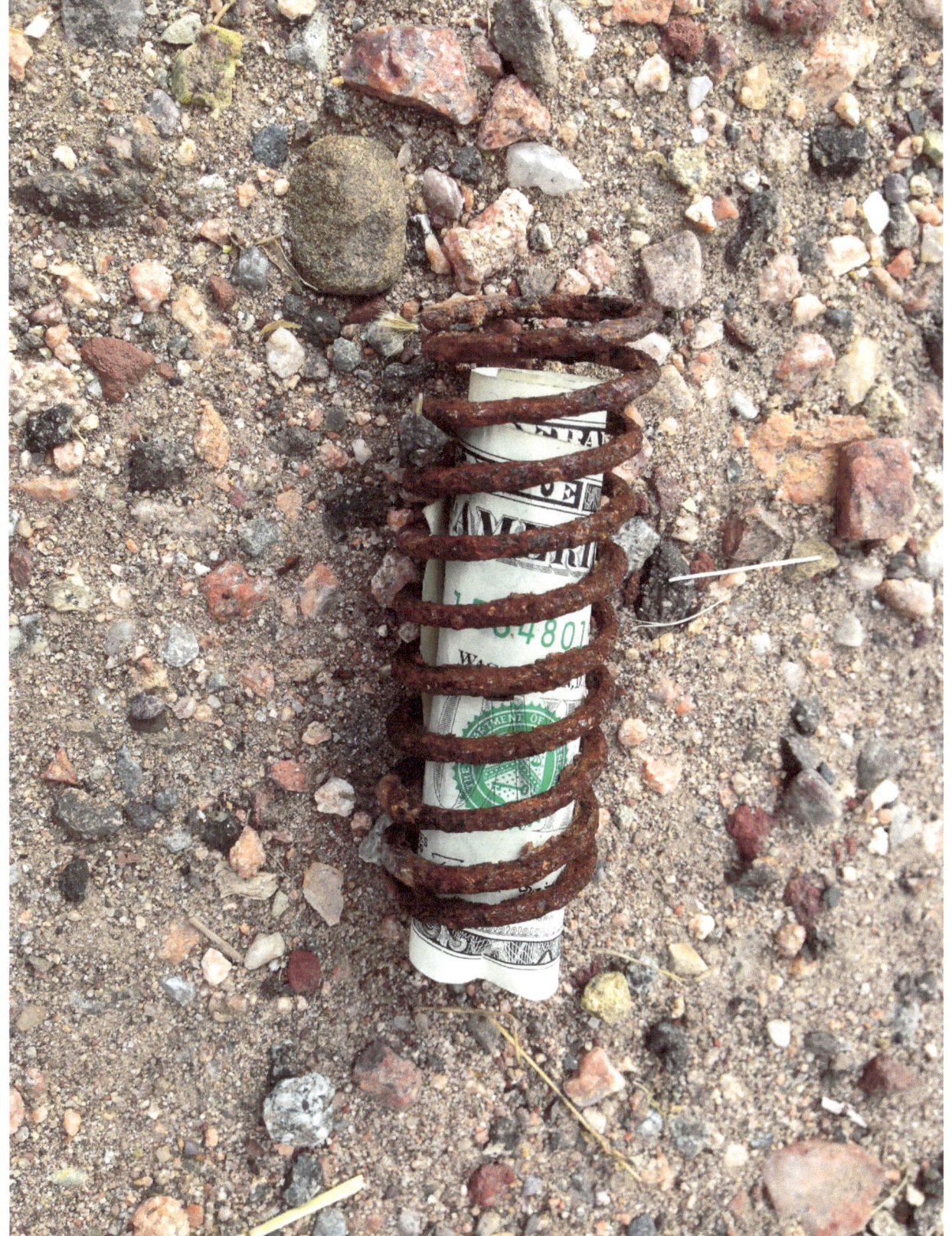

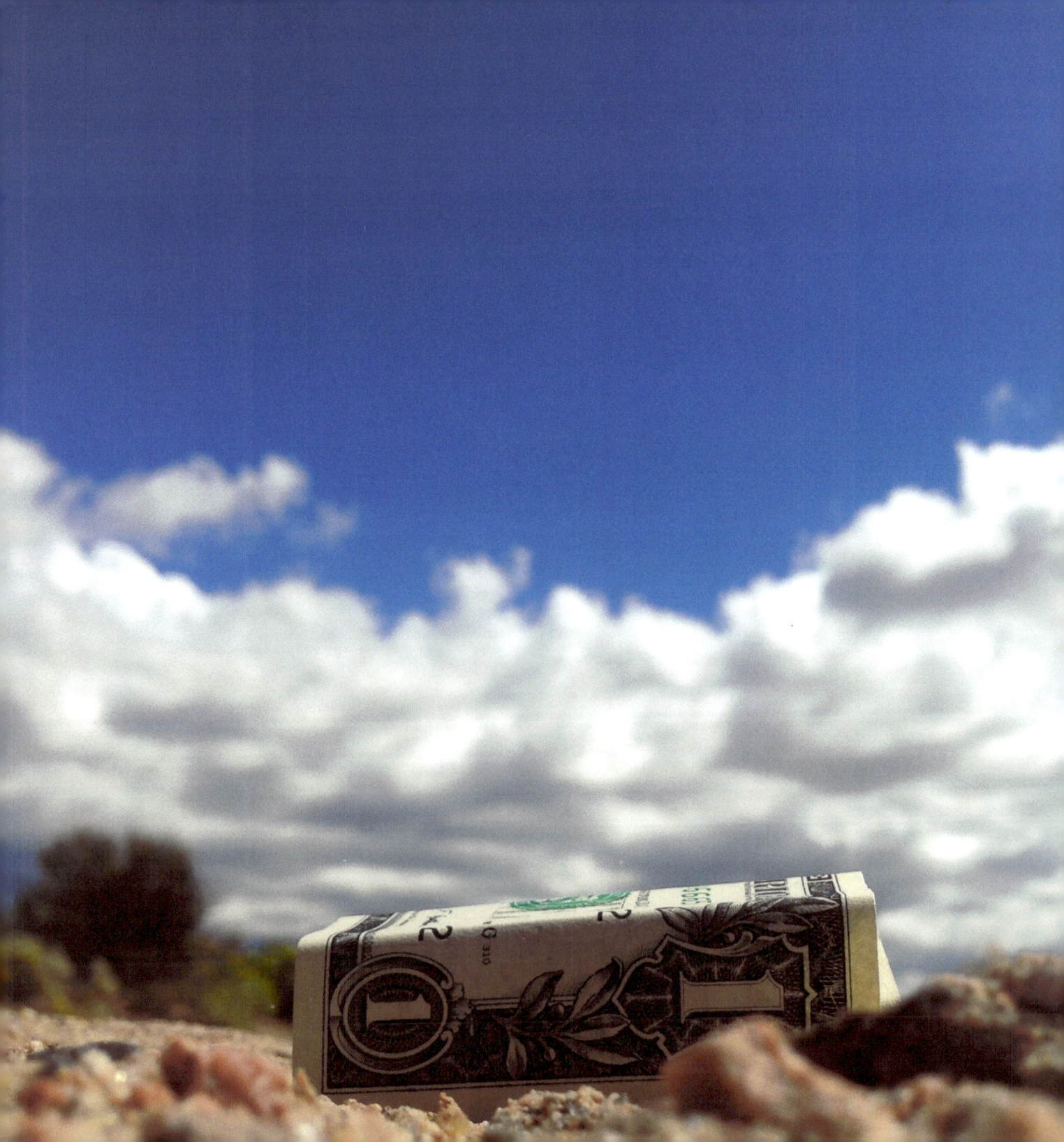

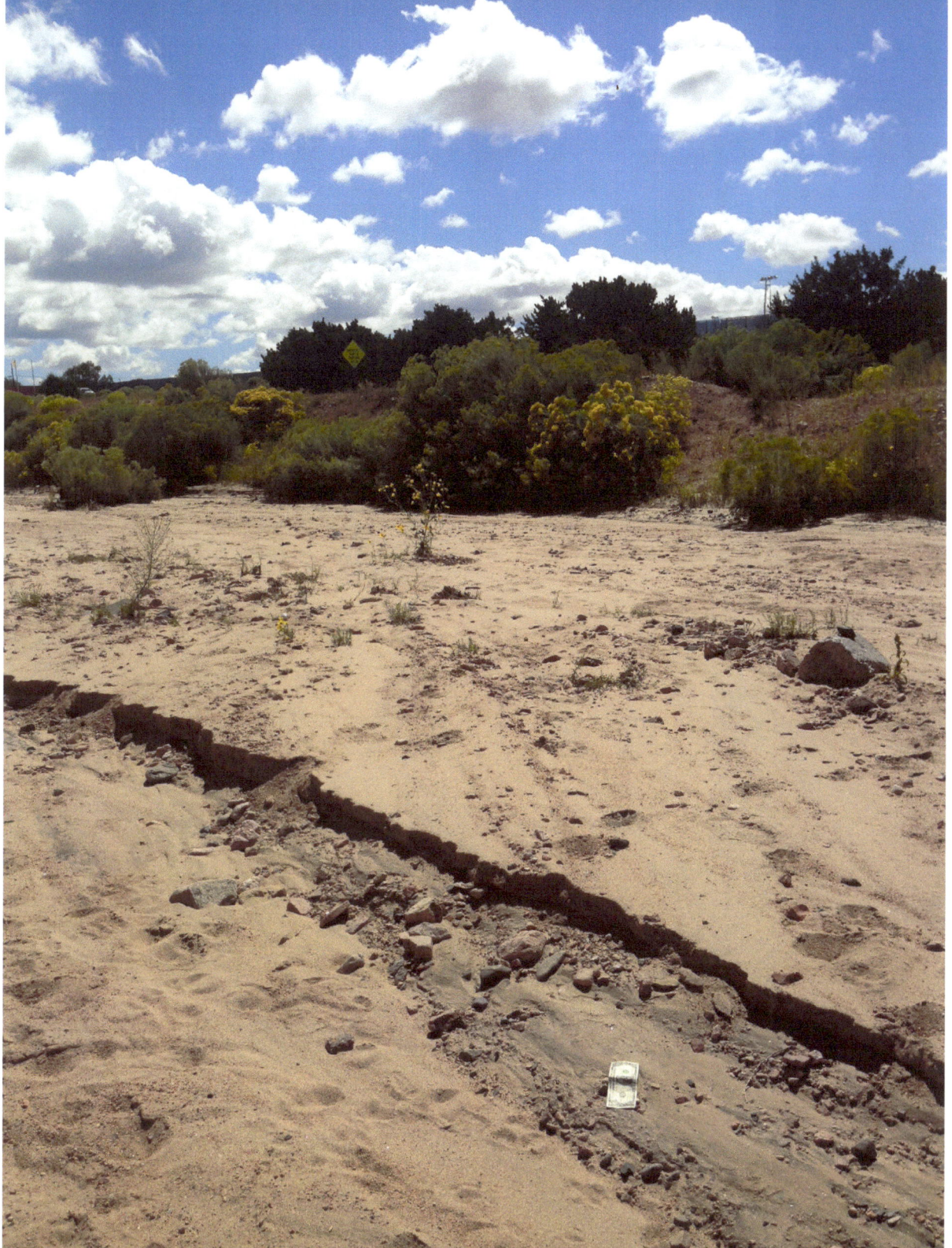

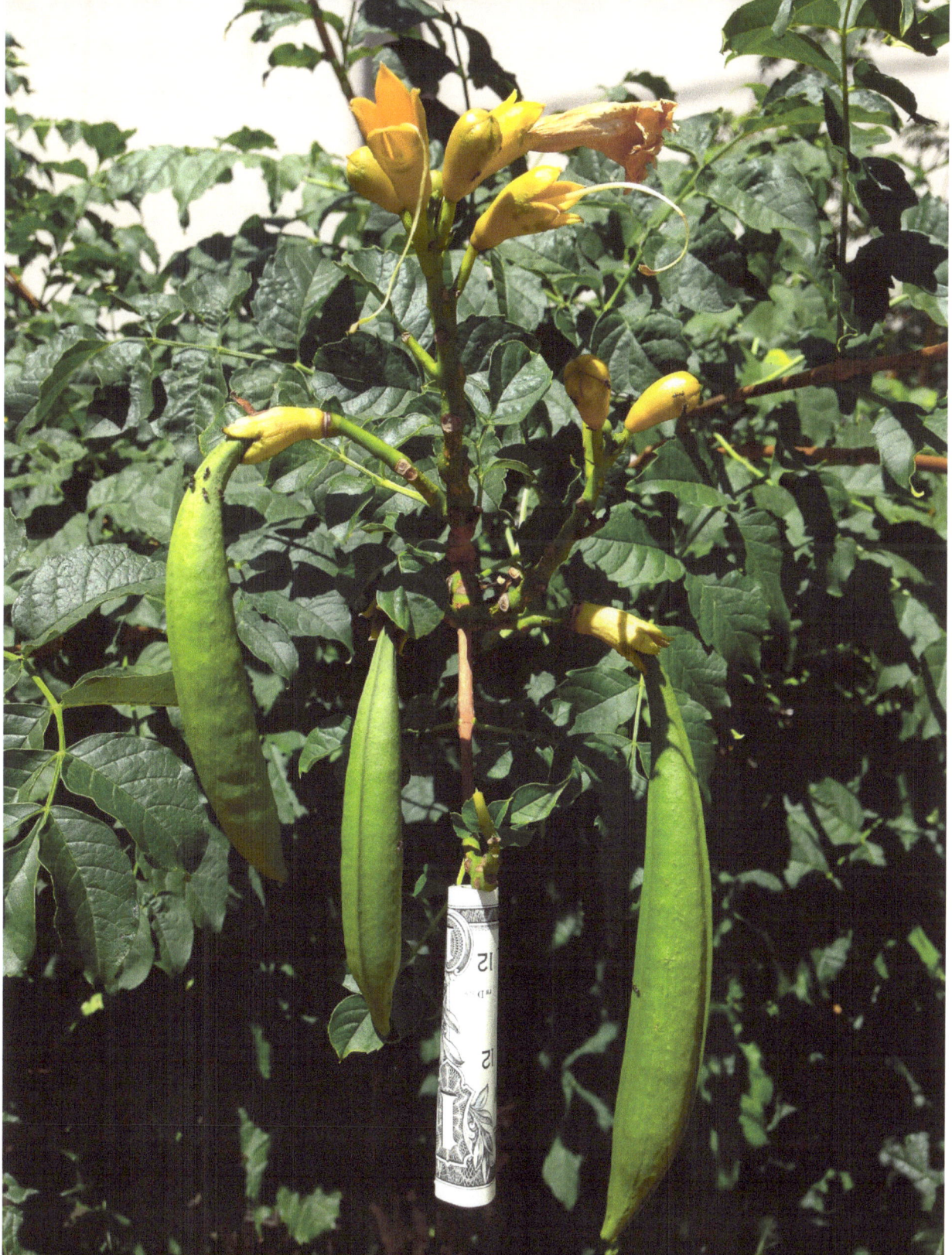

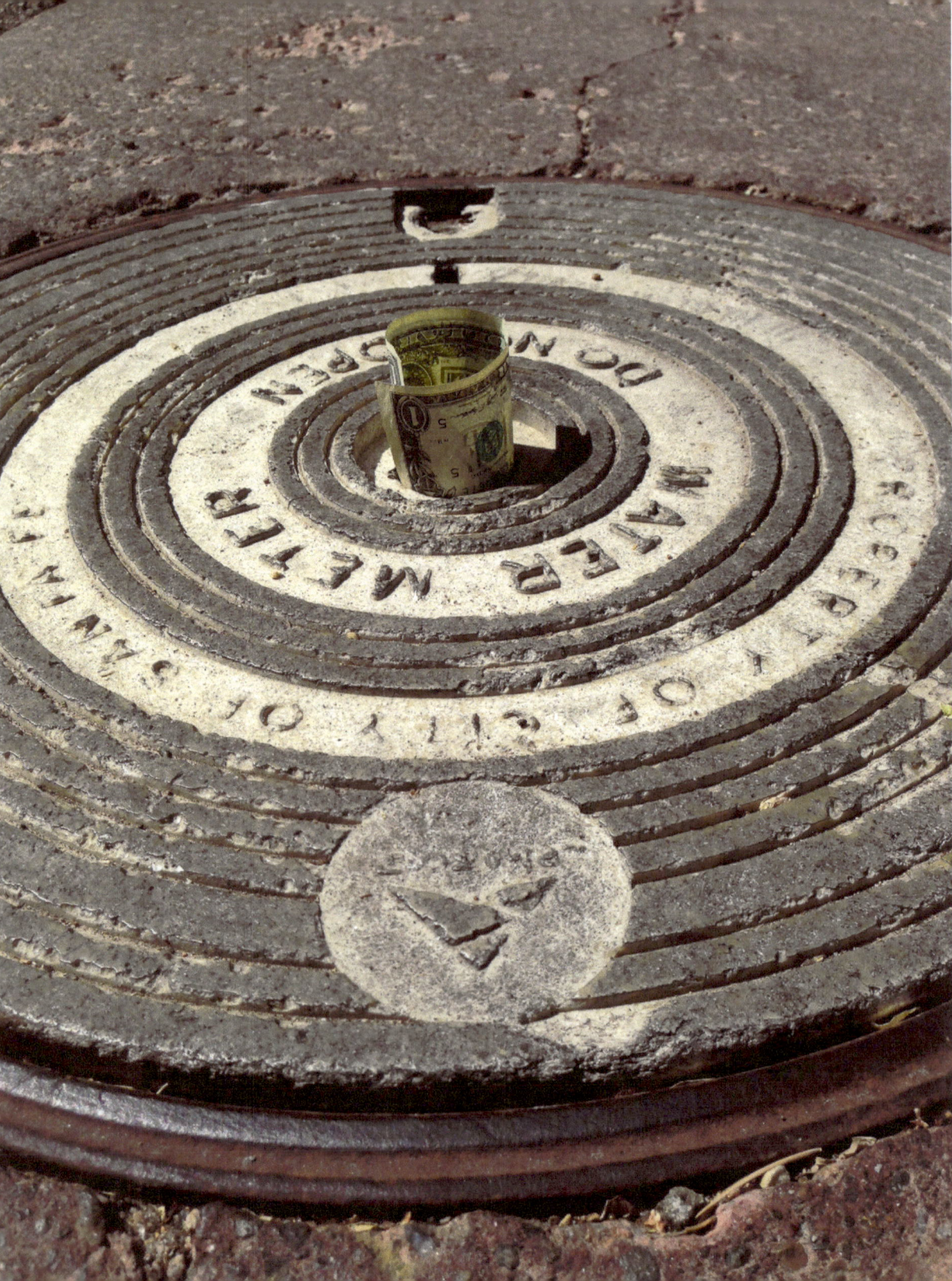

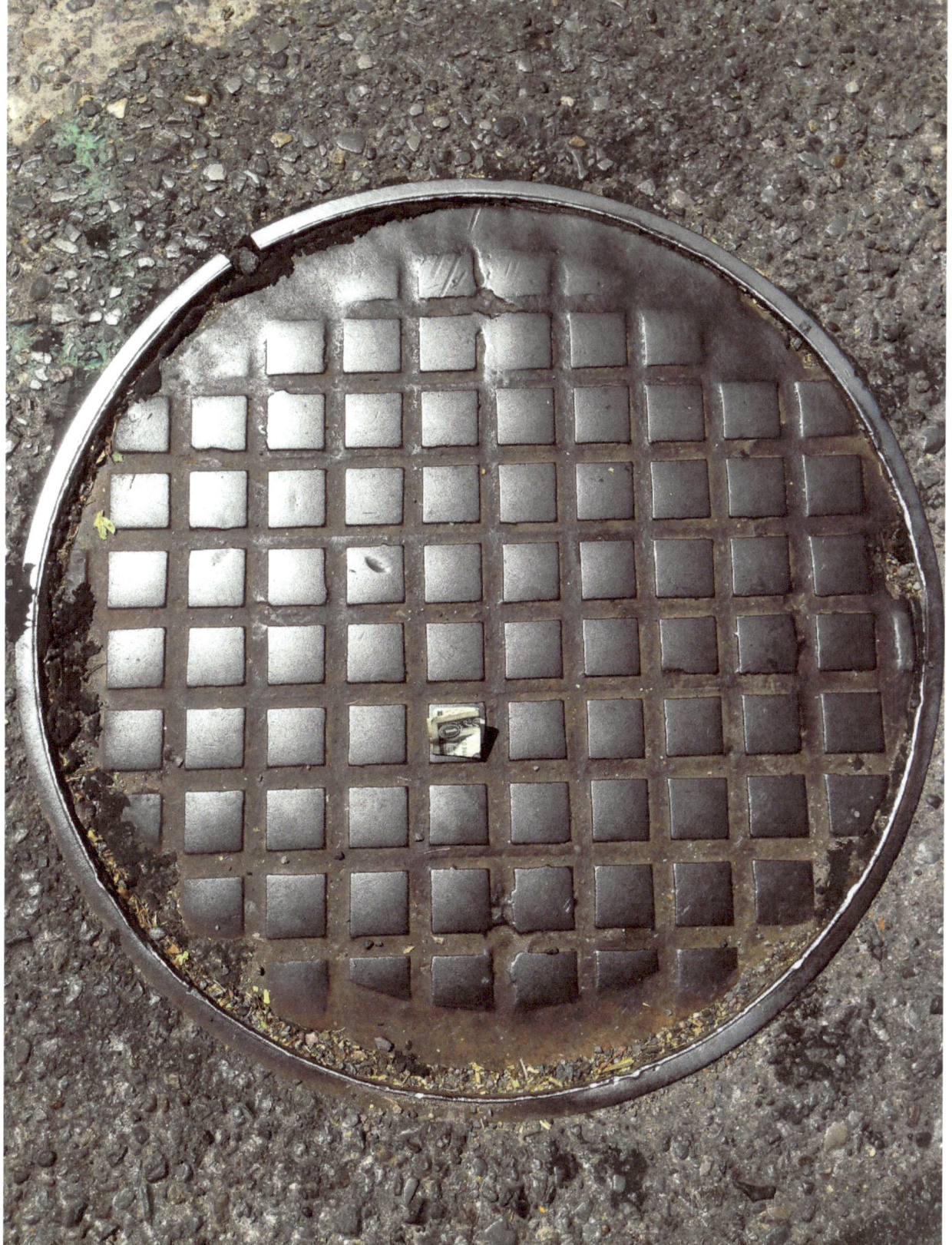

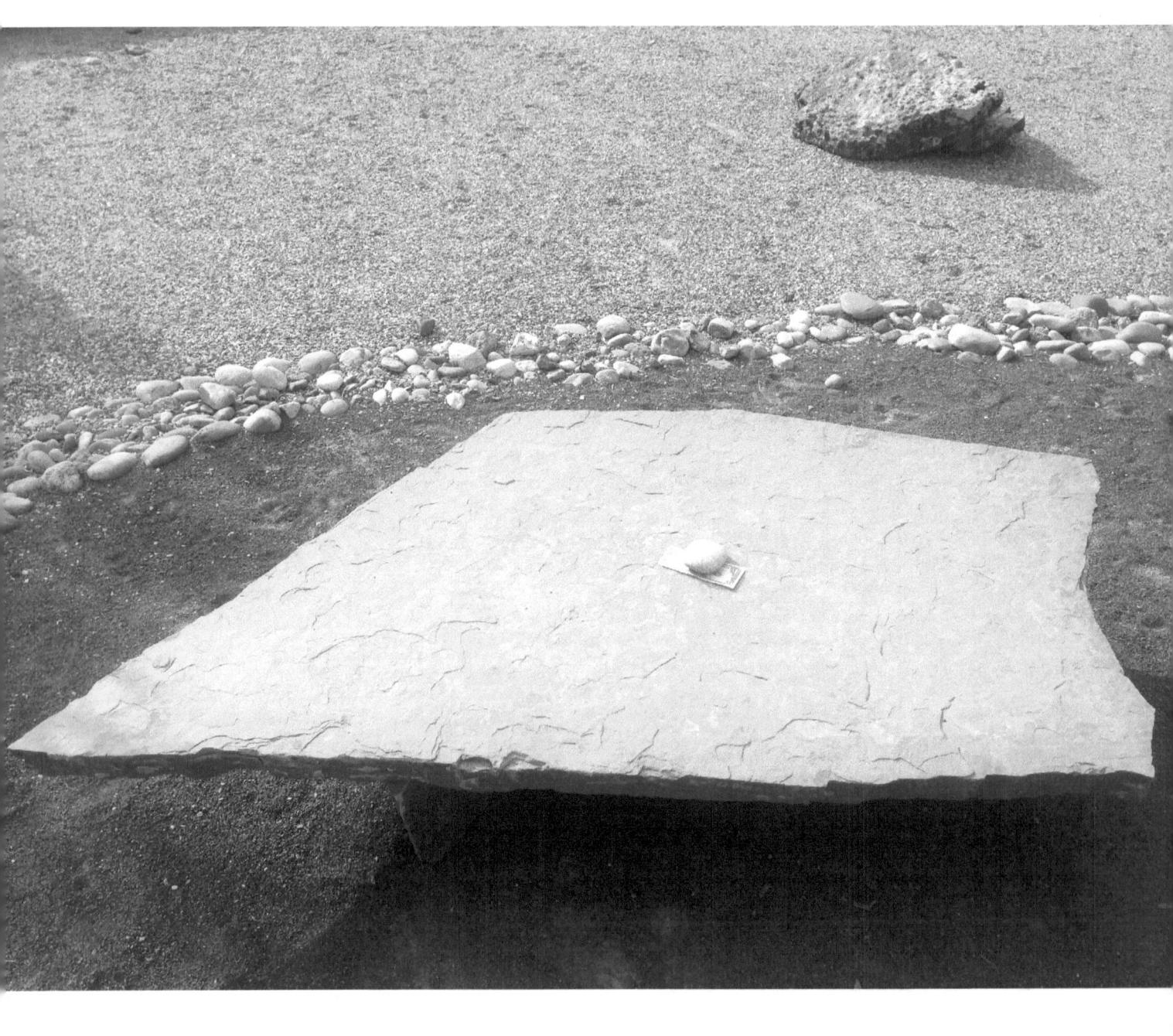

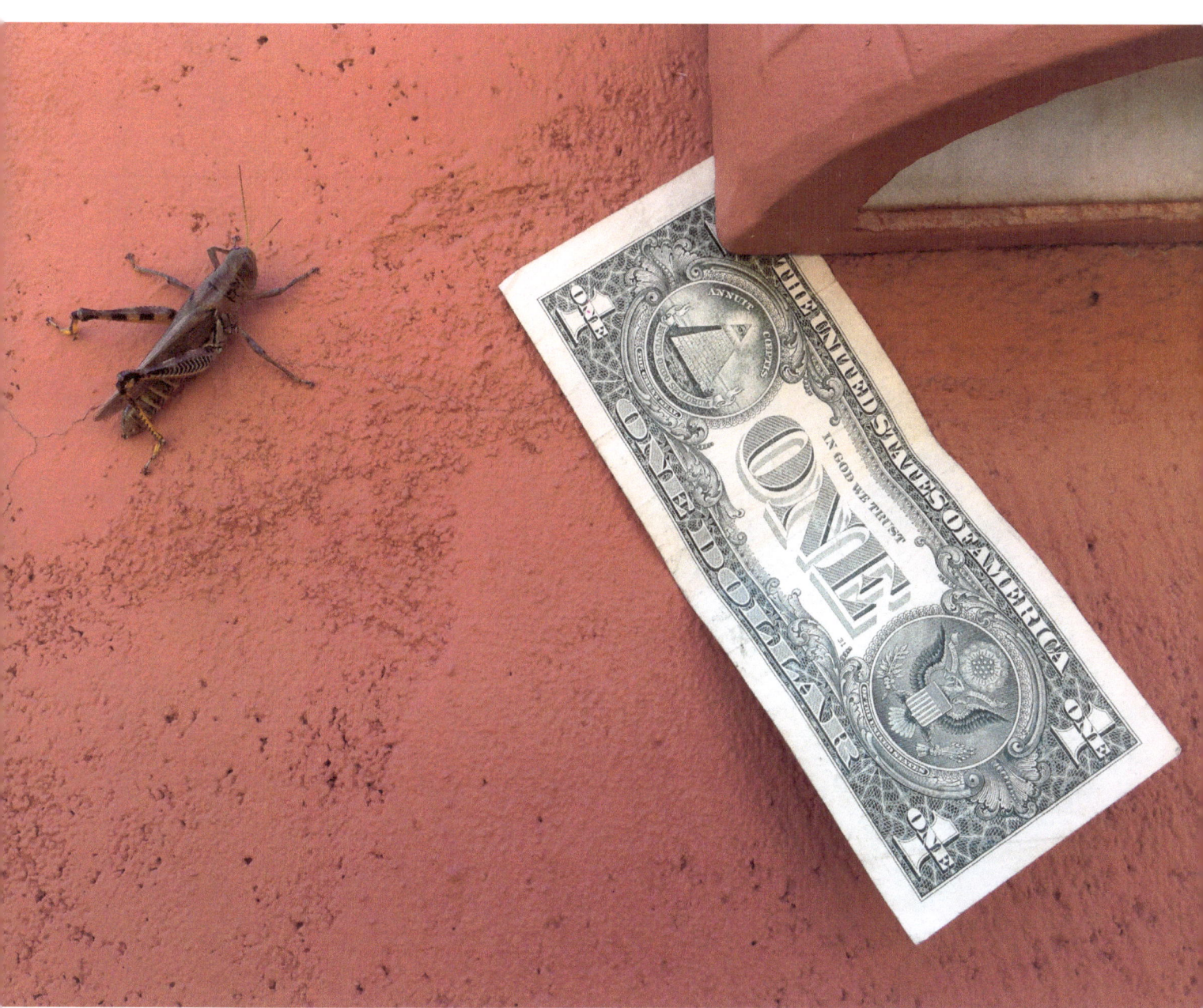

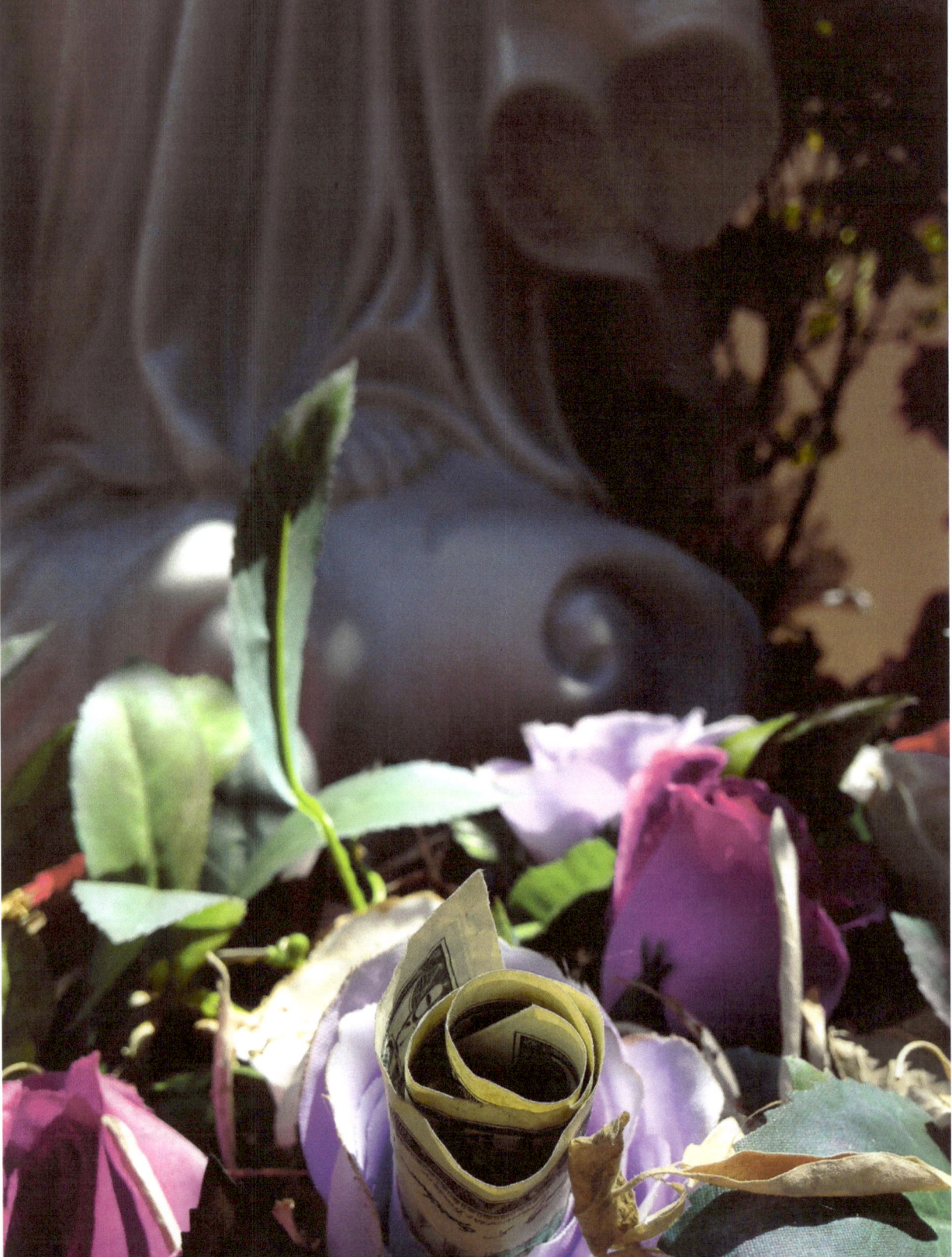

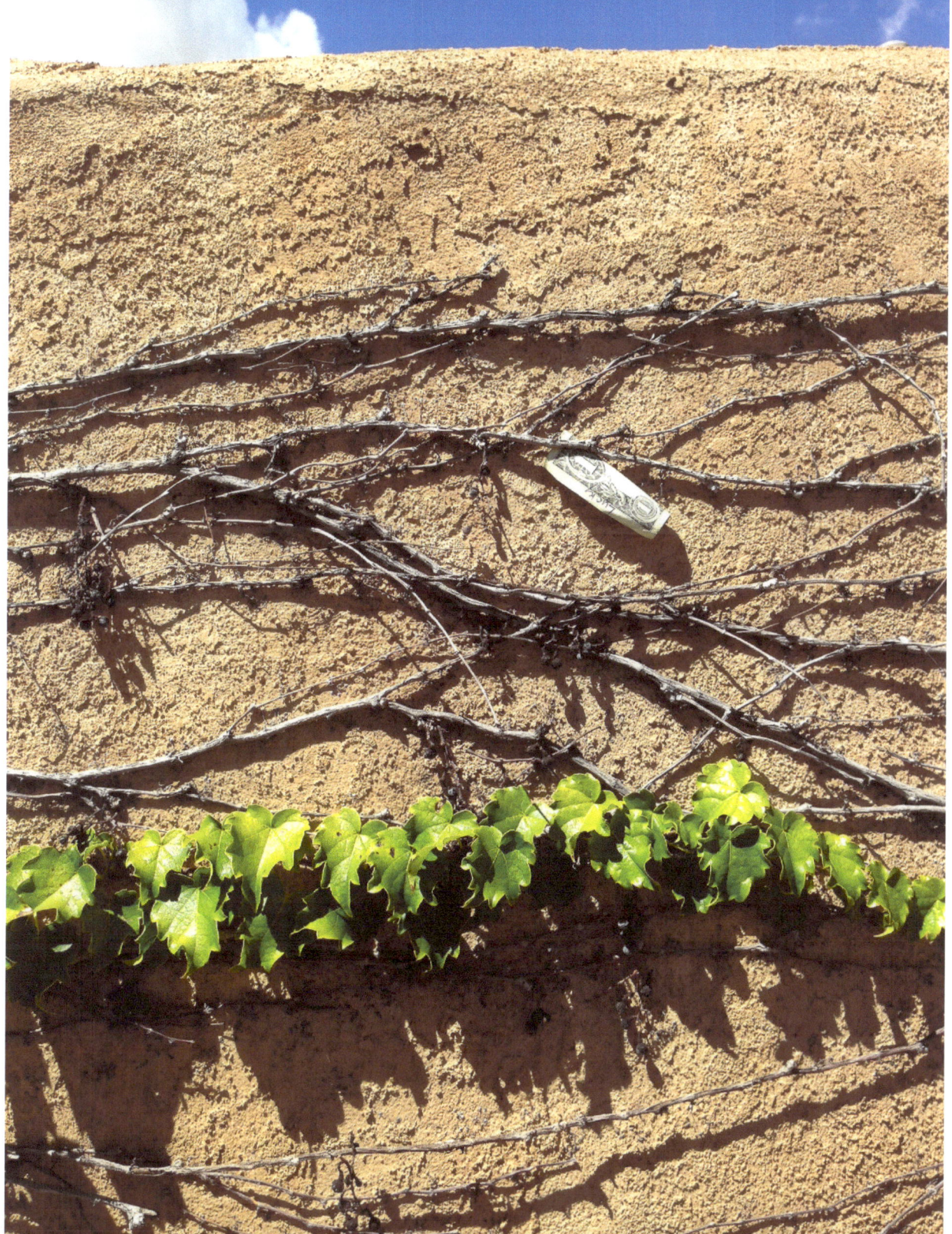

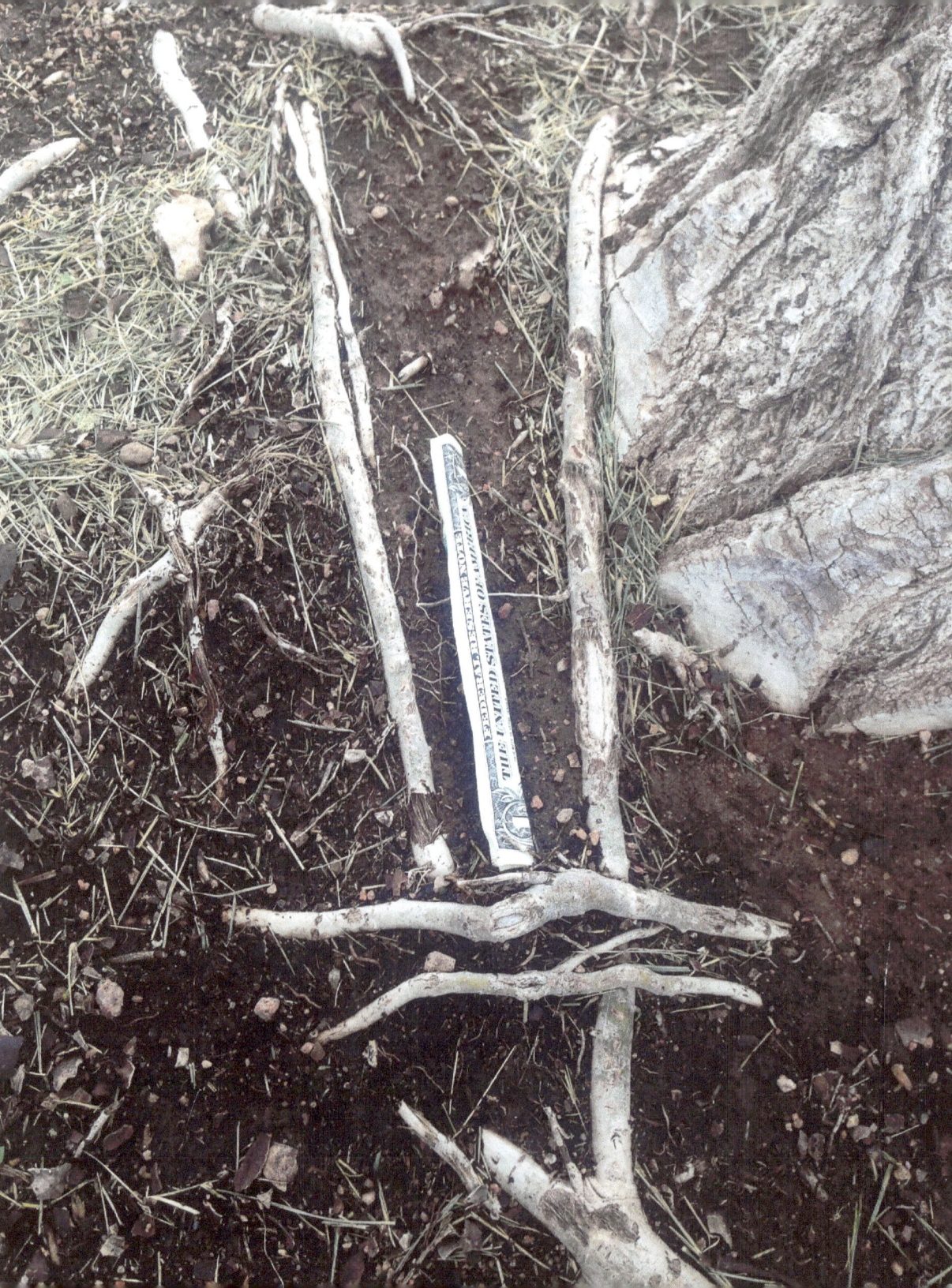

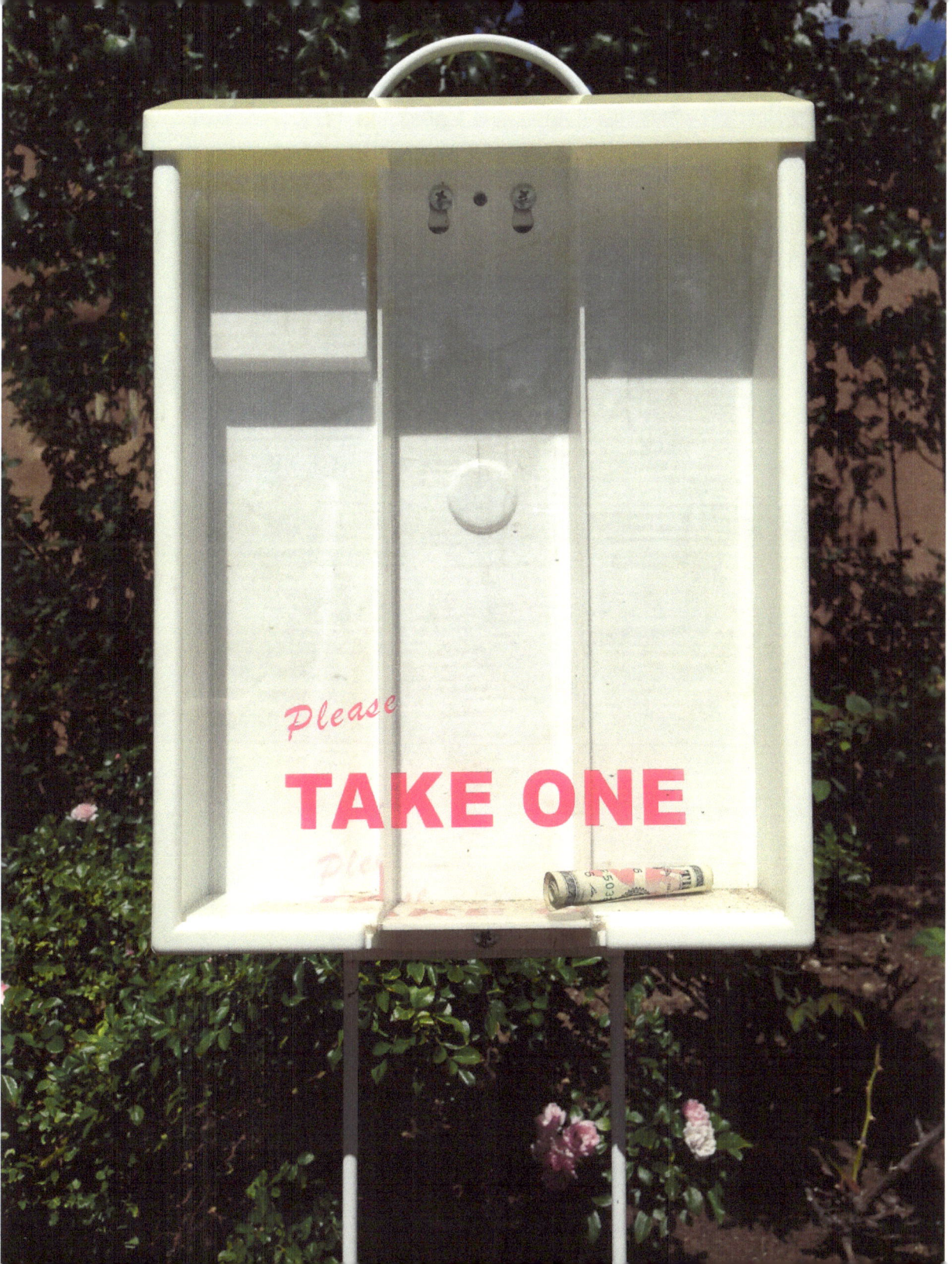

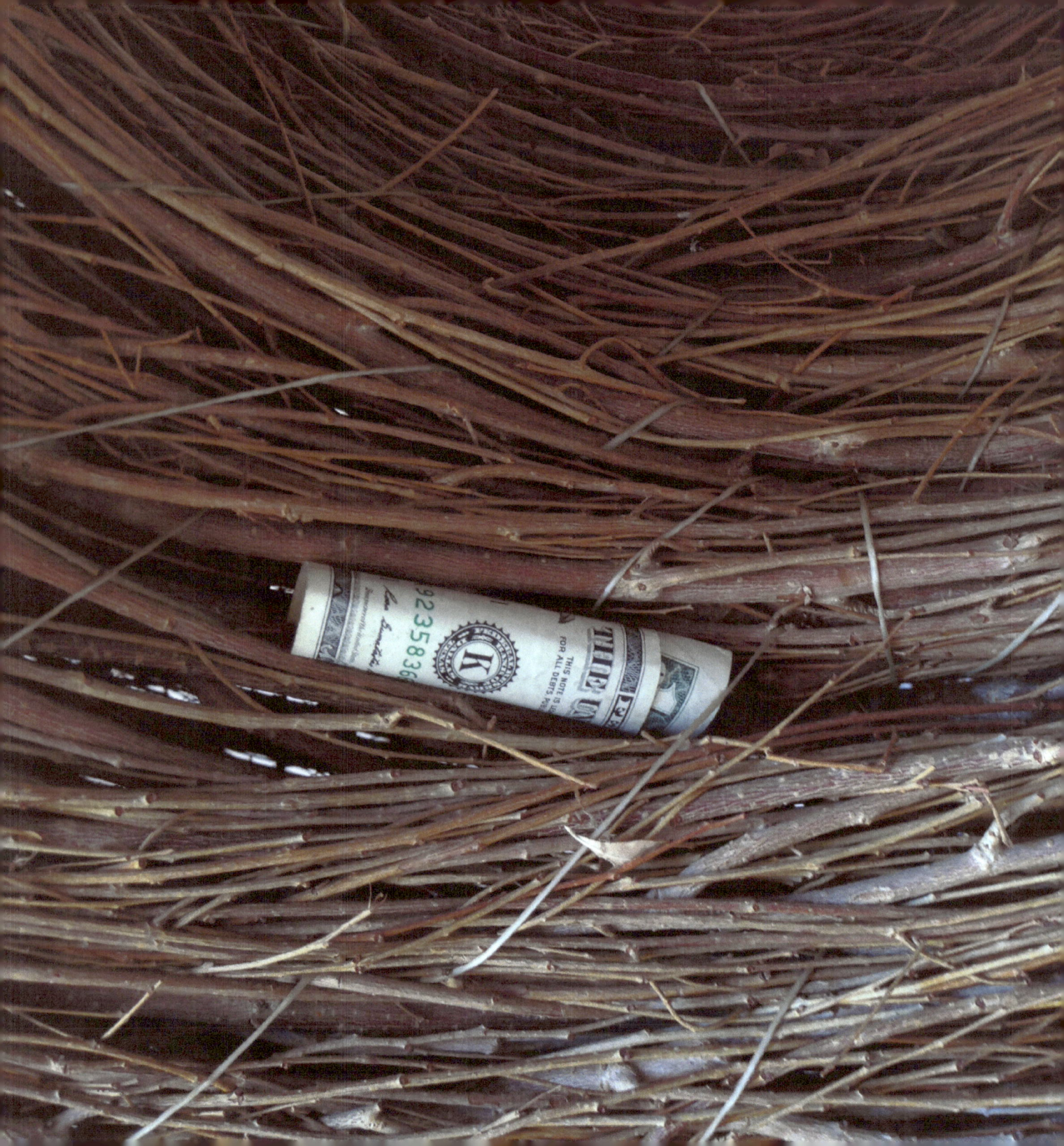

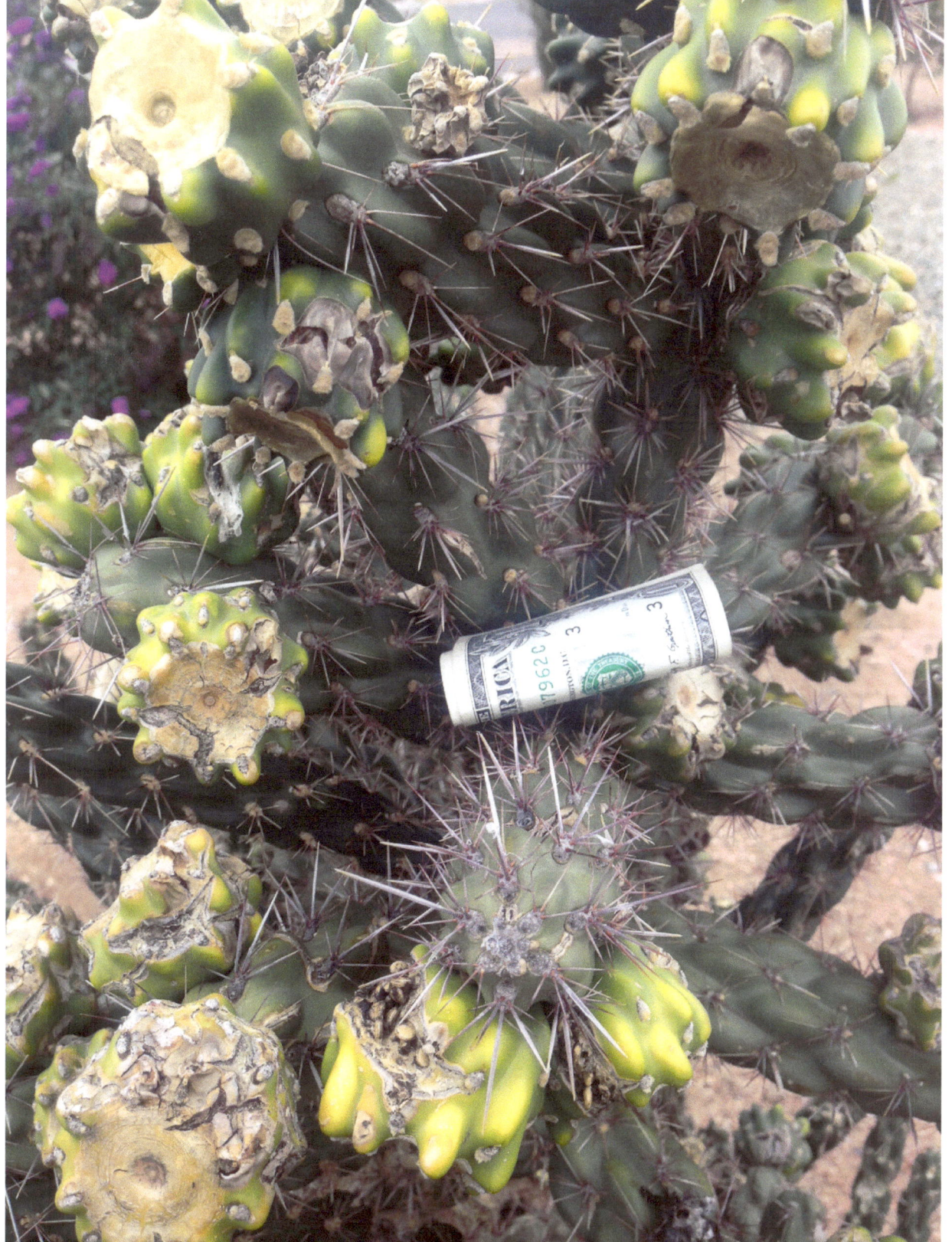

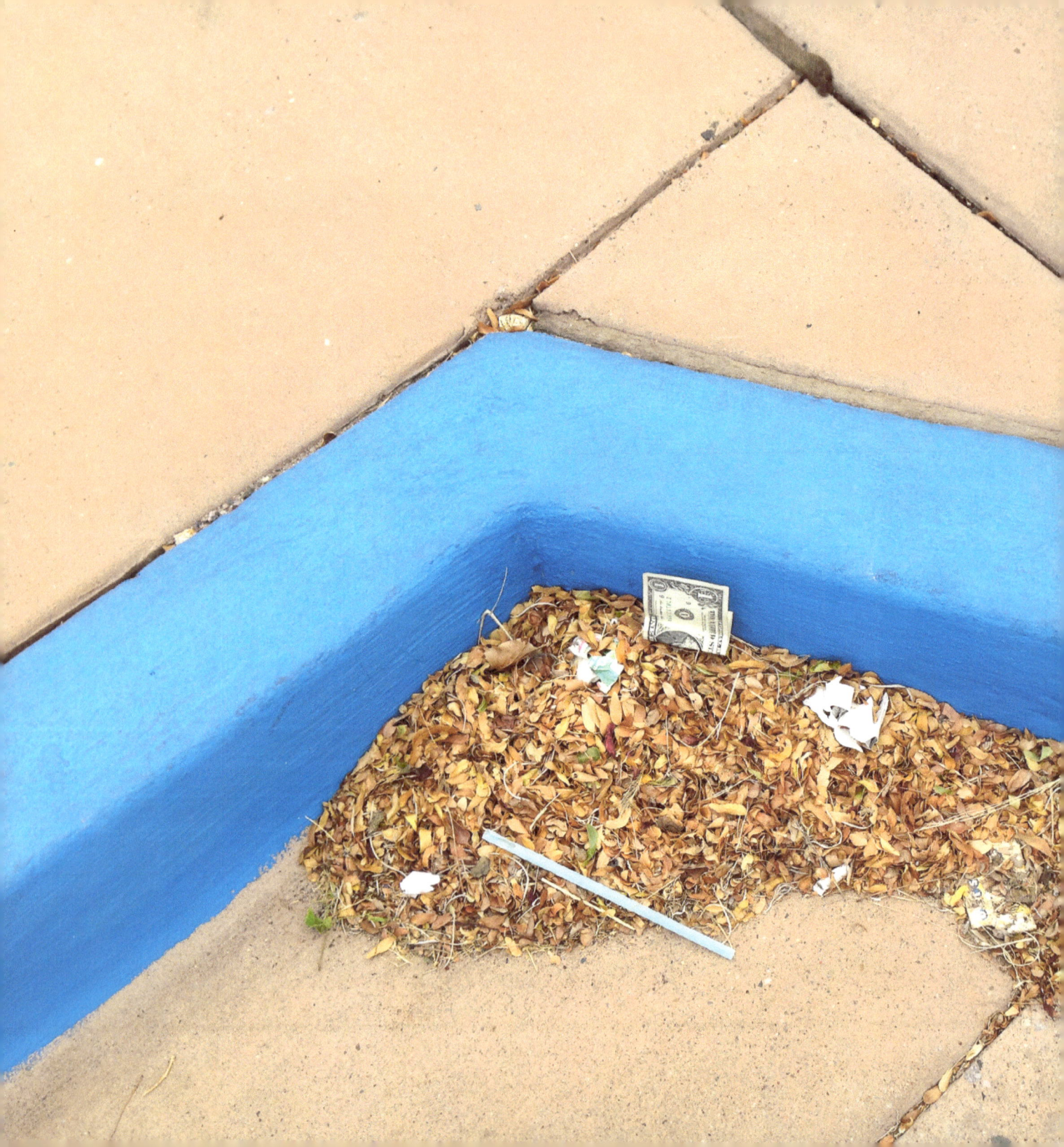

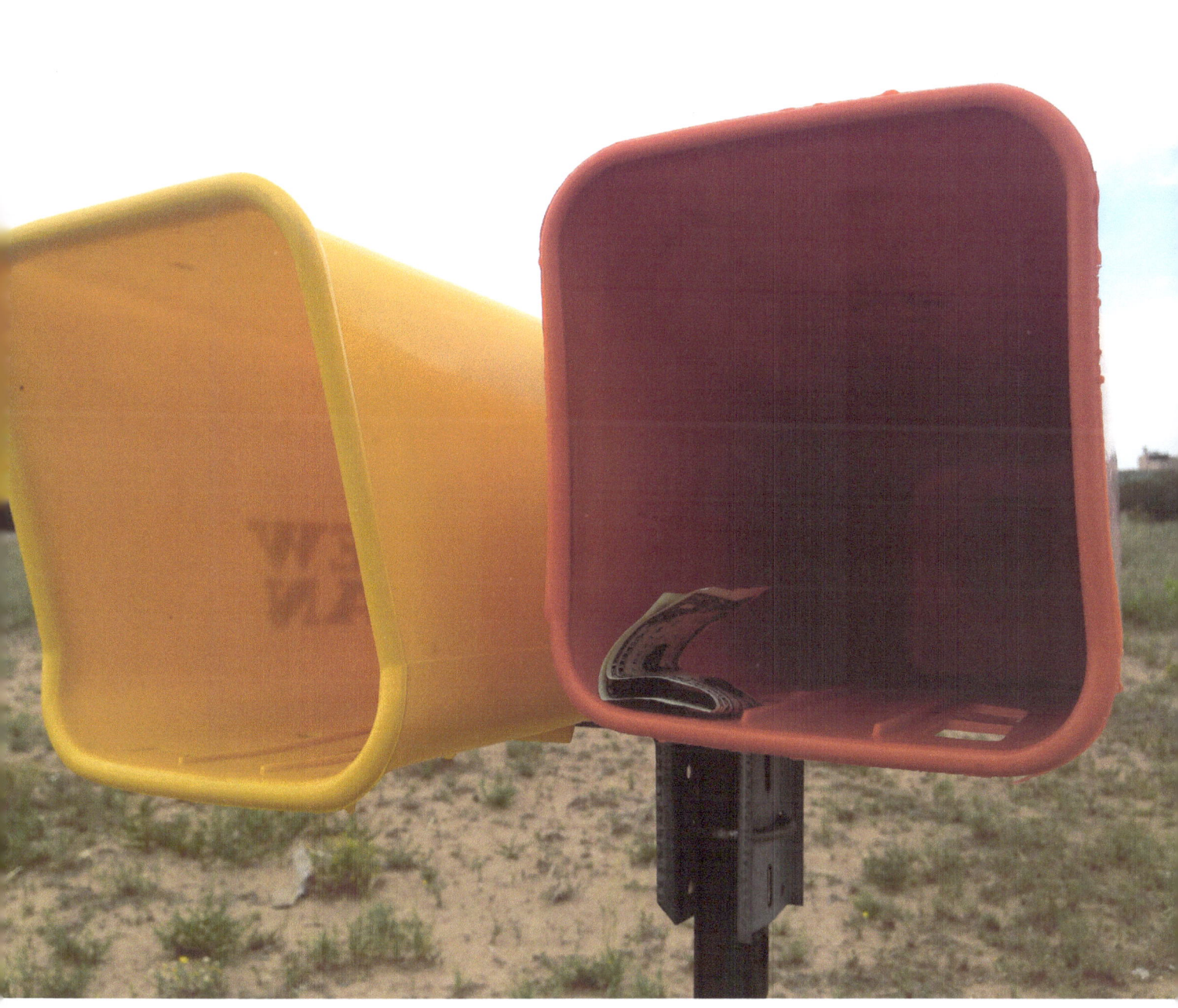

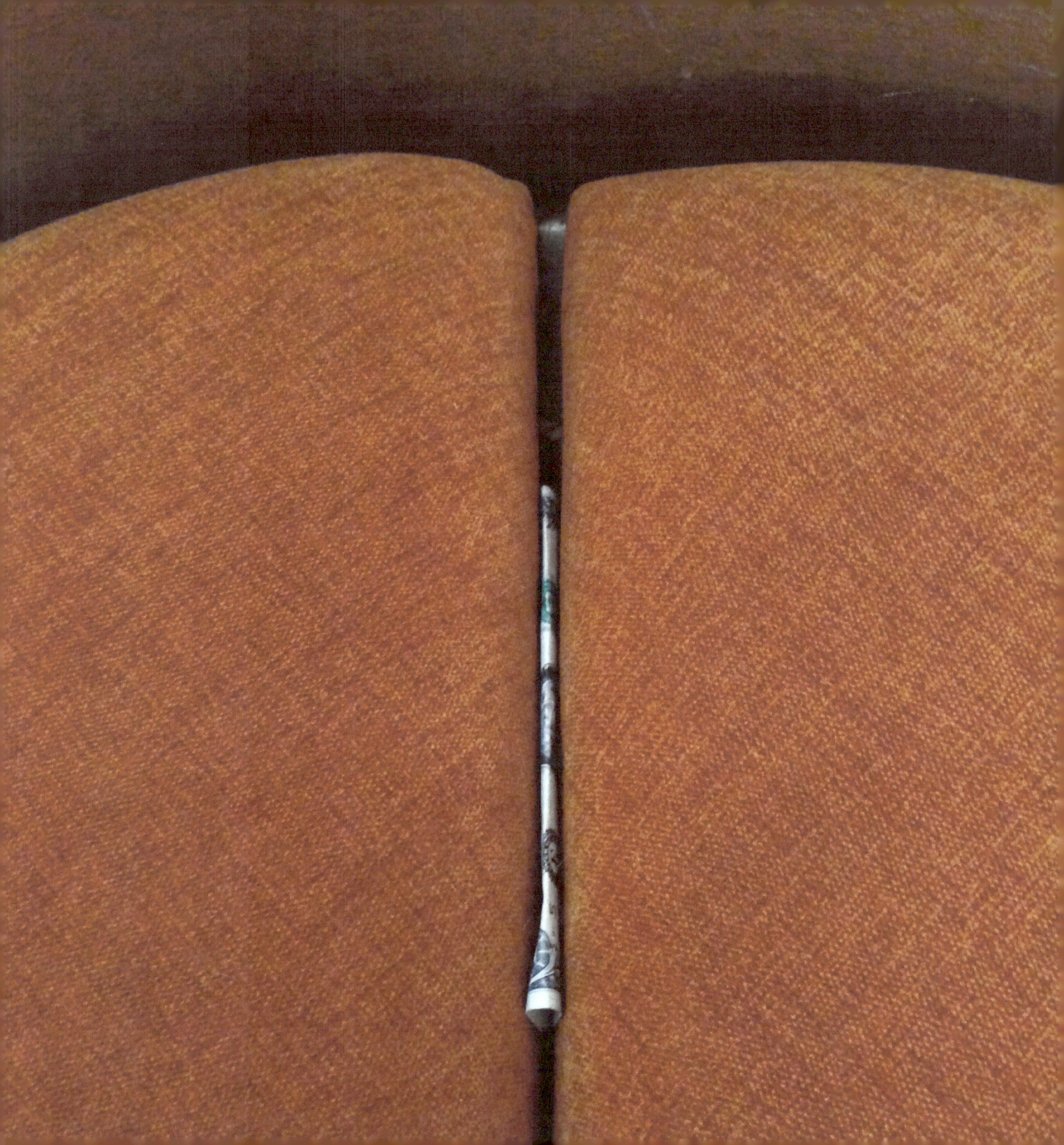